Forget the Third Arrow and Behold the Old World Order

Also by Susan Carpenter

Special Corporations and the Bureaucracy: Why Japan Can't Reform
(Palgrave Macmillan, 2003)

Why Japan Can't Reform: Inside the System
(Palgrave Macmillan, 2008)

Japan's Nuclear Crisis: The Routes to Responsibility
(Palgrave Macmillan, 2012)

Japan Inc. On the Brink: Institutional Corruption and Agency Failure
(Palgrave Macmillan, 2015).

Forget the Third Arrow and Behold the Old World Order

A journey into the depths of Japan Inc.

Susan Carpenter

First published 2017 by Kaikaku

ISBN 978-1-5272-0671-7 (paperback)

ISBN 978-1-5272-0673-1 (ebook)

To

While living and working in Japan for a number of years I recognized the invaluable and, indeed, remarkable contribution by the Japanese to the international community in almost all fields of human endeavor.

Contents

Acknowledgements

I would like to express my appreciation to Roger Dahl for generously allowing me to reproduce his cartoons on pages 1, 243 and 260. Dahl is the highly-regarded cartoonist for the *Japan Times*. His latest book *Roger Dahl's Comic Japan* is published by Tuttle.

Similarly, I would like to thank David Donar for his cartoon which is reproduced on page 109. Donar's cartoons can be accessed on his website Political Graffitti.

Acronyms and Abbreviations

AIST......................National Institute of Advanced Industrial Science and Technology
ALIC ....Agriculture and Livestock Industries Corporation
ANRE...................Agency of Natural Resources and Energy
BOJ ....Bank of Japan
CHUDEN.............Chubu Electric Power Co.
CPI ....Consumer Price Index
DBJ ....Development Bank of Japan
DPJ......................Democratic Party of Japan
EC ....European Commission
EPA......................Economic Planning Agency
EPDC ....Electric Power Development Co.
EXIM ....Export-Import Bank
FAZ ....Foreign Access Zone
FBR......................Fast Breeder Reactor
FDI ....Foreign Direct Investment
FILP ....Fiscal Investment and Loan Program
FSA ....Financial Services Agency
GDP......................Gross Domestic Product
GHLC...................Government Housing Loan Corporation
GPIF....................Government Pension Investment Fund
IAI........................Independent Administrative Institution
IBJ........................Industrial Bank of Japan
IMF ....International Monetary Fund
JAEA....................Japan Atomic Energy Agency
JAERI...................Japan Atomic Energy Research Institute
JAMA...................Japan Automobile Manufacturers Association
JAPCO ....Japan Atomic Power Company
JASME.................Japan Finance Corporation for Small and Medium Enterprises
JBIC ....Japan Bank for International Cooperation
JDB ....Japan Development Bank
JETRO..................Japan External Trade Organization
JFC.......................Japan Finance Corporation
JFTC.....................Japan Fair Trade Commission
JGB ....Japan Government Bonds
JH.........................Japan Highway Corporation
JHF.......................Japan Housing Finance Agency
JNEPA..................Japan Newspaper Editors and Publishers Association
JNOC....................Japan National Oil Corporation

JOGMEC..............Japan Oil, Gas and Metals National Corporation

Keidanren.............Japan Business Federation

KEPCO ....Kansai Electric Power Co.

KYUDEN.............Kyushu Electric Power Co.

LDP.....................Liberal Democratic Party of Japan

MAC ....Ministry of Agriculture and Commerce

MAFA..................Ministry of Agriculture, Forestry and Fisheries

MCI.....................Ministry of Commerce and Industry

METI...................Ministry of Economy, Trade and Industry

MEXT ....Ministry of Education, Culture, Sports, Science and Technology

MHLW ....Ministry of Health, Labor and Welfare

MLIT...................Ministry of Land, Infrastructure and Transportation

MM ....Ministry of Munitions

MOC ....Ministry of Construction

MOD ....Ministry of Defence

MOF....................Ministry of Finance

MOFA..................Ministry of Foreign Affairs

MOX ....Mixed Oxide Fuel

NHK....................Nippon Hoso Kyokai

NPL.....................Non-performing Loans

NRA ....Nuclear Regulatory Authority

NSK.....................Nihon Shimbun Kyokai

NTT.....................Nippon Telephone and Telegraph

OECD..................Organization for Economic Co-operation and Development

PKO.....................Peacekeeping Operations

QE ....Quantitative Easing

QQE ....Qualitative Easing

SCAP...................Supreme Command of the Allied Powers

SDF ....Self-Defence Force

TEPCO................Tokyo Electric Power Company

TSE ....Tokyo Stock Exchange

UDC ....Urban Development Corporation

UNCTAD ....United Nations Conference on Trade and Development 34

URO ....Urban Renaissance Organization

USTR ....United States Trade Representative

WTO....................World Trade Organization

YODEN................Shikoku Electric Power Co.

Introduction

Forget the Third Arrow and Behold the Old World Order: a journey into the depths of Japan Inc.

This book's commentary demonstrates: i) the consequences of historic protectionist trade policies and isolationism for Japan's current economy; ii) the factors which contribute to the self-perpetuating nature of a system which frustrates reform; iii) the resurgence of a strong nationalism; iv) the enduring relationship between government and business; v) an understanding of the similarities with other non-market driven economies where government and business are intertwined; vi) the parallels between the experience of Japan following the 1990 Financial Crisis and events in the West since 2008. The book explains how my experiences in Japan Inc. allowed me to predict what is happening currently regarding US-Japan trade relations, to predict the expansion of Japan's military and to predict that nothing fundamental would change in Japan's political economic system.

Prior to entering Japan Inc. at the height of the asset-inflated bubble in 1988, I had lived in Japan during two significant periods; the Vietnam War, directly after the abolition of the gold standard and during the first oil crisis when the Ministry of International Trade and Industry (MITI) restructured its industrial policy to focus on high-tech industries and nuclear energy. Readers will first journey with me and the Japanese through Japan's post-war political economic development as I adapt to the socio-political society. These experiences enabled me to enter the innards of the political economy.

My employment in the private sector and government agencies allowed an intimate view of corporate Japan and government agencies during the two "lost decades." By 1996 I was convinced that Japan Inc. was suffering from systemic failure and that, contrary to assurances from the Japanese government, Japan's economy would not recover from the impacts of the bursting of the asset-inflated bubble in 1990. I predicted a prolonged recession and that, owing to continuous political turmoil and the ministries' tight control over industrial production and domestic markets, the government would not succeed in implementing structural reforms. Structural reforms and the deregulation of markets would be more image than substance. In other words, there would be little change and, as importantly, the political environment would move backwards towards a version of the pre- World War II model.

During my employment in Japanese corporations and government agencies in the late 1980s and 1990s I was frequently asked by Japanese how I was able to be in positions deemed appropriate for Japanese. My rote answer was that my skills met the specific requirements of the positions. When western journalists and business owners asked how I was treated as a female staff I replied that their question would best be posed to Japanese female staff because I was trying to emphasize that my experiences were substantially similar to Japanese employees. However, the same questions still persist.

Surprisingly, I was never asked the most important questions; what did I see and what was I exposed to while I was working in Japanese private and public sector corporations. What I was exposed to was the consequence of years of concentrated effort to expand my responsibilities and build interpersonal networks in the corporations.

Until recently, the overwhelming consensus among the international business community, the IMF and the OECD was that the Japan Inc. model had propelled Japan's post-war success in the global marketplace and that after the bursting of the asset-inflated bubble in 1989 the government would take measures to deregulate markets and initiate fiscal reforms in order to stimulate a floundering economy.

However, what I was experiencing from 1990 onward was the steady deterioration of the world's second largest economy because of the insularity and the rigidity of the Japan Inc. system. No one inside or outside Japan seemed to recognize the seriousness of Japan's postponement of structural reforms and the failed attempts by government to correct its recessive economy. Furthermore, the United States was actively involved in the support of the post-war system because Japan was its key ally in the Pacific and the location for its numerous military bases.

Nevertheless, the image of success breeds success and the Japanese elite government officials and business owners, basking in these images, remained over-confident and complacent despite the financial crisis and the politicians' inability to reach a consensus on policies that would bring about fiscal consolidation. Japan was locked in a system which was rigid and inward and nothing significant in the political economic system would change because the very rigidity of the system prevented the accommodation to rapidly changing needs on the home front and weakened the country's ability to withstand both internal and external crises.

My work in big business and government agencies made me privy to a Japan Inc. which was very different to what I had experienced while living in Japan for seven years before entering a Japanese company. I was fluent in Japanese and comfortably integrated in the Japanese political society as a foreigner, or at least, I thought so.

In the summer of 2001 I was conducting a program for Japanese small and medium sized business owners at Hofstra University located in Long Island, New York. One of the participants was a Japanese woman who had been sent by an affiliate of Nippon Telephone and Telegraph

(NTT), a huge corporation managed by the former Ministry of Post and Telecommunications. Although NTT was in the process of privatization, the government owned one-third of equity in the holding company. Several years earlier after graduating from a university in Tokyo, the woman entered the company's Strategy Division. She confided to me that she had never really known her own society until she had entered a Japanese corporation.

I presumed that as a Japanese who had been raised and educated in Japan she would have adapted quickly to Japanese corporate culture. I had also presumed that having resided in Japan for seven years in circumstances comparable to middle class Japanese prior to entering a Japanese firm and that having reasonable fluency in the Japanese language would help me to avoid a significant degree of corporate culture shock. However, it was not until I began working for Japanese corporations that I saw Japan Inc. unmasked.

An essential criteria was that I would be the first foreign employee in a conservative Japanese company because I recognized that foreigners who worked in Japanese firms left because they had experienced what they considered to be discriminatory practices and harassment due to misunderstandings arising from poor communication and ignorance of the Japanese corporate system. On the other hand, Japanese management was reluctant to hire foreigners because they were unable to adapt to regulations thus disrupting the workplace. Mutual misunderstanding was also prompted by cultural differences. Japan was an ultra-conservative and insular society and Japanese corporations operated very differently from western corporations.

Foreigners saw Japan as a "westernized" country and a democracy and anticipated that management would accept them as equal to Japanese staff. What they did not understand was that Japanese corporations were hierarchical and that they would be considered new staff and expected to adhere to instructions from their superiors and abide by corporate etiquette. Many foreigners were frustrated that they were not accepted for their skills and many experienced what they considered to be demeaning treatment.

I hoped to enter a corporation where the staff had no previous exposure to foreign staff and, therefore, few preconceptions. Entering a conservative Japanese company as the first and only western staff would enable me to adapt smoothly to the corporate system without promoting misunderstanding. I did not presume that the Japanese staff would relate to me as a foreigner but I did assume that I could make them comfortable with my presence and integrate in the workplace over a period of time. However, I failed to consider that fluency in the written language could pose other problems which are detailed in the book.

In the Beginning

I lived in circumstance similar to the Japanese middle class. The small Japanese-style homes lacked storage space and freezers were out of the question. Refrigerators were half the size of the American brands and without freezer compartments. Refrigerators with freezer space for ice cream and ice cubes were considered luxury items. There was no central heating or ovens because of high energy costs.

Frugality dominated our budgets with the quality of food taking precedence over the amount on the plate. Imported produce such as oranges, which I had consumed daily in the US and took for granted, were sold at three times the price and domestic produce could often be as expensive. Shoppers habitually examined domestic products, comparing one piece of fruit or vegetable with another for several minutes before making a purchase. In the 1970s this practice extended to packaged meats and fish. And the import duties made foreign foods too expensive for daily consumption. Although beef imports from Australia and lamb from New Zealand could be sourced, US beef was almost non-existent. I became obsessed with going to markets, not to shop, but to observe consumer buying patterns.

It was difficult to fathom why Japan, having achieved by 1975 the world's third largest GDP (after the US and the Soviet Union) would continue its mercantile policies and protect domestic markets from foreign competition and why we consumers had to pay premium prices for imported goods. But I gradually began to recognize that in order to stabilize Japan's economy and to promote rapid economic growth, the US opened its markets to Japanese imports, which the Japanese government took full advantage of while keeping tight control over domestic markets. The government's policies not only shielded industry from foreign competition but, also, our choice of products which were limited to goods primarily produced in Japan.

The government proselytized that the Japanese language was so difficult that foreigners would be unable to fully understand the intricacies of the Japanese social political system let alone the issues regarding the protection of domestic industry from foreign competition.

It was not until I began working in Japan Inc. that I realized that what was perceived outside Japan as a maze-like distribution system which frustrated entry was not nearly as complex as presented by the Japanese government.

This xenophobic firewall prevented Japanese corporations from accessing foreign corporate strategies and corporate governance, promoting domestic consumption and stimulating competition among domestic producers. Indeed, opening up markets was the key to encouraging structural reforms of a lopsided economy.

I never intended to publish articles or books in order to set the record straight but the data I collected during my employment provided sterling examples of how the 1990 financial crisis impacted the Japanese corporate sector and why the Japanese government would be unable to implement structural reforms. However, I was in a quandary as to release the information without compromising myself or my colleagues.

I concluded that the most effective way to bust the myths about the infallibility of the Japan Inc. model that had been perpetuated over the years was to publish books in an academic context to stimulate a realistic understanding of Japan Inc. Nevertheless, I was exceedingly reluctant to embark on an academic career because the process to publishing would require at least four to five years of intense labor. As it turned out, it took 15 years.

The Academic Route

I succeeded in publishing four academic books after receiving a doctorate at the University of Edinburgh. However, to publish books that were acceptable to the academic community the work had to be placed in the context of existing academic literature. My problem was that relevant academic literature in English or in Japanese simply did not exist. In other words, I was entering virgin territory.

Each book gave a comprehensive analysis of Japan's political economic landscape at the time of publishing. In the first book *Special Corporations and the Bureaucracy: Why Japan Can't Reform* (Palgrave, 2003) the section "Forecast for Japan: too little too late?" states: "At the time of writing the forecast for Japan's future as a global economic power is bleak."

I sent a copy to the late Chalmers Johnson, a Professor of Political Science at the University of California who was considered the guru of Japanese industrial policy and a China specialist. He wrote the bestsellers *MITI and the Japanese Miracle* (1979) and *Japan Who Governs?* (1995). I was immensely grateful when Johnson congratulated me for getting out a book about a subject of which there was little writing in English and which was at the "very heart of Japanese government."

His message made me determined to forge ahead with *Why Japan Can't Reform: Inside the System* (2008) which argued again in the conclusion "Too Little Too late: what ministerial policies have wrought" that: "even if the Japanese initiated structural reform of the administrative system, the reforms would come too late to bring the economy back on track. That prediction still stands."

The book argued that the Japan Inc. model defied structural reform and frustrated the implementation of economic and social policies that could resolve the problems that had challenged the Japanese for years.

Japan's Nuclear Crisis: The Routes to Responsibility (2012) assessed the impact of Japan's 2011 nuclear crisis on the Japanese political economy and defined pertinent political and economic elements intrinsic to the political economy to reveal why the Fukushima nuclear plant was still operating despite numerous problems that had been plaguing the reactors since the 1980s. The book exposed the Ministry of Economy, Trade and Industry-affiliated agencies which have been at the core of the nuclear and electric power industries since the 1950s.

Japan Inc. on the Brink: Institutional Corruption and Agency Failure (2015) contended that due to entrenched vested interests in Japan's political economy and the rigidity of the Japan Inc. model structural reforms and the essential "third arrow" in Abe's Abenomics would not happen. And as a result, Abenomics was merely a combination of reckless monetary policy and ambiguous fiscal policies which would fail to regenerate Japan's fragile economy and cut sovereign debt.

My forecasts have proven substantially correct and I now feel that the time is right to share with readers the same information regarding what was transpiring during Japan's first and second "lost decades" but in a different context. Although the contents in my academic texts may be regarded as exposés of corruption in government and industry, this book is empathetic to the behavior of the majority of ministry officials and to the views of the Japanese regarding their political society.

The book is tightly drawn with events stated at the beginning referred to in subsequent chapters. Although the book is by no means a personal story, I hope that by incorporating anecdotal materials readers will be able to engage in what was transpiring at the time and to understand that post-war Japan's economic development forged a rigid government and corporate system that was supported by mercantile policies, a system which became Japan's Achilles Heel by the 1980s.

1

In the Beginning

In November 1966 my husband and I loaded all of our possessions on a State Line freighter to embark from San Francisco on our journey to Japan. The ship sailed beneath the Golden Gate Bridge at dusk, arriving five days later in Honolulu, where it docked for several days before heading for Midway.

The weather was balmy, the sea changed from an icy blue to a gentle green hue and jumping fish entertained us as we stood on the deck gazing out at the endless expanse of ocean lulled by gentle waves capped with white froth. As the boat approached Midway, we saw the remains of B-29 bombers resting in the shallow emerald green waters, a poignant reminder of the Battle of Midway. The ship was the only commercial freighter allowed to dock because it delivered provisions to the US naval base. Passengers were permitted to disembark and walk around the island which was inhabited by the military and wives of the officers. As we strolled on the white sandy beach we passed a woman sitting on a bench looking intently through binoculars at the ocean. When we asked her what she was looking at she said that she was searching for the glass fish balls used by fisherman to weigh down their nets. When she spotted one she sent a sailor under her husband's command to collect it. She decorated her basement rump room with the balls, her main hobby while she was living on the island. The short stopover at the base was my first exposure to US military bases in the Pacific but it did not prepare me for what I was to experience in Japan.

The ship entered Yokohama Bay at 2am. The night was crystal clear. We could see a myriad of tiny lights floating on the water and as we slowly drew nearer to the port we realized that the lights were coming from the lanterns used by the fishermen on their small boats to attract fish. We disembarked from the ship at 6am after our passports had been checked. We were sponsored by the senior partner of a San Francisco law firm specializing in maritime law, which was the first American law firm to enter Japan. Our sponsor was also the first foreigner to receive a law degree from Tokyo University,

The storage agency which would store our possessions until we found housing sent a truck to meet us at the dock and collect our goods. The driver and his partner kindly offered to take us to the hotel located on the outskirts of Kamakura where we planned to settle. Kamakura is located about an hour's train ride from Tokyo and is located on the Shonan Peninsula. The city is a popular summer resort known among Japanese and foreigners alike for its beaches and its tourist attractions such as the huge statue of the Hase Buddha, the Zen Buddhist monasteries and Hachiman, the Shinto Shrine. There are many villas which were owned by wealthy families before the Second World War but were now leased to the Supreme Command of the Allied Powers (SCAP) personnel during the Occupation and to the American military for R&R during the Vietnam War.

We knew only a few basic expressions in Japanese and within a few hours after arriving, I made my first error. A typhoon had hit the area before our arrival and the weather was hot and humid. The hotel, which was located directly across the road from a beach, catered to summer tourists. There were no other guests and the atmosphere in the dining room was eerie. When a young waitress took our order I asked for a Coca Cola to cool down. Curiously we waited for 20 minutes before the waitress returned with our order. I was shocked when she placed in front of me a steaming cup of cocoa. Evidently, the Japanese pronunciation for Coca Cola was simply *Cora*. I was too embarrassed by my first language bungle to ask for my original order and drank the piping hot drink while perspiring profusely.

After lunch we took a trolley to town and wandered around this cultural mecca in search of a Japanese chocolate bar in order to compare it with Hershey. I tried a bar elegantly packaged in a green box decorated with red leaves and labeled Ghana which was produced by Lotte. The price was the same price as a Hershey bar but I was disappointed because the chocolate was oilier and less sweet. I also tried traditional Japanese cakes of rice flour and sweet red bean paste and I was hooked. Although I soon became accustomed to Japanese brands of chocolate, I also developed a penchant for Japanese sweets and cakes.

As remains the case today, Japan's political economy is fairly controlled and recognized as being xenophobic. It was difficult to find a rental because Japanese landlords were reticent to let to foreigners who, compared to the Japanese, did not keep their property as tidy. It was definitely discriminatory but logical as well because the Japanese are generally fastidious. My husband's acquaintance in Kamakura introduced us to a real estate agent who catered to foreigners and whose landlord clients were willing to rent property to foreigners. The landlord required a sponsor together with a guarantee payment, which is still the case today. My husband was determined to live in a traditional Japanese-style dwelling. The house he fancied was located in Inamuragasaki a 15-minute trolley ride from Kamakura and stood at the top of a flight of 50 stone steps and quite isolated. It had been built before the war with wooden floors in the hallway and kitchen and tatami floors throughout the other three rooms.

The beach of Inamuragasaki was nearby where a famous battle in 1333 ended the rule of the Kamakura Shogun who kept 50 pug dogs in his kennels. It was said that the echoes of the cries of soldiers defending the Kamakura government against invasion could be heard during bad storms.

Our beds were Japanese futon on the tatami floor and getting up on a winter's morning was like breaking through a wall of ice. We placed sturdy Aladdin kerosene stoves imported from Great Britain strategically in each room to provide the only source of heat but we were advised not to use the stoves for more than two hours at a time because of the danger of carbon monoxide poisoning. A coal stove was stoked each time we needed hot water for the Japanese-style bath, and a small electrically generated hot water heater placed above the kitchen sink taps provided hot water for washing the dishes. The kitchen faced northward which was freezing during the winter months while the room where we entertained guests faced to the south which was typical in Japanese homes.

There was a roofed veranda which was also home to a variety of insects. My husband who had lived in the tropical paradises of Tobago and Hawaii was amazed by the size of some of them, including centipedes, praying mantis, huge roaches and hairy creatures with many legs that were harmless but unattractive. During the hot and humid summer months we were serenaded by hundreds of chirping cicadas. Abandoned cats with their tails chopped off roamed around our untended garden.

Becoming accustomed to insects, hot and soggy summers, cold winters, climbing up the stone steps while lugging packages and cooking on two propane burners in an icy kitchen, took some time but our neighbors and the majority of Japanese lived in similar conditions. However, unlike our neighbors two plain clothes policemen visited our home twice annually to check on us and to ask questions on the activities of foreigners who were living in our area. As far as we knew there were no foreigners living near us.

Food Glorious Food

Food plays a central role in Japanese society and housewives traditionally spend a good portion of their household budget on food. Until the late 1980s frugality dominated with the quality of food taking precedence over the amount on the plate. Shoppers habitually examined products, comparing one piece of fruit with another or one vegetable with another vegetable for several minutes before deciding on a purchase. In the 1970s this practice extended to purchases of packaged meats and fish because the import tariffs made foreign products too expensive for daily consumption. Meat was very expensive and, although beef imports from Australia and lamb from New Zealand could be sourced, US beef was almost non-existent. Observing household buying patterns became a hobby and a visit to a market was not necessarily related to buying groceries.

Nevertheless, it was difficult to believe that Japan's industrial complex and infrastructure had been devastated by the war. The Korean War (1950–53) spurred the production of armaments in Japan's decommissioned factories and raised exports to the American military. The 1964 Tokyo Olympics promoted a flurry of construction. Preparations for the Olympics included catering to the needs of thousands of foreign visitors, most of who had never held chopsticks or chewed on a morsel of sushi. Foods from abroad such as cheeses, biscuits and cereals, chocolates, canned goods, wines and spirits were imported to Japan by the large trading companies. The Japanese, feeling the first flush of prosperity since before the war, also purchased these imports. They liked what they tried and the demand for imported foods increased.

In order to stabilize Japan's economy and to promote rapid economic growth the US opened its markets to Japanese imports of which the Japanese government took full advantage while keeping tight control over domestic markets. The government's policies not only shielded industry from foreign competition but, also, Japanese consumers' choice of products which were limited to goods primarily produced in Japan. However, there were inexpensive canned goods from Rumania and Bulgaria, although not sold in the US due to the Cold War. Imports of processed foods, teas and coffee were distributed by the large trading companies such as Itochu, Mitsui and Marubeni. Often the products' labels indicated that the distributors were manufacturers of goods such as steel and unrelated to the food and beverage industries.

There was rice called "Specially Chosen Rice" (*tokusen mai*). The name was specifically given to rice grown domestically in prefectures renowned for rice production such as Niigata Prefecture but we heard that some of the special rice was actually from California and sold on the black market. Because imported rice was banned due to strong lobbying by rice farmers, who were receiving substantial subsidies from government, the claims were difficult to confirm.

I experienced the same lifestyle as a typical Japanese housewife. Domestic foods suited Japanese palates and ours as well. The small homes lacked storage space and freezers were out of the question. Refrigerators were half the size of the American brands and without freezer compartments. Refrigerators with freezer space for ice cream and ice cubes were considered luxury items.

Since we lived on the outskirts of Kamakura our access to markets was limited and we depended on the village greengrocer and fish monger for provisions. The milkman delivered bottles of milk to our home. We made the occasional hour train trek to Yokohama to a street where a supermarket catering to foreigners sold a variety of western imports but for a price. The area was called Motomachi where westerners were allowed to reside (the foreign ghetto) when they ventured to Japan to provide services to the Japanese in the late nineteenth century as part of the push by the government to modernize Japan's industry to join the ranks with western nations. A cemetery for foreigners was located on the hill above with graves dating back to the 1870s.

There was a significant German presence in the larger cities, indicating Japan's long relationship with Germany including its first constitution after the Meiji Restoration, which was based on the Bismarck constitution. The Meiji government dispatched Japanese to Germany to study science, medicine and engineering and until the mid-seventies, patients' medical records were written in German. German brewers went to Japan to teach the art of beer brewing and German butchers taught the Japanese ham and sausage production. In the 1930s, Japanese engineers were sent to German to study automobile design. Some German foods and beverages became staples in the Japanese daily diet. German restaurants, bakeries and coffee houses were prevalent and Germans seemed to be the most favored of foreigners as opposed to Americans despite the popularity of American pop culture.

The only sacrifice for us was not being able to drink the usual morning orange juice. Due to the high tariff on oranges a glass of fresh orange juice was $5 and we were forced to substitute Taiwan bananas. But domestically grown fruit was also relatively expensive compared to US produce, although US grapefruit were sold at almost the same price as in the US because they were not grown domestically. The Japanese *mikan* controlled the markets while Navels and Valencia oranges, priced at $3 per orange, were left to rot on the shelves. *Mikan* juice from Ehime Prefecture, one of the primary orange-growing regions besides Shizuoka Prefecture, was sold in cans but foreign residents considered that there was no substitute for Valencia from Florida. The high tariffs were the result of the policies of the Ministry of Agriculture, Forestry, and Fisheries (MAFA).

Major Japanese wine and liquor producers were importing and distributing foreign wines, fortified spirits and blended whisky in the 1960s. Bottles of Johnny Walker Red and Black labels and Chivas Regal were much sought-after for corporate gifts and for special friends. But the domestically produced wine was inferior to the wine imports because Japan's humid climate was not conducive to the cultivation of grapes for wine and producers mixed their wine with cheaper grape juice from Hungary and Bulgaria.

The Clothing Conundrum

The yen/dollar exchange rate was exceptional at ¥360 per dollar. Joseph Dodge, the chairman of Detroit Bank, was SCAP's economic advisor who planned policies to revitalize and stabilize Japan's economy. Known as the Dodge Line, the policy also acted to promote Japanese exports in overseas markets. Since we received funds from the US we benefited considerably.

The majority of consumers' expendable income was still limited through currency regulation but foreign luxury brands had already entered Japan through either licensing agreements with Japanese producer-distributors or through joint ventures with the Japanese companies controlling 51 percent of the shares. Christian Dior licensed Kanebo, the venerable textile company and the oldest listed company on the Tokyo Stock Exchange, to copy and sell its fashions in one of its outlets in the Ginza. Dior also licensed Kanebo the rights to manufacture nylon stockings for the Dior brand. Since foreign apparel entered the market through licensing agreements and was manufactured in Japan, the clothes were produced specifically for the Japanese stature. I purchased a Dior tweed coat for a pittance but the sleeves had to be lengthened.

Footwear produced in Japan also was sized according to Japanese feet. Japanese or foreign residents with longer and narrower feet were at a disadvantage and experienced difficulties sourcing domestically manufactured shoes. My husband and I brought most of our clothes with us but my husband had to go to a tailor to have his shirts made to fit his taller frame. Tariffs on leather goods such as handbags and shoes were high and receiving any leather goods from the US was a luxury we could ill afford.

Learning the Language: a 15-year struggle

A month after our arrival we began studying Japanese privately with two teachers to whom we were introduced at a Japanese language school for Jesuit priests who were sent to Japan to teach at Jesuit universities and private high schools for boys. The director of the Juniso School was a Jesuit priest from the Basque country in Spain who spoke five languages, including Japanese. Our teachers who instructed the priests lived in Kamakura. They also taught Japanese at Sophia University, a Catholic university, in Tokyo. The text books had been written by Anthony Alfonso an American Jesuit priest who was a professor of Japanese at the University of Michigan and at Sophia. *Japanese Language Patterns* was considered for the next 30 years as the quintessential Japanese text book for spoken Japanese. It was rumored that Alfonso had suffered a breakdown subsequent to publishing the book in 1966.

The text book for written Japanese (*kanji*) was authored by my Japanese teacher, Kazuaki Niimi and together with "Japanese Language Patterns" was used for years at such universities as California and Michigan. Both Alfonso and Niimi taught Japanese in the Department of Japanese at the Australian National University in Canberra.

Niimi's home was located in the district of Zazengawa ('meditation river') appropriately named because of the many Zen Buddhist monasteries in Kamakura. I visited him once weekly for two-hour lessons conducted in a traditional Japanese room with tatami floor. I sat on a cushion with legs tucked under body facing Niimi across a low wooden table. At the end of each lesson, Mrs. Niimi served tea and Japanese rice crackers or cakes or yogurt that she had made.

Mr. Niimi was a superb teacher. He told me that in order to build a vocabulary and understand the nuances of the spoken language it was paramount to becoming fluent in the written language. He presented me with his kanji manuscript prior to its publication. Niimi's instruction and manuscript initiated a 15-year struggle of learning around 3,500 kanji so that I could read post-Meiji literature in the original by famous authors and correspond with close Japanese friends while I was living away from Japan. It was a daily ordeal memorizing each kanji, writing and rewriting by hand on special practice paper. It was impossible to foresee that the written language, which gave me access to great literature as well as to the nuances of daily life would one day be a tool giving me entry to Japanese companies and access to information not usually available to foreigners.

With a Little Help from My Friends

The generosity of new and accepting friends aided the process of integrating into Japanese society. Our rental was divided by a wall into two living spaces. We were fortunate to live next to a young couple with two children and a little dog. The husband's father had been an ambassador to France but it seemed as if the family was struggling financially. Mr. and Mrs. Saida were devout Catholics and the little boy attended a parochial school. Mrs. Saida taught English at several schools in order to afford the expensive tuition fee.

She introduced me to a large private girl's high school in Kita Kamakura, which was one station north of Kamakura and where most of the Zen temples were located, to give private piano lessons to students who wanted to enter first-tier music schools in Japan and in the US. My degree in piano from the Julliard School of Music was enough to gain employment because the school was as well-known as Harvard. I was pleasantly surprised that even Japanese who had no knowledge of music were impressed with the label, which also significantly eased entrance in Japanese corporations even though music was not involved in the work. I began to understand that in Japanese society where one received a degree was as important as one's skill sets.

We met our closest friends by coincidence during our first year in Japan when we were visiting Kyoto to see the Zen Buddhist temples and monasteries. One early morning we were waiting at the front gate of a temple known for its pine tree. A man and woman in their early sixties were also waiting to enter. They introduced themselves in hesitant English as Mr and Mrs Hibi and we replied in hesitant Japanese. By coincidence the Hibis lived in Kita Kamakura and they invited us to visit them at their home. Their house sat on top of a hill just a five minute walk from the train station and from Engakuji, a famous Zen Buddhist monastery.

I was reluctant to contact them because my Japanese was still basic and communication could be uncomfortable for them. Six months passed until one day outside the entrance of Kamakura Station on my way to the Kita Kamakura High School I felt a tap on my shoulder. Turning around I saw Mrs. Hibi's smiling face. She had been trying to locate me and insisted that I visit her the following week for tea.

The Hibis built the house to escape to the countryside because their home in Tokyo had been destroyed during the war by fire bombs dropped by the American air force. The house was large by Japanese standards with a big garden tended by a gardener. A housekeeper cleaned and cooked twice weekly. The lounge area was heated by central heating, a real luxury in comparison to our house.

That first visit initiated the beginning of a long friendship which was based on mutual interests, humor and a devotion to the consumption of Japanese traditional sweets. My relationship with Mrs. Hibi profoundly influenced the way I adapted to Japanese social mores and values. She was a gracious hostess who was an avid reader of Japanese literature, which she preferred to domestic responsibilities. My determination to learn written Japanese was inspired by Mrs. Hibi's love of literature and I wanted to read the same books in Japanese.

The first book she recommended was *Mon* (the gated entrance to Buddhist temples) by her favorite author Natsume Soseki, which is set at Engakuji. It took me an entire day to read one page, constantly referring to a Japanese dictionary. But I completed the book and went on to read a number of Soseki's works as well as Mrs. Hibi's other recommendations. My visits with her focused on sitting on the lounge floor, listening to classical music and laughing at silly things while consuming quantities of Japanese cakes served with green tea followed by western cakes with English tea.

She was self-effacing and did not speak much about her background other than that her father was a university professor in Tokyo and that her grandfather was the first consul general to Beijing during the Meiji Period. His grave was in Beijing. One of Mrs. Hibi's most treasured possessions was a splendid large Chinese calligraphy her grandfather had sent to his family and which decorated the Japanese-style room in her home. She boasted that the some of the finest things in Japanese society had been imported from China. My other Japanese friends who were also well-educated shared Mrs. Hibi's values. Therefore, my initial impression of how the Japanese related to the Chinese was entirely positive.

On New Year's Eve the Hibi's entertained us with a special meal which Mrs. Hibi had prepared, followed by a visit to Engakuji to hear the monks ringing the giant temple bell 88 times. We returned to their house for the mandatory bowl of noodles at midnight to signal longevity. On New Year's Day Mrs Hibi served the traditional cold lunch in lacquered lunch boxes she had prepared the day before. I always helped with the washing up in the cold north-facing kitchen. Even though she was not an enthusiastic cook, thanks to her patient instruction, my repertoire of Japanese dishes increased considerably.

Whenever I visited the Hibi's for a meal or for tea, Mrs. Hibi gave me boxes of expensive biscuits or Japanese rice crackers or canned crab all stamped with the Mitsukoshi logo. Mitsukoshi is one of Japan's oldest department stores where Mrs. Hibi seemed to purchase most of her clothing during the sales. Years later a friend told me that Mr. Hibi's ancestors were among the stores' founders in Osaka during the seventeenth century. Since Mr. Hibi was from Osaka and since I was served dishes cooked in the Osaka style, I presumed that the information was correct.

My husband and I reciprocated with Western-style meals at our house. I served Spaghetti Bolognese or a minced beef recipe on dishes that did not match, which they enjoyed immensely because it was a respite from their usual cuisine. There was also the welcomed element of informality. Mr. Hibi had a good sense of humor but it was not until I could speak Japanese that I was able to communicate easily with him. We stayed at the Hibi's home many times. They also entertained my parents on a visit to Kamakura and visited us for a week in San Francisco.

The Outsiders

The word for foreigner in Japanese is *gaijin* which can also be translated as "other person" or "outsider." We had numerous adventures as a consequence of not fully understanding the language and not having integrated into the culture. Some were rather unpleasant because of the way Japanese perceived foreigners but we tried not to take this personally because it was a part of the society.

Our ignorance also prompted some experiences which were very comical. Nevertheless, these experiences also prepared me for future work in Japanese corporations and understanding how to relate to Japanese staff who had never associated with foreigners or who had limited exposure to foreigners. As importantly, I became inured to what most foreigners would regard as discriminatory behavior. Japan was to be accepted on its terms if one wanted to establish a comfort zone.

While the Hibis were a part of mainstream society, three female friends suffered the consequences of not being one of the crowd. Our sponsor introduced us to a friend who had been married to a Japanese diplomat who was posted at the United Nations in a very elite position. However, the marriage was an unhappy one and she requested a divorce, despite the social ramifications. She returned with their young daughter to her family's estate in a town located near Kamakura. Since her father owned newspapers and a golf course near Mt. Fuji and was very wealthy, she was well-taken care of. However, the woman admitted that the divorce had stigmatized her among her social circle and that it would be difficult to marry a Japanese again. On the other hand, her sister, who was determined to become a "princess" one day, married a member of the Toshiba family.

One of my first impressions of Japanese society was that many Japanese appeared to have either poor dental habits or poor diets because their teeth were capped with silver and gold. The woman explained that instead of treating tooth decay through preventive measures Japanese dentists tended to drill or extract teeth that were regarded as remotely rotten. She kindly introduce us to her British dentist in Tokyo who was excellent and refrained from removing or drilling my teeth.

My exposure to less positive aspects of Japanese society occurred when we met another woman one afternoon on a commuter train returning to Kamakura from Tokyo. She had noticed us while we were having coffee at the German Bakery, a popular confectioner in Tokyo, where she was the hostess. She invited us to her home in Kamakura to meet her German mother and Japanese father.

Her German mother had been divorced from the German ambassador to Turkey in the 1930s before she remarried her father who managed the silver mines during the Japanese occupation of Manchuria where she was born. At the end of the war her parents fled Manchuria with her and her grandmother in tow and only the clothes on their backs. When they arrived in Tokyo they were impoverished. The parents took out a loan and opened a German restaurant which became a favorite eating establishment in Tokyo among ministry officials. They sent their daughter to an expensive private girls' parochial school from which the Empress had also graduated. Although my friend was very attractive, compared to Japanese females her body was voluptuous. During her teenage years, she had experienced sexual harassment while riding on subways and even when walking down a street. When we met her she was in her early thirties and had yet to marry. Her parents were very worried and were searching for a match. Two years later they found her a husband who moved into their home, which was a new build and quite spacious. The relationship was not particularly happy and we never met the husband.

Mama-san

Our friend introduced us to one of her friends whose husband, who was the president of the sewing machine division of a large Japanese manufacturer, had built a spacious modern house in an area between Kita Kamakura and Kamakura where they lived with their boxer dog. The animal substituted for a child because they were having problems conceiving. At the time, household pets were relatively uncommon. The couple finally had a little girl several years later.

The husband was often away on business but the couple invited us one autumn as their guests to the mountain resort of Zao in Yamagata Prefecture known for its hot springs and skiing where we had the opportunity to become better acquainted. The tatami mat rooms in the traditional Japanese inn were well-appointed and we enjoyed the baths and the Japanese cuisine. The following morning we accompanied them in a chauffeured car to a gated estate nearby. A middle-aged woman and an elderly woman, both in kimono, were solemnly standing in front of the gate as we approached. The husband got out of the car and went up to them to chat for about ten minutes before returning to the car for the drive back to the resort. I guessed that the elderly woman was his mother but the other woman remained a mystery. I wondered why our friend did not join him. I was to learn the true nature of the couple's relationship several years later. The husband dropped the three of us at the inn before leaving on another business trip.

We visited the temple Yamadera where the illustrious seventeenth century haiku poet Matsuo Basho wrote his famous Frog Haiku. I purchased a slab of polished grey slate on which his hand-written poem is transcribed. It is still among my positions in its original wooden box.

The following morning we travelled to Sendai where our friend took us to meet her husband's old friend, the owner of a pachinko parlor. The middle-aged woman had met the husband in Harbin during the war. She greeted us in front of the parlor and guided us inside for a brief tour. Koreans are usually the proprietors of pachinko parlors but I was unsure of her nationality. It was the first and last time I entered a pachinko parlor but despite the early hour, men were standing in a trance before the machines trying their luck.

The woman escorted us upstairs to her apartment above the parlor. The front door opened into an interior, dominated by red walls and heavy black ebony furnishings. A high-pitched voice of a child or an elderly woman repeatedly sneezing and calling out in a very high voice, "Mama-san! Mama-san!" came from another room. We followed the woman into the room to the voice. To our utter astonishment, there was a big iron cage hanging from the ceiling. Standing on a rung in the cage was a large jet-black Minna bird wagging its head as it sneezed, chirping "Mama-san! Mama-san!" We tried unsuccessfully to suppress our laughter.

The woman took us to a Chinese restaurant for dinner before escorting us to our hotel. The next day we visited one of Japan's oldest Zen Buddhist temples before taking a boat ride around the major tourist attraction Matsushima, the small uninhabited islands covered with pine trees.

Language: 101 mistakes!

The number of errors I made during the first three years exceeded belief. Some of the mistakes related to the misinterpretation of English words that had been abbreviated by the Japanese in order to ease pronunciation. The incidences were comical, embarrassing and could be expensive as well. A few months had passed after our trip to Yamagata when the wife offered me a *misshin* at a reduced price. Presuming the *misshin* was a washing machine, overjoyed, I accepted. She called me the following week to announce that the *misshin* would be delivered to her house by one of her husband's staff. It was perplexing because washing machines were usually transported directly to the home by truck and installed. I visited her at the appointed time and was ushered to the tatami mat Japanese-style room, which was used on special occasions.

A gentleman in a suit was kneeling on a cushion in front of a low table. But the medium size case on the table was far too small to contain a washing machine. I kneeled on a cushion across the table from him. My friend settled next to me wearing a very pleased expression on her face. The man opened the case to reveal a sewing machine, which in Japanese is called a *misshin*. Unable to conceal my shock, I sputtered out in English that I did not sew, which was not what my friend was expecting to hear and not what I had intended to say. Although the gentleman did not understand English, my friend seemed to understand the expression of dismay flickering across my face. Her face darkened. I quickly recovered my composure. I knew that if I did not thank my friend and the employee profusely for the *misshin* and purchase it on the spot, her husband would lose face. I carried the case home, ¥40,000 poorer. I did not open the case until we were preparing to return to the US a year later. Fortunately, I was able to resell the *misshin* at the same price.

Before returning to the US I tried unsuccessfully to contact our friend. Although Mrs. Hibi had never mentioned that she knew of the couple, she told me that the wife was one of the president's mistresses and that she had been in a protracted argument with one of his other mistresses who lived in the nearby town of Ofuna. Evidently, the president had cut off our friend's accounts at the local merchants causing her to accrue substantial debts at many shops in Kamakura. Fearful of being arrested, she refused to leave her house or answer her telephone.

We were still ignorant about the common practice at the time by wealthy businessmen to have mistresses. I then considered that the middle-aged woman standing in front of the gate in Yamagata was the president's real wife and that the woman who owned the pachinko parlor may once have been a mistress whom he had set up in business.

Is There a Doctor in the House? Hit and Miss

My husband became unwell and since the standard of medical care in Kamakura in the 1960s was inadequate to deal with my husband's illness we commuted to Tokyo, first to St. Luke's Hospital, which was purported to have more modern facilities. Nevertheless, the doctors were not up-to-date with his type of illness and my husband ended up in an American Seventh Day Adventist Hospital for treatment. My own experience at St. Luke's is memorable.

When I felt sharp pains in my lower back and developed a mild fever I went to St Luke's Hospital and was seen by a nurse. She insisted that I did not have a fever but that westerners had higher body temperatures than Japanese. The physician on duty prescribed a sulphur drug. Within several days, the back pain worsened and I took the two-hour trip to St Luke's again. The diagnosis was inflammation of the kidneys. Again, I was prescribed sulphur tablets. The pain became unbearable and I also had difficulty breathing. This time I went to the Seventh Day Adventist Hospital for a diagnosis, which was not only nephritis but, also pleurisy. I was kept in the hospital for ten days before being released.

A taxi collected me for the ride to Tokyo Station but on the way, the driver hit a small pick-up truck which turned over. Fortunately nobody was injured. The taxi driver, apologizing profusely, hailed another taxi. When I reached the train station I found that my wallet was missing but, fortunately, I had enough money for the train ticket.

Although I had suffered considerably from the delay in treatment and a lost wallet, there was a happy ending. A few days later, I received in the post a packet containing my wallet intact along with a letter of apology from the taxi driver who had discovered the wallet, which had fallen out of his taxi during the confusion. Twenty years later when I returned to Tokyo to work I was to experience a similar episode.

A Close Encounter with the New Komeito Party

The New Komeito Party (NKP) is currently in coalition with the Liberal Democratic Party (LDP). The original party was an offshoot of the Soka Gakkai, a lay Buddhist organization based on Nichren Buddhism and founded in the 1930s. The organization developed rapidly after the war primarily due to the sponsorship from Japanese on lower incomes. The organization published magazines and brochures advocating devotion to the church's precepts. Believers who contributed to the Soka Gakkai coffers were promised successful and lucrative careers. The political party, the Komeito ('Clean Party') was established in the 1960s and it evolved to include other right-wing parties since the 1990s. According to NKP officials, the Soka Gakkai and the NKP are independent organizations. Nevertheless, the Soka Gakkai and the NKP meet biannually and the majority of NKP members belong to the Soka Gakkai.

My first exposure to the Soka Gakkai was in 1969. It was common to see young male American missionaries from the Baptist Church or Seventh Day Adventist Church in black suits and ties making the rounds of neighborhoods and going from door-to-door to distribute literature with the hope of bringing new members into the flock. However, it was not common to see members of the Soka Gakkai visiting homes. But one day I received an unannounced visit from our next door neighbor's cleaner who was accompanied by two gentlemen wearing suits. I was alone when she and her friends knocked on the back door of the house as a sign of respect. Unable to speak English, she offered Soka Gakkai literature in English. I knew that the Komeito Party, was directly connected to the Soka Gakkai and was momentarily at a loss of how to deal with the situation. In order not to disappoint or humiliate the cleaner I told her that I was an American citizen and that if I participated in any political activities or voted in foreign elections I could lose my American citizenship. The cleaner and her friends vehemently denied that the Soka Gakkai was a political party but I insisted politely that the Komeito Party was associated with the religious organization. I hurriedly produced my passport and opened it to a page which stated something about not participating in foreign elections. To my relief, neither the cleaner nor the gentlemen could read English and departed without further protest.

US-Japan Relations: unwilling bedfellows

We relied on the Armed Forces Radio which mainly broadcast news on the US and music programs which were programed for the military. Although the Occupation had ended, the Vietnam War was in high gear. The constant presence of American military throughout Japan was a painful reminder for many Japanese of their country's defeat and the Occupation. I saw the war from very different perspective than Americans in the US because Kamakura was located near Yokosuka, a town that hosted a major American naval base where thousands of US naval personnel were stationed. The servicemen who returned from Vietnam on R&R were as young as 16 and the anxiety of having to return to the front was evident.

There was a palpable anti-American sentiment. Prime Minister Eisaku Sato (1964–72) was forced to close Tokyo University for a year in 1969 because of student protests against the US-Japan Security Treaty and Japan's support of American military engagement in Vietnam. One afternoon on our way to Tokyo we were stopped on the platform of Kamakura Station by police in riot gear who requested our passports and cautioned us not to travel to Tokyo because there was an anti-American demonstration in Tokyo.

Yukio Mishima (1925–70) was one of Japan's greatest writers of the twentieth century and nominated three times for the Nobel Prize for literature. He was born into a family of bureaucrats and was a nationalist. He enlisted in the Ground Defence Force in 1962. In the same year, Mishima formed a small private army of which most of the members were students and pledged to protect the emperor, whom he felt exemplified the Japanese spirit. On November 25, 1970, Mishima, accompanied by four members of his army, tried to instigate a *coup d'état* at the Self-Defence Force headquarters in Tokyo. They broke into the commandant's room and held him hostage. When Mishima read his manifesto to the soldiers who had congregated below, he was jeered at. Humiliated, Mishima returned to the room and committed suicide.

I conducted in-depth interviews in 1994 with Japanese officials in the Ministry of International Trade and Industry (MITI) who were children in the 1950s and 60s. The interviews included questions related to their impressions of America during their childhood. Their answers revealed the general reaction of the Japanese to the American Occupation and to the US military bases located throughout Japan.

A MITI "elite" career officer aged 46 stated:

> The Japanese saw America as the ideal country. Japan was supported by a large amount of American aid. Men from the Occupation Forces were in the town where I was living so I saw American troops often. The men had splendid physics. I thought that the bases were very luxurious. My main impression was the gap between the poverty in Japan and the abundance. I didn't see any resistance to the Occupation but the Japanese, who were attending elementary school and who were of a slightly older generation than I, felt great sadness at the loss of Japanese traditional values. Some authors like Yukio Mishima and Shintaro Ishihara saw the Occupation Forces as conquering devils and Japan as a pitiful nation. The Japanese, particularly at that time, were simply trying to survive so there was a strong feeling that America was supporting Japan. Social values completely changed. In a word (and this is true for the entire world), Americanization was taking place and, consequently, Japan was inside this giant wave.

A MITI non-career officer aged 36 told me:

> Although I was born quite a while after the end of the Second World War, the American Occupation Forces were still in Japan. My first sense of America was that America defeated Japan in the war. Until Japan's definitive defeat, Japan had never lost a war. There was an army base in my neighborhood. I was very small so I don't remember seeing soldiers, but I saw many American civilians in my area. My impression was that Americans were very large and that America was a powerful and wealthy country. Americans lived very wealthy existences with

big cars and shopping centers. They were independent! The Americans who lived in my town looked well-off and lived in spacious quarters. On the other hand, Japanese lived in a small area in cramped quarters.

An officer who was 31 confided:

> My father was in the Second World War. I didn't hear specific things about the war, but I often heard about Japan's poverty because of the loss of the war and how everybody suffered. Rice and food were at a premium and it was wasteful to leave anything on one's plate. Subjects such as war dead [and] the peace pact were not discussed much. Only after Japan became richer was there talk about how Japan broke the peace. There was also ambivalence about the US. The Japanese lost self-confidence because of the loss of the war. Self-confidence was also lost because everyone stopped telling their children about Japanese culture, Japanese values and how they wanted their children to live. My father kindly taught me various things but he didn't speak about Japanese culture, civilization or social values. I think that this was true for most Japanese households.

Yukio Mishima was one of former Tokyo governor Shintaro Ishihara's closest friends. Ishihara's initial exposure to the United States was during the war when his neighborhood was strafed by American aircraft. Ishihara claimed that the aircraft flew so low that he could see pictures of naked women and cartoon characters painted on the sides of the planes. His book *Japan Can Say No* (*No to Ieru Nihon*) was a collaborative effort with the late Akio Morita who was Sony Corporation's founder and chairman. Published in 1989 the book was a bestseller. Ishihara argued that the United States regarded Japan as a subordinate and that this attitude was related to racism.

2

The Second Time Around:
Where Oh Where did the Green Grass Go?

After spending two years in California recovering from what would turn out to be a chronic illness, my husband was impatient to return to Japan. We packed our belongings for a second attempt in 1972.

At the end of the war Japan's primary industry was agriculture. In the late 1950s when Japan began its period of rapid economic growth, thousands of young high-school graduates living in farming and fishing villages left for the Tokyo–Osaka–Kobe regions to seek better-paying jobs in retail shops, factories and small businesses. The mass migration resulted in the loss of population in communities outside of the industrialized areas and the overpopulation of big metropolises. The majority of farmers who remained in the rural areas were middle-aged or older.

By 1970 it was difficult to believe that Japan's industrial complex and infrastructure had been devastated by the war. The 1964 Tokyo Olympics had witnessed a spurt of infrastructure construction and industrial development in the metropolitan areas and rural areas. Towns were connected by a haphazard array of new small dwellings which were constructed without any consideration for design and which blighted the once lusciously green countryside and farmland that had been snatched up by land developers.

During the second period from 1971–76 we first returned to Kamakura before moving six months later to Shizuoka Prefecture about 100 km south of Tokyo and the small farming village of Sawaji which was 15 minutes by bus to Mishima city. We stayed with the Hibis for three weeks before we managed to find a rental located near the famous giant sculpture of Buddha (*Hase Daibutsu*). As was the case in Inamuragasaki, the hot water for the kitchen was supplied by a small gas-fitted hot water heater attached above the sink facet and ignited manually by a flick of a switch.

One afternoon in April we heard the humming of helicopters overhead and went outside to investigate. Our neighbors told us that the Nobel Prize recipient for literature Yasunari Kawabata who was also a Kamakura resident had committed suicide. Traffic jammed the roads leading to the town and helicopters transporting the media hovered overhead. Kawabata had been suffering from depression after his close friend Yukio Mishima had committed suicide the previous year.

I had experienced strong earthquakes in San Francisco but our first one in Japan occurred a few months before we moved to Mishima. We had been cautioned to turn off the gas before leaving the house to avoid fire which often occurred following an earthquake. The quake was long and rolling and strong enough to shake the front fence violently. However, there were no reports of damage.

It was a crucial period in Japan's post-war industrial history. Japan had achieved the third highest GDP in the world (behind the US and the Soviet Union respectively) but the bureaucratic government system was still firmly entrenched due, in part, to the United States' post-war policies at the time. The policies were profoundly influenced by the beginning of the Cold War in 1945.

Eisaku Sato, Japan's longest serving post-war prime minister (1967–72) and the brother of Prime Minister Nobusuke Kishi (1957–60), owned a home in Kamakura. Kishi's political ideology significantly influenced his grandson, Prime Minister Shinzo Abe, and played an important role in the United States' objectives to install an ultra-conservative ally in the Pacific in order to protect the region from communist expansion. Kishi's post-war political career is also indicative of how the "reverse reforms" during the Allied Occupation effectively perpetuated Japan's wartime government administration of the economy and an ultra-conservative political environment, which enhanced the power of the bureaucracy, thus forging the Japan Inc. model.

Prime Minister Nobusuke Kishi is credited with being the father of the Liberal Democrats (LDP) and one of the king-pins of what is known as the "1955 political system" that was based on the collaboration between politicians, businessmen and bureaucrats and banked with huge sums from the private sector. The LDP controlled the National Diet for 38 years until 1993 and from 1996–2009. Abe's LDP roots and his right-wing political philosophy are inherited from his grandfather. Now that the LDP once again holds the majority of seats in the National Diet, it is likely that a version of the 1955 political system will continue.

Nobusuke Kishi the Powerbroker of the LDP

Kishi was a talented elite official in the Ministry of Commerce and Industry (MCI), the forerunner of the Ministry of International Trade and Industry (MITI). Since the Meiji Period the Japanese military had protected Japanese interests in Taiwan and Korea. After Japan's expansion into Manchuria during the First World War, General Hideki Tojo ran military operations in Manchuria until the Second World War. He supported Kishi who was sent by the MCI to Mukden in Manchuko, a puppet state in Manchuria which was formed by the Japanese army in collaboration with the Chinese imperial government after the Manchurian Incident. While in Mukden Kishi skillfully manoeuvred the distribution of capital to cultivate right-wing nationalists and allies in small and medium sized businesses. Kishi was an expert at money laundering no matter how large the amount. It was rumored that, through his connections with the opium trade, Kishi engaged in both legal and illegal transactions for both public and personal purposes with simply a telephone call.

In November 1943, MCI merged with the Cabinet Planning Board to form the Ministry of Munitions (MM) to improve the production of military supplies. When General Tojo became Prime Minister in 1941 he appointed Kishi as cabinet Minister of Commerce and Industry and in 1944, Kishi was also appointed the director of MM.

Before the outbreak of the war, Kishi had formed the Association for the Defence of the Fatherland. When he returned to Tokyo in 1939, he extended his network and won a seat in the National Diet in 1942. In 1944 he established the "Kishi New Party." Its members were Kishi's political and business right-wing associates from Manchuria and elite control bureaucrats and right-wing military personnel. His money power base were the directors of the public companies in Manchuria and the non- *zaibatsu* independent businesses that had reaped profits through Kishi's agendas.

Japan surrendered to the Allied Powers on 2 September 1945. The period 1945–52 is commonly referred to as the Allied Occupation. The occupying counties were the United States, Great Britain and Australia but Great Britain and Australia sent far fewer troops than the United States, which was commanded by Douglas MacArthur, Supreme Command of the Allied Powers (SCAP). The United States was determined to create a Western-style capitalistic and democratic society. Wartime government officials were purged as Class A criminals and executed, Tojo among them. Kishi was purged as a Class A war criminal and imprisoned in Sugano prison in Tokyo for three years.

SCAP intended to reform Japan's wartime economic system by systematically disbanding the military and the ministries. MM along with the Home Ministry and the Military Police were abolished in 1945. Policies also included dismantling the *zaibatsu* (family-owned conglomerates) established before and after the Meiji Restoration such as Sumitomo and Mitsubishi because of their full participation in the war effort. The US initiated a new constitution to introduce democratic principles such as freedom of speech, free elections and female suffrage. Labor unions were allowed to reorganize and the Socialist and Communist Parties that had been banned during the war were also given the right to reorganize. The new constitution which removed the Showa emperor as the formal head of state, replaced the Meiji Constitution. The Ministry of Defence was abolished and the controversial Article 9 renounced Japan's right to wage war. However, the beginning of the Cold War in 1945 with the Soviet Union, the communist-backed General Strike by the Government Workers' Union in 1947, the Korean War (1950–53) and the perceived threat of communist expansion in East Asia persuaded SCAP to reconsider a number of the intended reforms in order to cultivate an economically strong and politically conservative ally in the Pacific where the United States could base its military operations in the Pacific and its military hardware. In 1947 the Diet banned strikes by government workers and in 1948 the Wage Control Program replaced free collective bargaining.

SCAP recognized that fundamental to a swift recovery for Japan's devastated industrial complex was the expertise of the ministry officials who had managed Japan's wartime economy. It reinstated former ministry officials, thereby preserving Japan's pre-war institutions and the economic system. SCAP's staff ignorance of the Japanese language and the social system compelled them to rely on existing institutions, namely the bureaucracy, to implement policies.

The nature of bureaucratic rule and the persona of the ministries remained intact because the officials who planned Japan's post-war industrial policies were former MCI and Ministry of Finance (MOF) officials. Kishi's ministry, the Ministry of Commerce, was the forerunner of the Ministry of International Trade and Industry (MITI), which was established in 1947. The first officials previously had worked for the MCI and the Ministry of Munitions alongside Kishi during the war. MITI's remit focused on the planning and implementation of industrial policy. The two economic ministries, the Ministry of Finance (MOF) and the Ministry of International Trade and Industry (MITI) were credited with being at the helm of Japan's industrial resuscitation.

Survival of the Fittest

When Kishi realized that he would not be executed, he planned tactics that would lead a right-wing conservative party to power, an organization which would also include right-wing socialists and conservatives. When he was released from prison in 1948, he was forbidden by SCAP to enter public office again. However, the order was soon rescinded by SCAP as a part of its "reverse reforms."

Kishi first re-established his Kishi New Party and integrated it with his "Association for the Defence of the Fatherland" to form the "Japan Reconstruction Federation," which included some of the former members of a pre-war conservative party and elite bureaucrats. He consolidated the federation with the well-established ultra-conservative parties whose objective was to revise the new constitution and the security treaty to allow Japan to rearm in order to defend itself. His younger brother Eisaku Sato, who was Prime Minister Shigeru Yoshida's protégé and chief cabinet secretary, urged Kishi to enter the Liberal Party, which was established by Ichiro Hatoyama, who was slated to become Prime Minister in 1946 but was purged by SCAP and prohibited to enter politics for five years. Kishi understood that in order to realize his ambitions he had to enter mainstream conservative politics and requested an introduction to Shigeru Yoshida who served as prime minister from 1946 to 1947 and from 1948 to 1954.

Yoshida invited him to become a member and Kishi won a seat in the National Diet in 1953. Kishi made a power-play within the party by accusing Yoshida of being in the lap of the Americans and the British. He succeeded in undermining Yoshida's leadership by courting senior members of the party as well as business leaders to form a new government. Calling for a new conservative party, together with 200 politicians he created the "New Party Formation Promotion Council." Yoshida reacted by expelling him from the Liberal Party.

In 1954, Kishi and his party joined Hatoyama and other Liberal Party members and, combining a strategic alliance with the Socialists formed a separate faction, the Democratic Party. Together they won 185 of the 467 seats while the Liberal Democrats lost almost half of their seats in the Diet. Hatoyama succeeded Yoshida as Prime Minister in 1954. However, Hatoyama was reluctant to merge the parties with the Democratic Party faction because he sensed that he could lose control, but Kishi's political acumen and determination paid off and the Liberal Democratic Party was established in 1955 with Kishi at the center.

Kishi had finally achieved his goal. He had succeeded in incorporating the existing conservative parties, right-wing and more moderate factions into a single conservative political party which would dominate Japanese politics for 38 years. Hatoyama suffered a stroke in 1954 but continued to serve in office until 1956 before resigning. He was replaced by Tanzan Ishibashi, who, also due to illness, resigned after just 63 days. On 25 February 1957 Kishi became Japan's 56th and 57th Prime Minister.

Manipulation of Fear

Kishi shrewdly manipulated America's intense fear of communism in the United States (1947 Truman Doctrine) and communist expansion in Asia to push his ultra-conservative party to power. America was instrumental in guaranteeing that LDP politicians would dominate the National Diet in the first election. Communist-backed labor union protests were suppressed and the Central Intelligence Agency (CIA) funneled money to the LDP in the 1950s and 1960s in order to ensure a strong, conservative government. The CIA had created a fund, known as the "M Fund" which was organized from the sale of confiscated Japanese military supplies, industrial diamonds, platinum, gold and silver which had been stolen in occupied countries and the sale of shares of the dissolved *zaibatsu*. Kishi, who was strongly supported by the United States as Prime Minister, was a recipient of CIA funds which were funneled through LDP coffers. The US State Department announced in July 2006 that by 1964 President Lyndon Johnson had officially stopped payments for "covert programs of propaganda and social action to encourage the Japanese to reject the influence from the left." However, the fund effectively continued during Japan's post-war period to support the LDP.

MITI's administrative jurisdiction encompassed the retail and manufacturing sectors, the energy sector, small businesses development and promoting international trade. MITI's mercantile policies protected domestic industries within its jurisdiction from foreign competition in order to catch-up and overtake the United States as a global economic force to be reckoned with.

My husband and I experienced the government's protectionist policies, farmers selling their land to real estate developers and the acceleration of nuclear power plants on earthquake-prone zones.

Country Life

Sawaji's primary crops were *mikan*, rice, horse radish, ginger root, persimmon and white radish. Our cottage was located on agricultural land owned for centuries by Ryutakuji, a famous Zen Buddhist monastery which gave us permission to live in the cottage on the condition that we upgrade the interior at our own expense. Farmers living in the area volunteered to tend Ryutakuji's rice fields.

Mt. Fuji towered regally behind the cottage, a truly magnificent view. Clouds covered the top and each day Fuji-san wore a different cloud-hat. The dirt road led to Hakone National Park through cedar forests and past hog and honey farms. My husband had photographs of his father sitting on the veranda of the Fujiya Hotel with two American colleagues who were sent to Tokyo by Price Waterhouse to teach Japanese banks western accounting methods in the 1920s. The hotel was a popular venue in Hakone for its hot spring baths and we had spent a few days there during our first period in Japan. The only other guest was a pilot in the United States Airforce who was due to go to Vietnam on his first mission. He confided that he was extremely concerned about duty.

The rustic environment of our new home was a sharp contrast to Kamakura. The monastery sent craftsmen to repair the shoji screens which divided the rooms and to replace the battered tatami floors with new tatami mats. We installed a Japanese bath and a tile floor and cleaned up the kitchen which had two old propane gas hobs for cooking. Similar to the Kamakura house, we used canisters of propane gas for cooking. With the exception of the bath water which was heated by stoking a coal stove, personal hygiene was a cold water affair. There was an electrical outlet in the kitchen where we put a small refrigerator and an outlet in the adjacent room where we put a Pioneer radio and phonograph console. Again we used several kerosene stoves for heating. Sadly the Aladdin brand from Great Britain was no longer available and we relied on Matsushita (Panasonic) which seemed to dominate the market. I stood next to the stoves to keep warm, resulting in red patches on my legs and swollen red toes which my husband unceremoniously called "pigs." We used the non-flush, hole-in-the-floor sand toilet which was cleaned monthly by the "honey bucket truck" and sanitized with antiseptic fluid. It was environmentally friendly and better than a flush toilet if cleaned regularly.

Country life was tough going. We lived half-a-mile from the bus to Mishima. The bus stop was next to a tiny shop which sold newspapers, milk, bread and other essentials. The public telephone box stood in front of the shop and since we did not have a phone we relied on the public phone. Real estate developers had recently constructed a small estate nearby with monotonous stucco box-like houses. The residents purchased groceries, meat, fish, sandals, home electronics and kimono from newly established shops.

For those of us who lived outside of the village we could rely on vendors passing by on motorbikes daily selling fresh tofu and piping hot yams stored in steam ovens. The vendors announced their approach with sad whistle-like tunes that had probably been used for many years, a reminder of what Japan was like before the war. There were also vendors selling brooms and bamboo poles for hanging the wash or drying white radish or persimmon, and, occasionally, a man selling his knife sharpening services made the rounds. They announced their approach with taped recordings of themselves singing out their wares.

On our walks along the road leading to Hakone we stopped at the hog pens to look at the animals whose eyes mournfully expressed their acceptance of their fate as sausages and bacon. We passed a strange wooden shack on stilts with a bicycle parked beneath. The sign read "Yakult." A Japanese yogurt producer founded by a Doctor Shirota in 1935 had set up tiny outlets in villages. A Japanese company Calpis also produced a yogurt-based beverage that, when diluted in hot water, was a delicious beverage in winter and, with ice, a cold summer drink.

But what I enjoyed most while in Sawaji was the daily announcements from Mishima city hall at noon over loud speakers to farmers in the field. There was a weather report, reminders of meetings and the latest farming news. But it was the song which preceded the announcement that I eagerly awaited because it was an old folk song played languidly on a harp. If the days were warm I would sit on the wooden veranda (*rokka*) to bask in the sun while listening to the mournful melody.

Konosuke Matsushita (1894–1989), the founder of Panasonic and a devout Zen Buddhist, was regarded as the guru of modern Japanese industrialists. He was an important patron of Ryutakuji, offering substantial contributions to the monastery's purse and sending his staff to practice meditation. He had no particular interest in religious practice until the age of 37. At the urging of a friend, he attended a service at a Buddhist temple. The atmosphere and the sincere devotion of the congregation brought him great consolation and inspired him to develop a personal ideology which supported his propensity to work overtime. Spiritual benefits could be reaped not only from prayer but also from the daily, diligent execution of one's duties.

He regularly attended religious retreats at Buddhist monasteries, prodding his employees to participate in order to restore inner peace and to improve concentration. What was good for the soul was also good for sales. The enthusiastic found solace but the less willing realized only pain, sitting in cross-legged silence for eight hours a day for seven days.

Nixon's Shock Doesn't Shock

Our budget was not affected by the "Nixon Shock" in August 1971. The "Nixon Shock" refers to the end of the Bretton Woods system of fixed exchange rates and the Gold Standard on which currency standards were based. The Bretton Woods Agreement in 1944 established the US dollar as the only national currency backed by gold. The other currencies were valued against the dollar and countries could trade their dollars for a fixed amount of gold held in the US.

In the early 1970s the Vietnam War caused a rapid rise in inflation in the United States, which was also experiencing pronounced trade and budget deficits. The dollar that had been valued at $35 per ounce of gold was weakened by America's inability to cut government spending and reduce its trade deficit and budget deficit, which President Richard Nixon claimed was causing the inflation. As the government continued to print more money to fund operations in Vietnam and inflation continued to rise, countries began exchanging dollar assets for gold and America's gold coverage dropped to 11 percent. In August 1971, without warning, President Richard Nixon imposed 90-day wage and price controls as well as a 10 percent import surcharge. This action effectively made the dollar non-convertible on the open market. Even though the import surcharge was dropped five months later, there was a general revaluation of currencies. By 1976 there was no longer a fixed exchange rate.

The MOF suppressed the yen, which had been ¥360 per dollar for 22 years, to ¥308 per dollar. The government's fiscal stimulus together with the Bank of Japan's lower interest rates acted to prevent the yen's rapid appreciation. The currency finally stabilized at ¥300 per dollar. Although the yen appreciated almost 50 cents to the dollar the prices of exports to the American market were relatively unaffected. MOF and MITI officials felt that as long as Japan ran a trade surplus with the United States, they were in control of the economy and their administrative territory. Japan continued to hoard its dollar assets in the United States, considered a safe haven, while controlling the yen in Japan. The yen's appreciation did not seem to affect the Japanese people who, encouraged by the government, were saving much of their income. By the 1970s, the savings rate had peaked at almost 30 percent, the highest in the world.

Foreigners in their Midst

Farmers, who had profited from the sale of their property, replaced their centuries-old farm houses with new-builds complete with modern conveniences, including flush toilets. The toilets were manufactured by Toto, a company founded in Kitakyushu in 1917 to become the world's largest toilet manufacturer by the 1990s.

A neighbor who was a farmer and who had sold some of his land to real estate developers replaced his traditional thatched-roof farmhouse with a new stucco dwelling. He proudly gave us a tour to show us the amenities he had installed. Several rooms had central heating and the flush toilet was a Toto toilet sporting a heated cover to warm the toilet seat. All very high-tech but a bit sad from a presumptuous foreigner's perspective because of the loss of the traditional Japanese way of life.

We never encountered any discrimination during our time in Sawaji or Mishima. In Mishima we were treated as if we were Japanese. Although there were few foreigners living in Mishima, once the staff in supermarkets and our bank found that we spoke Japanese they were very welcoming. On the other hand, the residence in Sawaji were reticent to engage verbally even while waiting for the bus. We assumed that their exposure to foreigners had been limited.

The cottage was surrounded by *mikan* orchards tended by an aging couple whose backs were bent from carrying heavy loads of oranges for years. I took the liberty of bringing them tea and rice crackers on a lacquered wooden tray to introduce myself in the typical Japanese fashion. Although they accepted my offering they seemed somewhat flustered, probably because they had never been approached by a *gaijin*. I left behind the tea pot and cups on the tray and returned to the cottage. A few days later I discovered the lacquer tray inside the entrance with a pile of *mikan*. Intermittently there were gifts of preserved fish, a delicacy, or rice crackers. But our communication continued with silent gestures.

The ice wall finally melted when I happened to be following school boys returning from school. Our house sat on a hill overlooking the rice paddies and dirt road to the estate. As the boys neared the hill, one of them pointed to the cottage and shouted to his friend, "Do you know if foreigners are living up there?" Laughing, I shouted in Japanese, "This foreigner lives up there!" The boys turned around in amazement to see the "foreigner." From that day conversations at the bus stop commenced.

Nevertheless, I would have preferred that one incident had not occurred. The freezing winters took its toll on our health and I developed kidney problems again. My husband visited the monastery to ask the head monk about a doctor in the area. The monk offered to introduce us to his acupuncturist whose practice was located in the seaside fishing town of Numazu about a one hour train ride from Mishima. The monk credited the acupuncturist with healing all of his aches and pains. My husband gratefully accepted. Since I had never experienced acupuncture I was willing to try it to alleviate the pain.

When we arrived at the office, there were several patients waiting for treatment. While my husband stayed in the waiting room I was taken to a treatment area where I was instructed to remove my trousers and shirt and to lay down on a long mat on the tatami floor. Five minutes later an older gentleman entered with a portfolio of needles. I immediately recognized that he was blind, causing me great concern. I was unaware that at the time many acupuncturists in Japan were blind. The man first felt my thin arms and legs, pronouncing that I was underweight. If he had examined my stomach he would have reversed his diagnosis. Without regard for my kidney infection, he proceeded to inject needles into my arms, legs, stomach, neck and head. As he turned the needles I experienced shooting pains. Despite a high-pain threshold I could not help but cry out. He tried to calm me during the treatment and I tried to remain as stoic as possible.

After returning home I took off my clothes to reveal large bruises covering my arms and legs. Naturally, I did not want continue the treatments but, although my husband understood that bruising should not be the consequence of an acupuncture treatment, he worried that if I did not have a second treatment the head monk would lose face. On the second visit the pain from the needles was worse and I kept yelling to the extent that when I exited the treatment room the patients in the waiting room looked at me as though I was a hysterical foreigner. My husband could see that the bruises were worse and decided that it would be best to terminate the treatments.

Oil Shock!

Although we were not directly affected by the "oil shock" which began in October 1973, the newspapers reported the unfolding drama from the Japanese perspective. The Organization of Arab Petroleum Exporting Countries (OAPEC), consisting of OPEC, Egypt, Syria and Tunisia had announced an oil embargo to protest the United States' military support of Israel during the Yom Kippur War. The embargo lasted until March 1974 but it was considered by many countries, including Japan, to have been caused by the United States' control of oil prices and the "Nixon Shock." The end of Bretton Woods and the dollar's devaluation impacted negatively on oil exporting countries, namely the Arab States.

In January when Prime Minister Kakuei Tanaka (1972–74) met with Henry Kissinger he was unable to receive a guarantee from the United States for a steady supply of crude oil in return for Japan's support of American policies. The Japanese government felt compelled to take a pro-Arab stance and Japan was thereby recognized by the Arab nations as pro-Arab. Although the embargo ended in March, the price of crude oil rose from $3 to $12 per barrel and the yen appreciated to ¥260 per dollar.

The papers carried photographs of housewives stampeding to supermarkets to empty the shelves of sugar and toilet paper. The gas man from the estate who delivered the propane monthly told us that he and other business owners in town were relieved that the oil shock had occurred because they assumed that the sudden decrease in oil imports would force the government to slow down the pace of rapid industrial development and that the Japanese would have a brief respite from continuously pushing their economy forward. Contrary to expectations that the sudden rise in prices would cause inflation, Japan's economy slumped into a period of stagflation.

Government at the Controls

Kamakura had become an emotional and intellectual comfort zone but it also served to conceal a more realistic perception of the daily struggle of the Japanese to peddle along their rapidly expanding economy. The government had no intention of slowing down. Steel, automobiles, heavy and home appliances, petrochemicals, auto-tires, synthetic fibers, aluminum, non-ferrous metals, plate glass, pulp and paper, the industries in MITI's administrative jurisdiction, were among those directly affected by the oil embargo and the subsequent increase of petroleum prices.

The crisis forced the government to recognize the county's vulnerability and take immediate measures to rationalize oil in order to decrease the demand for both gasoline and electricity. The newspapers reported the reaction to the crisis and the effects on the Japanese economy which had until then depended on the manufacturing and export of energy-intensive industries. Since Japan imported around 90 percent of fossil fuel the government controlled the distribution of oil to industries deemed important such as the automobile industry while simultaneously subsidizing the energy-intensive ones, which would become known as "sunset industries." MITI also introduced a new source of energy.

In 1973, the government announced that nuclear energy was a national priority. In order to continue economic expansion and overtake the US economy the government had to reduce industries' reliance on fossil fuels. In 1974, the "Three Power Source Development Law" was enacted to subsidize local authorities that were willing to host nuclear power plants

Nuclear in Our Neighborhood

The town of Hamaoka (merged in 2004 with Omaezaki) is located in the Tokai region at the southern tip of Shizuoka Prefecture and 125 miles northeast of Tokyo. Tokai is Japan's major industrial and manufacturing region with densely populated cities which are supported mainly by the manufacturing sector. Car manufacturers with extensive operations are Toyota Motor Corp., Honda Corp., Mitsubishi Motors and Suzuki.

Hamaoka was impoverished when the residents accepted to host a nuclear power plant in 1969. Seismologists had warned the government in 1970 before the license for the construction of Hamaoka Nuclear Power Plant No. 1 reactor was granted to the Chubu Electric Power Company (CHUDEN) that the proposed site was near two seismic fault lines and that a major earthquake in the Tokai region was overdue. While we were in Sawaji we experienced our second earthquake in the late afternoon. The tremor was so severe that the huge temple bell in the monastery confines which monks normally rang three times daily, chimed independently for three minutes.

Regardless, CHUDEN received the permit and commenced construction and the plant was commissioned in 1976. Three more reactors were commissioned and, despite seismologists' claim that Hamaoka was the most dangerous plant in Japan, a fifth reactor was commissioned in 2005. Although two reactors have been decommissioned since 2009, a sixth reactor has been under construction since December 2008 despite the warning from seismologists that an earthquake of the magnitude of nine (such as the one that occurred in 2011) would trigger the evacuation of more than 28 million residents in Tokyo. Operations were suspended after the Fukushima nuclear crisis but as I predicted in *Japan's Nuclear Crisis* Hamaoka will go online despite anti-nuclear protests.

I continued Japanese lessons with Professor Niimi, making the two-hour train journey fortnightly, passing the towering Soka Gakkai pagoda in Gotemba. I had become fairly fluent in Japanese and wanted to work in a Japanese company but, unfortunately, my husband had been hospitalized twice while in Mishima and after four years of dealing with health issues we made the difficult decision to return to the US.

3

Holding Out for the Dream Job

We relocated to the Napa Valley, California, the premier wine producing region in the United States. Besides grapes and wine, the area is also known for its hot springs and popular among sufferers of chronic diseases for the mud baths and mineral water. In 1880 Robert Louise Stevenson who suffered from Tuberculosis took an extended eight month honeymoon with his wife Fanny Vandegrith at the Calistoga Hot Springs before moving to an abandoned cabin near the Silverado Mine where he wrote the novel *The Silverado Squatters*.

By the mid-1970s, many Japanese had sufficient expendable income for a honeymoon to Hawaii or a trip to the US and Europe. Explanations written in Japanese at key tourist attractions in the larger cities on the east and west coasts indicated a major increase of Japanese on holiday. By the early 1980s Japan had become the world's second biggest economy and the producers of luxury goods such as Tiffany and Cartier began to cater to Japanese tourists, hiring Japanese staff to ease sales transactions.

Americans could be forgiven for thinking that the Japanese were wealthy because they were flocking to jewelry, handbag and shoe shops to purchase expensive name brands. However, if Americans went to Japan and purchased the same items they would have understood why most Japanese consumers were confined to purchasing domestic brands while spending their income on luxury goods overseas. The high tariffs which were levied on imported goods, including leather products, jewelry and apparel, made the same luxury items unaffordable to the majority of Japanese. Besides import duties, the wholesaler's costs were incorporated in the price of the imports.

We saw a significant rise in Japanese home electronics and car imports. The United States' open markets to Japanese imports and the continuation of the favorable exchange rates put Japanese producers on an even playing field with their American rivals. By the mid-1970s the Japanese automobile industry was taking full advantage of the oil shock and, hot on the heels of Chrysler and GM, aggressively pursued American consumers who were beginning to appreciate the fuel-efficient engines as well as the lower prices. Honda first entered the American market via its motorcycles, which proved to be very competitive with the heavier Harley Davidson. German car manufactures also benefited with sturdy and reliable fuel-efficient Volkswagens and Audis.

Anticipating a Wine Boom

I saw that a market for foreign wine was steadily growing in Japan and that Japanese tourists were beginning to visit wineries in the Napa and Sonoma Valley. I decided to establish a small company which would provide tours of Napa Valley wineries specifically for Japanese tourists and businesses which wanted to invest in wineries located in the region.

In the 1960s the only place one could buy a decent bottle of wine in Japan was at Western-style hotels. Suntory's classic was a sweet red similar to the Communion wines which were introduced to the Japanese in the sixteenth century by Portuguese and Spanish Catholic priests. Imported German and Austrian wines like Blue Nun, a Liebfraumilch, also catered to their preference for sweet wines, which remained popular until the mid-1970s. As an alternative, diners could bring their own bottles to the restaurant and pay corkage. Wine-lovers could also find imports in department stores or they could go to a local liquor shop to buy domestic vintages produced by the two largest producers in Japan, Suntory Inc. and Sanraku Inc. Imported wines and blended whisky, such as Chivas Regal and Johnny Walker Red and Black sold at premium prices.

Nevertheless, as early as the 1964 Tokyo Olympics there were signs that eventually wine would find a proper niche in the Japanese market. It was simply a question of exposure to options. Only a few would dare to predict that within 30 years not only would many Japanese be taking wine seriously but, also, would be enjoying a California Cabernet with Japanese cuisine. As Japanese companies began to internationalize and establish corporate offices overseas, their employees who were seconded abroad for three to five years drank fine wines which were unavailable in Japan. Furthermore, Germany, Austria, Italy and France had become popular tourist destinations where Japanese could enjoy wine with their meals.

In 1972 a Suntory television commercial urging people to "drink wine on Fridays" triggered a mini-wine boom. By 1979, the younger generation, especially women, were drinking a glass or two of wine at bars and in restaurants, usually the sweet variety.

Ironically, although the rise in consumption of domestically produced wine raised profits, it also created a shortage of Japanese grapes. There were not enough grapes to go round and bulk grape juice from Romania, Hungary, Germany and Austria was blended into the domestic wine. The labels on the bottles of some domestic wines do not indicate that 90 percent is reconstituted grape juice and water.

There were no guided tours in Japanese and the majority of Japanese tourists were not fluent in English. I decided to design a tour in Japanese. Initially I visited a number of wineries where there were tours in order to gauge which ones would be applicable to both Japanese corporate executives and tourists. The Louis Martini Winery and the Beaulieu Winery offered excellent one hour tours daily as did Shramsberg Vineyards, a sparkling wine producer, founded in 1862. Robert Louis Stevenson befriended Shramsberg during his honeymoon, recording the visit in *The Silverado Squatters*. In 1969 President Richard Nixon served the wine at a State Dinner honoring Premier Chou-En Lai in Beijing.

I met a housewife who catered private functions and proposed a joint venture where she would provide lunch following the tours which included the wines from the wineries toured that day. She enthusiastically accepted and I designed a brochure in Japanese intended for wineries, hotels and travel agencies located in the Bay Area.

The three wineries permitted me to record their tours which I transcribed into Japanese. The process took six months. Unfortunately, before the tours began the caterer pulled out due to family issues. I planned to initiate the tours myself but my husband's health continued to deteriorate and we moved to San Francisco. Nevertheless, my efforts were not in vain because the project served as a catalyst to gaining entry as the first non-Japanese employee in Japan's largest domestic wine producer several years later.

Farewell to a Friend

The Hibis intended to visit us in the spring of 1980 but in February we received an unexpected telephone call from their son with the news that his mother had died following an emergency operation at Kamakura Hospital. Although he tried to reassure us that their house was also our house, we were inconsolable. I wrote to Mr. Hibi a letter of condolence and he replied giving details of her funeral. She was buried in the family plot in Engakuji monastery, a poignant reminder of one of her favorite books and her favorite author. I could never have predicted that this event would directly affect another event while I was working for a Japanese wine producer ten years later and influence my decision to create a brief academic career at a Scottish university 18 years later.

Holding Out for the Dream Job

I was offered a position in a San Francisco law firm on the condition that I receive a law degree with the firm paying the tuition fee. It was very tempting because within two years I would be earning a lucrative salary and supporting us comfortably. Nevertheless, I wanted to work in a Japanese importer and distributer of goods, preferably foods and beverages because I had, along with Japanese consumers, experienced highly tariffed imported goods and high prices of domestic goods due to the government subsidies. But I did not understand the intricacies of the distribution system and government regulations which was fundamental to keeping Japan's markets tightly regulated and, for all intents and purposes, closed to foreign direct investment. I wanted to know why Japan's markets were still protected and why the government was continuing its mercantile policies which frustrated the competition among domestic companies and the development of domestic consumption. The policies seemed to be self-defeating.

Hopefully, in the end, my responsibilities would provide a foundation for a future job in the United States Trade Representative (USTR) in Washington, DC. I presumed that, in addition to a significant exposure to the effects of Japan's trade policies, my fluency in Japanese and relative ease working with Japanese would be an invaluable asset to the USTR.

However, in order to cultivate a thorough knowledge of Japan's distribution system and market access it was vital to enter a large Japanese company to observe directly the effects of government regulations on market entry and to participate in negotiations with foreign suppliers to learn Japanese negotiation methods. Therefore, I chose to wait for an opportunity.

One criteria for the job was that I would be the first foreign employee in a conservative Japanese company because I was well-aware that foreigners who worked in Japanese firms left because they had experienced what they considered to be discriminatory practices and harassment due to misunderstandings arising from poor communication and ignorance of the Japanese corporate system. On the other hand, Japanese management were reluctant to hire foreigners because they were unable to adapt to corporate regulations thus disrupting the workplace. Mutual misunderstanding was also prompted by cultural differences. Japan was an ultra-conservative and insular society and Japanese corporations operated very differently from western corporations.

Foreigners saw Japan as a "westernized" country and a democracy and anticipated that management would accept them as equal to Japanese staff. What they did not understand was that Japanese corporations were hierarchical, that they would be considered as new staff and expected to adhere to instructions from their superiors and abide by corporate etiquette. Many foreigners were frustrated that they were not accepted for their skills and experienced what they considered to be demeaning treatment.

I wanted to enter a corporation where the staff had no previous exposure to foreign staff and, therefore, few preconceptions. By entering a conservative Japanese company as the first and only western staff I would be able to adapt smoothly to the corporate system without promoting misunderstandings. I did not presume that the Japanese staff would be able to relate to me as a foreigner but I did assume that I could make them comfortable with my presence and integrate in the workplace over a period of time. I did not consider Japan a "foreign society" but I failed to anticipate that fluency in the written language could provoke other problems.

A Window of Opportunity

To keep up my Japanese I commuted weekly to the University of California in Berkeley for Japanese lessons with a tutor whose husband was an American whom she had met in Japan when he was teaching English. American men in the 1970s and 1980s were attracted to Japan's remarkable transformation from a war devastated state to become the third largest economy in the world. Dissatisfied with their lives in the US and opposed to the Vietnam War they longed for acceptance in a political society that seemed to echo their own values. The move to Japan was an escape from their own society. Generally, they were employed as English language instructors. Some men married Japanese women in order to integrate into the society and alleviate loneliness. Many of the women preferred Americans because they wanted to escape from the strictures of their society and live in the US. Nevertheless, the men were not fully accepted by their in-laws and, sadly, their wives were considered as outsiders and no longer true Japanese if they followed their husbands to the US.

The tutor, realizing that I was fairly fluent in written Japanese, suggested that we collaborate in a new translation of a short story by Miyazawa Kenji, one of Japan's most famous authors. *Night of the Milky Way Train* has a poignant beauty and is very popular in Japan. Even though we completed the translation, the tutor was unable to find a publisher.

As I had predicted, confident of an expanding market for foreign wine during the next decade and taking advantage of very low interest rates courtesy of the Bank of Japan (BOJ) which had lowered rates in 1985 due to the Plaza Accord and the floating of the dollar, Japanese wine producers began purchasing or investing in vineyards located in famous wine producing regions such as the Bordeaux and the Burgundy regions of France and in the Napa-Sonoma Valley. In 1986, Suntory, a family-owned firm, considered to be the producer of the finest domestic whisky and wine, purchased Chateau St. Jean, a Sonoma winery, and invested millions of dollars in replanting vineyards and grounds. However, it sold the winery in 1996.

Although not engaged in wine production, Otsuka Pharmaceuticals, Japan's third largest producer of pharmaceuticals and the first to build a research facility in the US in 1983, purchased a California winery. Established in 1921, the multinational company also has a food and beverage division which produces snacks and sports drinks such as Pocari Sweat. CEO Akihiko Otsuka referred to wine as a healthy alternative to hard liquor and stored a collection of Bordeaux in a cellar in the Otsuka Pharmaceutical Research Center at Lake Biwa, near Kyoto.

In 1986, Otsuka purchased Ridge Winery, which is located at an elevation of 2,600 feet on top of Monte Bello Ridge in the Santa Cruz Mountains near San Jose. Two of the owners who were former presidents of Syntax, a pharmaceutical firm which had a joint venture with Otsuka Pharmaceuticals, knew that Otsuka was a collector of Bordeaux. When Otsuka visited Ridge, he liked what he saw and purchased it.

By sheer coincidence, in the summer of 1987 my translation partner introduced me to a Japanese friend, a woman who operated a tiny promotion firm in Japan. The woman wanted to introduce me as a future employee to the soon-to be new director of the wine division at Sanraku Inc., a subsidiary of Ajinomoto, and Japan's largest domestic wine producer.

When the tutor's friend visited San Francisco we met. She told me that the vice president of Ajinomoto Tadao Suzuki had taken the helm of its subsidiary Sanraku, Inc. Ajinomoto is the sole producer of the flavor enhancer monosodium glutamate. The woman explained that Suzuki intended to convert Sanraku, a conservative, unsophisticated producer of low-end Japanese spirits, whiskey and wine into a market leader, focusing on wine, and with name recognition to rival Suntory. In order not to be out-gunned by Suntory, in 1987 Sanraku Inc. purchased Markham Vineyards which is located across the road in St. Helena from Louis Martini Vineyards.

Prior to 1987, Sanraku was importing and distributing wines and liquor from France, Austria, the Netherland, Germany, and the United States but Suzuki was determined to up the game by giving Sanraku Inc. a full corporate make-over. Its parent company, Ajinomoto, and its lenders had the capital to finance the operation. For moral support Suzuki brought along with him some of his former colleagues from Ajinomoto to manage various divisions, including the wine division, general affairs, finance and human resources. His soon-to-be director of the wine division was the director of the mayonnaise and soup division.

The woman was attractive, single and about 35, which by Japanese standards was beyond the age considered appropriate for marriage. She had earned a degree in politics from Waseda University, a first-class private university in Tokyo.

Her fashion statement was flamboyant by conservative Japanese standards. A bit rebellious, she smoked, and her vocabulary bordered on the irreverent, often in the masculine vernacular, illustrating that she was a member of a new breed of Japanese women, independent from traditional social mores and men.

Her father and her grandfather were engineers, her grandfather having studied automotive design in the 1930s in Germany at Porsche. I assumed that she was financially independent and able to defy the accepted social etiquette at the time. She mentioned that her mother had died and shortly afterwards her father remarried, triggering a turbulent relationship with him, which may have influenced her rebellious attitude towards men.

She did not divulge information about her profession nor her financial backing. She first met the future director of the wine division at a promotional event for Honda motorcycles that was sponsored by Ajinomoto. Dressed in black leather motorcycling gear, tight breeches and jacket, she was particularly enticing. They went out drinking afterwards and became friends but she did not confide details regarding their relationship.

Too Good to Be True?

Ostensibly it seemed like a fine opportunity even though the wine trade had been hit by a scandal around that time. The Japanese are fastidious consumers. Half of a dead rat in a jar of Skippy Peanut Butter in the 1950s did not faze Americans but in Japan a jar or bottle with a hint of anything foreign will be withdrawn from the market. In this case, Austrian wine had been contaminated with antifreeze and the wine market withered. It took several years and a concerted effort among foreign wine associations and domestic importers and producers to revive trust among Japanese wine drinkers.

After she returned to Tokyo I was very apprehensive because the job had yet to be created. When she returned to San Francisco in September with three other colleagues, two women and a man, all in their thirties I began to worry. Evidently they were on a marketing survey trip or at least this was what they told me. I was invited to spend several days with them as their tour guide. The first day they hired a car and drove across the Golden Gate Bridge to the nearby posh seaside town of Sausalito where we stopped at a well-known hotel for lunch on the roof-top veranda. The group marveled at the yachts anchored in the harbor below, the stunning views of San Francisco and the Golden Gate Bridge.

What was striking about their behavior was their complacency and arrogance, a sign of what was occurring among youth in Tokyo. Their manner seemed to be a deliberate denial of refinement which is commonly associated with Japanese culture. Their language was laced with slang and colloquialisms, which are now a part of the daily vocabulary. It was at the height of the "bubble" and it seemed as if their budget was bottomless. I wondered who was supporting the expense account.

After perusing the lunch menu they ordered some of the most expensive items with a bottle of wine. They smoked while they picked at their food, leaving most of it on their plates, suggesting that the Japanese, at least the Japanese in the big cities, were now nouveau riche, conspicuous consumers, and in the process of discarding the "less-is-more" foundation of Japan's cultural heritage. But I had not been to Japan for 12 years to experience this evolution. The following day I took them to Fisherman's Wharf before they returned to Tokyo. It was not until I went to Tokyo for the interview that I saw the impact of the "asset-inflated bubble" on Japanese consumer culture.

The potential position at Sanraku presented an invaluable opportunity to work in a conservative Japanese company and to engage in work that would provide an intimate view of distribution, business development and corporate strategy. Suntory had already internationalized and was employing a number of foreign staff. I waited expectantly for word from the woman who finally contacted me at the end of the year with the good news that I would be interviewed at Sanraku in February. Elated, yet cautious, I made preparations for the trip, sorting out a tourist visa. I contacted Mr. Hibi whom I had not seen since 1976 to ask if I could stay with him during the interview period. He had married his secretary a year after his wife's death, much to his children's dismay. Nevertheless, he was very pleased that I was coming to stay with him.

4

How I Got the Dream Job

I arrived at Tokyo Haneda Airport at 6pm. Despite being jetlagged, as soon as I made my exit from the airport I felt right at home. Tokyo smelled exactly the same as it did when I departed 12 years earlier. I took a taxi to a business hotel located in Nihonbashi in the vicinity of Ajinomoto's headquarters where Sanraku was ensconced and where the firm had reserved a room for me.

Tired and anxious about the interview, I alighted from the taxi and carried my luggage to the hotel reception. At that very instant, I realized that I had left my handbag in the taxi and I ran out to catch the driver before he took off but, to my horror, he had already left. My handbag contained my visa, passport and my wallet with all of my money. In desperation, I hurried to the nearest police box to report the situation to the officers on duty. The policemen told me that they would immediately contact all of the taxi companies in the Tokyo metropolitan area and as soon as they heard anything they would call the hotel. The hotel reception kindly registered me even though I had no identification other than that Sanraku had made the reservation. The receptionist assured me that I would be called as soon as the police or a taxi company contacted them. I was relieved that I could communicate in Japanese because otherwise I would not have been able to express the urgency of the situation.

Since it was already 8pm I knew that I would probably not receive word until morning. But I thought that, although the bag might not be returned, remembering my previous experience

20 years earlier, there was a good possibility that the bag would be returned. I spent a restless night waiting for a call which came at 7am. The bag had been recovered by a taxi company and that I could collect it. I debated about the type of gift to offer the taxi driver and whether a traditional gift of a large tin of Japanese biscuits from a well-known shop or whether cash was more appropriate on this occasion. I decided on an elegantly wrapped large box of a variety of Japanese rice crackers and biscuits. I opted to take a taxi since I was unfamiliar with the area where the company was located. Tokyo is a huge city and the ride took 30 minutes. As I had thought, the bag's contents were intact. When I presented the biscuits to the manager, thanking him profusely, his expression fleetingly registered both disappointment and contempt since he had expected cash from an American.

The Interview

The next morning I went to Ajinomoto's corporate headquarters for the interview. The building was located on Showa Blvd in Kyo-bashi in the Ginza where a number of corporate headquarters and commercial buildings also straddled the wide avenue. The drab white building with a cornerstone inscribed with the date of the company's establishment in 1907 had been built in 1972. After a receptionist dressed in the Ajinomoto company uniform announced my arrival, a second receptionist from Sanraku came to usher me to Sanraku corporate headquarters on the fourth floor and to a large private room. She brought me a cup of green tea and instructed me to wait for a few minutes. The windowless room was a typical arrangement for business meetings. I sat at the end of a long sofa in front of a rectangular wooden coffee table on which was placed a heavy crystal ashtray. To the right was a large easy chair. I was dressed conservatively in a dark green kilt skirt, white cotton blouse and a dark green cardigan which I had knitted.

After waiting nervously for about five minutes the door opened and a balding gentleman in his mid-fifties wearing Japanese leather sandals, usually worn at home, shuffled in. He handed me his Japanese business card identifying him as the director of human resources. Sitting in the arm chair and puffing away on a Japanese brand cigarette (Cherry or Peace) he spoke perfunctorily in informal Japanese with a quizzical expression on his face. His accent indicated that he was not from the Tokyo area. I had anticipated that the company had been well-briefed regarding my background and my credentials and that the interview was merely to confirm details. But the director spoke to me as though I was an oddity. I began to suspect that no one had told him anything about me as a potential employee. I also suspected that he had never interviewed a foreigner nor had he associated often with foreigners. After the 20-minute interview the director told me to wait and left the room.

As ten anxious minutes passed and as I started to worry that I would not be offered the job the director entered the room again, this time followed by two middle-aged gentlemen and an older man. Bowing, they handed me their Japanese business cards identifying themselves as Sanraku executive directors. They were friendly but appeared puzzled as well. The interview was conducted in Japanese because no one spoke English, which was fortunate because at least I could prove that I was fluent in their language. I related my education, my background and my years in the Napa Valley. When I was asked about wine in general I was effusive about the growing wine market in Japan and the Japanese' penchant for fine wine. I was also asked about California wine which I predicted would become popular and gain a niche in the Japanese market. I was pleasantly surprised that they were impressed that I was a Juilliard graduate because most

Americans had never heard of the school. Their reaction could have been related to Sanraku's rival Suntory's advertising campaigns which focused on the arts.

Towards the end of the interview the HR director leaned forward and uttered the word *kiboo*, which in Japanese can be translated as "hope," "desire," or "objective." I had no clue to what he was alluding and, in desperation, I glanced at the business cards I had placed on the table in front of me. The director sitting beside me was in charge of corporate strategy. I blurted out that I hoped to contribute to Sanraku's new marketing strategy as a member of the wine division, which seemed to satisfy the executives. The director of HR stood up and told me that I would meet with the director of the wine division at the end of the week. Evidently, the executive board wanted to meet me initially before going on to the final stage with the new director of the wine division. I checked out of the hotel and took the train to Kita Kamakura for a reunion with Mr. Hibi.

A year later a young woman entered the wine division as a trainee. We exchanged experiences about our interviews, which were remarkably similar. The HR director had been at Ajinomoto before following Suzuki to Sanraku. The fact that he was a native of Niigata explained his speech pattern. She was also confused about *kiboo* but finally realized that he was referring to the amount of salary she expected to receive. We laughed every time the HR director passed our division. Mr. Suzuki had been at the helm less than a year and I am still incredulous that I had managed to secure the job.

A Reunion

After the interview I went to Tokyo Station and took the train to Kita Kamakura and to "my home." It was a tearful homecoming. Mr. Hibi greeted me emotionally and, for a moment, it seemed as if I had never left my home. But as soon as I was seated on the familiar sofa in the familiar lounge beside Mr Hibi, I felt an incredible emptiness, realizing for the first time that Mrs. Hibi would not appear. Although his children were opposed to his second marriage, Mr Hibi was in his mid-seventies and did not want to move because he could visit their mother's grave often while being cared for. Mr. Hibi brought out the plum wine, which Mrs. Hibi had made and enjoyed with me. Although I stayed in "my room," the room was no longer mine.

The following day, I accompanied Mr Hibi to Engakuji to his wife's grave in the family plot. Mrs. Hibi had never mentioned her relationship with the monastery but it seemed the perfect spot for her because of her humble nature and her love of Natsume Soseki. The graveyard was ancient and crowded with the graves of famous Japanese politicians and writers. Mrs. Hibi's grave stone had been carved by an illustrious Zen master who was the head master at Engakuji for many years. Mr. Hibi, placing fresh flowers on the grave, told me that I could visit any time I wished and that I should mention the Hibi name to the gate keeper at the cemetery entrance because he would let me pass without paying the entry fee. I could not have foreseen at the time that Mrs. Hibi's grave would play a role while I was employed at Sanraku.

As we walked to other monasteries in the vicinity I confided that I was concerned that the job offer was ambiguous but he assured me that the position was mine. Several days passed before I received a call from Sanraku to schedule an interview with the incoming director.

I went to the corporate headquarters to meet the new director who was in his mid-fifties. He was short and rather portly. Fortunately, the interview was merely a formality as if my position had already been decided. He was very cordial and positive about having me as a member in his division. He requested that I return to the States and await further notice because the company would apply for my sponsorship in order to obtain a work permit. But I feared that circumstances could change at any time and that I might be sloughed off. In other words, as an ignorant foreigner I presumed that unless a contract was in hand the job was not guaranteed. I told the new director that I would try to have a friend to sponsor me which would speed up the process of obtaining a work permit for a foreign staff.

I returned to Kita Kamakura and asked Mr. Hibi if he would act as my personal guarantor because I would feel far more secure if he sponsored me. He was a successful businessman with excellent connections and I did not feel that my request was an imposition since he regarded me as a close friend. He graciously accepted.

I remained in Kamakura for a week, waiting for the illusive contract, biding my time by visiting old haunts and an old friend who lived in Kamakura proper. Kamakura Station had been rebuilt and the supermarket where I had shopped in Motomachi had opened a branch behind the station. There were also new tennis courts. I was unable to find my friend's house because new homes had sprouted up on new streets. To facilitate the search I went to a rice and sake shop in my friend's neighborhood to ask directions. Since the proprietor made deliveries to homes in the vicinity he knew where my friend lived.

No Trespassing

I returned to Engakuji where I had been many times. I went to see the Sharidan, a National Treasure which was built by Chinese and Japanese Zen Buddhist monks in the thirteenth century. The building was rebuilt in the sixteenth century after burning down. Engakuji sustained 30 practicing monks who meditated in the Sharidan. Only male monks were allowed to enter and it was off-limits to laymen except on special occasions. Women were forbidden. It was February when traditionally the monks went to their respective temples and families for a two month respite from the strenuous practice. I passed through Engakuji's main gate and went to the rear of the monastery where the Sharidan was located. Within the monks' living compound the wooden structure stood elegant in its simplicity. The entrance to the compound was protected by a low bamboo fence. Written in Japanese in black ink on a wood block was the warning, "No Trespassing."

I peered inside the compound to see if anyone was around. Only one white cotton undergarment was hanging on a pole, proof that the monks were off on their winter break. I tentatively climbed over the fence and as I approached the building, I heard hammering and men's voices. Holding my breath, I peeked inside to see carpenters repairing the ceiling. They did not notice me creeping nervously inside onto the dirt floor. I could hardly believe my luck and for ten minutes I basked in a thousand years of spiritual energy as I gazed transfixed at the slightly elevated wooden platform where the monks chanted prayers and meditated daily. But I knew that if I stayed any longer I would be caught. Reluctantly, I left and climbed over the fence thinking that I had managed to escape without being noticed. As I began walking towards the monastery's main entrance I heard the sound of clacking wooden sandals behind me. I glanced around to see a monk in his robes pursuing me, his arms folded across his chest. He shouted angrily in Japanese that I should not have entered the compound. Frightened and feeling a tad guilty I promptly answered in English that I did not understand Japanese and made my escape.

Mr. Hibi called Sanraku several times to enquire about the contract. He told me that, although the HR knew that he would be sponsoring me, it would take several months to process a work permit. I returned to San Francisco to wait nervously for word and for the contract. Without a firm contract and with new management, my future job was still an uncertainty. In order to impress upon Sanraku that I was waiting, I sent in hand- written Japanese the latest news about the wineries and forecasts for the 1988 vintage in the Napa-Sonoma Valley.

Finally, in June I received word that Sanraku had obtained the work permit and that I could come. Overwhelmed with relief I made hasty preparations and collected the visa at the Japanese Consulate and packed my bags.

I arrived six weeks later during the hottest and muggiest period of the year. The year 1988 saw the beginning of a rash of political scandals that served to unhinge Japan's political system because of the involvement of numerous high-ranking members in the LDP and elite civil servants.

The Recruit scandal hit the front pages of the major dailies. The scale of the massive insider trading and corruption scandal brought down Prime Minister Noboru Takeshita's entire administration, the resignation from office by many key politicians, and the arrest and indictment of powerful businessmen. The episode was a good example of collusion between cross-party ultra-conservative politicians, bureaucrats and big business and of money politics during Japan's post-war period.

The scandals that plagued Prime Minister Kakuei Tanaka (1974–76) during and after he was in the prime minister's office were regarded as political corruption, involving primarily politicians. The Lockheed bribery scandal in 1976 was covered by the international press because the case went to trial and Tanaka was sentenced to four years in prison for accepting $3 million from the Lockheed Corporation for convincing ANA to order passenger planes from Lockheed instead of from McDonnell Douglas. Abe's uncle former Prime Minister Eisaku Sato (1964–72) was also implicated with Lockheed officials in separate bribery cases.

The Recruit scandal, involving 155 prominent figures, was regarded as the most pervasive of all time and much bigger than the Lockheed scandal. It was credited with ending the 1955 System and the reign of the LDP, spurring the defection of LDP members to form splinter parties such as the New Japan Party in 1992 and Morihiro Hosokawa's installation as prime minister in August 1993.

The Japanese electorate generally regarded politicians as corrupt and not in the same league as bureaucrats who were considered beyond reproach. But elite civil servants were now vulnerable to public scrutiny and no longer off-limits to interrogation by prosecutors.

5

The Dream Job

The Ajinomoto Connection

Sanraku Inc., formerly known as Showa Brewery, was established by the Ajinomoto Corporation in 1934. In 1935 Showa began producing alcohol and, in 1946, *shochu*, a popular Japanese distilled spirit made from fermented sweet potato or rice with 25 percent alcohol content by volume. In 1961 Showa Brewery purchased Mercian Winery and then merged in 1962 with Nisshin Brewery to purchase Ocean Co., a whisky producer. In 1985 Showa's name was changed to Sanraku Inc. The English translation of Sanraku is "three pleasures," the company producing wine, *shochu* and a blended whisky, considered a "working man's whisky."

The English translation of Ajinomoto is "essence of taste." The multinational produces the flavor enhancer Accent, otherwise known as monosodium glutamate (MSG), and holds the sole patent on the fermentation process for its production. MSG is commonly used in Asian cuisine. Saburosuke Suzuki established Suzuki Seiyakusho, a pharmaceutical company, in 1907. When Dr. Kikunae Ikeda, a chemist, acquired a patent for his invention of the fermentation process for MSG, Suzuki purchased a joint share in the product and received a permit from the Ministry of the Interior to produce MSG under the label Lady&Aji-No-Moto. Suzuki began production in a small factory in Zushi, a town located two hours south of Tokyo and where the Imperial Family has a summer villa. In 1909, after the company won a bronze medal at the first Japanese Invention Exhibition, it launched its brand Aji-No-Moto which became the corporate name as well.

Aji-No-Moto entered Taiwan in 1910 and in 1912 began selling wheat starch to spinning companies. The company expanded operations in China in 1914 and in 1917, Suzuki established S. Suzuki & Co., the origin of the present Ajinomoto Group. Although Suzuki opened sales offices in China, Singapore, Taipei and New York in the 1920s and 1930s, the offices were closed at the end of the war. After the war, in 1947, Ajinomoto resumed exports to the United States and began to trade publicly in 1949.

From 1951 onward Ajinomoto developed into a multinational company, its group of subsidiaries manufacturing a full range of products, including salad dressing, soups, seasoning, cooking oil, pharmaceuticals, fertilizer and animal feed. It launched Knorr's Cup-a-Soup in 1964 and engaged in numerous joint ventures with foreign food producers in Japan to produce such products as Kellogg's Corn Flakes, General Foods Maxim Coffee and DANON dairy products. In 1982, it began exporting its product Aspartane to the United States and NutraSweet to Switzerland.

Tadao Suzuki, Saburosuke's grandson, was Ajinomoto's Vice President before transferring to Sanraku as its CEO in 1987. Although he wanted wine and spirits to be Sanraku's core business, Suzuki also intended to expand Sanraku's fish feed and chemicals business, which were also specific to Ajinomoto's business interests. Suzuki was determined to achieve his objectives swiftly through substantial financing from Sanraku's parent company and Ajinomoto lenders to transform Sanraku Inc. into a company which rivalled Suntory its main competitor.

Prior to Tadao Suzuki's entrance, Sanraku had been importing and distributing wines and liquors. It was the agent for Tio Pepe Sherry from Portugal (1972), Gustaf Adolf Schmidt wines from Germany and Tokai wine from Hungary (1973) Jim Beam Brands (1977), and Remy-Cointreau and Maison Albert Bichot (1982). Louis Martini Vineyards located in the Napa Valley, was also included in the wine portfolio.

First Day on-the-Job

I stayed again at a business hotel courtesy of Sanraku because I had yet to find permanent accommodation. My first morning was devoted to my formal introduction to corporate staff. During the afternoon I would be taken to look at flats in the metropolitan area.

I was introduced to the nine staff in the wine division. Although not wine connoisseurs, they were Sanraku old-timers who had forged tight sales networks with retailers, hotels, bars and restaurants. An attractive and stylishly dressed woman in her mid-fifties was the only female middle manager (*kacho*) in the wine division or, for that matter, in the entire company. There were three male employees in their late twenties, two full-time salesmen and one secretary, a female in her early twenties.

A young man came from HR to formally present me with my long-awaited contract stamped with the head of HR's seal together with the company handbook which listed the corporate rules and regulations and the annual schedule. Everyone seemed pleased to meet me. Staff were seated at long tables with the directors of each division at the head and the division's middle management (*kacho*) seated next to him. Since I was a new employee I was placed at the bottom end of the table.

Staff told me that in order to modernize Sanraku's corporate culture, its management and working practices, Suzuki immediately employed two staff from McKinsey and Co. to engage with the wine division staff for a year. The male and female consultants sat at my desk but they rarely communicated with staff, preferring to observe daily operations in silence for one year before departing. Chuckling, the *kacho* opened the desk drawer to reveal the pencils they had left behind. Whether or not McKinsey's recommendations were deemed realistic, Suzuki had sent out a clear message to personnel that the times were changing. Nevertheless, the Sanraku old-timers did not anticipate any major changes.

I was escorted to the other divisions by my director where I formally introduced myself in Japanese to the staff in each division in the traditional way, holding my contract before me while bowing respectfully. This procedure was repeated until my director had introduced me to the three other divisions located in the same room; liquor, the alcohol division which was in charge of the production of *shochu*, and a luxury goods division. With the exception of the luxury goods division where there were only two members, a director and his young female secretary, there were approximately 10–15 staff per division. The division for procurement and distribution, which collaborated with the wine division in the procurement and distribution of imports, was located in an adjacent room.

I was taken to the floor above to be introduced to the finance division and to the Sanraku upper management who had interviewed me in February. Finally, I was introduced to Mr. Suzuki in his executive office. He was very gentile and more sophisticated than his staff, including the director of the wine division. Although he had been briefed about my entry in his company he appeared slightly perplexed about me and my role. It was not until a few months had passed that I realized that my role had not been discussed in detail and that apparently, he was content to rely on Sanraku staff until he firmly held the corporate reigns. It was still early days.

Returning to the wine division I was unpleasantly surprised to find that on top of my desk was a pile of literature in Japanese about Sanraku and Sanraku's winery, Mercian, which was located in Yamanashi Prefecture where Suntory also operated its winery. The male *kacho* in charge of Sanraku's Markham in the Napa Valley, preferring to keep me in the position perceived as the primary role of a foreign bilingual, requested that I transcribe some of the literature into English for marketing brochures to be given to foreign clients. However, I knew that once I began translating I would be expected to continue. Luckily, due to extenuating circumstance, I was able to postpone the exercise.

Finding a Flat

The same man from HR came to collect me to take me to see rentals available to foreigners. He explained that Sanraku would subsidize 85 percent of the monthly rent while I would pay 15 percent. I was delighted to learn that the subsidy was not included in my salary. The man showed me several flats which were about 40 minutes commute from the office. They were shabby with two to three rooms carpeted with old tatami mats. The kitchen appliances were old and greasy.

The rents were inflated not only because of the bubble economy but, also, because landlords took advantage of foreign tenants and of the corporations which subsidized the rents. I doubted whether the HR staff could afford to live so close to the office. He probably lived with his parents or lived on the outskirts of Tokyo. I felt pressured to choose a flat soon even if the flat did not suit my criteria in order to integrate into the company quickly. Also, I feared that the fellow might report to his colleagues that I was being difficult. However, in retrospect, I could have made a final decision after seeing as many as ten flats and, most likely, my companion would have been happy to be out of the office for a few days. But since a new position had been created for me I did not want to cause any undo problems and enter as inconspicuously as possible. The initial impression of Sanraku's first foreign staff had to be entirely positive.

The following morning I returned to the office. Only five feet separated the divisions. The alcohol division was adjacent to the wine division and directly behind me sat a Sanraku employee who was in his mid-fifties and near retirement age. He was a chain smoker, puffing continuously on strong Japanese brand cigarettes. I was engulfed in a cloud of smoke but since he never spoke to me, not even a greeting, I presumed that he was disgruntled with a foreign woman brought in by a new management who were taking over a company where he had been employed his entire career. Despite suffering from asthma I remained silent.

Although the literature on my desk I was supposed to translate was easy to understand, the male staff spoke rapidly and since they came from various regions their accents and some of their vocabulary also posed big problems. When I was asked if I understood, I nodded in the affirmative but I wondered if I would survive the first month. Fortunately, the literature provided much of the vocabulary used by the sales staff and within a few months I was able to adapt, but not quite. The salesmen sometimes used vernacular expressions such as *yatsu* which ordinarily means "young guy." I would look around the room but could not spot a young man. As I became more familiar with my colleagues I finally drummed up the courage to ask the young secretary the meaning of *yatsu*. Laughing, she said that the term referred to liquor bottles. At that instant, I considered myself a full-fledged member of the wine division. Numerous incidences like this provided a foundation for future work and helped to establish a comfort zone in the work place and in subsequent Japanese corporations because the use of specific vocabulary differed according to the industry.

In the afternoon I went with HR to view more flats. The first flat was as depressing as the flats he had shown me the previous day. As I became increasingly worried that I would not be able to rent something hygienic and located closer to the office, he took me to see a small studio flat that had just been built for women tenants. The building was a squat grey concrete, two-story bunker-type structure with four flats on each floor. Concrete stairs to the second story climbed up the side of the building but there was no roof to shield tenants from the rain. The flats were fronted by steel doors. Located in Sangenchaya, a popular neighborhood in Tokyo and one stop to Shibuya, a major shopping district in Tokyo, the flat, although somber and utilitarian was immaculate and convenient to shops. There was an eight-minute walk to the Sangenchaya subway station and only one transfer to another main subway line which stopped at a station close to the office.

The landlord was a woman in her fifties and lived a few doors away from the new building. She had never rented to a foreigner and met us at a second story flat to assess whether she would consider renting to me. The steel door opened to reveal a small living space with wooden floors. The Japanese expression "as narrow as a cat's forehead" (*neko no hitai kurai semai*) describes the flat perfectly.

The entrance led into a tiny unit kitchen. Above two gas hobs for cooking was a cabinet for storing dishes and cutlery and a second cabinet for storing provisions. Below was a compact refrigerator. Directly across from the cooking area was a unit bathroom which was slightly raised above the floor for good reason. The toilet was flanked by a sink and a narrow shower which was without a shower curtain. The floors were plastic and the narrow shower was also plastic. In the center of the floor was a drain which accommodated the excess water from the shower. Although a fan was installed to remove the moisture during a shower, using the toilet afterwards could be a wet experience for both feet and bottom. At the opposite end of the room glass sliding door, opening onto a tiny balcony, provided the only source of sunlight. There was enough space for a single bed or futon, a small dresser and a low table. The view from the roof was of Sangenchaya.

At first, the landlady was reluctant to rent to foreigners primarily because of the difficulties communicating. However, my fluency in her language and my ability to relate to her made her comfortable. She decided to accept Sanraku's guarantee and the key money. She offered to order a low make-do plywood table which I could sit at using cushions while eating or watching television. It was a barebones existence. The rent was far less than the other flats and I accepted quickly so that I would be considered accommodating at the outset.

Commuting on a "killer train"

The streets near my flat were lined with small shops and a supermarket where I purchased essentials and cleaning products. I purchased a compact television at my neighborhood electronics shop to ensure quick repairs if necessary. There was a tofu shop and a Japanese version of a take-away, which sold tasty hot Japanese dishes, including rice. A laundromat was a few blocks from the flat.

I stayed at the hotel for another week, spending mornings out of the office while I shopped for a bed and a dresser which I found at a furniture store in Shinjuku, a central district known for its department stores as well as for discount electronics shops. The most elegant shopping area in Tokyo besides the Ginza was Omotesando which was on the way to the office on the same subway line. The supermarket in Yokohama where I had shopped for my husband had also expanded to this neighborhood and I could purchase favorite American brands and navel oranges but for a price.

My initiation to corporate life differed considerably from my expectations. Japan had effectively become my home and Japanese my second language and there was little to adapt to in terms of daily life with the exception of the commute to Showa Doori. I should have used the trains before renting the flat. The trains during rush-hour were called "killer trains" (*satsujin densha*) and for good reason. When I arrived at the platform at 8am, the rush hour, I discovered that there were four rows of commuters packed together in front of me. When the train arrived it was already full of passengers. Regardless, the conductors on the platform mercilessly shoved the first row of commuters onto the cars before the doors shut. Another train arrived a minute later and the conductors shoved a second wave of commuters onto the cars. I was pushed along with fellow commuters onto the third train. Passengers were packed like sardines in a tin. My arms were glued to my side but since I was held up by the other passengers it was impossible to fall. I could barely breathe. The train arrived seven minutes later at Omotesando where I transferred to the Ginza Line, which fortunately arrived at the opposite platform. I had no control over my body as I was swept out of the car by a wave of humanity across to the opposite platform onto a waiting train. There was no time to react. It was a matter of survival. I was numb by the end of the ride. I could not conceive of having to commute in this manner for years and remain remotely human.

I tried to make the daily commute as bearable as possible by gazing at the advertisements hanging in the car. Some of the seated male passengers read newspapers which carried photos of naked women or violent and pornographic comic books. Some of the whiskey and bank advertisements enlightened because they used photographs of westerners together with concocted catchphrases in English. Mitsubishi Bank released one with a smiling young blond-haired, blue-eyed man in a business suit with the phrase in English "Fresh Man" splashed across the top. Supposedly, the objective was to project the image of Ivy League upper class confidence and success.

Corporate Shock

I had assumed that I hardly resembled a Japanese but since I was small in stature compared to many westerners working in Japan and had black hair I was often mistaken for a Japanese from behind. Also, my Japanese friends and colleagues would assert that I was "more Japanese than they were," implying that my demeanor was subdued. Of course, this was a misinterpretation but in many ways this perception significantly helped me to engage in the workplace. Nevertheless, I increasingly became aware that I was indeed considered useful as the "white face" representative of the corporations where I worked. And there were instances at Sanraku when male staff focused on my bust or my legs even though I always wore a conservative blouse and skirt. Nowadays Japanese females are taller, generously endowed and have beautiful limbs, illustrating a change to a western diet heavy with dairy and animal products. But foreign women are still considered special in the sexual sense.

I wore good shoes to the office but after several pairs of shoes from the US were trampled on, I decided to break with tradition and wear trainers on the subway, changing them to proper shoes when I arrived at the office. After six months arriving at the office in trainers female employees followed suit. I had started a trend. Once I encountered Mr. Suzuki in the elevator getting an early start while I was still wearing trainers. Embarrassed, I sputtered out an apology which my boss waved off. He had attended North-western University in Chicago and was used to the fashion statement. He had also discontinued the traditional company uniform for female staff. Only the women at the Ajinomoto reception desk on the ground floor wore corporate uniforms. The morning pre-work group exercise routine and chanting the corporate slogan was also discontinued in order to westernize the environment.

Employees were provided monthly with subway and train passes as well as meal tickets for the commissary located in the basement. Social security tax was withheld from wages. I initially went to eat lunch in the cavernous commissary which served both Ajinomoto and Sanraku staff. It was canteen-style where kitchen staff served up typical Japanese lunches of fried fish, noodles, rice, tofu and boiled vegetables. I paid with the meal ticket and sat beside a few male members from my division who ate quickly in order to go on personal errands before the end of the one hour designated lunch break. Female employees rarely frequented the commissary, preferring to go out together for a more palatable lunch of sandwiches and a good gab or bring their own packed lunch. Later I joined them and also took advantage of the break to get a free lunch of food samples at one of the department store food halls located in Nihonbashi and the Ginza.

"Whereabouts Unknown"

My efforts to be as inconspicuous as possible were hampered by a tall, lanky young male employee about 18, who had recently entered Sanraku after graduating from high school. He was in the finance division on the second floor but whenever he spotted me he would shout "Hi, Susan!" which was annoying at first, but I began to see that he was a lovely, highly intelligent fellow who was bored with his duties but whose potential Sanraku had no interest in developing. He told me that he was the oldest of seven children and that he supported his family. Sometimes, he came down to the wine division to break the tedium to chat or to ask questions about the US and California and to take sweets which I kept in the bottom drawer of my desk for staff in order to create a rapport when I first arrived.

Although half of the staff returned to their desks at 1pm, the *kacho* and directors were often absent, not to return until 3pm–4pm. When I inquired why nobody was around the secretaries' giggling coquettishly, replied, *Yukue Fume* or "Whereabouts unknown" which could be interpreted in a number of ways, including having a coffee or going on a personal errand or, perhaps, engaging in something more risqué. When my superiors returned they would stay on until 7pm or 8pm.

In all fairness, the *kacho* who were salesmen were often visiting bars, liquor shops and restaurants because Sanraku's business was primarily with these trades. The salesmen also were pressured to go drinking with clients and commonly suffered from alcoholism. Sometimes I accompanied a salesman from the wine division to an outlet and invariably one of the secretaries would chirp, "Come back soon!" or "He's so lucky to have a date with Susan san!" which brought unwanted attention.

From 6pm onward was considered overtime and staff collected time-and-a-half to support their families. Also, employees were reluctant to leave before their directors. However, it was a trade-off because many faced two-hour commutes to their homes on the outskirts of Tokyo, arriving too late to see their children. Although they may hastily slurp down a bowl of noodles at a platform kiosk before boarding the train, their wives waited for them with suppers prepared earlier in the evening.

Trial-by-Fire

I did not have a computer nor did I know how to use a computer. Within a few weeks after entering Sanraku a *kacho* decided to send me to an NEC school for a two-week crash course. The Nippon Electric Company (NEC) was, at that time, the largest producer of PCs and semi-conductors in Japan and furnished all of the PCs to Sanraku. The program was in Japanese and the keyboards were marked with Japanese characters which were manipulated manually to create Chinese characters, depending on the vocabulary. I doubted whether I would ever be able to learn the system, let alone operate a computer, within a few weeks. There were only three other Japanese students attending the class. At first, I missed some of the instructor's rapid-fire Japanese but, fortunately, the manual was also in Japanese, which was easy to understand because manuals tend to be simple and childlike and often illustrated with cartoon-like characters which are helpful, especially in the NEC manual. After the class I returned to the office merely to show my face and to ensure that my desk was still there. It was "trial-by-fire" and I anticipated that when I had completed the course I would have to operate my first NEC PC.

There was no PC at my desk and I moved to another area in the office to use one. Mr. Suzuki requested a year-end greeting to foreign clients and the wine division director occasionally requested letters to CEOs of foreign liquor firms. Some of the communications revealed Sanraku's corporate strategy in which I would not have been included otherwise. When I was asked if I needed any tools to help me with my marketing responsibilities, I boldly requested the heavy Sunday edition of the New York Times, assuming that I would not receive it. Evidently, the expense was not an issue and a copy appeared on my desk each week.

Suzuki's Corporate Strategy

Within months after entering Sanraku, due to a series of events, my responsibilities provided a continuous respite from duties usually associated with foreign staff and changed the way I would engage in the company. Better still, the work forged the way to be involved in Japan's distribution system for liquor and food and for a potential job in the USTR.

Mr. Suzuki's determination to internationalize the wine division made my remit wide-ranging; i) assist and participate in meetings and negotiations involving the conception, development, promotion and marketing of both imported and domestic products; ii) engage in market research, conducting on-site surveys and evaluating pertinent economic information from a variety of industrial and proprietary sources; iii) liaison activities with foreign producers dealing with Sanraku which included preparing and conducting market research tours, meetings and conferences for foreign corporate officials. I also participated in numerous wine events as a Sanraku representative.

These responsibilities afforded me the rare opportunity to monitor and evaluate the product distribution system, particularly the role of the wholesaler, and to perform analyses of Japanese demographic trends and consumer buying patterns. As importantly, I experienced how a large Japanese company was managed on a daily basis in terms of structure, organizational behavior and practice and saw directly the many issues related to corporate expansion in general during the bubble years amid Japan's volatile economic environment.

I translated the wine division's marketing strategy for foreign clients:

> The loosening of restrictions for obtaining a liquor license has opened up the flow of liquor onto the general market. The market for ordinary consumers has experienced a rapid growth due to a change in eating patterns (i.e. the tendency to eat outside the home in gourmet restaurants). Considering these factors and looking ahead to the future, Sanraku intends to acquire the top share in total wine sales not only for Mercian domestic wine but, also, for imported wine.

> The Japanese diet has become extremely varied, including many gourmet and international food products and Sanraku is promoting wine as a part of the daily diet. Because of its affiliation with Ajinomoto, a major food corporation, Sanraku has the means and funds to emphasize its strong relationship to the food industry and, therefore, promote wine as an accompaniment to food.

1. Domestic Wine: Targeting its Select Brand for household use, Sanraku also plans to catch hold of the wine drinkers by producing wine-like products, including Vino 5.

2. Sanraku is seeking to raise the Mercian Brand image and "cost merit" by strengthening its Mercian network overseas and establishing the quality controlled MG Brand in the imported wine market.

3. Imports: In the midst of the expanding import market, Sanraku plans to increase its share rapidly by handling world-famous brands.

Peachy Keen on OLs

Shortly after my arrival I was invited by two young male employees from the liquor division to join female support staff in the tea room to taste test six clear liquids served in small glass cups. They explained that the beverage they were concocting would be marketed to office ladies (OLs). In the late 1980s young women between the ages of 18 and 26, who were mainly support staff in companies, were vigorously courted by not only confectioners but also by liquor producers. OLs were earning a good income but in order to economize many lived with their parents instead of renting their own apartments, an expensive proposition in Japan. Frugal (but only up to a point), they invariably spent some of their monthly salaries on sundries, mainly food and clothing. The wine and liquor industry, anticipating that OLs would acquire a taste for fruity white wine and low alcohol beverages, dashed off an array of products.

We tasted each liquid tentatively, assessing it for sweetness. The men refused to divulge the ingredients but several months later the finished product was being merchandised in a four-ounce pink can and heavily promoted in a television commercial featuring a popular starlet to launch Peachtree Fizz on the market. The drink was a mixture of white liquor, produced by Sanraku and a peach schnapps, one of Sanraku's imports from the Netherlands. Supporting print advertisements and a hot-pink vending machine featured the same starlet. Some Sanraku executives questioned whether consumers preferred the starlet to the drink. Nevertheless, Peachtree Fizz was a resounding success. Following the launch, the two young inventors were presented at a brief ceremony with jackets bearing the Peachtree logo, hardly a substitute for royalties. One of the vending machines was on exhibit in the office and I asked the young man from the finance division to pose next to it while I took his photo.

The taste test episode served as an introduction to the other female staff who were in their twenties. Raised on a diet of American Pop Culture and Hollywood movies they confessed that they had anticipated that I would be blond and blue-eyed and taller. Bowing deeply, I expressed my apologies for having disappointed them. They burst out laughing and our relationship was on solid ground.

The Beaujolais Debacle: the wine division's worst nightmare

Sanraku's first triumph with Peachtree Fizz was tempered in November with a major crisis revolving around the late delivery of Beaujolais Nouveau from France and which impacted negatively on Suzuki's plans to re-orchestrate Sanraku's corporate image. I had yet to drink the wine because it was considered too young for good drinking and prompted headaches.

Japanese wine producers and importers had made a concerted effort during the late1980s and 1990s to entice potential wine drinkers to buy their first bottle and to sip their first glass of wine. Marketing and promotion were extremely creative in 1988 and 1989 with big, pushy promotional campaigns for bringing Beaujolais Nouveau to the masses.

Although Takashimaya and Daimaru, two of Japan's most prestigious department stores, had been carrying Beaujolais Nouveau for over 15 years, sales were unremarkable. However, in order to introduce wine to the Japanese, who preferred beer and sake and otherwise known as "wine-beginners" in June 1988. Sanraku brought in a Summer Nouveau from Australia. Sales were so successful that feverish preparations were made by the domestic wine producers, including Suntory, to launch an all-out media campaign for Beaujolais Nouveau. It not only appealed to the agrarian roots of the Japanese, but also to their traditional love of festivals and celebrations dedicated to the first arrival of new crops of the season such as rice and tea. The Beaujolais Nouveau party was considered a logical extension of a festival welcoming the first sake.

Their bottles of the Australian Beaujolais on display in the wine division but I was not involved in the campaign which had begun before my arrival. The campaign progressed on schedule and a complete success was anticipated for not only the 1988 season but for subsequent seasons as well. Sanraku along with the other main wine importers placed large orders with wine merchants in France. The wine was scheduled to arrive from France on the day before the third Thursday of November and delivered to hotels, restaurants and department stores, which geared up for record sales. The countdown to 12:01 a.m. began. But the wine division's worst nightmare commenced when the wine failed to make an entrance at customs.

Because the sun rises in the East, Japanese celebrants would be the first to taste the new wine before everyone else in the world. And given the Japanese sense of timing, it was of crucial importance that the new vintage would be flown directly from France in time for the celebrations. Unfortunately, it was too much too soon for the France-Japan collaboration. The French were overwhelmed by the coordination problems of air-lifting hundreds of cases of the wine half-way around the world in a single day. The Beaujolais Nouveau did not arrive until the following day. Sanraku also had simultaneously launched a Mercian brand Beaujolais Nouveau to take advantage of the event even though the quality was questionable.

When the director of the wine division realized that the French Beaujolais Nouveau would not arrive at Customs on time for distribution to Sanraku's customers he called an emergency meeting with all wine division staff, including Suzuki, and a *kacho* from the distribution division who was overseeing the operation's logistics. Since Suzuki had not been advised of the situation earlier, he was outraged. The incident was the first time that I witnessed a number of examples of Suzuki's isolation from Sanraku's daily operations and key decisions taken by middle management without first consulting with the CEO. However, Suzuki's isolation from staff was specific to CEOs and chairmen in large Japanese corporations who confer mainly with upper management who are fed information by division directors.

It was also the first time I had witnessed the lack of "information-sharing" between divisions in Japanese private and public corporations. Evidently, the distribution division delayed informing the wine division that the wine would be delivered a day late. In other words, there was no coordination between the wine division and the distribution division (i.e. "information-sharing"). The distribution division *kacho* attempted to justify his division's ineptness by intimating that the French wine merchant may purposely have delayed the arrival of the wine in Singapore where the flight from Paris was refueled because the French did not want the Japanese to be the first to drink the wine. However, there was no evidence to corroborate his suspicions.

Appalled by the mishap, Suzuki, pacing agitatedly around the room, suggested options that would minimize the damage in terms of large financial losses suffered by Sanraku's clients and damage caused to Sanraku's reputation and corporate image. My director, who accepted part of the blame for the debacle agreed with Suzuki that he, Suzuki, the Sanraku upper management and the directors from other divisions would travel throughout Japan during the week to personally apologize to Sanraku's clientele.

I was dispatched to conduct surveys at Tokyo department stores with managers in the liquor departments to get their assessment of Beaujolais Nouveau. Their answers to my questions revealed that the managers were unanimous about the boom being the result of the push by mass media and that the Japanese were always significantly influenced by media. The manager of Takashimaya's liquor department explained:

> College students want to give the impression that they are wine experts so they drink Beaujolais Nouveau on November 17. It gives them status, the same as when they are drinking Corona Beer or Wild Turkey. The mass media latches on to this and takes the message to consumers who then request that restaurants, which would not ordinarily carry such low-class wine, serve Beaujolais Nouveau. In France, the restaurants control what its patrons drink; "This is what we offer so please choose from our selection." Restaurants in Japan cater to the whims

of their clients. The customer controls what the restaurant offers. Beaujolais Nouveau has snob appeal.

The manager at the liquor division at the elegant and venerable Mitsukoshi department store said that Japanese were wine snobs and that Beaujolais Nouveau resembled Valentine's Day, a mass media event:

> Sanraku should know why Beaujolais Nouveau is so popular. It is one of the companies which pushes and advertises it. Its popularity is mainly due to mass media. It is not good wine and the wine department tries to persuade people to drink better wine. The wine beginner tries local wine. Mercian is watery, has no bouquet and is high in alcohol also. The company shouldn't even produce it!

I was sent to represent the wine division at a tasting event at the elegant Ochanomizu Hotel to offer samples of the Mercian Beaujolais Nouveau. My constant smile concealed my embarrassment and the photograph of me serving a "wine-lover" appeared in the December issue of the wine magazine Vinoteque.

The following year the grave illness of Emperor Hirohito necessitated the postponement of the Beaujolais Nouveau festival by one week in November. It was perplexing to see that staff were unconcerned about the Emperor's health, complaining that waiting for his impending demise was a major inconvenience and a loss of business. The Emperor succumbed during the weekend following the third Thursday.

I was equally saddened when department stores and supermarkets remained open for business. The dirge from Tchaikovsky's *Sixth Symphony* was piped through loudspeakers, an acknowledgement of the end of an era spanning 63 turbulent years. I lamented the fact that government policies to overtake the United States economically to prove to the world that Japan was a force to be reckoned with had eaten away at the less-is-more frugal society that once was a primary attribute of Japanese culture and its traditional values. Within 20 years Japan had effectively become a nouveau riche throw-away society. The younger generation was focusing on the future and the creature comforts, travel and shopping afforded by new wealth rather than on a past that for many was bleak and highly controlled by the government. The present represented the loosening of strictures on the society and far more freedom.

Their apathy to the Emperor's death was mainly because the majority of them were born after the war and were ignorant of their past because their history books conveniently ignored much of the detail regarding Japan's engagement in the Second World War. Furthermore, SCAP had removed the Emperor as Japan's head of state and the constitutional monarchy was dissolved along with the military. The old constitution was replaced with a new constitution prohibiting Japan from waging war and exporting military hardware. Emperor Hirohito was a reclusive figurehead who symbolized the past, the war and much suffering. Following the war, he became even more remote from society because he was no longer the head of state.

If Suzuki had been a Fly on the Wall

Suzuki entered Ajinomoto in 1951, after graduating from the School of Economics at Keio University and then attended North-western University in Chicago. He became a director in 1971 and then Vice President in 1981. Despite his education abroad, his business acumen and his former position at Ajinomoto, Suzuki was still a member of the traditional Japanese corporate establishment.

In terms of economic degrees, the private universities, namely Keio, Hitotsubashi or Kyoto, traditionally outranked the other universities and the technical colleges from where the majority of the Sanraku employees had graduated. The Keio old-boy network was specific to certain industries such as the finance sector. Presidents and upper management in the retail banks are often graduates of Keio University, a private university recognized for its economics faculty. Suzuki and the Ajinomoto directors, who transferred with him to Sanraku, had received economics degrees from Keio. The Dai-ichi Kangyo Bank (DKB) was staffed with Keio graduates and Sanraku staff's wages were transferred monthly to Dai-ichi bank accounts.

The DKB was the result of a merger in 1971 of Dai-ichi Bank and Nippon Kangyo Bank, government bank which had been the lead underwriter of war bonds during the Second World War, until it was later privatized. Dai-ichi Kangyo became the largest bank in terms of assets and deposit market shares. It was the only bank to have branches in all of the prefectures. The bank also managed the national lottery system.

The men who emigrated from Ajinomoto to Sanraku knew even less about wine than the wine division staff. The new director of the wine division who had been the former director of the mayonnaise and soup division at Ajinomoto had a penchant for sake and karaoke bars. His second-in-command, who was seconded from Ajinomoto was a marketer for Cup-a-Soup, was out of his depth when it came to persuading Japanese to drink more and better wine. However, Suzuki was supported by the expectations of future success because the 1970s and 1980s economy had created consumers with growing disposable incomes and who were willing to be wooed by imaginative marketing and promotion campaigns to purchase high-end goods.

Suzuki and his colleagues from Ajinomoto were approaching retirement age, which gave them seniority in the management. After their retirement as directors of their divisions they would serve as executives on Sanraku's board of directors. Cliques (*batsu*) or old-boy networks exist in every society and can create a back-scratching, mutual obligation-mutual protection system in both business and government, especially in Japan where relationships are often forged during university years. The university in itself is a brand and future employment and even social status can hinge on where one has been educated.

If Suzuki had sat at desks in the various divisions observing Sanraku staff six months prior to his decision to diversify and expand operations, he would have recognized the significant differences in the corporate culture of Ajinomoto and its affiliate. He would have been better able to gauge the pace by which Sanraku staff would adapt to the change of management and their new responsibilities and the timeframe for achieving his goals. On the other hand, Sanraku staff, who had graduated from regional universities and technical colleges and on much lower incomes, would be uncomfortable sitting beside Suzuki whom they regarded as elite, urbane, wealthy and second-in-command at Ajinomoto, They would be reluctant to share information about personnel in the other divisions and their private personal concerns. Therefore, bringing in former colleagues from Ajinomoto to chair some of the divisions in order to restructure Sanraku would prove to be ineffective unless Suzuki himself was intimately involved in operations as well.

6

The Martini Marathon

After contracts are signed the producers of famous brands often travel to Japan to meet with the importers for the formal launching of their products. When Sanraku's clients visited corporate headquarters, Suzuki promoted the image that Sanraku was a sophisticated company with an expertise in marketing foreign wine while possessing well-established sales and distribution channels. There were media events, elegant meals at French and Italian restaurants and traditional Japanese inns, sightseeing tours throughout Japan and market tours of retailers located in key cities to show how Sanraku was planning to market their clients' products. Suzuki personified a Japanese CEO who was urbane, literate and well- versed in Western consumer culture.

A few weeks after the Beaujolais Nouveau crisis elaborate preparations were underway for a visit by Louis Martini and his wife Elizabeth for a series of seminars regarding the new vintages of Louis Martini wine. The Sanraku sales offices in Tokyo, Kyoto, Osaka, Hiroshima and Fukuoka arranged seminars to be presented by Louis Martini to the wine trade, including restaurants, bars, department stores and liquor shops where Sanraku's business was the strongest.

Louis Martini Vineyards was one of Napa Valley's oldest and most revered family-owned wineries that had been established by Louis Martini's father in 1933 in anticipation of the end of the Prohibition. Louis Martini was reputed to be among the top wine makers in California. Well-recognized for its Cabernet Sauvignon, the winery owned over 900 acres of premium vineyards in the Napa-Sonoma Valley. Considered one of the finest red wines produced in the Napa Valley, my father had served Louis Martini Cabernet Sauvignon frequently. I was excited about the prospect of meeting Louis, if only briefly, because the wine division *kacho* in charge of the account was scheduled to accompany him on his tour of Japan. Since I had recently entered the company I was unaware that the *kacho* was focusing entirely on Markham and, no longer wanting to market the Martini label, he excused himself a week before the Martini's arrival.

Sanraku was investing considerable capital in replanting vineyards and upgrading Markham's production facilities in order to produce in record time a Merlot for the Japanese and US markets. The *kacho* was also involved in the purchase and refurbishment of Chateau Reysson in the Bordeaux. Both purchases were structured by Mr. Suzuki's wife's relative who had been given a top position in the finance division. The *kacho*, by positioning himself with the relative, would be able to forge a new post for himself and, as importantly, escape from corporate headquarters when traveling to California and France.

Even though my job description was to market California wine I was surprised when I was asked to accompany the Martinis so soon after entering Sanraku. But it was a mixed blessing because after the Martini's arrival I soon realized that there would be substantial pressure to perform well due to high expectations from management. I was determined to receive a five-star approval rating so that I could continue to perform similar duties in the future.

When Mr. Martini visited Sanraku in November he had retired as the CEO, leaving his daughter Carolyn to manage operations but remaining as chairman and the figurehead of the winery for several years. It was the Martinis' first visit to Japan. They stayed at the five-star Imperial Hotel. Sadly, the original building designed by Frank Lloyd Wright had been removed and replaced by a modern structure that was indistinguishable from other hotels in the city but the Martinis were pleased with their accommodation. Prior to arriving at Sanraku, the female *kacho* who also was to accompany the Martinis on their ten-day visit took them to the Mercian Katsunuma Winery in Yamanashi Prefecture.

Upon their arrival at corporate headquarters, the Martinis were greeted warmly by Suzuki at a press conference organized for the wine trade. After posing with Suzuki for photographs to be used for full-page adverts in liquor magazines, Martini was interviewed by the wine and liquor magazine *Wands*. I was introduced to Louis and Elizabeth who were delighted to know that my father's wine cellar was stocked with Martini wines and that I had lived near their home for seven years. Despite the personal connection, I managed to maintain corporate etiquette as a Sanraku staff and was careful not to usurp my superiors, namely the wine director and the woman *kacho* who had been actively involved in the marketing of wine imports for Sanraku.

I accompanied them with the wine division director and woman *kacho* for lunch hosted by Mr. Suzuki at an elegant French restaurant which served, at Suzuki's request, several of the Martini wines being launched on the market. The meal was the first of a number of gastronomic events I attended but since they were related to my duties I was unable enjoy the delicacies. The lunch was the first time I had heard Mr. Suzuki, the *kacho* and the director speak in English which was passable.

In the afternoon we returned to the office where Martini gave a second interview with the wine publication *Vinotheque*. In the evening the wine division director played host with the wine division staff at dinner at a fashionable Italian restaurant. The Martinis were suffering from jet lag and deferred the night sightseeing tour of Tokyo until the end of their stay which was fortunate because I had to collect them at 9:30am sharp to take them on a tour of Tokyo department and liquor stores to view how Sanraku was going to market Martini's six varieties of wine. I had planned to arrive a few minutes early to wait in the lobby for the Martinis when they came down from their room but I was surprised to find them sitting in the lobby awaiting my arrival. I had learned an important lesson; always arrive ten minutes before clients.

We joined members of the wine division for lunch at an Italian restaurant, hosted again by the division director. In the afternoon Mr. Martini gave a lecture to the Japanese Sommelier Association at the Prince Takanawa Hotel where Sanraku had a large account. The lecture was followed by yet another dinner at the hotel served with Louis Martini wine.

On the third day the director and I took Martini to other large department stores to view his wine. The bottles were proudly displayed on the shelves in full view of Japanese wine-lovers which both Mr. Martini and I presumed was the way Sanraku intended to market his wine. Afterwards the Martinis and I were driven in a chauffeured black Toyota Crown with a white lace curtain across the rear window not only to shade the passengers from the sun but, also, to indicate that the passengers were either upper management or corporate clients.

We drove around Tokyo and environs for sightseeing. Since I had previously visited these spots I was able to explain the historic significance. It was also a convenient time to chat about the Napa Valley and California. The Martinis were very curious to know how I got the job and remarked that with my skills I could be successful as a consultant to foreign firms.

The itinerary was well choreographed. Throughout the whirlwind ten-day tour Martini visited a number of department stores and liquor shops to be shown Sanraku's marketing and distribution strategy. My role was to act as the Martini's guide and interpreter while the female *kacho* would interpret at Martini's seminars during his visits to Kyoto, Osaka, Hiroshima and Fukuoka and Kumamoto in Kyushu. I was expected to interpret the branch salesmen's comments on our visits to various liquor outlets where the Martini wine was launched. Wherever Martini visited, his bottles of wine were on full display on the shelves in front of the bottles of domestic wine, including Mercian.

The Kyoto branch manager hosted a dinner for the Martinis at a traditional Japanese inn where Martini wines were served alongside the traditional sake. Mr. Martini's six foot four inch frame towered above the Japanese salesmen and he later confided that he felt awkward removing his shoes before he entered the inn. His shoes, lined in a row with the other diners, looked like a giant's slippers. He had to bend down to avoid hitting his head on the low beams in the seventeenth century building. When he tried to sit on the usual cushion before the low table in the private dining room he was unable to kneel on his knees in the proper Japanese fashion and sat uncomfortably with his legs stretched out under the table. Nevertheless, the Martinis enjoyed the elegant Japanese cuisine and the sake.

We stayed at the beautiful Miyako Hotel, an experience I would never have been able to afford. I will always remember the marigold-colored carpets lining the hallways. The *kacho* and I shared a room and she invited me to join her for a massage but I excused myself because the next day would be an early start for Okayama, the capital of Okayama Prefecture.

The Martinis relished their rides on bullet trains, our primary transport. I joked that it was the only way to fly. We stopped briefly at Okayama Castle and then we were chauffeured part way across the Seto Bridge, which connected Honshu to Shikoku, Japan's fourth largest island. The bridge was the world's longest two-tiered bridge with a span for trains and a span for automobiles. There was little traffic, prompting me to explain that the majority of commuters preferred taking the ferry rather than paying the steep bridge toll.

Then it was onto Hiroshima where we visited department stores and liquor outlets. While Mr. Martini was giving a seminar at the Hiroshima Grand Hotel I took Mrs. Martini to Miyajima, an island located in the Seto Sea and where the elegant world heritage site of the 1,400-year-old vermillion lacquered Itsukushima Shinto Shrine looms out of the water. Deer were roaming wild around the island.

In the afternoon we took the bullet train to Fukuoka, Kyushu for the final seminar and an introduction to the Sanraku branch office and visits to liquor outlets. The *kacho* returned to Tokyo, leaving me to attend the Martinis alone, putting extra pressure on me to ensure that everything that the wine division had arranged was adhered to and that the Martinis enjoyed their trip.

On the way to Kumamoto to see Sanraku's large *shochu* plant we stopped for a night at a traditional Japanese hot spring resort in Beppu to take the sulphur baths and where an oenologist from Sanraku's R&D facility in Fujisawa, a town close to Kamakura, met us. Speaking in excellent English, he took Mr. Martini to the bar to discuss vintages and grape growing while Elizabeth and I took the baths. We emerged later in cotton kimono robes to collect the men for a superb Japanese dinner of stewed wild boar (*botan nabe*) which is a Kyushu specialty. The oenologist, a lovely gentleman in his forties, took photos of Elizabeth and me in our kimono and invited me to visit him and his family in Odawara, a town near Fujisawa also known for its hot springs. His wife was an accomplished cook and prepared my favorite Japanese dishes when I visited. The oenologist said that he was relieved he did not have to work at corporate headquarters under the watchful eye of upper management.

Corporate headquarters can be high-pressure workplaces because of the monitoring by upper management and high expectations of workers. Branch offices that are located in other cities or preferably in other countries alleviate the pressure from constant scrutiny. The less communication with headquarters, the more independence from corporate regulations. The downside is that the opportunities for promotion in corporations are often based on the ability of staff to forge strong interpersonal relationships with upper management at headquarters.

The next day the oenologist joined the three of us to be chauffeured in the black Crown Prince to Mt. Aso to see the still active volcano. Martini asked for my assessment of the California wine market in Japan. I explained that California wine accounted for only 17 percent of the market in contrast to French wine which accounted for over 30 percent. I emphasized that, altogether, wine consumption comprised only 1 percent of Japan's total alcoholic beverage market.

Martini inquired how Sanraku planned to market California wine in general and to promote his brand. I told him that Japanese considered French wine to be more elegant and that preparing a meal to accompany the wine required time and effort. On the other hand, California wine was considered inferior to French wine and this negative image persisted. Our conversation inspired my suggestion that Sanraku publish a small cookbook to promote his brand as an elegant addition to a meal which could be prepared at home on top of the stove within 30 minutes, using inexpensive ingredients that were easily available at the neighborhood market. The cookbook would portray the brand as informally elegant and the cuisine together with Louis Martini wine would transport the housewife and her husband, who had returned home after a stressful day at his office, to sunny California. The cookbook would be distributed to liquor shops and department stores where the Martini brand was being retailed.

Martini and the oenologist enthusiastically supported my proposal. When Martini informed Suzuki at the final meeting with the wine division staff that his company would assume 50 percent of the cost of the cookbook, Suzuki and the wine division staff seemed equally enthusiastic. The go-a-head was exactly what I needed to confirm my position in the wine division or at least this is what I assumed.

Before taking leave of Sanraku, Mr. Martini asked what he could send me to show his appreciation for taking care of him and Elizabeth on the exhausting journey. Without considering the expense, in jest, I requested navel oranges. On 29 December I received at my flat an effusive letter of thanks from Mr. Martini, informing me that the oranges would be delivered in January to my flat. Although he had sent a letter to Mr. Suzuki to express his appreciation for the warm welcome provided him and Mrs. Martini, he understood that a personal letter sent to me at Sanraku would create an uncomfortable situation for me. I rationed myself to one orange a day, savoring each bite.

A Riddle

A week after the Martini's departure I visited the department stores to check on Martini sales. I was shocked to see bottles of Louis Martini were tucked behind Mercian wines (labeled Chateau Mercian and Bon Marche) on the shelves and barely visible to shoppers. If Martini's agent had returned a few weeks following the launch to the department stores and liquor shops in Tokyo, Osaka, Kyoto and Fukuoka, anticipating that he would see bottles of Martini wines on display, he would have been disappointed.

Foreign producers of food and beverages who want to enter the Japanese market may prefer to appoint agents to represent them when contacting prospective importers and to attend negotiations for contracts. The agents may have a number of clients on their roster and scout foreign markets for potential importers. The agents are concerned primarily with the initial stages of entry with the objective of sealing a transaction on behalf of their clients. Large trading companies that have international operations, such as Mitsubishi, Mitsui and Marubeni search for products deemed suitable for the Japanese market and will introduce the producers to importers. However, producers of name-brand products will contact importers directly or will be contacted by importers who manufacture similar goods and who can offer not only distribution and sales channels but also marketing expertise.

Martini's agent while representing the American beef industry also acted as the agent for other California wineries. At his annual meeting with the Sanraku wine division to discuss the sales for 1990 and future sales for FY1991, he was informed that the stock of Louis Martini wine was no longer sufficient to support the increasing sales of California wine and that Sanraku was expanding its California presence in the market. Perhaps aware that Martini's price and quality were comparable to the soon-to-be released Markham merlot, the agent offered to introduce his California clients whose wines were cheaper. Or perhaps the agent was unaware that Sanraku's Mercian wines, which were cheaper than both Martini and Markham, were also competitive with California brands and were receiving the star treatment.

Clearly, Sanraku's marketing strategy for foreign wines was secondary to the promotion of its domestic brands. It was obvious that key to Suzuki's objectives was to upgrade the Mercian brand image and "cost merit" by strengthening its Mercian network overseas and establishing the quality controlled Mercian wine within the imported wine market. Nevertheless, this strategy was puzzling because of the comments from the department store liquor department managers revealed that consumers considered the Mercian brand as inferior. Suntory was ranked as the superior producer of domestic wine and whose imports were top of the market. I suspected that Sanraku was planning to eventually replace Martini with Markham due to the similarity in quality and price. I tentatively suggested to the wine division director that until Markham's wines were mature, which would take several more years, Sanraku should consider continuing to import Martini wines to bridge the gap. Although Sanraku wanted to expand its portfolio of California wines, I guessed that the price range would be lower than that of Markham and

Martini. Nevertheless, Sanraku's marketing strategy of foreign brands simultaneously promoted and protected its domestic products.

Trial-by-Fire: cookbook hell

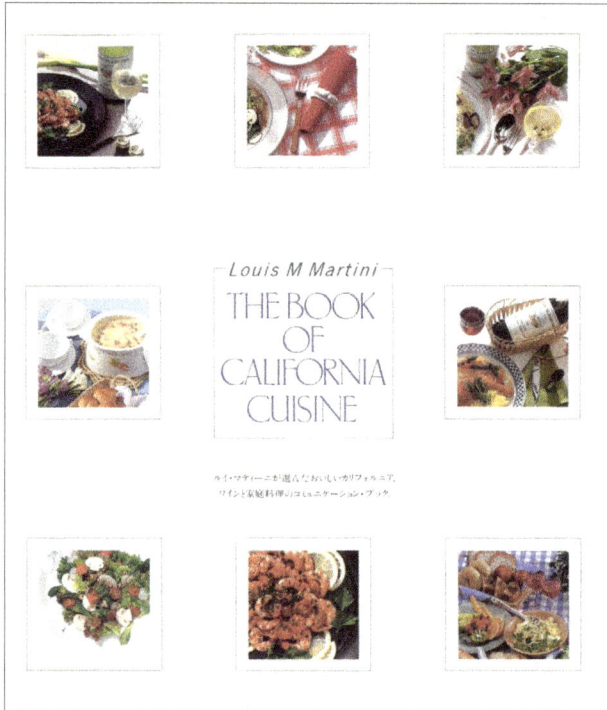

The wine division had been caught by surprise when Martini announced his desire for me to design a small cookbook in Japanese. Since the cookbook had been authorized and Louis Martini was footing over half of the bill the wine division director and female *kacho* were compelled to comply despite the competition with Markham. But their enthusiasm dwindled after Martini returned to California, leaving me to push the project alone. Staff did not expect that the book would ever be completed. But I was committed.

Sanraku's marketing budget had traditionally included setting up booths at various trade fairs and exhibitions for the wine trade in areas where Sanraku's sales offices were located. Sanraku joined with other wine producers for wine tasting events for its retail clients to plug Sanraku's most recent imports and domestic blends. Similar to other liquor producers, Sanraku also published print adverts in trade publications and popular magazines for both its domestic and imported brands. However, other types of promotion were rarely considered. Generally, Japan's two largest advertising companies, Dentsu and Hakuhodo, engaged in the majority of projects for Sanraku but the *kacho* introduced me to the director of small marketing firm, which, as I was to discover, had little experience in the promotion of foreign products.

The budget allotted for the cookbook allowed for only the services of this small firm to assist me in the planning and implementation of the cookbook. The *kacho* participated at the initial session in mid-January when I discussed with the firm's manager the cookbook's objectives. I had understood that the company would provide the layout, arrange for the photo shoot and that I would compose the recipes and personal greeting from Elizabeth Martini in Japanese and provide the food for the photo shoot. I explained at the meeting that the theme would be California and that the recipes would be ostensibly Mrs. Martini's. The preparation time for the simple and uncomplicated meals would be no longer than 30 minutes so that wives could relax with their husbands and friends over a glass of Louis Martini wine and enjoy the meal as well. In reality, the dishes were based on my recipes which I had prepared often for my friends and husband on two gas burners. Electricity bills were still high, making ovens a luxury for many who preferred small microwaves. The meals were to be accompanied with a salad and rice or bread and coordinated with a specific Martini wine. With the exception of one dish, the ingredients would be void of meat because beef, due to the import quotas and tariffs, was too expensive for household budgets and lamb from Australia and New Zealand was still unpopular.

Two weeks passed before the second meeting with the firm. I was appalled that the layout did not resemble anything that I had requested and clearly the firm's staff like most Japanese had never been to California and perceived the state in the context of a Disneyland and a Fisherman's Wharf. Although a cheap option, the firm was unsophisticated and totally out of its depth and I realized that if I did not take a hands-on approach the cookbook would never materialize. Complimenting them on their efforts I suggested that in order to expedite matters I would design the layout since I was from California and was familiar with many regions besides Disneyland. It was the first time that I designed a layout for a cookbook that I had presumed would serve as a prototype which Sanraku could use for other imported wines and for Markham. I was determined to keep my promise to the Martinis and, also, to expand my job description in order to illustrate to a future employer, hopefully the USTR, that my responsibilities were relevant to the position's criteria.

Since Japanese imagined French cuisine as elegant and California cuisine as McDonalds and Kentucky Fried Chicken I struggled to find a cost-effective way to change the image, or, at least, to attempt to change the image. I managed to source from a photo library scenes of stately homes located in US, most of them in California, to insert at the top of each page devoted to a main dish.

A month had passed since the initial meeting. The promotion firm sent me copies of the recipes to proof read but there were numerous errors which needed correcting. I was introduced to the cooking school where the photo shoot was scheduled to discuss in detail the logistics of preparing the dishes for the shoot and the table settings for each dish. I planned to purchase the ingredients on the day of the shoot. All was going smoothly until the big day.

I managed to purchase the ingredients with the exception of sliced roast beef and bagels for the picnic scene. I finally found the beef at one large department store but there were no bagels in sight. The photo shoot was due to take place in the late afternoon and time was of the essence. A last ditch effort for sourcing bagels at Takashimaya in Nihonbashi was successful. I scurried across Tokyo, a 40-minute train ride, to the cooking school to find that some of the school's cutlery and crockery were unsuitable. I galloped to a department store in the area to source cups and other accoutrements, which delayed production by several hours.

The preparation of the dishes and the layout of the food went well but the roast beef I had purchased four hours earlier was turning brown under the hot lights. I knew that the beef would turn even darker but there was no time to go across town to purchase more. A bottle of Louise Martini wine was placed beside each of the five dishes. The five bottles of the wine were photographed for the final page.

Another week passed before I received the color photographs of the dishes on the table settings according to plan. A few days later I received mock-ups of the book in black-and-white to which I made corrections and returned to the agency. The following week I received a colored mock-up of the cookbook and showed it to the *kacho*, expecting her to be very satisfied with the results. But she merely pointed to one of the bottles of wine pictured on the final page stating that the label had been recently changed. Aghast that she had not informed me, I immediately contacted the agency to request a second photograph. Another week passed.

The *kacho* was sitting across the desk from me when the one thousand copies of the cookbook were delivered to her one afternoon in March. Spotting her as she quickly put them under the table and unable to contain my delight, I asked if I could look at them. Reluctantly, she handed the cookbooks to me. I realized later that she may have expected to take the credit for producing the first piece of promotional material that exceeded flyers or brochures or single page print adverts or, perhaps, she had been ordered not to distribute material that promoted an import which Sanraku did not want to promote. Since Martini shared 50 percent of the budget the bill was only $1,000 per 1,000 copies or ten cents per copy.

I requested that the cookbooks be distributed as soon as possible to the Sanraku branch offices. I also contacted Sanraku's branch managers to tell them to expect delivery of the cookbooks. My previous meeting with them facilitated our communication and they seemed as enthusiastic as I was. The little book proved so popular that within six months a reprint was ordered and one thousand copies were distributed again. The Martinis were very pleased and asked for copies to be sent to their winery for Japanese tourists. Elizabeth wrote to me that a Japanese woman tourist burst into tears of joy when she saw the cookbook, claiming that no other winery she had visited had offered literature designed just for Japanese. Sadly, the cookbook was regarded as material suitable for only one winery and not for marketing other brands, which was an expense that perhaps during the bubble years Sanraku could justify.

The endeavor for producing a seven-page promotional cookbook had taken a grueling three months and I was out the office much of the time. I was careful to conceal my relief at having accomplished the assignment as best that could be expected with the support available. Nevertheless, without considering my hard labor, some of the staff resented the fact that they were unable to escape headquarters as well. I became conscious of a latent jealously among colleagues who had been at Sanraku far longer than I and whose salaries were lower than mine. A few may have mistakenly entertained the notion that I would usurp their position in the wine division. I was merely surviving.

What's Really Cooking? Gustav Adolph Schmitt wants the cat but Sanraku doesn't

Rudolph Schmitt, the CEO of the German wine maker Gustav Adolph Schmitt, which was established in the seventeenth century, visited the wine division in 1990 to discuss improving promotional methods for his new brands that Sanraku was launching on the market. Since the wine had been in the wine division's portfolio since the 1970s Schmitt was candid about his concerns about his brand's position amidst the rapid addition of other brands. The discussion focused on the design of a label and the promotion of a new Liebfraumilch. Mrs. Schmitt who also attended the meeting mentioned that she owned cats.

Conveniently forgetting the trials of the Martini cookbook, I suggested a black cat on the label and promotion of the wine by naming the cat and producing a serial cartoon based on the cat's travels to Japan, an affair with a geisha cat and a violent encounter with a band of wild cats. I also suggested that she send family recipes for a small cook booklet. She sent recipes while I composed names for the cat as well as a draft of the story-line for the cartoon. Some of the names I suggested were Tommy, Hans, Victor, Kristof, Amos and Rudi. Since the Japanese enjoyed animal adventure tales I recommended "The Adventures of Rudi." Unbeknownst to my colleagues I tacked on my mother-in-law's family name to Rudi's last name:

Born of royal blood (house of Von Springer) Rudi is the oldest of six kittens.

Episodes 1–3: Childhood

Episode 4: teenage and young adulthood (i.e. playboy era)

Episode 5: Courtship and introduction of fiancé: Lily, Marlene, Margit, Christina, Gabby

I recommended a three-year campaign.

I also suggested that Mr. Suzuki appear in magazine adverts on behalf of the label. Mr. Schmitt enthusiastically endorsed my recommendations. However, after Schmitt returned to Germany, the wine division became less positive. The director of the wine division requested that I send a letter on his behalf to Schmitt thanking him for his marketing suggestions which he found very interesting. He requested that Mr. Schmitt send him further details. The promotion did not progress beyond the preliminary stage.

7

Sanraku Snares Glenfiddich
A Third-Party – Party

Getting to know the third party in the party: non-tariff barriers

The salesmen at the branch offices were old-timers whose territory covered most of the Kansai region. Before Suzuki's takeover they had been selling mainly Sanraku spirits, Mercian wine and the small portfolio of imports to bars, restaurants, small retailers and department stores. The Martini trip eased communications with them from corporate headquarters and I was invited to participate at events in Osaka with the branch manager.

The success of the Martini visit served to instill some confidence among Sanraku staff that I was able to operate confidently in their environment. I accompanied salesmen on their visits to the liquor outlets and liquor wholesalers. I also engaged regularly at wine promotion events, giving me the opportunity to visit numerous retailers to gauge market access by foreign producers and consumer buying patterns. But the most enlightening excursions were to the wholesalers. Through these visits I learned about the distribution system which foreign producers regularly attributed to the barriers they encountered when entering the Japanese market.

Until the late 1980s the wholesale-distribution system was feudalistic and very insular. The relationship between importers-wholesalers-retailers was based on networks that were established between the parties prior to war and which were to continue after the war. The relationship gradually relaxed, not through deregulation, but through the changes in the wholesale business.

I accompanied the wine division sales *kacho* on some of his visits to wholesalers to discuss new imports and to hear the wholesalers' forecasts about sales to the retailers and on-premise establishments. The wholesalers' offices were sometimes located next to their storage units outside of Tokyo and we took long subway rides to the destinations because private cars were considered too expensive for personnel on the lower rungs of the corporate ladder. One memorable visit was to a wholesaler's office on the outskirts of Tokyo. Dressed in a kimono, he sat on a cushion on the tatami floor next to a round hibachi, which is a large charcoal burner lined with heat proof material, serving both as a heater and as an ash tray. The salesman sat on a cushion while I, a respectful female, kneeled on a cushion. The scene transported me back to pre-Second World War days as the salesman chatted with the wholesaler, both of them puffing away on Peace cigarettes. But it was only a brief encounter with the past.

I learned that foreign producers usually entered a third-party distribution arrangement with Japanese companies who generally shared the costs of promotion while marketing and distributing the goods. The distributors may manufacture products that are similar to that of the importers. Likewise, distributors may not be involved in the same business but are linked through equity and directors to the large trading companies, who act as the importers. Foreign liquor and wine producers usually depended upon the third-party distribution system.

The importers' agents met the shipment at the port of call to take the goods through customs and the wholesalers collected the goods to store in warehouses because often the importers' facilities were not large enough for the inventories. The wholesalers delivered the goods directly to the retailers and to on-premise establishments on behalf of the importer, in this case, Sanraku. Besides duty, the wholesalers' costs were incorporated in the price of the imports.

The salesman expressed surprise when the kimono-robed wholesaler proudly showed us bottles of wine sporting his own label. The times were indeed changing. The national wholesalers (there are also regional and local ones) were also entering the wine market during the bubble years with their individual labels. Foreign producers were beginning to contact wholesalers directly to sell and distribute their brands while wholesalers were also contracting foreign producers to produce wine for their own labels. The foreign firms were located mainly in Hungary or Romania where production costs were far lower than in the more popular wine producing regions. The quality of the wine was questionable but the price per bottle undercut both domestic and imported brands because price did not include the wholesalers' fees. Nevertheless, the wholesalers' long-term relationship with their importer clients dictated that goods were delivered as promised. The signs that the old distribution system would gradually change in favor of the consumer were undeniable but not because of government deregulation but because wholesalers wanted a piece of the market and were competing with the importers for whom they were also providing services.

Suntory was distributing a top-end champagne, Ballantine Whisky and Freixenet Cava. From 1988–90 Sanraku, in order to expand its presence in the whisky and wine market, negotiated contracts with Glenfiddich Scotch Malt Whisky, Champagne Pommery, Torres Rioja and Babycham. I participated in all of the negotiations.

Sanraku was approached by the agent for William Grant and Sons, an independent family-owned distiller, to import and distribute Grant's blended whisky. But Suzuki did not stop at a blended whisky and managed to sign a deal with the company to import and distribute its popular Genfiddich single malt Scotch whisky, the first single malt to enter the Japanese market. It was a coup for Sanraku because the distiller was said to be the third largest Scotch whisky producer in the world with over 10 percent of market share.

Alexander Gordon, the Chairman of Glenfiddich, attended the Glenfiddich launch in Japan with his wife Linda in March 1989. The budget for the high-profile four-day launch of the brand was sizable by any standard but Suzuki was intent on upgrading Sanraku's image of a domestic producer of wine, base alcohol, low-end whisky and *shochu*.

The four-day event was choreographed similarly to the Martini visit. Mr. Gordon (known as Sandy) was escorted to various branch offices as the figurehead of Glenfiddich. I had anticipated attending only the initial reception but the Gordon's itinerary was revised at the last minute and I was asked to accompany the Gordons during their trip. I was also to chaperon Linda while Sandy attended functions.

Glenfiddich was a major client and since I knew nothing about whisky production or of Scotland other than kilts, bagpipes and shortbread I envisioned high-level anxiety and sleepless nights. The Gordons arrived in Tokyo on 4 March and went directly to the Okura Hotel, a five-star hotel comparable to the Imperial Hotel where the Martinis had stayed. The director of the liquor division, who also had been a director at Ajinomoto, spoke English and chaperoned the Gordons but much of the time I was with the Gordons alone.

A series of formal functions announced to the liquor trade the entry of Glenfiddich. The initial reception at corporate headquarters was attended by media and photographers. Mr. Suzuki welcomed the Gordons and Sandy responded in kind, posing with Suzuki for photographs. In the evening Mr. Suzuki hosted an elaborate dinner serving Glenfiddich and cheese as the final course. Sandy was duly impressed.

The following day I arrived at the Okura at 8:50am sharp ready and waiting for the Gordons when they stepped off the elevator. The liquor division director collected us in a car to take the Gordons to Meiji Shrine, a park and Shinto Shrine in the center of Tokyo and then left me to show them around Tokyo, while he returned to the office.

With the exception of business meetings, wherever he went, Sandy wore binoculars and was raising them constantly to his eyes. Curious, I asked him what he was looking at and he pointed to birds. He was an avid bird watcher and travelled all over the world to view birds. His revelation was most welcome because my husband was a member of the Audubon Society in the US and after I entered Mercian, I became a member of the Wild Bird Society of Japan. I had no time to participate due to the workload but because I had lived in the countryside in both Japan and the United States I was familiar with certain breeds of birds and, therefore, able to relate with Sandy through a common interest. The anxiety level began to dissipate gradually. Suzuki hosted yet another lavish meal that evening.

The next morning we were chauffeured to the Hakone hot spring resort for more sightseeing with the liquor division director acting again as chaperone. I was very familiar with the area because it was only a few miles from Mishima and my husband and I had stayed in the same hotel where his father had stayed in the 1920s. The Gordons invited me to their hotel room for a drink before meeting the director in the hotel restaurant. The room looked out over a vast garden and Sandy went outside searching for birds. He served Linda and me a special Glenfiddich Scotch. On subsequent evenings I went to their hotel room for a Glenfiddich cocktail hour before dinner.

The liquor division director joined us for the trip to Kyoto by bullet train for more sightseeing followed by a visit to the Sanraku's Osaka sales office where Gordon appeared at yet another launch reception hosted by the branch manager whom I had met with Martini. Sandy was taken to large department stores and liquor shops to view Glenfiddich displayed boldly on the shelves and to speak with sales staff about the future marketing of the brand.

The day after we returned to Tokyo it was arranged that I would escort the Gordons to my "home town" of Kamakura, driven in Mr. Suzuki's silver Mercedes by his personal chauffeur. It was my first and last ride in a silver Mercedes. Since the liquor division director did not attend I suggested that we divert briefly for a visit to Engakuji and the grave of my closet friend. When the car arrived at the entrance for vehicles I announced the Hibi family name to the gate keeper who waved the driver through without paying the entry fee. The chauffeur remained in the car while I escorted the Gordons to the ancient graveyard and Mrs. Hibi's grave. It was the first time that they had visited a Buddhist monastery. Enraptured with the natural beauty of the ancient cemetery and the monastery grounds, they appreciated the opportunity to see the graves of venerable politicians and writers. Sandy was looking constantly through his binoculars at birds while Linda snapped photographs. We wandered around Kamakura where I introduced them to Hachiman Shrine before heading back to Tokyo for yet another dinner.

The next day I attended Linda while Sandy was at a function. We met a Mercian senior executive and a William Grants and Sons representative for lunch at a famous tempera restaurant in downtown Tokyo. We sat on high stools before a bar where the tempera chef cooked the ingredients in front of us and served each piece to be eaten while piping hot. I was seated between Linda and the Mercian executive who did not speak English. The tempera looked delicious but I was unable to touch the tender morsels that were piling up before me because I was interpreting Linda's and the executive's conversations. By the end of the lunch I had managed to gobble three pieces of cold tempura in order to impress upon my friends that I had eaten at one of Tokyo's exclusive tempura restaurants. After lunch I guided Linda to the nearby Asakusa Kannonji, Tokyo's oldest temple, built in 628AD. Mr. Suzuki hosted another dinner that evening and since I did not have to interpret I could enjoy the meal.

On the final day, the liquor division director who was a devout Catholic took the Gordons to the St. Ignatius Church in Tokyo where he was a parishioner. Word had it that he was appalled that I had taken the Gordons who were Christians to a Buddhist monastery. To apologize for my blatant lack of regard for their religious beliefs he took them to his church.

Before their departure to Hong Kong, Sandy and Linda visited corporate headquarters to thank Suzuki and his staff for their warm hospitality, expressing their confidence that Sanraku would provide fine support for Glenfiddich in Japan. They presented me with a copy of *The Diary of an Organist's Apprentice at Durham Cathedral 1871–1875* and invited me to visit them in Scotland at their home outside of Glasgow.

Glenfiddich Revisited

Shortly after the Gordon's departure I returned to some of the outlets to see if Glenfiddich was still being presented in the same way. Not surprisingly, the bottles were displayed alongside the bottles of domestic blended whiskies.

Foreign companies, while regarding Japan as a potentially lucrative market were concerned that the distribution system hampered penetration and considered that importers who also produce similar products were the fastest route to entry. However, relying on importers who produce competitive products may not be entirely in their interest. Although the initial entry may be successful, sales may dwindle due to circumstances that could have been avoided if, prior to entering into an agreement, the foreign companies had sent staff to Japan to observe how the potential importers were marketing and distributing their foreign clients' products in conjunction with their own goods. Additionally, doing some research on the importers' corporate management and corporate strategies concerning the development of their domestic business would provide a better understanding about a future relationship, which can be costly in terms of output for advertising and marketing, 50 percent of which is often assumed by exporters.

Gordon delegated the responsibility for monitoring operations to the William & Grant agent. The agent's territory covered the company's Asian markets and trips to Japan to assess Sanraku's marketing and distribution of Glenfiddich were intermittent. If the agent had visited the same outlets where Gordon had been escorted in Tokyo, Osaka, and Kyoto, shortly after Gordon's departure, he may have questioned the presentation of the first single malt whisky to enter the Japanese market.

Nine years passed before I contacted Sandy Gordon in December 1997 when I was visiting Edinburgh to consider Scottish universities for doctoral study. He recognized my voice immediately and advised me to apply to the University of Edinburgh's School of Management. I waited until I received my doctorate in 2002 to contact the Gordons again with an invitation to dine at my flat to celebrate. Since Linda was unwell and unable to climb stairs Sandy invited me to his home for lunch, which he cooked and served. I spent six hours with the Gordons, eating a delicious lunch of vegetable soup, salmon and apple pie, sipping Glenfiddich and looking at several volumes of photographs of our excursion. I was amazed to see that many of the photographs were of me with the Gordons, who stated that the brief tour was one of the best trips they had ever taken. Sandy expressed disappointment regarding the sales of Glenfiddich in Japan and that Suntory was slated to become the distributor.

Babycham: my one and only?

In 1989, Hiram Walker Allied Vintners which was a part of Allied Lyons (now a part of Pernod Ricard) approached Sanraku regarding marketing and distributing Babycham. Allied Lyons was the world's second largest producer of wine and spirits, including Ballantine's whisky, which was being distributed by Suntory. The company owned Showerings, the British company that was producing Babycham and Britain's third largest producer of pear cider. The sparkling cider with a 6 percent alcohol content was packaged in 800 ml green bottles with a cute chamois logo on the label. In Britain the drink had an aura of the 1950s when men took their dates to the neighborhood pubs for an after-dinner drink. The popular phrase "I'd love a Babycham" was used for years to market the drink.

Members of the wine division, including myself, were unfamiliar with Babycham but after a tasting the consensus opinion was that Babycham would be popular among women aged 18–30, or older, but for different reasons than in Great Britain. At the time, there were few foreign imports on the market of fruity flavored carbonated low alcohol drinks targeting women who could not tolerate higher alcohol beverages and who were not beer drinkers. Babycham would be the first pear cider to enter the market. I suggested that the green bottle with the chamois logo on the label was a vital marketing tool because it was cute and "British" and would definitely appeal to young women as much as the cider. We decided to give Babycham a test run.

Sanraku announced to its branch offices that samples of Babycham were to be tested for two weeks to calculate the drink's popularity. At the end of June, Jack Cupples, the Showerings International Marketing Development Director visited the wine division with the director of Hiram Walker Japan to discuss the logistics of distributing samples of both the sweet and dry Babycham to various outlets. At the meeting I emphasized that the chamois label and green bottle would be key to the marketing campaign and that the inclusion of a small token with the logo would serve to promote the product at the early stages.

The wine division salesman whom I had accompanied to the wholesalers and I took Cupples to department stores and bars in the Tokyo-Yokohama area. One bar in Yokohama which did business with Sanraku catered to a young cliental, serving cocktails and wine. It was a mini-den of iniquity. Cupples gawked at the décor, an array of lewd statues of naked female figures with upper torsos devoted to pigs' heads and large breasts, horse heads mounted on large breasts, and statues of mythical animals painted in psychedelic colors. A Harley Davidson motorcycle was on display for good measure. The bar manager was serving Babycham and seemed optimistic about future sales.

As I had predicted acceptance of the brand among young women was positive. The following October, Cupples accompanied David Gwyther, Showering's Managing Director, to the formal launch of Babycham and for meetings with the wine division to discuss the fall promotional campaign.

The visit was choreographed similarly to the Martini and Glenfiddich visits but since Babycham was not regarded as a luxury brand or as a wine, Suzuki was not as involved with the proceedings. I was elected to attend to the Showerings directors, escorting them first to Tokyo and Yokohama retailers, including bars and convenience stores where the green bottles of the pear cider were on full display. I took them to Osaka to meet with the salesmen in the Sanraku branch office. It was my third liaison with them and together we guided Gwyther and Cupples to various outlets, recommending marketing strategies and the types of outlets and on-premise establishments where Babycham would experience good sales. The Osaka branch manager hosted a dinner for them which included, of course, a libation with Babycham.

The following day was spent in Kyoto for meetings with salesmen at the Kyoto branch and for lunches and dinners at traditional Japanese inns. The elegant Japanese cuisine was accompanied with Babycham. An afternoon focused on sightseeing courtesy of the branch manager and his salesman, first to several famous Zen Buddhist monasteries, followed by a tour of the War Museum known now as the Kyoto Museum for World Peace. The exhibits included Japanese submarines and aircraft with the former version of the Japanese flag painted on their sides, torpedoes, various types of Japanese military hardware and uniforms from the Second World War. There was also the body of a British fighter plane that had been shot down over the Pacific. The two British and two Japanese men were too young to remember the war and although they seemed very interested in the displays, I could not discern their private thoughts as they walked through the exhibition together.

After returning to Tokyo, the directors were entertained with a lavish dinner at which Suzuki presented them with gifts to commemorate their visit to Japan and to celebrate Showerings' subsequent relationship with Sanraku. Mr. Suzukuki had asked me to purchase a suitable gift for Gwyther and I chose a large book of Japanese prints, which seemed to please Gwyther.

In March 1990, Cupples paid a fourth visit for a meeting with the wine division followed by a dinner hosted by the director of the wine division. He targeted convenience stores and on-premise establishments as the most important market for Babycham and visited more bars in Yokohama that were said to be popular among young office workers. Sanraku also opened a booth for Babycham at Japan's largest annual food and drink exhibition. Afterwards we went for a meal with a wine division employee to an Italian restaurant to toast with Babycham and eat pasta.

Babycham Revisited

Cupples tried to control the promotion and marketing as much as possible, requesting monthly statistics on sales and detailed reports on Showerings' marketing campaign. Showerings had invested considerable capital at the initial stages, assuming over 50 percent of the expense for promotional materials, which included pens stamped with the chamois logo and flyers in Japanese. Nevertheless, if Cupples had returned to Japan to monitor sales at the outlets and on-premise establishments in the cities where he had been escorted, he would have seen that Babycham was not the only fruit-based, low alcohol drink on the market and recommend that there was the risk that his product would be in danger of being lost among other similar drinks which contained the same alcohol content and which had been launched by domestic producers, including Peachtree Fizz.

[In March 1991 H Clifford Hatch, the finance director of Allied Lyons resigned after auditors disclosed that the books carried "abnormal" exchange losses totaling £150 million. David Gwyther and Showerings marketing director Gray Oliver also resigned from Showerings amid a shake-up of board members.]

8

A Foreigner in the Inside

In addition to the New York Times I also requested a membership of the Foreign Correspondents Club in Japan which is located in Hibiya on the ninth floor of the Imperial Building (*Teikoku Biru*). The majority of journalists posted in Japan by foreign media are members of the club which has offices worldwide. I attended interesting presentations by journalists who had published books regarding subjects, not always on Japan. The presentations were scheduled in the evenings following a light buffet supper. I had the pleasure of meeting James Sterngold one of the correspondents for the New York Times. The chief correspondent was David Sanger. Many of the articles regarded US-Japan trade issues. Both journalists were excellent writers but I occasionally disagreed with their analyses.

Foreign journalists posted in Japan frequently asked me about my experiences as a foreigner in a Japanese company and my treatment as a female employee. I replied that since I had lived in Japan seven years prior to entering the company there were not many unknowns. If they wanted to know how I was treated by management it would be wise to first ask Japanese staff about their treatment.

When I interviewed an American CEO of a large construction company in 1995 he said that prior to 1989 and the bursting of the asset-inflated bubble there was a lack of coverage in the American press about Japan:

> The American press and business publications built this myth (and maybe the Japanese had something to do with it) of quality and better management. Now we are coming around to saying, "Maybe this myth is a myth."

Foreign journalists often struggle to access news due to the press club system. The foreign media has been objecting for many years about the barriers and is obliged to work within a certain context and conditions and reporting is confined to accommodating these conditions. Their publications may not assess the entire story and their analyses of current events may also be incomplete.

The efforts of academics and commentators to access reliable information is further complicated by the insularity of organizations and their reticence to open their doors to outside observation by both Japanese and non-Japanese. The Japanese social political system is relatively opaque compared to those of Western industrialized nations and gaining a solid understanding of a given environment can be difficult and time-consuming.

In *Japan's Nuclear Crisis*'s chapter entitled "Information-Sharing is Not a Buzz-Word in Japan: Press Clubs Insulate an Insular Political Economy," the section "Press clubs: information cartels control the flow of information" explains that the formation of press clubs can be traced back to 1890, around the same time Japan's new bureaucracy was established to modernize a feudal Japan. Japanese reporters insisted on entry into the sessions held by the Imperial Diet. Since then, press clubs have served as the major purveyor of information from the ministries and from the Diet to both Japanese and foreign media.

Reporters, commentators and journalists who belong to news organizations and who are covering government activities are assigned to press clubs (*kisha kurabu*) which are located in offices that are set up to gather news from major organizations such as the ministries, the Prime Minister's office, political headquarters, local parliament and police headquarters, as well as consumer, entertainment and sports organizations.

There are now approximately 1,000 press clubs located throughout Japan with members ranging from approximately 15 to 20, with the major Japanese dailies regarded as regular club members. The Prime Minister's Club can have over 500 members and the Diet Club can have as many as 5,000 members. Some institutions such as the Japan Broadcasting Company (NHK), the ministries such as the Ministry of Public Management, Home Affairs, Posts and Telecommunications also operate their own press clubs. Japan Railroad (JR) and the power utilities have press clubs. Reporters and journalists representing domestic and foreign media are assigned to one club and can remain in that club for their entire career.

The members of press clubs receive information first. There is a close interpersonal relationship between reporters and their press clubs which prompts reporters to cooperate in the manner of questioning the news source and the way that the information is released to the public. If reporters incur disapproval from the press club they may be sanctioned. They may even be expelled from the club.

The Japan Newspaper Association or Nihon Shimbun Kyokai (NSK), also known as the Japan Newspaper Publishers and Editors Association (JNEPA), plays a fundamental role in choosing which newspapers, journals and television stations can enter a specific club. The NSK was founded by Japanese media on July 23, 1946. It is an independent organization based on voluntary membership. The members include the major dailies throughout Japan and television stations, which are also affiliated with the newspapers. The new members, including news agencies and broadcasters, are chosen by the board of directors and must abide by the Canon of Journalism.

Since the NSK decides on who enters which press club, accessing information is controlled and, therefore, restricted. The interlocking and vested corporate interests strengthen the press club system because the major newspapers are directly or indirectly linked to broadcasters, namely television and radio stations. Japan has five national newspapers; the *Asahi, Yomiuri, Mainichi, Sankei* and *Nikkei*. There are two major news agencies, Jiji Press and Kyodo News. Six broadcast companies constitute the government's public broadcasting system: Nippon Hoso Kyokai (NHK), TV Asahi, TBS (Tokyo Broadcasting System), Fuji TV, NTV (Nippon Television) and TV Tokyo. These organizations tend to control the activities of the press clubs. The direct and indirect institutional connections support the approach of Japanese mass media's conveyance of information to the public and Western journalists often comment on the homogeneous nature of news reporting by Japanese media. Japanese and foreign news providers who are not members of the press clubs experience difficulty accessing primary data.

The Other Side of the Coin

Nevertheless, Japanese journalists will struggle to cover issues in the United States. An interview I conducted with an economics correspondent from the government-funded NHK posted in New York in 1994 revealed his difficulties in accessing stories in the United States:

> When American journalists cover America, they have the advantage. When Japanese journalists cover Japan, we have the advantage, not only because of language but, also, because we have many friends. It is true that in Japan, we can visit company executives' homes at night on the so-called "night round." This sometimes allows us to get an exclusive or an "off-the-record." So, open press conferences are not as common as in the United States because the important questions have already been asked. I go to Wall Street to meet many American bankers, security companies and American economists. It is very difficult to enter this silent circle. Although I can get interviews, in order to access good information I must have a friend among them. Still, as a journalist, I don't approve of any barriers to foreign journalists. We have to change our ways and make all information available to everyone.

A Foreigner in their Midst: the positives and the negatives

In 1988, Sanraku entered into a number of import and distribution third-party ventures with the luxury brand Champagne Pommery, Scotch whisky maker William Grant, Torres, the largest producer of Rioja in Spain, Cordoniu Cava and Cruz Domaine de France. And taking advantage of Ajinomoto's presence in China, a key market where it had manufacturing facilities and excellent distribution channels, Sanraku began to import wine from Gu Yue Long Shan located in Shaoxing Province in 1990. The company also invested in a joint venture with an Australian winery in the Hunter Valley, New South Wales to produce wine for export to Japan.

Following the Glenfiddich launch I began participating routinely with members of the wine division at negotiations with foreign wine producers. Occasionally, large trading companies that had international operations such as Mitsui and Marubeni would introduce foreign wine producers who wanted distribution in Japan. The producers either had contacted the trading companies directly or the trading companies had scouted producers whose wines were considered suitable for the Japanese market. If the wines received high marks at a tasting a meeting was scheduled with the producer and representatives from the trading company sitting across the table from the wine division. Preparations for the meetings were often at the last minute and haphazard. Although schedules had been printed, the statistical information from Sanraku's branch offices regarding inventories and sales was missing and the director had to improvise. In other words, the statistics were ambiguous.

I invariably received queries from the trading company representatives about how I was able to enter Mercian and serve in a position which traditionally would have been appointed to Japanese staff. Probably the representatives had never encountered a foreign woman involved in negotiations and who was comfortable in their environment. The exporters as well as foreign press correspondents also commented on the unusual nature of my job. Realistically, if it were not for the Plaza Accord and the BOJ's monetary policy, I would probably not have had the opportunity to work in an unsophisticated and conservative company attempting to internationalize. I began taking photographs of my environment and collecting documents related to my work to comprise a detailed portfolio.

When Cruz Domaine de France, which represented many of the smaller French vintners internationally, came to call, my colleagues exclaimed, "The French are coming! The French are coming!" They were arrogant, perceiving the Japanese as wine novices and unable to differentiate between fine and mediocre wines. During a tasting we found that one of the Cruz wines was corked [wine becomes acidic when air seeps through the cork]. When we informed Cruz management who were attending a negotiation session, they appeared confused, as though we had imagined that the wine had turned. Even after they tasted the wine, they insisted that the wine was not corked. We refused the wine and requested a new shipment.

Cordoniu and Freixenet were Spain's largest Cava produces. Since Suntory was importing Freixenet Sanraku courted Cordoniu. Negotiating directly with the Spanish producers at meetings was straight-forward but sending FAXs to Spain (email was virtually non-existent at the time) was another matter. It seemed as if there was a religious holiday celebrated weekly for a saint's birthday and Spanish wineries turned off the FAX machines on those days. If there was an urgent communication we had to remain at the office late into the evening to ensure that our FAX was received in Spain,

Champagne Pommery was a valuable client because Suntory was also marketing and distributing a top-end Champagne. The house posted a young Frenchman in the wine division as its representative for the first few months to ensure that marketing was implemented accordingly. He was very popular among the young female staff.

Until 1989 there was no consumption tax in Japan. Instead, a luxury tax was included in the retail price of the goods. In 1989, the luxury tax was revoked and replaced with a 3 percent universal income tax. The meeting to discuss the revaluation of the prices of imports, particularly Champagne Pommery, one of the more expensive items in the wine portfolio, revealed the pressure to compete with Suntory. Since the Japanese tended to consider higher priced wine such as champagne as superior, the consensus was to set the price of Pommery slightly higher than Suntory's champagne.

I received occasional requests from Suzuki and wine division *kacho* to translate their communications with foreign producers and consultants. The work gave me access to information regarding the wine division's business development and overtures to foreign wine producers. At times, FAXs and other materials while being distributed to the other members of the division were withheld which was isolating. But my curiosity was cured with casual visits to the central files to look at faxes and other communication, which concerned operations about Mercian's two foreign wineries, future alignment with Australian wineries, and overtures to California wineries such as Gallo and Robert Mondavi. Evidently, Martini did not satisfy Sanraku's thirst for California wine, which, as yet, had only a tiny slice of the wine market.

"Face Blend"

I participated in wine exhibitions where the attendees were Japanese representing the wine trade. However, on one occasion Mercian set up a booth at an exhibition at the American Club where westerners who worked in the branches of foreign firms or embassies were the majority of members. The club is located adjacent to the Russian Embassy in Tokyo's Rippongi district, known for its night life and expensive real estate.

I arrived at the club before my colleagues and sat in the lobby to wait for them. Until the exhibition, with the exception of foreign clients, I had associated primarily with Japanese. As club members strolled through I received a major shock. The members were tall, Caucasian, with blond or brown hair. For what seemed to be an eternal minute I was unable to distinguish one person from another because they all looked alike. Their faces were the same and they all wore the same expressions. I was probably experiencing what Westerners experience due to lack of exposure; all Asians look alike. In China this is known as "face blend."

At the booth, my colleagues who had little exposure to westerners expressed surprise that the attendees were larger than me. When we returned to the office after the exhibition I related my confusion when the people entering the club were white and had the same faces. My colleagues exclaimed, "Now you're one of us!" It was a momentary acknowledgement of belonging to the group.

A Foreigner's Faux Pas: "Information-sharing" is not a buzz-word

Loyalty to the group is vital to the stability of the group. An employee is reticent to disagree openly with his superior's decision for fear of antagonizing him or falling out of favor because the other members of the division may distance themselves thus isolating him from the group. Since the Japanese identify themselves as members of groups and feel protected as such, isolation for them is an exceedingly unpleasant prospect. Behavior considered to be out of order, even mild descent, may provoke isolation by other members of the division, who will move to protect their superior in the hope that he will regard them as loyal and reciprocate appropriately in the future. Despite the image of tranquility there is a muted tension that workers learn to accept. Although I was considered an "outsider," in order to integrate into the group I was careful to hide any negativity.

However, group unity tends to encourage group insularity thus preventing staff from sharing information with employees from different divisions. There is a muted fear of raising suspicion among the members of their own division if they share information with other divisions, even though not relevant to their own. "Information-sharing" is not yet a buzz-word in corporate operations.

Mercian's divisions were entities unto themselves with the directors forging strong relationships with their staff. The exchange of information between divisions was done only when deemed mutually applicable. Not realizing the consequences, I made a corporate etiquette blunder by passing on to other divisions newspapers or journal articles with information I considered not relevant to my division but which could be pertinent to the liquor division or the luxury products division or the procurement and distribution division. When I was asked by one of my division's *kacho* the nature of the information I had offered another division, I gave him a copy of the article to assure him that the information was not applicable to our division but that it was useful to the other division. But he remained suspicious. Nevertheless, I learned that being a foreigner could be advantageous as well because I was able to operate outside of the considered norm and had some leeway to move between divisions and to communicate more freely with other staff. However, I was cautious to be as inconspicuous as possible.

The Unanticipated Negatives

Acceptance was intermittent. My male colleagues, forgetting that I was "one-of-them," would utter derogatory remarks about foreigners, especially, about the physical attributes of western women. The overtly racist and sexist comments were comparable to comments made by Westerners regarding Asians and I did not take their attitudes towards non-Japanese, including Chinese and Koreans, personally. One afternoon I answered a phone call for a *kacho*, replying briefly to the caller's question before passing on the call. The *kacho* reassured the caller that I was not Chinese but an American.

Racist comments regarding Japanese were common among foreigners working in Japan. I was making the rush-hour commute home on the train when I was stunned to hear three Australian businessmen standing in the center of the car loudly mouthing racist remarks in English about the Japanese. I was mortified. Although no one reacted, some passengers must have understood the obscene language.

Some foreign clients assumed that since I was a westerner like themselves I was more comfortable culturally with them and, therefore, willing to divulge information about Mercian's plans for importing their competitors' products and future strategies regarding their products. I was taken for meals occasionally by clients' agents after meetings with the wine division in order to find out any information that had not been discussed at the meeting. I was amazed at their audacity. As a Mercian employee I was loyal to my employer and, as importantly, I did not want to risk losing my job and cutting the networks I had established within the company.

Since all females may receive comments of a sexual nature from male staff on the work place or sexual overtures they prefer to turn a blind eye because they do not want to cause disruption on the workplace in order to keep their jobs. In the case of some societies, foreign women are regarded according to a different criteria. Although not prevalent now, Japanese female staff in American companies were most likely to experience discrimination because they carried the image of being sweet and fragile and would acquiesce to sexual overtures. In Japan, foreign women, particularly attractive young women, are considered by Japanese men to be outside the "norm" and fair game.

I had assumed before entering the company that because of my age I was immune to this behavior but since I appeared to be younger than my age I was considered approachable. After entering Sanraku, male staff asked me if I liked Japanese men and I replied positively because I wanted to integrate and to get on with the job. Regardless, I never considered ethnic differences so my reply was honest. Furthermore, the remarks from male staff, who had not generally been exposed to foreign women on the workplace, were not malicious and occasionally meant as a compliment, depending on the vocabulary.

Disco in Rippongi

There were numerous adventures in Tokyo, most of them related to work. There were episodes that illustrate my inexperience regarding Tokyo-life and which, in retrospect, were quite comical.

It was in the autumn of 1989 when the female *kacho* suggested that I attend a wine promotion event organized by the California Wine Society which would be held that evening nearby in the Ginza. She said that it would be a good way of meeting people. I suspected that she had been invited but did not want to go because she commuted to Fujisawa which took almost two hours from Tokyo Station. Since my remit was marketing California wine, attendance seemed logical but I was reluctant because I was tired after a long day and wanted to return home.

Grudgingly, I went directly from the office in my business attire. Several steep steps from the outside of the building led into the venue. At the entrance two young assistants were seated at a reception table, registering visitors who were crowding into the narrow room. Bottles of California wine from various wineries were opened on a long table for the promotional tasting offered by two representatives from the California Wine Society. Compared to the French Wine Society promotion events, this one was rather drab but given the fact that California wine was still a relative unknown, the budget was limited.

As I sipped a glass of Cabernet Sauvignon a well-dressed Japanese man approached me holding a glass of red. He was about two inches shorter than me and, speaking in impeccable Japanese, he said that he was a wine-lover and was interested in trying California wine. I wanted to leave as soon as I had finished drinking the one glass when he abruptly asked me if I would like to go to a disco. He seemed entirely respectable and since I had never been to any disco I was curious and it was still early evening.

The disco was located in Rippongi, which, besides the American Club and the Russian Embassy, was home to foreign and Japanese corporate offices. Rippongi is also the posh night-club neighborhood, popular among Japanese and foreigner corporate executives and office workers alike. Sake bars serving morsels of fish and chicken and innards on skewers, karaoke bars and Mah-jong clubs jostled for position on the narrow streets, declaring their specialties with garish neon signs. Some shops were opened during the bubble years. The area was blanketed in a gaudy haze, a den of iniquity where frequenters were briefly released from the strictures of social scrutiny.

The man led me down a hill and into a side street lined with clubs, among them the Java Jive Disco. It was an alternative world, an escape to a Caribbean island with sand strewn on the wooden dance floor surrounded by beach deck chairs. Stripped beach umbrellas perched on top of low tables next to the chairs shaded exhausted dancers from the bright lights overhead. A Jamaican band played Reggae tunes while dancers swayed to the music. The man brought me a Pina Colada decorated with the commensurate miniature umbrella. He asked me for a dance and when we danced our feet crunched on the sandy floor. I was so engrossed in my surroundings that I forgot to feel uncomfortable until we took a break and returned to our chairs.

Wondering what would happen next, giving him the benefit of the doubt, instead of asking him if he was married I asked if he had a family. He replied that he had a son who was 17 and who lived with him. He added, without hesitating, that his wife was a surgeon and that he was an eye surgeon who specialized in eye cancer. He said that he practiced at the National Cancer Research Institute located in Tsukiji where the St Luke Hospital and the fish auction house were also located. He was a member of a tennis club and he enjoyed bird watching and travelling to exotic places to photograph birds. Although his background was impressive, he was unabashed about taking a foreign woman to a disco.

I was about to politely take my leave when he asked me if I would like to go to a Kabuki performance at the National Kabuki Theatre. I had always wanted to attend a performance in the traditional Kabuki Theatre so I took the risk and accepted, which I later regretted because it triggered a series of strange incidents which could only happen to a naïve foreigner in Tokyo. The doctor enhanced the invitation with a promise to introduce me to his friends at the theatre.

Kabuki: not a safe bet

We arranged to meet on a Saturday morning at his laboratory in the institute where he would show me a film of his recent trip to India to look at wild birds before heading to the theatre. When I arrived at the hospital, the main floor was vacant of staff and there was no one at reception. I took the elevator to the floor where the laboratory was located to find that there was no staff around nor were there employees working in the spacious laboratory. The doctor, leaning against a long white counter and wearing a white laboratory technician's coat, was waiting for me expectantly. He took me to an adjacent room where he had set up a movie projector, a screen and two chairs in front of the screen. After I was seated he brought me a cup of green tea and proceeded to operate the projector. The film was 16 millimeter and in color, which intensified its morbid nature. Concealing my repulsion, I watched for 30 minutes vultures pecking away at the corpses of large animals like hippos and elephants and the remains of humans who had been partially cremated on funeral piles floating down the Ghandi River. The entire film was of birds of prey pecking at corpses. At the end of the film he asked me if I found the film disturbing. I retorted that the film was beautiful, a reaction which he had not anticipated. He was mildly disappointed.

On to the Kabuki Theatre where, judging from a courteous greeting from a well-dressed, middle-aged woman, the doctor was perhaps a patron of the theatre. Unfortunately, the doctor's friends were not there. The doctor ushered me to a box seat. A Noh play preceded the Kabuki drama. Since the language was in ancient Japanese, a translation ran across a screen above the stage. Kabuki actors are male who play both male and female roles. The stars have loyal fans who applaud when they enter the stage. An intermission followed the first act and the doctor took me to a dining room where lunch was served in three-layered lacquer boxes, each layer offering Japanese delicacies. The price of a box seat ticket and the lunch must have easily been $200.

After the Kabuki, the doctor took me to a French restaurant in Omotesando. We drank fine wine with the meal, finishing with cheese and biscuits. When the cheese arrived, the doctor loudly complained to the young waitress about the quality of the cheese and demanded another selection. I was taken aback by his behavior because the cheese seemed perfectly acceptable and, also, Japanese rarely complain about service even if the quality is poor. Furthermore, his language was very impolite. I was embarrassed because I would not have complained myself. As we left the restaurant he offered to introduce me to his friends again and invited me to another performance of Kabuki. I accepted because I assumed that I would meet people who were most likely well-educated and interesting.

When I met him the following Saturday at the theatre he was alone and I wondered if he had ever intended to introduce me to anyone. We saw Kabuki in box seats but the lunch was a simple meal in the usual wooden one-layer lunch box. Leaving the theatre the doctor asked me if I would like to go ballroom dancing and offered to introduce me to a club. Concerned that he had contacts at Sanraku and, not wishing to upset him, I accepted reluctantly.

Like Java Jive, the ballroom was another world. I left my coat and handbag in a locker before entering the ballroom dancing. The whole scene was reminiscent of the 1950s when the Japanese were becoming "Americanized." A live band was playing Glen Miller and Benny Goodman ballads. The musicians were middle-aged and older. The dancers, escaping to their post-war past, were mainly in their sixties, the women in taffeta dresses and the men in tuxedos, a single flower pinned to their lapels. High bar tables dotted the dance floor where dancers drank cocktails capped with the usual miniature umbrellas. The doctor brought me a drink before asking me to dance.

His face hit directly at my bust line and he was enjoying himself. I was not. When the dance ended I politely called it a night and he escorted me to the subway while confiding that his wife was not interested in sex. I replied that his situation did not relate to me and hurried off. He did not contact me again until a few months later when he invited me to play tennis at his tennis club. Fortunately, the oenologist had invited me to join his family in Odawara to go mushroom-picking. The doctor never called again. In retrospect, I had indeed taken a risk because I could not confirm if the man was actually a doctor. He could have been support staff because I never met his colleagues. Also I never knew if he spoke English because he always communicated in Japanese.

A Dentsu Mini -Drama

Another adventure occurred when the director of corporate strategy whom I met at my interview invited me to join him and an executive from Dentsu for dinner one evening. He had also invited two young Japanese female staff who turned down the invitation. Despite misgivings, I accepted because the director had been very kind at the interview. After dinner the executive offered me a ride home in a taxi and since Sangenchaya was 40 minutes from the restaurant and it was late I gladly accepted. On the way, the executive asked me if I would like to play billiards. In order to pry myself out of an awkward situation I hesitantly asked him about his children. He had several. I asked if his wife worked and he replied that she stayed at home to take care of the children. When the taxi arrived at Sangenchaya Station I requested that the taxi stop at the main road leading to my street. As I was alighting the taxi the executive asked me if I was not worried about the late hour and walking home alone. I assured him that the neighborhood was very safe. The executive angrily retorted, "I guess I won't be seeing you again!"

9

Corporate Culture
The strength of Japan Inc.?

Until recently, the common perception among the international business community was that the Japanese corporate system was one of the major strengths of Japan's political economy, that the system fostered loyalty among staff, and that the constant effort to integrate staff into the corporate culture secured a stable working environment. The lifetime employment system initiated after the war by large corporations to ensure a stable workforce promoted the image of caring and nurturing employers whose fate was tied to that of their employees. In-house arbitration resolved issues between management and staff. The popular notion of Japanese corporate life is group unity and commitment to hard work to achieve corporate objectives. Until recently, employees participated in daily exercise routines before starting work and management gave daily pep-talks to inspire commitment to the company. Year-end bonuses are distributed to deserving employees and division directors take staff out drinking regularly at the company's expense after working hours to encourage good communication and group harmony.

Konosuke Matsushita's style of corporate management became popular among foreign businesses in the 1980s, particularly in the US even though the methods did not altogether suit Americans employees.

As an engineer, an inventor and founder of Matsushita Industrial Electric Company Ltd. (now Panasonic) Matsushita was intimately involved in all aspects of his company. His treatises on management, productivity, employee development, employee welfare, and guiding enterprises through crises were the bibles for Japanese businesses. Many of the books were published by the Peace and Happiness Through Prosperity (PHP) Institute, which Matsushita founded on November 3, 1946, in order to resuscitate the Japanese psyche crushed by the war. The institute provided a positive environment in which professionals from the public and private sectors could conduct research, collect data on economic trends, engage in business consultation, and create educational programs. As president, Matsushita poured his efforts into the institute and he thrived on a non-stop lecture circuit to preach his methods until his death at the age of 94.

Matsushita established his Institute of Government and Management in 1979. The institute incorporates Matsushita's personal philosophies and values that were promoted by the PHP. The Institute's "Basic Principle" encourages "deep love of our country and our people and the contribution to the peace, happiness and prosperity of all people." The curriculum includes Zen meditation and the Martial Arts. Former DPJ Prime Minister Yoshihiko Noda (2011–13) and a number of his cabinet ministers were graduates of the institute.

Prior to entering Sanraku I had considered that I was acclimated to the strictures of the Japanese social system but it was not until I worked in the company that I realized that my acclimatization had been superficial at best. The Japanese social system is a rigid hierarchy, built from group upon group but there is no single group that is directly on top of another. In other words, the structure of the system resembles a pyramid of horizontal groups. First and foremost, the Japanese identify themselves not as individuals or through their occupations but as members of groups, for example, corporations, government and educational institutions, divisions within organizations, societies, and even home towns. When I asked Japanese about their professions they often referred to their employers first. Even university degrees are not as important as the ranking of institutions where the individuals received their degrees. Today only 30 percent of Japanese put themselves before the group.

The Japanese corporate system is a hierarchical structure and the seniority system still prevails in many institutions, especially in the ministries. Although the popular concept among non-Japanese is that corporate structure is a "bottom-up" operation, it is definitely a "top-down" affair. Upper management is usually composed of the oldest members of staff who have devoted their entire careers to the same organization and who delegate daily operations to division managers. The divisions are structured as hierarchies as well. The division managers who assume much of the responsibility of operations within their division will delegate the work to middle management (*kacho*) who then instruct lower staff who do the legwork.

Sanraku's Corporate Culture: true to form

Mercian's internal structure was hierarchical and human resource management was based on the seniority system with promotion generally unrelated to an employee's achievement. Sanraku guaranteed lifetime employment and staff received generous welfare benefits. With the exception of the wine division female *kacho* who had worked in Sanraku for some years there were no other women in management positions. Two women were recruited by the wine division as "wine advisor"' to receive on-the-job training but it was doubtful that they would be promoted. With the exception of a few external officers, most members of the board were appointed internally.

Besides hiring the consultants from McKinsey and Co., Suzuki made some token gestures such as replacing the morning exercise routine with soft, languid music piped through loudspeakers after lunch. But instead of energizing staff, the music signaled a post-lunch siesta. Also, employees were no longer required to wear uniforms. However, these changes were minimal at best. Even though Mr. Suzuki was trying to modernize HR management methods, he still adhered to corporate tradition. Year-end corporate parties were essential. Mr. Suzuki organized ice-skating parties at a Prince Hotel, which most of Sanraku's staff felt obliged to attend.

Although the New Year holiday began on 31 December and ended on 5 January, Sanraku employees were required to arrive at the office on 3 January at 8:30am to hear Suzuki's formal New Year's greeting, a tradition in many Japanese corporations. After a few hours of toasting to the New Year with Sanraku sake or whiskey everyone retreated to their homes. Most employees, especially those who had over an hour's train commute, would have preferred to have spent the day with their families.

The director of the spirits division (Peachtree Fizz) took his division for a week-away at the Sanraku country retreat to build team spirit and loyalty through group training, which included team games and hiking. The staff returned unshaven, exhausted and hoarse from shouting their pledges of loyalty to each other and to the company. Their exhaustion was partially due to late nights of drinking and toasting to each other, which was probably the best part of the retreat. When PeachTree Fizz proved a success the two young staff who invented the drink were presented at a brief ceremony with jackets bearing the PeachTree logo in recognition of their achievement. Although there was the possibility that they received bigger winter bonuses, their endeavor was considered a team effort.

The forays to bars after-hours arranged by the division directors were ostensibly planned to promote team spirit. As a member of the wine division I was obliged to participate in these after-hours excursions and I must admit that, even though I did not socialize with my colleagues on the workplace, my communication with them improved immeasurably during the after-hours bar hopping arranged by our director. Nevertheless, it was evident that the event was a showcase for him to perform before a captive audience at karaoke parlors. He hailed from downtown Tokyo where his father owned a business producing silk rope ties for kimono.

The division would congregate at an Italian restaurant for a good meal toasting with lager, usually Sapporo Black Label, followed by wine. The first destination was a karaoke bar where we dutifully took turns singing. I favored Japanese pop songs, which delighted my colleagues, who opted for American and British pop songs, especially "All the Lonely People" by the Beatles. The second destination was another karaoke bar for another song fest and more whiskey accompanied by bowls of a potpourri of dried cuddle fish, rice crackers, peanuts and chocolate. The women staff ordered Japanese tea with dried barley because its pale brown hue was similar to whiskey, which they disliked intensely. I managed to excuse myself from going to the third karaoke bar because my last train home departed at midnight.

The Rotation of Staff

Even though there were four divisions in the same room and about 70 employees, the divisions were entirely separate entities with the directors forging strong relationships with their staff. The rotation of staff was one of the more intriguing aspects I witnessed in all of the institutions where I worked and was one of the most frustrating to observe because individual talent and expertise were wasted due to the corporate structure. When a director received notice that he would be transferred to another division, he prepared himself psychologically by gradually disengaging from his division several months prior to the actual transfer. After moving to the new division, he would no longer communicate regularly with the staff in his former division, even though the division was located in the same room.

The director of the luxury goods division, whose family had owned the Mercian winery before it was purchased by Sanraku, became the deputy director of the wine division a year after I had entered. Realistically, he should have been the director because of his extensive knowledge of the Mercian Winery operations but the hierarchical corporate structure, the deputy director's age and his relationship with Suzuki dictated his position.

Utilization of Returning Staff

I interviewed in 1994 the Vice President of the North American branch of a major trading company. He had previously been seconded to the Chicago branch for three years. When asked why the Japanese struggled to internationalize he addressed the issues experienced by Japanese corporate personnel who were seconded abroad to corporate branches:

> The rotating staff, even if they spend five years here, upon landing at Narita Airport, once they go through the doors of Narita, they forget everything they experienced during the last five years. They must be real Japanese. That's the only way to live in Japan. The only way to live in Japan is to forget everything one has experienced. It is not only true in ordinary Japanese society, but it is also true in Japanese companies, even in my company. No matter how many thousands of workers are sent to no matter how many countries, the Japanese will not develop an international point of view and will not become international. If one considers that the Japanese people live entirely on trade, Japan cannot afford to be isolated.

After Sanraku purchased Markham Vineyards in 1988, a male employee in the wine division, who had entered the company several years earlier, was chosen for secondment to the winery for two years with his wife and child. During that period he studied the winery's daily operations, and assisted in the refurbishment of the plant, the replanting of the vineyard and the finances. Importantly, he engaged with various ethnic groups living in the Napa Valley while improving his English. It was an invaluable experience not to be wasted when he returned to corporate headquarters.

Upon his return he visited the wine division and other divisions where he received a warm welcome. He returned a week later after he had settled his family. Although he commuted daily to the office, he remained idle at his desk without assignment. The same routine continued for three weeks before he was transferred to another division where his responsibilities were only superficially related to his training in the Napa Valley. It was an unfortunate waste of knowledge-transfer and a waste of human resources.

Generally, the effective utilization of experience is not considered. I was appalled at the waste of the expertise of a recently retired gentleman who was made an "advisor." He visited the division frequently to speak with the staff. He was very knowledgeable about wine, about how trading companies survived after the war dealing on the black market, and about the distribution system. However, the number of visits gradually decreased due to the reorganization of the company. For whatever reasons, perhaps his age, he was no longer considered as useful as an advisor and staff gradually isolated themselves from him. Although he appeared to accept it, he must have felt a degree of humiliation.

Getting to Know You

Most of the smokers preferred smoking in the tea room rather than at their desks. Even though female staff preferred to smoke separately, I deliberately pretended to smoke in the tea room in order to speak with the old-timers. Initially they were shy but after a while they warmed up. When I asked them if they enjoyed their working environment they invariably answered, "Human relationships can be stressful," reflecting the ongoing struggle to control behavior in order to preserve group unity and harmony.

Although the rigidity of the system could be stifling, discouraging personal development, some employees were satisfied. However, others expressed the desire to have the option of migrating to another company but they were reticent to make the move because they would be forced to start again as new staff members at the bottom of the ladder in the new corporation and accept a much lower salary, regardless of their maturity and the skills that they had accumulated while working for their former employer. They also inferred that the companies to which they were applying might be suspicious and question their motives for leaving a company mid-career and their willingness to take the risk. There might also be issues of loyalty to a new employer and technology transfer. Another concern was that the employee's company might be informed about their application to other companies because of the connections between the corporations through interlocking directors and equity.

A year passed before the young secretary in the luxury goods division invited me to dinner with her family who lived in Tokyo. She had been reluctant to invite me because she thought that I was more affluent and better educated and, therefore, of a different class from her family. She and her brother were single and still lived with their parents in a three-room flat in an old apartment complex. Rents in Tokyo at the time were exorbitant because of the real estate bubble but the woman's father wanted to remain in the city to be closer to his work.

Her mother prepared a delicious meal which she served in the same room where the family also slept. I was also eating my meals on the floor in my flat which was about as narrow as a cat's forehead (*neko no hitai kurai semai*). If the girl had known my situation she would have invited me to her home sooner. The secretary's parents had never engaged with a Westerner before but we had a lovely evening chatting about all things Japanese, including Japanese sweets. Since I received no invitations from other staff, I assumed that their perception of my background was unfortunately similar to the secretary's.

An Invitation from the Boss

Mr. Suzuki invited me and the wine division director for dinner at his home located in Denenchofu, an affluent district in Tokyo in the autumn of 1989 to thank us for our work. It was a gesture I deeply appreciated. Mr. Suzuki answered the door and, showing us into his living room to low tables where the food was to be served, he told us that his wife was in the kitchen preparing the meal. But the director whispered to me that most likely the Suzuki's cook was in charge. Mr. Suzuki was a gracious host. While we were sipping the cocktails he prepared and served, Mrs. Suzuki entered the room to welcome us. She was very attractive and relatively younger than her husband. An avid golfer, she played golf almost daily, which was a very expensive hobby in Japan. Mr. Suzuki served the meal on ceramic ware which Mrs. Suzuki had made. Since the director and Mr. Suzuki had been colleagues at Ajinomoto, the conversation was relaxed. Mrs. Suzuki spoke glowingly about her trips to San Francisco.

10

I Christen Thee Mercian Inc.

New Digs and New PCs

Suzuki's takeover and corporate make-over included moving offices to a newly constructed building located in the center of the Ginza district within walking distance of Japan's flagship department stores, premier restaurants and hotels. By spring, staff was comfortably settled in the new environment and along with management from Ajinomoto and the press we attended the lavish inaugural reception. A larger-than-life color photograph of a starlet holding a glass of Mercian wine was draped over one side of the building.

Although the configuration of the office was altered, all of the divisions remained in the same room. Thankfully, employees were required to smoke in a separate tea room and I was no longer enveloped in a smoky haze. The meeting and reception rooms were well designed. The new wine tasting room proved to be a sound investment. Equipped with individual spittoons, the wine division assessed the quality of the wine samples sent by foreign producers, who approached Mercian for sales and distribution in Japan, and estimated the number of years the wine could be laid down before release within five years.

New IBM computers replaced the NEC computers. Evidently, the director of HR, without consulting Suzuki, had decided to replace all NEC with IBM. I learned several years later that the replacement signified that in the 1980s IBM, along with other subsidiaries of foreign multinationals, had placed large numbers of retired bureaucrats on their boards. IBM hired officials from MITI, MOF, the BOJ and the Science and Technology Agency. IBM Japan employed more retired senior bureaucrats than any domestic firm in order to ease entry into the information service business sector and to compete with MITI's baby Fujitsu for a larger market share. The meeting and reception rooms were well-appointed.

No sooner had Sanraku moved office when I experienced a third earthquake, a sharp tremor which lasted an interminable two minutes. Everyone in the office dove for cover under their desks. To my colleagues' dismay, in an attempt to calm everyone, I remained standing and jokingly declared "If we must die let's die together!"

Name-change

Although Mercian was the second largest wine producer in Japan, consumers still regarded Suntory as the premier wine maker whose wine was considered to be superior. Suzuki was determined to hammer a new corporate name into the minds of consumers. In conjunction with moving corporate headquarters he initiated a corporate name-change.

In the spring of 1990 surveys were conducted throughout Japan on Mercian's name recognition and Mercian's corporate image. Ninety-nine percent of the 358 people surveyed recognized Sanraku as an old and traditional Japanese liquor producer and Suntory as the wine producer. Fifty-eight percent of 210 respondents were unaware that Sanraku produced wine and that Mercian was a part of Sanraku. Suzuki felt that because Mercian already had name recognition, creating an entirely new name would confuse consumers and was convinced that if the Mercian brand was to vie for top position in the wine market, the Sanraku corporate name would have to be Mercian. In June, Suzuki announced at a press conference that Sanraku would henceforth be known as Mercian Inc.

Nevertheless, the survey sample was not large enough to allow a solid assessment of the name-change and senior executives were concerned that the name "Mercian" would have a negative connotation among wine consumers (due to the name-change Sanraku will henceforth be referred to as Mercian).

All that Glitters is Not Gold

I spent the weekends wandering around Tokyo and environs to observe with wonder at a nouveau riche society. During the 12 years I had been away Tokyo had become a capital of opulence, reminiscent of the Roaring Twenties and the 1929 stock market crash. There were new office buildings and four star hotels operated by large Japanese retailers and real estate developers, a telling sign that the economy was overheated.

Tokyo and the large metropoles did not represent the economic conditions in other cities, especially those in regions that were distant from the capital and in the agricultural prefectures. Foreigners who visited the larger cities and towns either on business or on holiday saw the glitter and assumed that the Japanese had achieved astounding success economically and that the Japan Inc. model was infallible. The general consensus among the Japanese who were receiving large year-end bonuses was that they were enveloped in an era of prosperity.

Famous designer-brand boutiques were installed in every department store. The large trading companies, in league with the retailers, imported apparel and leather goods. Despite prices that were far dearer than in the countries of origin, shoppers were willing to spend hard-earned income on a bottle of champagne at the Clicquot Champagne boutique in Mitsukoshi. The branch of the Seibu Department Store in Hibiya devoted an entire floor to wine and wine tasting.

Shoppers waited patiently in long queues at the Fouchant Bakery in Takashimaya to buy one loaf of French bread. Although I knew that taking photos in department stores was taboo, I used my foreign face to quickly snap photos of the phenomenon before being cautioned by security guards.

Japanese designers to promote their brands as synonymous with imported luxury brands priced their apparel at approximately the same level as their foreign competitors. Michelin Star French restaurants and Italian bistros suggested an economy that was vibrant and expanding.

Maxim's was a place to be seen with corporate clients. The streets were dotted with foreign fashion and jewelry boutiques, elegant Japanese stationery shops, home-ware shops and Japanese traditional cake shops which also sold selections of French and German freshly baked goods to compete with the French and German patisseries. Some of the stores sported marble floors and pillared interiors and Japanese queued in front of the counters of famous Japanese bakeries to purchase newly released pastries, which could be equally as expensive.

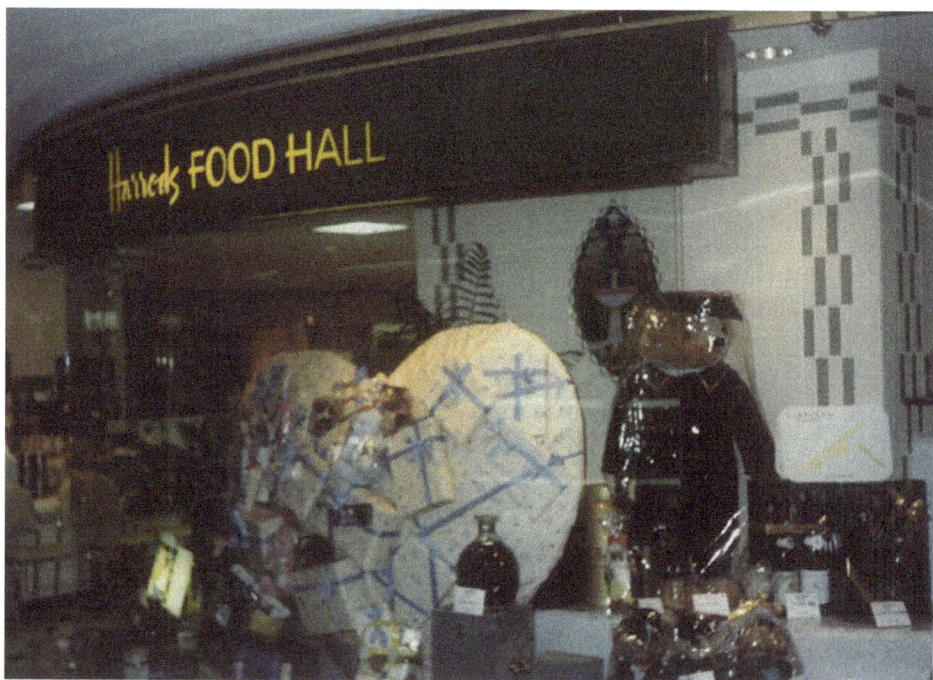

My forays to the large department store food halls to observe consumer buying patterns proved to be a gastronomic adventure as well because each stall served samples of their foods, which invited serial grazing from Japanese shoppers, including myself. I soon dismissed lunch in the commissary to enjoy the samples of cakes, traditional sweets and the regional foods. It was a welcomed hour's break.

Supermarket shelves displayed almost everything that a Japanese housewife could wish for, including domestic cheeses and butter from Hokkaido produced by Trappist monks. There was Kobe beef for a price, New Zealand and Australian lamb and a bit of US beef. Domestic companies were also copying foreign brands but these products were also sold at premium prices.

New products displayed on shelves for only three months were removed if sales were slow and replaced with new products. I was interviewed for the first issue of a youth- oriented magazine *Hey Tom*! It appeared on newsstands only once to be discontinued because the number of subscriptions and sales were considered to be too low.

The Toto corporate showroom located in Omotesando an exclusive shopping district in Tokyo was illustrative of the bubble economy. Toto had developed from a manufacturer of utilitarian toilets to a designer-manufacturer of toilets and bathrooms that were fit for emperors and Sultans. The showroom was a display of decadence, providing visitors a brief respite from the tedium of the workplace. The toilets were covered with gold and silver-leaf. Some of the toilet lids were embossed with semi-precious stones and the baths were inlaid with intricate ceramic tiles.

Overkill: The Beer Boom

The research and development of new products and marketing strategies by the domestic food and beverage industries were indicative of the economic environment during the 1980s. There was intense competition between domestic producers for a piece of the domestic market and producers, sparing no expense, went to extremes to carve out a niche in the already crowded arena.

Besides sake, beer has been the beverage of choice among the majority of Japanese males since German beer brewers entered Japan during the Meiji Restoration to teach the Japanese beer brewing. Traditionally, a meal commenced with a glass of beer.

The big four beer brewers, Kirin, Asahi, Sapporo and Suntory were engaged in an ongoing struggle to dominate the beer market. Their strategies encompassed not only a wide range of promotional activities but also the continuous launch of new brands. Due to low interest rates competition became more heated in the late 1980s and early 1990s. In 1982, costs for advertising and promotion had been approximately $350 million. By 1991, these expenditures had jumped to $1 billion.

In 1987 when Asahi Beer launched its smash hit "Super Dry" Kirin, Sapporo and Suntory countered by courting both male and female consumers through newly constructed beer halls. Sapporo's Bavarian style Sapporo Lion had been a popular after-hours gathering place for many years. Sapporo's new establishments were giant beer hall/restaurants which were creative versions of the traditional beer hall and where patrons could escape from the pressures of the workplace, eat reasonably priced food, and drink Sapporo Black Label. While promoting the producers' beers, the halls simultaneously promoted beer as a perennial beverage.

Kirin and Suntory opened beer halls near Osaka's main train station. The Kirin Lager Jungle-da was a cavernous 21,000 square feet and seated 600 patrons who could meander through a tropical rain forest and cross rushing streams over rustic bridges. Customers enjoyed listening to a live band while eating a variety of cuisines and drinking the house specialty, Kirin Lager. Kirin also opened a huge complex in Nagasaki which was modelled after a Dutch village. Its Beer Village in Yokohama sported a mini-beer museum, a video library, a beer-tasting corner, a restaurant where 11 kinds of beer were served and two garden areas. The public could tour the plant to see how the beer was brewed.

Kirin introduced a new service enabling customers to order draft beer through their local liquor stores which was then delivered directly to them within three days. During 1986–91, the four companies had collectively released 60 brands which served not only to confuse consumers but to overcrowd the market. Producers eliminated many of the brands after only a few years on the market.

Overkill: Chocolate Madness

I was content with the confections that I had enjoyed in the late sixties but by the 1980s the confectionery industry was releasing a host of reduced sugar (but chocolate-covered) products onto the market, targeting the new breed of consumer – the young, single, working woman.

Japan's economy, continuing its expansion, created better job opportunities and rising salaries. However, in order to avoid the burden of paying notoriously high rents, many young people opted to remain at home with their parents, taking advantage of free room and board. Their disposable income was spent primarily on clothing, cosmetics and comestibles. The confectionery industry wooed women with ad campaigns, innovative packaging, test marketing and sampling at supermarkets and department stores. Marketers used mass media effectively with television personalities promoting the products.

If products failed to receive quick acceptance, they were pulled from the shelves and replaced with new products such as chocolate-covered pickled white radish. In the 1980s Lotte marketed single-servings of chocolate ice cream wrapped in gold kimono-like covers. Meiji marketed "Fresh," a milk chocolate bar. The Belgian chocolate manufacturer Godiva gained entry to the market by introducing solid chocolate golf balls to Japanese golfers.

Home Alone: TV Adverts Entertain

I usually returned home by 8pm, too tired to do anything else but eat dinner and watch television adverts, which were my chief source of evening entertainment. The adverts were often better than the programs and I would switch between channels to catch as many ads as possible. Two favorites were for a canned coffee sold hot at vending machines and Levi Strauss's "American Legend, My Mind Levi's." I could not foresee that this penchant for watching adverts would prove to be beneficial in my future employment.

When I was in Japan in the 1970s, Levis were a rarity. When I returned in 1988 Levi 501 jeans had become a fashion statement. I was particularly interested in Levi's entrance into the Japanese market because of my personal friendship with members of the Haas family who own Levi Strauss Inc., a San Francisco company. Two daughters of the former CEO and Chairman, Walter Hass Jr. were students in my middle and high school and two cousins were close friends. The Haas Foundation is well-known for its support of numerous causes, an example of which is the large contribution to the University of California Business School renamed Haas School of Business in memory of Walter Haas Sr. who graduated with a degree in 1907 and who founded Levi Strauss.

Bob Haas, who was the CEO in 1988 and his wife were enamored with Japanese art and antiques and collected many objects for their home. Their interest began in the late 1960s when Levi Strauss was considering entry into Japan. It opened a sales office in 1971, Levi Strauss Ltd, and a distribution center near Tokyo in 1978. The innovative structuring of logistics and its distribution center in the early 1980s helped to achieve direct sales to retailers but it was not until the mid-1980s did Levi's take off in Japan.

Levi Strauss had such a strong brand image in the United States that for many Americans, Levi's was synonymous with jeans. Therefore, it could be assumed that Levi Strauss would be ahead of the game in any country where Levi's were sold. However, when the firm opened its Japan branch office, Levi Strauss Limited, in 1971 (predecessor to Levi Strauss Japan K.K., established in 1982), it found stiff competition from Japanese manufacturers, and it had to concentrate its efforts on establishing a strong brand image with which the Japanese consumer could identify, enabling them to differentiate Levi from other brands on the market.

A television advert also played a significant role in raising Levi's profile in Japan and in other Asian markets. Japanese advertisers are so adept at creating a strong brand image without directly alluding to the product that, at times, it is difficult to differentiate between the two. Where does illusion end and reality (the product) begin? A fine example of the use of this technique was the Levi Strauss Japan K.K. television ad campaign, "American Legend" which was launched in 1978. A Japanese young man in a white T-shirt and Levis sits in a meditative state on a bench in a bare room. There is no sound. Life-size photographs of famous Hollywood movie stars such as James Dean and Marilyn Monroe wearing Levi 501 jeans hang on the wall behind him. Captions in English run under the man's figure, reading: "My Mind James Dean" or "My Mind Marilyn Monroe" or "My Mind Clark Gable."

Although I wore Levi's, I purchased the hot canned coffee at vending machines situated on train platforms not to drink but to use as a hand warmer on those cold evenings waiting for a train.

11

Marketing and Advertising Strategy

What's it all about?

The wine division had been promoting wines for many years but the expansion of the line of alcoholic beverages and the purchase of two wineries represented Mercian's attempt to catch-up with Suntory.

But Suntory was an entirely different animal. Since the 1890s Suntory's core competence had been alcoholic and non-alcoholic beverages. The company is owned by the Torii family who established their winery in 1899. Suntory built Japan's first whisky distillery in 1923 and is considered Japan's finest whiskey producer. Suntory had been in the wine business since the 1920s, developing into a sophisticated marketer of liquor and wine. In 1963, although Suntory entered the beer brewing industry as a latecomer, initially producing a draught beer in 1967, the company quickly became recognized as a major contender in the competitive beer market. Suntory also developed a line of non-alcoholic beverages. In 1984 it engaged in a licensing agreement with the premium ice cream producer Häagan-Dazs, one of its numerous ventures with foreign producers in the food and beverage industry. In 1985 Suntory entered a partnership with Château lafite Rothschild and also purchased Château Lagrange and over 50 percent of Château Beychevelle. Suntory Vineyards and research center are located in Yamanashi Prefecture where the other large Japanese wine producers' vineyards are located. Suntory's wine is said to be made entirely from their domestically cultivated grapes.

Suntory's corporate investment in advertisement and marketing was substantially more than Mercian Inc.

Suntory's Marketing Strategy: sipping sophistication, sipping elegance

In terms of marketing and promotion Suntory concentrated its huge marketing and advertising budget on wine, whisky, beer and soft drinks. The advertising and marketing campaigns for wine and whisky focused on the arts and culture since the 1920s when the Torii family began supporting educational and social welfare programs. As the years progressed, Suntory's patronage came to encompass the full-fledged funding of the arts and literature and wildlife conservation.

Corporate identity is immersed in a potpourri of cultural activities and Suntory's philosophical theme "Enjoyment of Daily Life," together with its advertisements, cleverly exploited its corporate identity to promote its products. As an example, a well-known Japanese author approached Suntory in the 1980s suggesting that he do a commercial for whisky in Japan. His theory was that Suntory and writers were intimately related because both were the producers of "culture." The spot was successful. The writer's recently published novel received valuable publicity and the writer's calm soliloquy about the "Enjoyment of Daily Life" stamped an indelible literary image on a bottle of Suntory. Other writers have since joined his ranks, further enhancing this image. A scene in the American film *Lost in Translation* replicates the television advert with the protagonist, played by the actor Bill Murray, sitting in a chair, holding a glass of Suntory whisky and mouthing a few words in Japanese.

The Suntory Museum of Art was opened in Tokyo in 1961 and the Château Beychevelle International Center of Contemporary Art was opened in 1989. In 1986, Suntory Hall was inaugurated in Tokyo and is regarded as one of the finest concert venues in Japan. The 2,006 seat hall was built to commemorate Suntory's sixtieth anniversary of its whisky production and the twentieth anniversary of its beer brewing operations. The hall also includes a 450 seat recital hall. Suzuki copied Suntory by opening an art museum in 1990 in Nagano Prefecture naming it the Mercian Musée d'Art Karuizawa.

Mercian's Marketing Mix: cheap and cheerful

Suzuki's strategies were designed to: i) expand the portfolio of mid to high-end imported wine and spirits; ii) purchase wineries in famous wine producing regions iii) develop wine-based drinks, targeting young women and men with limited income. With the exception of Martini and Pommery, most of the new products targeted younger and less sophisticated consumers. Catching up with Suntory proved a strain on the wine division staff. Consequently, marketing was uncoordinated, haphazard and expensive. My recommendation that marketing and promotion of a brand over the long term would be cost-effective received a cool reception.

In 1988 Suntory, which also operated a flower business, released a wine instilled with the essence of flowers in bottles that were painted with specific flowers such as cherry or lemon blossoms. While Suntory was marketing the flower infused wine Mercian was marketing wine in milk cartons ("bag in box") and several other drinks targeting young women. Vino 5 was a concoction of wine diluted with fruit juice and water and packaged in a pint-size carton and sold mainly in convenience stores. I was asked to compose catchphrases in English for stickers on the cartons, which became a hobby.

Even though consumers may not understand the meaning of the words, expressions created from a foreign language bring an image of internationalization and promote a momentary escape from reality. French, English and German were popular languages for catchphrases. Among foreign males the black T-shirt with the logo "Asahi Super Dry" in Japanese characters is very popular but most are unaware that Asahi Super Dry is a lager with a 6 percent alcohol content that was launched on the market in 1988 by one of Japan's three main brewers. At the time, most lagers had a 4 percent alcohol content. I composed the following phrases for Vino 5 specifically for the Japanese:

Drink to me only

First love

Love on the rocks

Lover boy

Drink to lovely nights

Lovely Lad

Cheers to oshare nights (oshare is "stylish" or "fashionable")

Oshare Dreams

Forever you Forever Me.

Vino 5 and We

Alive with Vino 5.

The spirits division also asked me to create some phrases for the label of a new brand of *shochu*. I composed several but I did not expect any of them would be given serious consideration. However, several weeks later, to my surprise, the division handed me a small sample bottle of the new brew. One of my phrases, "25 Cask-Aged *Shochu*" was printed on the label, a highlight of my job at Mercian.

Mercian was one of the four major producers of *shochu* and was steeped in the tradition of producing spirits and whisky for the working classes and had consumer-recognition as a producer of excellent shochu. But Mr. Suzuki's strategy called for the reduction of *shochu* production because he considered it to be a cheap, unsophisticated, blue collar drink. I saw this strategy as a major miscalculation of the future *shochu* market because the strategy did not consider the growing popularity of *shochu*-based drinks among Japanese youth.

A Private Tour of Mercian's Winery

Although the Martinis had visited the Mercian winery and vineyards in Yamanashi Prefecture, they never mentioned their impressions. However, Elizabeth included in her letter thanking me for dishes I had sent to her that she and her husband had visited the Suntory winery: "When we were in Japan we went for a tour of the Suntory Vineyards. Louis was very impressed by their vineyards, research and wine that they made from their own grapes, not the blends, etc."

I visited Mercian Winery for a private tour offered by the senior manager and wine maker. Until Suzuki stepped in Mercian's budget for R&D was small compared to Suntory's because Mercian was engaged in other businesses while Suntory's core competence focused on alcoholic and non-alcoholic beverages. Mercian's winery and the vineyards were on a smaller scale compared to Suntory's and the wineries in the Napa Valley.

The tour was a peaceful walk through Japan's wine making history but it also explained the struggle of oenologists in Japan to cultivate grapes for wine in a humid climate. I saw the new steel fermentation tanks and the modern grape crushing machinery but I could see the need for Mercian to top-up its wine with concentrated grape juice from Rumania and Bulgaria, the least expensive option.

California Here I Come: a visit to Martini

In September 1989 I convinced the director to send me to Los Angeles and the San Francisco Bay Area for a ten-day market tour of liquor retail outlets to interview store managers and photograph the shelves so that the wine division could see how the brands of wine were being displayed. Since there were few shops in Japan that focused on wine the survey would reveal which wines were popular and how floor space was utilized.

After arriving at Los Angeles Airport I first went to a DHL depot to collect two large maps of the Bordeaux and Burgundy wine growing regions which the French Wine Association's office in Tokyo had shipped to me when I asked one of the administrators if there were any maps of the regions. He graciously offered to send them to LAX. The maps are very beautiful and adorn my kitchen wall.

I booked a room at an inexpensive hotel in Los Angeles. To cut costs I stayed with my parents while I was in San Francisco. Fortunately, the proprietors of the upmarket wine shops in Beverly Hills and the large outlets in San Francisco and suburbs allowed me to take photographs of their establishments and conduct interviews.

Before departing Japan I had contacted Louis Martini to inquire if I could pay a brief visit. We arranged to meet at the Louis Martini Winery for lunch. The weather was warm and dry and the vineyards were almost ready for the harvest. Elizabeth and Louis welcomed me with a basket laden with fruits and vegetables from Elizabeth's garden. They requested more copies of the cookbook and then escorted me to the winery's large garden. There were no tourists around when a caterer laid out a delicious lunch for the three of us on the picnic table.

After lunch the Martinis gave me a special tour of the winery before taking me to their home. I recognized the building immediately because I had walked passed it almost daily during my years in St. Helena. Louis proposed that he take me to some of his vineyards to show me some varietals and I hopped onto his pick-up truck for a tour. Louis explained that the Martinis owned over 900 acres of vineyard in the Napa-Sonoma Valley.

When we returned to his home Louis took me to his wine library where bottles of wine produced over the years were stored according to the year they were produced. Asking me the year I was born he presented to me a bottle of Cabernet Sauvignon he had made that year. It was a generous souvenir and a finale to a memorable day.

After returning to Mercian I presented the wine director with an album filled with the photographs taken during the survey along with the receipts for expenses. The entire trip cost $2,000, including airfare, which was certainly cost-effective. He and the female *kacho* were dumbfounded that I had actually executed the marketing survey exactly as I had proposed because they had suspected that I had taken a holiday. They took me to Mr. Suzuki's office to present the album and to detail how wine shops and large liquor outlets were using floor space and the wines that were most popular among American consumers. Mr. Suzuki, although surprised, seemed pleased with the effort but I do not know how the survey was used or if, indeed, it was used at all.

In December 1990, the wine division met with Louis Martini's agent to discuss the sales in 1990 and to forecast sales for FY1991. The agent was told that the stock of Martini wine was no longer sufficient because of growing sales of California wine and that Mercian was expanding its California presence in the market. The Martini agent offered to introduce Mercian to other California wineries that produced cheaper wines than Martini.

We did not tell the agent that we were approaching Gallo, California's largest wine producer and also considering Robert Mondavi which was being imported and distributed by another Japanese company. Gallo was known at the time as a producer of jug wine for mainly home use and was in a lower price range than Martini. Since Markham wines were comparable in quality to Martini wines and in the same price category, it was improbable that the Martini label would remain a constant in the Mercian portfolio. The agent invited me for lunch to suss out Mercian's future plans but I preferred to simply enjoy the cuisine. Coincidently, Gallo purchased Martini in 2002 but the Martini family continued to manage operations.

Moving to new headquarters and a corporate name-change was an expensive proposition. Regardless, Mercian continued to expand the wine business, acquiring Calpis Co., the producer of a yogurt-based drink which I drank regularly in the same fashion as Americans drink Ovaltine. There was a synergy because Calpis' core product was the yogurt-based beverage, produced through the fermentation process. Calpis also had purchased top-of-the-line California boutique wineries. Mercian eventually engaged in third-party ventures with Gallo and Mondavi and, pushing full-steam ahead, invested in Australian wineries and the importation of Italian wine.

Corporate Strategies Frustrate Corporate Development

Within a year after entering Mercian I became increasingly concerned about the company's corporate strategy and questioned the use of budgets. There was also palpable resentment and anxiety amongst the old-timers who regarded Suzuki as an interloper who was bored and frustrated with his lack of responsibilities at Ajinomoto and had taken on Mercian as a "toy" to mould into his version of a Suntory. Staff also grumbled that Mercian was acting as Ajinomoto's real estate agent because of its recent purchases of Markham in the Napa Valley and Chateau Reysson in the Bordeaux. The dilapidated Markham was undergoing a total overhaul with the replanting of the vineyards and the installation of new production equipment. Chateau Reysson was also being given a complete face-lift.

I could only guess that the reason for Mercian Inc engaging in other businesses entirely unrelated to wine or to *shochu* and blended whiskey was that Suzuki was also committed to Ajinomoto's interests because he was partially dependent on Ajinomoto's corporate lenders. However, fish feed and pharmaceuticals did not have a symbiotic relationship with wine. What was Mercian's core competence? Was there a marketing mix or a marketing muddle?

Walking on Ice

When Mercian's foreign clients remarked that as a consultant to foreign producers attempting entry into Japan I would become a millionaire I replied that the Japanese were walking on a thin layer of ice, alluding to the overheated economy. Although in the minority, there were Japanese who also were deeply concerned about the overheated markets. I gauged the economy to be engulfed in an illusion of prosperity.

At a wine and food event in September 1989 I met the well-known food illustration photographer Ken Huang whose company Fotony served the large Japanese food and drink corporations. He generously invited me to his studio to watch him shoot a layout for the magazine *Vegeta*. When I saw the complexity of the process I realized that food photography was not only a technical feat but an art form as well. In December I received the copy of *Vegeta* which carried the photos he shot when I was at his studio and a beautiful book of his photographs which he had authored. Enclosed was a letter with his latest news. He ended,

"This year the Japanese economy in general has been prosperous. And so are we. A thick bonus is expected to be paid to workers throughout the country."

Writing on the Wall

Japanese businessmen were misinterpreting the 1988 bubble as a benchmark for future rapid growth in consumption. Unaware, or perhaps in denial, that the economy was overheated and that the markets would not be able to sustain the momentum, they continued to plough capital investment into the expansion of their group companies and the diversification of their businesses. Mercian was illustrative of this era.

As Mercian's president, and later its chairman, Suzuki represented the company at corporate events and entertained corporate clients while delegating daily operations to division managers. He attended only high-level corporate meetings on strategies which were planned at the division levels. He was fairly isolated from internal affairs and it appeared that significant information relating to operations was being filtered out by middle management. Suzuki would have been wise to take more control of the restructuring of the company and corporate management.

By June 1990 I sensed the beginning of a bumpy ride for the Japanese economy and keenly felt that Suzuki was diversifying into activities that were exposed to the impacts of an economic slowdown. Anxious to hit the ground running and play catch-up with Suntory Suzuki was overestimating the pace of consumption and the rate of growth of the markets he was targeting. Although some of the business risk was spread by expanding the animal feed business and adding other products to Mercian's portfolio, the diversification also served to muddy the waters during the beginning of a bumpy economic period by going beyond the company's traditional core competencies. Furthermore, Suzuki's ambitions for Mercian Inc. pulled former Sanraku staff out of their comfort zone. It was not a winning formula.

Within three years, the number of staff in the wine division had increased to 20. Four of the original staff had either retired or had been sent to work in branch offices, which was considered a humiliating step down the corporate ladder.

And although Suzuki could rely on Ajinomoto for some support and on loans from the major metropolitan banks, he could not rely on the management unless he observed operations and studied Mercian's accounts directly. Regardless, even in the best of times it would have taken a number of years to develop Mercian's business as a premier wine producer in the same league as Suntory.

Through my work I was experiencing an era of opulence as a consequence of ultra-low interest rates. Mercian represented Japanese companies that expanded and diversified operations after the bursting of the asset-inflated bubble without considering the consequences such as the deflationary impact on consumerism as well as a maturing consumer market and aging population. Mercian was an example of:

> A company's rapid over-diversification during the bubble years, the miscalculation of Japan's economic stability and the impact of the continuing recession on the domestic consumer market during the 1990s.

> The problems experienced by a subsidiary's parent company when taking over the management and operations of a company that had operated fairly independently for many years and which had a separate corporate culture and different objectives.

> The problems encountered by foreign producers entering the Japanese market through a third-party distribution system.

I recognized that Mercian Inc. was in a no-win situation and that the learning curve had peaked. I wanted to remain working in Japan mainly to view directly the unfolding drama but I knew that I would be hard pressed to find as challenging a job in a company that would include me as a normal staff. Furthermore, I suspected that I would struggle to gain employment in liquor producers-importers because I would be regarded with suspicion and not entirely trusted as a former employee of Mercian Inc. I reluctantly concluded that I should return to the United States and apply to the USTR because I had accumulated skills which I assumed were pertinent to the objectives of the agency.

While at Mercian I had come to understand that even though I had been hired to perform roles that were not performed by the other employees, I was still considered a recent employee and perhaps an interloper. Nevertheless, I realized the value of being regarded as a foreigner because I could bend corporate rules when necessary.

In June, to my colleagues' surprise, I announced my intentions of returning to the United States for personal reasons. Mr. Suzuki kindly wrote a positive letter of recommendation.

In 2010 the Tokyo Stock Exchange delisted Mercian Inc for false reporting of net worth. The issues which led to Mercian's failure are discussed in the final chapter.

12

Made in the USA?

I returned to San Francisco for several weeks before going on to New York to stay with my third cousin who lived in a white shingle house in a town next door to Greenwich, Connecticut where the GDP per capita was one of the highest in the US and from where Wall Street execs commuted daily to Manhattan. My cousin who was about the same age was an in-house attorney for GE Capital. She offered to introduce me to a close friend who was a partner in a large New York law firm on Lexington Avenue with a roster of Japanese corporate clients. Cyrus Vance, the former Secretary of State during President Jimmy Carter's administration, was the law firm's chairman. Japanese companies, on a buying spree in the US, were among the firms' most lucrative clients.

The partner suggested that I apply for work as an assistant to partners who were engaging with the firm's Japanese clients to help facilitate the negotiations. But I knew that even though I would be dealing with Japanese businesses, the relationship would be superficial at best. I declined the offer even though the salary would be higher than Mercian's and the standard of living would also be more comfortable.

I briefly considered getting a law degree because candidates with my credentials were uncommon. After visiting Columbia University to enquire about the criteria for acceptance I was urged to apply despite my age. However, a law degree would take four years, consequently isolating me from corporate Japan and the drama that inevitably would unfold. I continued to stay at my cousin's house while looking for employment.

ESP!

I was going through withdrawal symptoms from the wine division so during one hot and muggy morning in Manhattan I collected maps and information on the Napa Valley to send to Mercian. I thought about the deputy director whose family had owned the Mercian Winery before Sanraku had purchased it. It was unfortunate that Mercian had not sent him to see Markham and I hoped that one day I would be able to be his guide around the Napa Valley wineries. By 2pm my dress was damp with perspiration and I decided to return to Greenwich instead of waiting until 5pm, my regular commute time. The train departed from Grand Central Station. Holding the bag with the maps for the wine division, I waited in a queue at the information booth under the giant clock to find out the time of the next train. A gentleman with greying hair and wearing a grey T-shirt was standing in front of me. In a soggy daze I did not notice anything peculiar about him until he turned around. Looking at me he exclaimed in Japanese, "Susan! We've been trying to contact you!" The man was the deputy director of the wine division. His face was ashen.

Since I had been thinking about him that very day and was holding a bag full of materials for the wine division, for a second, I assumed that seeing him standing before me was perfectly natural. After we regained our composure, the deputy director told me that Mercian was having some problems with Louis Martini and wanted me to accompany him to the winery to sort out the situation. He asked me if I could meet him in San Francisco the next day and accompany him to Martini for the meeting. Mercian would pay for the entire trip and for my services. To the relief of the deputy director I accepted. My ulterior motive was to have the opportunity to guide him around the Napa Valley.

After an uneventful flight to SFO I took a taxi to the St. Francis Hotel where Mercian had reserved a room for me and a room for the deputy director. That evening we ate in the dining room to discuss the meeting agenda. The deputy director told me that when he called the wine division that evening to report the Grand Central Station incident everyone was aghast at what could only be described as an ESP event. The next morning we were driven by private car across the Golden Gate Bridge to Napa. The director was awed by the natural beauty and the space and the dry, sunny climate. The meeting with Caroline Martini went smoothly allowing plenty of time to show the director my favorite wineries. We had dinner at a restaurant in St. Helena before heading back to the hotel. As we parted company, I handed the director the bag of information I had collected.

The USTR Does Not Want Me!

I went to Washington DC and stayed for several weeks with my mother's best friend. Her husband had retired from the World Bank where he was one of its first staff and who had worked for the bank in India, Thailand and the Soviet Union. I had no contacts at the USTR and decided to apply for a low level position which initially would not have entailed negotiations or analyses of trade policy.

I was interviewed at the USTR offices by a civil servant in his fifties who was the director of HR. After reading my CV and asking some general questions he ended the interview by stating that the USTR did not need a staff who was fluent in Japanese because it was focusing on China, which was surprising, since Japan was the United States' largest trading partner and its chief ally in the Pacific. Furthermore, the USTR was constantly pressuring Japan to deregulate is markets for rice, beef, automobiles, insurance and pharmaceuticals, industries that were represented by powerful lobby groups. The officer was not interested in either distribution or non-tariff barriers. I suspected that trade negotiations were equally based on political necessity. Frankly, the rejection came as a relief because I had come to the conclusion that, although I was in the US, I would continue to work in a Japanese corporate environment. There were numerous Japanese North American headquarters located in Manhattan.

Bubble, Bubble: all you need is cash

The United States, due to events such as the end of Bretton Woods (Chapter 2), high government spending during the Vietnam War, high inflation and a stock market crash in 1973–74, suffered a recession (1973–75). Not having fully recovered from the recession, the United States encountered a double-dip recession in 1981–82. Although Japan was fast becoming the second largest economy in the world and "overtaking the United States," the Japanese continued to rely on the ministries and politicians to tightly regulate their industries and to continue mercantile policies, accumulating a large current account surplus while holding the yen in Japan.

After the termination of the fixed exchange rate in 1971 the currency market was unregulated and controlled by supply and demand. During 1980–85 the dollar appreciated 50 percent against the currencies of America's chief trading partners; Japan, France, Germany and the United Kingdom. The US was also experiencing a large and growing current account deficit. On the other hand, Japan and Germany held large trade surpluses. Protectionist trade policies and the appreciation of the dollar threatened to destabilize the foreign exchange market. The US pressed for a multinational intervention to control the appreciation of the dollar against other currencies and make American goods competitive in global markets.

In September 1985, the United States together with Japan, France, West Germany and Great Britain agreed on the Plaza Accord, signed at the Plaza Hotel in Manhattan, which effectively intervened in currency markets, floated the dollar and appreciated other currencies, including the yen. The US promised to reduce its government deficit and lower interest rates. Japan agreed to loosen monetary policies and initiate financial sector reforms. During 1985–87, the yen appreciated 51 percent against the dollar. In FY1986 Japan's exports plummeted by a third, a blow to its export-driven economy. To counteract the yen's appreciation the BOJ implemented expansionary monetary policies and eased interest rates in early 1986 from 5 percent to 4.5 percent and gradually to 2.5 percent by February 1987.

During the post-war period the central bank had dictated to each bank quarterly the amount acceptable for net lending (i.e. quotas) through the extra-legal policy tool known as "window guidance" (*madoguchi shido*). The banks were ranked accordingly, from the large metropolitan banks to the regional banks. The Bank of Japan's easy money policy triggered what is referred to as Japan's "asset-inflated bubble economy." Corporate over-expansion in Japan during the bubble years of 1986–90 was funded by substantial loans from national and regional banks. Many of the loans were underwritten by the spiralling value in real estate. This trend was accelerated by fiscal policies which included lowering taxes. Unfortunately, the banks lacked the skills to assess collateral and approved additional loans to valued clients without increasing the collateral because the BOJ had provided a safety net as lender of last resort since the late 1950s.

On the other hand, the extra-legal "window guidance" could pressure banks to hire retired officials, a system commonly known as *amakudari* or "descent from Heaven" (discussed in

Chapter 16). The BOJ would "punish" banks by reducing loan quotas, while taking no action against the borrowers to recover collateral, leaving "zombie" borrowers effectively bankrupt but still in business. Many retired bureaucrats from MOF and retired executives from the BOJ were employed in top management positions in metropolitan banks and financial institutions. As of 1992, there were 78 former MOF officials and 64 BOJ officers on the boards of 115 listed banks through *amakudari*.

During the 1990s a series of scandals linking the failure of financial institutions with MOF officials in the regulatory agency that monitored the *keiretsu* main banks and other financial institutions were covered extensively by the Japanese media. Nevertheless, *amakudari* continued.

Dazzle in the Big Apple and London Town: the sky's the limit

I was amazed at the extent of Japanese corporate investment in the US. During the bubble years, Japanese companies invested heavily in the purchase and construction of commercial and residential properties in Japan. As a consequence, the value of real estate throughout Japan, particularly in Tokyo, appreciated over 50 percent. Furthermore, Japanese companies purchased high-profile properties in Manhattan and Los Angeles. In October 1989, Mitsubishi Estate, an affiliate of Mitsubishi Trading Group, initially invested an estimated $846 million in cash for a 51 percent interest in Rockefeller Center, joining other business owners with whom it had previously purchased 6.1 percent of shares in 1984. The Exxon Building was purchased by Mitsubishi Real Estate Development Company of Tokyo for $620 million in 1986. Identifying itself as Japan's second largest real estate company, it also invested $500 million in Citicorp Plaza in Los Angeles, which it developed with the Prudential Insurance Company.

However, the purchases by Japanese companies of high-profile real estate and American movie companies during the bubble years also triggered a spat of public protests. After Sony Corp purchased Columbia Pictures in September 1989, Matsushita, to even the score, purchased MCA Entertainment in 1990. The $6.6 billion MCA deal included the concessions in Yosemite National Park. After considerable public outcry that Japanese companies were buying up pieces of the American landscape, US Interior Secretary Manuel Lujan launched an inquiry into whether entertainment giant MCA Inc. had violated its government contract to operate Yosemite concessions when it sold Yosemite Park and Curry Co., the concession operator, to Matsushita without Lujan's approval. The unwelcome publicity and pressure from Lujan lead Matsushita within two years to sell off the concessions, which included a hotel and tents, for $49.5 million to an American non-profit foundation where Lujan served as a member of the board. The foundation donated the concessions to the National Park Service.

More Bubble Stories: regional banks

Japan's big banks opened retail branches in the US during the 1980s, among them Dai-ichi Kangyo, Sumitomo and Daiwa Bank, which opened branches in New York City and in Los Angeles in the 1980s.

In an attempt to emulate the metropolitan banks, Japan's regional banks such as Kyoto Bank and Iyo Bank in Ehime Prefecture, anticipating that the Japanese economy would continue to expand, opened one-man branch offices in New York and Los Angeles with the objective of providing offshore support for small businesses based in their prefectures. Some of the banks operated offices for no other reason than to be seen as having "internationalized." The new branches also served to illustrate Japan's overconfidence and the need to be recognized as an economic force internationally.

The banks, which were very exposed to the real estate market, were left with a substantial body of non-performing loans or "bubble loans." It was estimated at the time that the top 21 commercial banks were carrying $100 billion at the end of September 1992, escalating 50 percent from the end of March and constituting one-third of their total capital.

Until the 1990s, all Japanese banks were assured that the government would support them and that both the BOJ and MOF regulators were their protectors who shielded them from close scrutiny by outside auditors. The banks were reluctant to disclose the extent of their NPL because it would be tantamount to admitting mismanagement.

Nevertheless, large corporations, flush with success in international markets during the 1980s, were investing capital to expand their subsidiaries in ventures that were beyond the subsidiaries' core competencies, basing strategies on forecasts of continuing growth in both foreign and domestic markets. Their loyal banks, who also owned equity in the companies and in their subsidiaries, were willing to continue lending without assessing collateral or the risks involved regardless of the accumulation of significant debt. Furthermore, the regulation of the banks both private and state by the Ministry of Finance and the BOJ, the lender of last resort, remained almost non-existent. Nothing changed despite public outcry. The banks continued to lend to their borrowers and the borrowers continued to expand operations while disregarding debts which they kept refinancing.

Sushi anyone?

The wave of Japanese corporate investment and operations in the US and Great Britain also brought opportunities to Japanese retailers and to small and medium sized business that were setting up shop to provide services to the large corporations. Japan's most prestigious department stores opened branches in New York and in London to retail Japanese foods and accoutrements to Japanese corporate executives. Mitsukoshi operated a branch in London, serving elegant and expensive Japanese cuisine to a loyal Japanese clientele working in Japanese ministries, banks and large corporations.

Manhattan and Los Angeles were the most sought-after destinations for small businesses which included office suppliers and real estate agencies who offered rental properties and relocation services at inflated fees to Japanese executives who were bringing their families with them during their secondment. There were small Japanese businesses that catered for corporate events, delivering standard Japanese lunch boxes to offices daily. Japanese sushi restaurants along with tempura and noodle houses proliferated and were not only a popular lunchtime destinations for Japanese but, also, for non-Japanese.

A branch of one of Tokyo's finest traditional noodle restaurants opened in Soho, Manhattan in 1991. I had met the owner in Tokyo at a California wine tasting event shortly before I returned to the US. He had graduated from the University of California with a degree in city planning but had ambitions of opening a branch of his family's noodle restaurant in Manhattan. I was eager to support him and offered to help with the promotion by introducing him to James Sterngold, the *New York Times* correspondent in Tokyo, and his wife.

The restaurant was located in Ogikubo, where, by coincidence, the hospital where I was treated for the kidney infection in 1969 was located. I suggested that I invite Sterngold and his wife to dinner at the Ogikubo restaurant. The UC graduate was overjoyed and offered to serve the three of us cuisine representing the specialties of the house. The elegant meal was based on buckwheat served in various forms besides noodles. It was one of the most delicious meals I had yet to experience. The Sterngolds were impressed and a week later James published an effusive half page review of the restaurant which included that a branch was due to open in Manhattan.

When my friend visited New York to hunt for property in Soho I took him to fashionable restaurants, mainly Chinese, to suggest wines and spirits that would enhance his menu. I was confident that his new venture would be entirely successful because of the maze of Japanese corporate headquarters in Manhattan whose executives missed their fine Japanese cuisine.

The family invested substantial capital to finance the refurbishment of a small installation in Soho, (which accommodated only 20 diners) and cover costly overheads, including the secondment to New York the chefs from the Tokyo restaurant and sourcing most of the ingredients such as the buckwheat from Hokkaido. Sterngold's article in the *New York Times* promoted the new establishment to the rich and famous from the world of art, music and fashion, and to Japanese corporate executives. The restaurant became the hot spot for Japanese haute cuisine.

The owner called me his "lucky star" and whenever I wanted to savor gastronomy at its finest I could always reserve a table even though the restaurant was fully booked. The owner served me new dishes and my favorite Japanese sweet at the end. I would never again experience the star treatment.

TV Asahi

After the interview at the USTR I continued to commute from my cousin's house to Manhattan daily to look for work. I went to a large branch of the Japanese book store Kinokuniya near Rockefeller Center and purchased a copy of a Japanese newspaper published specifically for Japanese residents and distributed weekly by the Overseas Courier Service (OCS). The paper carried a want-ad section for Japanese staff. After three weeks of commuting daily to Manhattan and purchasing OCS papers, I found an ad for an office manager at TV Asahi's North American headquarters. TV Asahi was one of the largest commercial stations in Japan and which broadcast the popular 10pm news. The station also collaborated with CNN and ABC.

The ad did not detail the job description but I anticipated that the work would not be challenging. I visualized interaction with Japanese reporters and journalists and instant access to news. I called the office and spoke to a man who spoke fluent English. He explained that a new bureau chief from Japan would be coming to New York the following week and would schedule an interview with me.

TV Asahi was located on the 27th floor of the International Building in Rockefeller Center, in which Mitsubishi Estate had a 51 percent stake. For the interview I took Mr. Suzuki's letter of recommendation and the Martini cookbook but I refrained from including detailed information regarding my work at Mercian because it concerned corporate business which was not in the public domain.

The interview took place in the reception room with a table, chairs and a television. The deputy bureau chief who was in his forties and had spoken to me on the phone accompanied the new bureau chief. Since the new chief interviewed me in Japanese I suspected that his English was not fluent. He was in his fifties and appeared to have a good sense of humor. The cookbook sealed the job. I began to explain the objectives but it was unnecessary because the chief understood immediately, praising the work as a fine piece of marketing material. I was surprised because I had received no comments, either positive or negative, at Mercian. The chief also recognized that I was comfortable in a Japanese corporate environment.

He explained that I would be responsible to him, assisting him with general office work and other duties. I accepted because he would be my boss. The chief had been the director of the award-winning 10pm news and the three-year secondment to New York was probably a reward prior to his retirement. My job would commence in several weeks after the chief had relocated to Manhattan from Tokyo.

I managed to find a studio rental in the *New York Times* real estate ads. The apartment was on the 17th floor of a building located on East 63rd Street between Second and Third Avenues and a memorable 20-minute walk to Rockefeller Center, down Park Avenue towards the Pan American Building on 34th Street. There was a concierge who told me that among the tenants were representatives from various countries to the UN and business executives, and that most of the apartments were condominiums.

The studio was larger than the Tokyo flat and, in comparison, the facilities were luxurious, with a full oven, a dishwasher, a large bathroom with tub and shower. But since I was unsure whether I would remain in Manhattan I limited my purchases to the bare essentials; a bed, a small dresser, a folding table for eating, a 12-inch television, and a telephone, which I placed on the floor beside my bed. I could not have foreseen that I would remain in the same apartment for the next eight years.

TV Asahi New York transferred its staff salaries to the Daiwa Bank branch on Fifth Avenue where I opened a checking account after closing my Mercian account at the New York branch of Dai-ichi Kangyo (DKB). The yen/dollar exchange rate conveniently brought a bit of extra cash for the bare essentials. When the asset-inflated bubble burst in 1989, the DKB carried a load of non-performing loans because of its risky loans to corporate clients and to Yakuza crime syndicates. Despite the scandals involving the MOF's monitoring of banks in the early 1990s, the DKB continued to conceal the extent of its NPL problem and lending without calling in debts.

The TV Asahi office was spacious. The room where all staff worked was equipped with three large televisions placed on a wall adjacent to the desks where, besides the bureau chief and deputy bureau chief, an American researcher in his late twenties and a part-time American researcher in her thirties worked. Neither of them spoke Japanese. There were two young attractive Japanese female reporters seconded from TV Asahi HQ and three male Japanese local staff who served as cameramen and film editors. They were married and had their green cards. The female reporters and the Japanese local staff went on the road often to film interviews and on-site reports throughout the US. Both women were trainees and were getting their initial experiences in TV reporting. One was the daughter of a TV executive and had graduated from a university in Washington DC.

The TVs were always tuned to the three commercial news stations -NBC, CBS and ABC to keep staff on top of daily news, regardless of whether anyone was watching. An editing room was next to the work space where one of the Japanese local staff edited film before sending it as live feed to TV Asahi HQ. Adjacent to the editing room was a sound stage where occasionally live interviews of newsworthy Americans pertinent to Japanese interests were conducted by the bureau chief. There was a utility room with a FAX machine which received requests from HQ for reports on hot topics.

The deputy bureau chief was also regarded as local staff. He had served as the bureau chief of TV Asahi's Washington DC bureau and, consequently, had a solid knowledge of Washington politics. Married to an American, he lived in a wealthy suburb on Long Island. TV Asahi HQ regarded the New York bureau as its primary North American bureau and, similar to most Japanese corporations, seconded its staff to serve in the top positions. However, the bureau chief relied on his deputy for his expertise and his English and for implementing the requests from HQ. Many of the decisions regarding hard-news coverage and who would facilitate the reports were in the hands of the deputy.

The new bureau chief was very astute and often made the final decisions. He also was the sole interviewer for the live broadcasts. In other words, the deputy chief remained behind the scenes even though he did most of the legwork.

The bureau chief and I had an excellent rapport. Initially the work was minimal, keeping track of business expenditures accumulated by the local staff and accompanying him to various venues in Manhattan to acclimate him to the city. Since my duties were relatively inconsequential I was concerned that I would not be exposed directly to daily news about what was transpiring in Japan. The staff never discussed Japanese politics or reacted overtly to the turmoil in the equity market perhaps because they had settled in the US. I was reluctant to ask questions. However, the *Asahi*, the *Yomiuri* and the *Nikkei* newspapers were delivered daily to the office which kept me abreast of politics and business.

The Persian Gulf War

In mid-January there was a radical change in the office environment. The Persian Gulf War began on January 16, 1991 when the US declared Operation Desert Storm to counteract Iraq's invasion of Kuwait on August 2, 1990 and its refusal to withdraw its troops from Kuwaiti territory. The declaration was accompanied by an airstrike by the US coalition warplanes on Iraqi military targets, including Baghdad.

On the evening of 16 January we gathered in the reception room to watch the live blow-by-blow coverage by CNN reporters from Teheran. I chronicled the event on a yellow legal pad. It was extraordinary. I was covering an American war for Japanese news station and listening to the comments of Japanese news reporters. The CNN coverage continued, not only garnering CNN a reputation for forging the way for live TV coverage of military action but, also, for a new format for news reporting. It was broadcast history in the making. TV Asahi's relationship with CNN blossomed.

TV Asahi HQ sent FAX after FAX to request both the reporting of the conflict and the monitoring of President George H. W. Bush and his military staff at the White House The bureau chief and his deputy immediately began discussing the logistics of sending to the Middle East the three Japanese local staff to cover the war. I was tasked with investigating visa applications to Iran, sorting out insurance for their equipment and facilitating their entry through customs. I had no knowledge of the processes entailed but I managed to simplify matters through numerous phone conversations. Fortunately, a Japanese travel agent was hired to implement. However, Iran would not allow Japanese or other foreign reporters into the country and the three staff were sent to Israel for three days to report on the conflict and to conduct interviews with Israelis to gauge their reaction to the war.

Upon their return to TV Asahi they edited the footage and sent it to HQ. The report was superficial and hardly justified the expense but HQ seemed satisfied with the result. Most of office time was spent watching CNN and the instantaneous coverage. The political cartoons published in Japanese newspapers were among my favorites and I began collecting them. The cartoons were not US-friendly regarding the United States' involvement in the war. One cartoon depicted President Bush in cowboy gear on a bucking bronco and lassoing a terrified Saddam Hussein. Another depicted weeds growing abundantly in front of a dilapidated White House with the words "The New World Order" scribbled beneath.

My exposure to tight border security was at a check-point at border controls set up to check passports and passengers' identities during a one-day trip to Toronto to take an HQ reporter who was visiting New York to renew his visa at the US Embassy. We boarded a plane at La Guardia, making an hour stopover in Montreal in order to have our passports checked. When I handed my TV Asahi business card to the officer, he asked me if I spoke Japanese. He was so impressed that he let both of us pass through without looking at our passports.

Et Tu Brute?

The deputy chief was on the phone constantly to TV Asahi in Washington DC and he tended to turn up the volume of the televisions so that his conversations in Japanese were relatively private. He may have been concerned that I might disclose the information to the chief. His resentment of not being the Bureau Chief was palpable when he mentioned the chief's lack of knowledge of American politics or his absence from the office ("whereabouts unknown") or his tardiness in the morning, perhaps due to a bout of drinking with HQ colleagues the night before. The deputy bore the brunt of the work, yet the chief had the final word and received all of the credit.

At the end of the war the bureau chief interviewed the Commander-in-chief, United States Central Command, Norman Schwarzkopf ("Stormin Norman") who had led the coalition forces in the war. The interview was transmitted live to TV Asahi Japan and its affiliates. As the director of the 10pm news he understood the added value of showing the staff working busily in the newsroom instead of moving the camera directly to the interview. We were instructed to sit at our desks looking occupied while the cameraman zoomed in for a ten-second shot. Evidently I was spotted because following the interview TV Asahi Osaka telephoned the office to inquire about my identity.

Schwarzkopf visited a second time for another live interview regarding his recently published autobiography *It doesn't Take a Hero.* The two Americans purchased copies and asked the general to autograph them. But I asked him to autograph my legal pad paper on which I had recorded the 16 January attack.

Hot News

The Japanese press and television broadcasting stations reported news about the United States that was often provocative. The deputy chief also selected these topics. The stories regarded crimes perpetrated against Japanese tourists and racial discrimination, drug culture, prostitution or abortion issues which could be construed as "scare-mongering" and creating the impression that the US was racked with social problems and a dangerous place to live. The objective was to counter the articles in the US newspapers, which were about the negotiations between the US-

Japan trade representatives as the US was pressing Japan to deregulate its closed markets. The two female reporters and the three local staff were on the road much of the time, returning briefly to edit the film and to feed it to Tokyo.

Although the deputy chief was married to an American, had young children and had lived in the US for a number of years he was hardly an admirer of the US, which probably was one of the reasons he had been sent to cover the US by TV Asahi. He revealed his pro-Japan stance one day after reading an article by David Sanger of the *New York Times* who covered Japanese politics and trade issues. The deputy could not contain his anger and blurted out that the article was biased because Sanger did not have his fill of Japanese women.

A young male researcher from HQ spent three months in the office for training. He often complained that Jews controlled the banking industry and the American press, pointing to the *New York Times* and the *Washington Post*. In all fairness, he was merely repeating what he had been taught in Japan and what was also the view of many Americans.

Drinks at the Algonquin with Japanese Journalists

There was no socializing after work until the Bureau Chief suggested that we go to the Algonquin Hotel for a drink. The Algonquin was the venue for the renowned Algonquin Round Table, which was established after the First World War in 1919 by a group of illustrious journalists, authors, literary critiques, playwrights and humorists who met daily for lunch. Among the members of the mutual admiration society were Dorothy Parker, Robert Benchley and Pulitzer-prize winners Robert Sherwood and George Kaufman. They played games, gossiped, and spouted witticisms and ideas. Since some members wrote newspaper columns the group became famous in the national press. The round table continued until 1929. The hotel earned the status of New York City Historic Landmark in 1987.

The Aoki Corp., a large Japanese construction firm, purchased the property with the Texas-based Bass Group in 1987 for $29 million. During the same year Aoki also purchased with Bass the Westin Hotel and resort chain for $1.53 billion with the Industrial Bank of Japan (IBJ) financing the transaction. The North American hotels included the Plaza Hotel in Manhattan. The Algonquin hotel had yet to be renovated when we visited and the interior was only a tired memory of the Round Table days.

I had assumed that I would be going to the Algonquin with American writers but instead I was accompanying Japanese news reporters.

The End but Not For Long

One morning in late November I arrived as usual at 8am to collect the FAX from Tokyo. HQ wanted to counteract President Bush's scheduled visit to Honolulu on 7 December to commemorate the fiftieth anniversary of the bombing of Pearl Harbor with an investigative report regarding alleged atrocities committed by American GIs in Iraq against Iraqi soldiers such as burying them alive in the desert. In all probability, the deputy chief may have been concerned that I had seen this FAX because several days later the Bureau Chief advised me that my contract would not to be extended. Since he was dependent on the deputy director, he had little choice. Although we had a good working relationship and he had never indicated any dissatisfaction, I was relieved to be released because the deputy's attitude impacted on the office environment. Sitting in front of three blaring televisions was like being in a torture chamber.

Without skipping a beat, I went to Kinokuniya for a copy of OCS. In the want-ads section was a small advertisement by an organization called "Ship Machinery" located at the Japan External Trade Organization (JETRO) office in New York requesting an assistant. I considered that the job would be a stop-gap until I found a better position and telephoned the contact number from TV Asahi. A gentleman answered in Japanese. Replying in Japanese I asked if the position was open to an American. He was delighted that I was fluent in Japanese and asked me to visit his office the following day for an interview.

JETRO New York's office was located on the 44th floor in the McGraw Hill Building, which was also in Rockefeller Center and owned by Mitsubishi Estate. I was escorted to a small one-man office and told to wait. The book cases were lined with volumes in Japanese regarding ships and transportation. There were also directories with Tokyo University (TODAI) written on the covers. Realizing that the man was a graduate of Tokyo University and that he was probably a civil servant from the Ministry of Transportation, I thought that it would be a refreshing interlude to work with an elite bureaucrat for a few months.

Ironically, President Bush cancelled his trip to Honolulu to avoid friction with its key ally in the Pacific.

Pop goes the Bubble

In May 1989, the BOJ began to boost the official discount rate from 2.5 percent to 3.25 percent and then to 5.5 percent. Stock prices fell to 50 percent of their value during the peak in 1989 and by 1991 the value of real estate fell heavily. In order to cover losses, companies began selling equities, triggering a downward spiral of the equity market.

13

The Japan External Trade Organization New York (JETRO)

In the late 1980s, although the Japanese were purchasing foreign luxury brands, there had been little change regarding the deregulation of domestic markets and in the number of non-tariff barriers. Entry into the Japanese market was still through licensing agreements or third-party ventures. I had been informed that the Japan External Trade Organization (JETRO) was the government-funded organization that promoted international trade and inward investment in Japan, which, at the time, was 2 percent of the GDP. Out of curiosity, on my way to a function at the Hotel Okura I stopped at JETRO's HQ in Toranomon near the US Embassy. However, there was a queue of Japanese waiting for service and I decided to postpone the visit.

While on the market survey trip to Los Angeles and San Francisco I discovered that JETRO had an office in San Francisco. I called the office and, identifying myself as an employee of Mercian Inc., I asked if I could drop by. I was invited to attend the final day of an exhibit of the products of small businesses based in Gifu Prefecture and several adjacent prefectures at the San Francisco Convention Center. The products had been brought over by the business owners with the objective of receiving orders from US retailers. JETRO had organized the show but the businessmen funded their trip and the shipping of their goods. An American in his late twenties who had taught English in Japan was a JETRO local staff. A Japanese male in his forties who had been seconded to San Francisco from JETRO Tokyo was in charge of the office.

I first went to the JETRO office on Post Street to collect some literature about the organization. Glossy brochures titled "JETRO in America" were placed on tables in the reception area, identifying JETRO as a "non-profit, government-supported organization dedicated to promoting mutually beneficial trade and economic relationships between Japan and other nations." JETRO had a network of 33 offices in Japan as well as 79 overseas offices in 56 countries. Worldwide staff totaled 1,300. The brochure listed seven offices in the US: New York, Atlanta, Chicago, Houston, Denver, San Francisco, and Los Angeles:

> where each has a comprehensive information center on U.S. Japan business and economic relations and offers American business people a variety of consulting services and other assistance. By far the major focus of our activities in the U.S. is helping American companies develop exports to Japan. Promotion of U.S.-Japan industrial cooperation, technology exchange and direct investment in Japan are also areas of significant activity. Over the years, JETRO has become a valued resource of thousands of American companies, particularly small and medium sized businesses new to the Japanese market. In addition to directly assisting private companies, we cooperate closely with national, state and local economic development agencies, as well as with industrial and trade associations seeking to promote exports to Japan.

The brochure related the types of services available to potential exporters:

> With a wide-array of effective export promotion services, a cadre of seasoned Japanese business experts and an extensive information infrastructure, JETRO is ideally suited to help American companies take advantage of burgeoning opportunities in Japan. From providing comprehensive market information to personalized consultation, representing products at key Japanese trade fairs to offering free temporary office space in major Japanese cities, we have what it takes to help American businesses get on the road to success in Japan.

The Ministry of International Trade and Industry (MITI) had established JETRO as one of its public corporations in 1956 to promote Japanese small business exports in international markets and to provide them with information regarding foreign markets. In 1958, JETRO created the Institute of Developing Economies (IDE) as a separate public corporation but it later merged with JETRO in 1998. In 1971, the International Economic and Trade Information Center was established.

Gifu Prefecture is known for products made from steel, namely, swords. The wares offered by the business owners from Gifu were knives and other utensils produced from steel. The business owners from the other prefectures displayed small wooden goods such as chop sticks and lacquer-ware. The products were not of the highest quality and pertinent only to niche markets. Disheartened from the lack of interest, the businessmen confided that they had sat in a room in the Convention Center for two days waiting for dealers to view the show but very few had turned up and they had yet to receive any orders.

I wondered why JETRO had invited these particular businesses to the United States in the first place, why JETRO had not promoted the show more vigorously in order to justify the businessmen's outlay and why JETRO had not counselled the businessmen on the US market so that they could decide whether their goods were appropriate. The businessmen and the two JETRO staff invited me to join them for dinner at a Chinese restaurant. Concealing their disappointment, the businessmen tried to enjoy their final meal.

JETRO was providing services that appeared superficial at best and the organization seemed to be inconsequential as a trade promotion organization in terms of promoting Japanese small businesses abroad.

A Wee Break?

I exited TV Asahi on 7 December and began working at JETRO for the Ship Machinery representative office during the first week of January. I closed my checking account at Daiwa Bank because I had sensed that the bank's management style was haphazard. My instincts proved correct. In late 1995, it suffered a $1.1 billion loss due to a rogue bond trader at the New York branch. Toshide Iguchi, who admitted to 30,000 unauthorized trades during 12 years in New York, was sentenced to four years in prison. Daiwa was accused of covering up the loss and ordered to shut down its US branches. Sumitomo Bank subsequently took over Daiwa's operations.

Iguchi published *Confession* in 1997 in which he condemned the bank for covering up the loss and accused prosecutors of a sloppy investigation. In an interview with *Bloomberg News* on April 30, 2014, Iguchi claimed that only 5 percent of unauthorized financial trading cases were reported.

The same brochures titled "JETRO in America" were placed on tables in the reception area of the office. An American woman in her fifties manned the reception desk and greeted me in a Brooklynese accent.

The Ship Machinery office was down a corridor from the reception where there were also five one-man offices assigned to officials representing MITI's industrial associations. There was a representative office for shipbuilding which was adjacent to the ship machinery office and representative offices for the Japan Bicycle Promotion Institute, which promoted Japanese bicycle exports, Japan Automobile Manufacturers Association (JAMA) and an association for the Japanese optical industry.

On the opposite side of the corridor across from the offices were desks with Apple computers where the secretaries who were assigned to assist each director worked. It was a drab, basic set-up. With the exception of one young American woman, the majority of assistants were Japanese women who were local staff in their late twenties and thirties.

My new boss did not promote ship machinery but rather boats and luxury yachts produced by the ship building industry, an industry that is highly subsidized by government (as it is in the US). His business card identified him as a JETRO employee. Beneath the JETRO logo he was identified as the representative for Ship Machinery. This was also the case for the officers representing the industrial associations to whom I was introduced. Even though they were representing their respective agencies they were considered JETRO staff. When I accepted employment in Ship Machinery, I was unaware that I also would also be regarded as a JETRO employee and not as an employee of Ship Machinery.

The officers appeared to have a relaxed work schedule and tended to arrive at JETRO around 10am to have a tea or a coffee and chat with their next door neighbors. They often were out of the office from early afternoon onwards. I rarely saw American visitors even though the officers had been seconded to promote their associations' activities. Since they communicated in Japanese and read Japanese newspapers I could not ascertain if their English was fluent.

The Lay of the Land

A few weeks after I began working a short, stocky Japanese gentleman in his mid-fifties, dragging his legs along with iron crutches, stopped at my desk and introduced himself as a Director in the Research and Planning Department. He invited me to go out for a drink after work at one of his favorite bars near the office. I accepted because I could ask him about JETRO New York's set up. Fluent in English, he was intelligent and well-educated. His face glowed with a smile much of the time, belying a very serious nature, and an inner pride tinged with cynicism that often got the best of him.

That evening he told me that he was born in Taiwan where, he claimed, his father was the Chief of the Secret Police during the war. He was an infant when the war ended and his family managed to flee back to Japan, his grandmother carrying him on her back. He had contracted polio as an infant, leaving him severely disabled. His legs were paralyzed, forcing him to wear a heavy brace and to use crutches to support himself.

The disabled in Japan were hidden away from society by their families who felt a sense of shame. During his childhood he was cared for by his sisters but, fortunately, in 1968, an American couple brought him to New York, supporting him until he found work, which was at JETRO New York where he had been ever since. MITI may have recognized his father's position and offered him a job at JETRO but I would like to think that MITI was fortunate indeed to have a bilingual as the in-house translator whom they could trust to facilitate its interests in the US and to help officials seconded to the New York office. He also made himself indispensable sorting out problems encountered by the officers and their families who had also relocated to New York from Japan.

The director would never have been able to develop his talent and achieve his full potential in Japan. His job at JETRO New York translating and writing documents for Japanese officials, while providing good income, also enabled him to have a successful career as a writer, publishing books about Japanese history and English translations of Japanese Haiku. He had a drinking problem that probably was the consequence of years of taking JETRO representatives to bars as a means of introducing them to the finer aspects of New York life while simultaneously establishing a secure comfort zone for himself. These continuous forays should have adversely affected his health but, surprisingly, with the exception of bad hangovers and arriving late to the office, he seemed immune from illness. I continued to join him on occasion for drinks or for a meal with other JETRO representatives, which was always entertaining.

He was embraced by a large coterie of friends, among them female admirers, who were attractive, young Japanese women studying at Columbia University. He also communicated with women via FAX or email exchanging risqué Haiku. Although he had lived in the US since the 1960s and was married to an American, similar to the deputy director at TV Asahi, he identified himself as a Japanese.

The following day the director took me to his office in Research and Planning, explaining that several years earlier JETRO had moved office to the McGraw Hill Building from a smaller office located in the Time Life Building a few blocks down Avenue of the Americas. Mitsubishi Estate owned both buildings at the time. Due to the increase of representatives from Japan (the "bubble" effect) the office was expanded. JETRO acquired the adjacent office that had been rented by another company and refurbished the premises to meet the requirements of the new representative offices.

The director's office was in JETRO's Research and Planning Division at the other side of the 44th floor and at the far end of the large room. The offices for the other directors were more spacious than the one-man offices on the corridor. The Executive Director of Research and Planning was seconded from JETRO Tokyo for three years. The other two employees who were also seconded from JETRO Tokyo worked in the adjacent office as researchers of US politics, foreign and trade policies. The officer seconded from the Economic Planning Agency (EPA) shared an office with a MITI officer, an engineer who searched for patents in Washington DC that were applicable to Japanese industry. The EPA, a MITI agency, was Japan's main collector of Japan's macroeconomic statistics. Next door was the office for officials from the Ministry of Agriculture and Fisheries.

The desks across the aisle from the directors' offices were occupied by an officer sent for one year from the Japan Finance Corporation for Small and Medium Enterprises (JASME), a MITI public corporation which was a state financial institution that was the consolidation of the Small Business Credit Insurance Corporation, Japan Small Business Corporation and the Textile Industry Restructuring Agency. There was a representative from the Ehime Prefecture government and an American male employee who assisted the three directors. He was a recent university graduate with a degree in Japanese studies and, as did the other American assistant, had taught English in Japan for several years.

The executive offices of JETRO's Managing Director and President were next to Research and Planning. The Managing Director was an elite MITI official, in his mid-forties, who was posted for three years to oversee office operations. The President was also a MITI elite official who was posted for two years to represent JETRO America to US government officials, business leaders and to American academia.

A Curious Situation

It was perplexing that some of the officials were identified as JETRO staff even though they were not connected to JETRO or to MITI's industrial associations and corporations. After doing a bit of research, I discovered that JETRO opened its first overseas offices in London and New York in 1959, registering in the United States as a public corporation and not as an agency of a foreign government under the Foreign Agents Acts of 1938, which caused some consternation among American officials. In 1976, the US Department of Justice sued the Japan Trade Council (established in Washington DC in 1958) for civil fraud, charging that MITI contributed 90 percent of the Council's funds through its JETRO New York office. Soon afterwards, JETRO reregistered as a foreign agent. Since JETRO USA is registered with the US State Department, it is able to host various agencies and organizations that are not registered. Industrial organizations that sent representatives abroad to promote products of industries and local businesses used JETRO branches as bases for their activities. During the economic bubble a number of prefectures, anticipating economic expansion, also opened one-man offices at JETRO's overseas offices to establish a presence without considering fully the objectives of their "presence."

MITI used the JETRO offices as listening posts, keeping track of foreign trade regulations, foreign and domestic policies that would affect the import of Japanese goods, industrial and environmental standards, and government patent applications in anticipation that new inventions could be applicable for Japanese businesses. JETRO staff also collected macroeconomic data and surveyed foreign markets on behalf of Japanese businesses.

By 1975, JETRO was operating 24 trade centers and 54 offices in 55 countries, testimony that Japan had become a major player in world markets. Besides the JETRO offices, MITI officers were loaned to Japanese consulates, embassies and Japan Chamber of Commerce offices for periods of two to three years.

The Manufactured Imports & Promotion Organization (MIPRO) was established in 1978 by MITI. MIPRO operated an office in Washington, DC where MITI officials and Japanese trade delegations visited regularly.

Too Close for Comfort

My boss was liberal for a civil servant. Even though he spoke to me in Japanese I assumed that he could communicate in English as well. He was very kind, generously topping up my salary on occasion. A Japanese woman in her thirties who was married to an American sat at the desk next to mine. She also assisted the representative collecting statistics and recording news from American trade journals. We received Japanese trade magazines and newspapers which reported blow-by-blow the consequences of the bursting of the bubble and the continuing political turmoil.

I attended several exhibitions of luxury yachts with him. My responsibilities were minimal perhaps because my boss would return to Japan at the end of March, which was disappointing. His replacement was said to be an officer representing the Ship Building Industry.

JETRO management exacerbated a latent xenophobia among the officers by releasing news bulletins about crimes perpetrated against Japanese tourists throughout the United States. The officers were continuously cautioned about racism, drugs and the proliferation of gun-related crimes in the United States. Consequently, the officers were always anxious about living in a country where they could be the victims of violent crime and tended not to stray too far from the office except on holiday with their families or on business trips. My boss also released a bulletin around the office claiming that on his way to JETRO he was chased by youths who taunted him with racially abusive language.

I had intended to remain at JETRO until I found a better position but when the officer who would replace my boss visited the office for a week in March for orientation I realized that I would have to leave. Although only in his mid-thirties, he reminded me of a lieutenant in a Japanese prisoner-of-war camp. The Japanese assistant had the same impression. However, she preferred to remain in her position because she had previously assisted several ship building officials and was accustomed to the work.

I asked my boss if I could transfer to another office after he left. He told me that it would be difficult because a transfer of local staff to another representative office was rare. I assumed that he was intimating "transfer of information" and "loyalty." But since I had been with Ship Machinery for only a few months and since the current representative from Kyoto Prefectural Government was due to return to Kyoto and his American assistant would also exit JETRO thus leaving a space, he promised to urge the Managing Director to allow the transfer.

The American assistants tended to leave JETRO at the same time as their directors. During their term their bosses would take them for lunch, offer gifts and even send them to Japan for holidays as incentives. It may have been that they were not entirely trusted to maintain confidentiality about their bosses' activities and might release some information to their bosses' successors who were seconded by the same organization. On the other hand, the assistants may have become attached to their bosses and because they had college degrees decided to either go to graduate school or find another job. Nevertheless, the Japanese local staff continued working for successive representatives.

I was pleased with the prospect of working for a representative of a prefecture government, especially Kyoto, a cultural Mecca and one of the most sophisticated of the prefectures with traditional businesses, some established in the seventeenth century, and multinational corporations such as Nintendo, Kyocera Corporation, Omron and Wacoal Corporation, the woman's lingerie manufacturer.

I first spotted the future Kyoto Prefectural Government Representative when he visited JETRO in March for a week of orientation with the outgoing Kyoto representative. A short, plump gentleman marched quickly down the corridor while nervously staring straight ahead. He appeared daily during the week before returning to Kyoto. I was relieved when the ship machinery representatives confirmed that I could transfer to the Kyoto office which was located in the expanded section of JETRO. According to the Ship Building assistant, the outgoing Kyoto officer was high-strung and irritable.

JETRO held a small farewell party for my boss which other officers and their Japanese assistants attended. I became better acquainted with them and more relaxed about wandering around the 44th floor to see where the other representatives worked.

The Japanese assistants congregated in a small tea room where I joined them during the interlude between my boss's departure and the arrival of the new Kyoto representative. Some had married American GIs or English teachers in Japan. Their spouses married in order to alleviate the loneliness, difficulties with the language and to try to assimilate into Japanese society. Their wives took care of their physical and emotional needs.

The Japanese women married Americans to escape the strictures of their regulated society for a freer lifestyle. But when their husbands returned to the United States, they were no longer dependent on their wives. Some of the marriages deteriorated, ending in separation or divorce. Although the women had received Green Cards they had difficulty functioning independently in American society.

Their education was no higher than high school or junior college. Although their English was satisfactory for daily life it was not sufficient for working in American companies. The women preferred working in a Japanese organization with other Japanese women for emotional support. Their skills were applicable for the undemanding work at JETRO but they were caught in an ambiguous existence because by marrying foreigners they were no longer accepted fully in Japanese society and were reluctant to return home. They were permanent ex-pats.

The secretary for the two executive officers, was a stylish Japanese woman in her mid-fifties, and sat at a desk in front of their offices. She considered herself in a different strata and rarely associated with the other assistants. Fluent in English, she had resided in the US for many years and, before moving to JETRO, had worked for a branch of a Japanese travel agency. She was very protective of her two bosses.

Taking a Wander

As a rule, the assistants remained at their desks while their bosses were present at JETRO but more often than not they were on their own and would visit each other to chat. Since the director of Ship Machinery was preparing to relocate his family to Japan I took advantage of his absence to explore the rest of the 44th floor. Their Japanese assistants informed me about their bosses' activities which provided a fundamental understanding of JETRO's functions.

JETRO New York was the largest JETRO USA office and reflected the structure and management of the other branch offices located overseas. However, this office was highly unusual because it housed a microcosm of around 40 officials sent to JETRO by government agencies, prefectural governments and industrial associations, which in Japan were separate entities and which rarely interacted.

Ensconced in the New York office during the 1990s before the merger of some of the ministries in 2001 were officials from MITI's corporations such as officers from EID/MITI, EXIM's Import and Investment Insurance Division.

The prefectural governments represented at JETRO New York included Kyoto, Osaka and Ehime. The public corporations of other ministries such as the Japan Highway Corporation (Ministry of Construction) and prefectural governments which were not attached to MITI were required to pay JETRO substantial fees for office space and secretarial support, which helped JETRO pay the rent as well as justify its budget. Regardless, these officers were expected to cooperate with MITI in research projects and promotional events that were unrelated to their responsibilities for their respective agencies.

The offices were managed by JETRO staff posted from Japan for three years while MITI managed operational budgets. JETRO staff cared for the needs of all representatives, including facilitating visas for the agents, applying for social security, health insurance, and procuring local staff to assist the officials with research and administration.

A partial wall separated these offices from the large Reference Library where business owners visited to collect information regarding market information and doing business in Japan. The central desk was manned full-time by a female in her mid-fifties who had emigrated from the Philippines and who had been working at JETRO for about seven years. She was friends with the receptionist. The two desks on either side of her were occupied by a Japanese male who was about to retire and a young Australian female.

A separate room was next to the library for the JETRO Trade Promotion Division where JETRO staff seconded from Tokyo were posted for three years to promote JETRO as the government-funded organization that assisted American small businesses to enter the Japanese market and coach them on doing business in Japan. The Executive Director was a JETRO officer who was a graduate of Tokyo University in Agriculture. He had established the Business Support Centers in Tokyo and Yokohama. Similar to the Executive Director of Research and Planning he was considered high on the totem pole at JETRO New York.

All of the officers, including MITI officials, were regarded as JETRO staff. As an example, an officer posted from the Ehime government identified himself first as a JETRO staff. Most of the officers' previous careers were unrelated to their work at JETRO New York and they had received little preparation regarding their future work before leaving Japan.

The requests from their home offices to investigate trade regulations, laws, current government policies, environmental issues and industrial standards were forwarded to consulting companies, some of which had been on contracts that had continued for years from director to director without any regard for the quality of the work. Other duties included guiding delegations of Japanese businessmen on tours of US regions, arranging meetings with American businessmen and government officials and entertaining Japanese government officials during their visits to the US.

The Best of Both Worlds

Transferring to the Kyoto Prefectural Government Office not only afforded me more time to search for a job with a higher income but, also, I recognized that I would never again have the opportunity to observe closely Japanese civil servants from numerous ministries and local governments. I was addicted to reading daily news reports and media commentaries and the Japanese media was having a field day covering scandal after political scandal. The economy was in recession

In 1989 LDP politician Sasuke Uno succeeded Noboru Takeshita as Prime Minister but resigned within three months after taking office due to a sex scandal involving his relationship with a geisha. Uno's successor was Toshiki Kaifu, another LDP politician (1989–91). Ironically, in November 1991, two months before I entered JETRO, Kiichi Miyazawa, who had been implicated in the Recruit scandal, became Prime Minister.

However, the struggle for power among factions in the LDP and the need for action to ignite Japan's flagging economy destabilized the political system. Some government members, wanting to distance themselves from scandal and attempt to initiate political reform, defected to form new parties. Morihiro Hosokawa, the former governor of Kumamoto Prefecture, founded the reformist New Japan Party with Hiroshi Kumagai, a former MITI official who had left MITI in mid-career to enter politics on the LDP ticket. Former Prime Minister Yoshihiko Noda (2011–13) was also a member. The party joined forces with the Japan Renewal Party, which was founded by another LDP political kingpin Ichiro Ozawa, and Tsutomu Hata.

During my brief period at JETRO five Japanese newspapers and magazines were delivered daily to the directors and I kept up-to-date on all issues in Japan. My PC's software programs were identical to Mercian's so I was in my comfort zone and in the best of both worlds; Japan and Manhattan.

14
Inside–*Inside/Outside* Japan

The Kyoto Prefectural Representative office was in the newly renovated section of JETRO New York. The assistant's cubicle which I occupied was outside of the director's office overlooking 49th Street. The Japan Highway Corporation Representative office (JH) was next door with the same arrangement. The American assistant, who had worked for the JH for several years, was in her early thirties and a graduate of an Ivy League university. She had a child with her former husband, who was Chinese.

The adjacent office was occupied by a MITI non-career officer, an engineer, who monitored American EPA regulations, small machinery production and the aeronautical and automobile industries. A Japanese woman who was married to an American assisted him.

A MITI career officer who was also an engineer occupied the next office down. With the support of consulting companies and an American assistant he monitored US politics. His male assistant was in his late twenties and had attended a university in Kyoto where he met his Chinese wife. Although he did not read, he spoke Japanese and we enjoyed chatting in Japanese.

At the opposite end were the offices of the two MITI Directors in Industrial Research. Both officers who were in their late thirties had law degrees from Tokyo University and were on their way up the MITI pyramid. Together with the Managing Director they were regarded as the top officials at JETRO. Their research was supported by an American male in his mid-thirties who had a degree in International Relations. He had been working for Industrial Research for about five years but he did not speak Japanese.

The secretary for the Industrial Research Division had worked at JETRO since the 1980s and considered her position to be a rank above the executive secretary. The two women did not engage with each other. She was very discrete about her directors' activities and doted on them. In her late fifties, despite a brusque façade she was kind. I never asked her about herself but she confided that she had married a GI with whom she had a child. She was currently living with a much younger Japanese man whose sister owned a Japanese restaurant in Manhattan.

EID/MITI occupied two offices and a large research area in the expanded section. A MITI career officer in charge occupied one office and his assistant, a non-career female officer, occupied the second office.

EID/MITI's budget of $175 billion ($1=¥120) for FY1992. The fund covered Japanese companies' losses in foreign countries resulting from bankruptcy, war, political instability, default, war, etc. The fund expanded to provide funds to foreign firms as well, including businesses that was unrelated to Japanese exports.

MITI's U-Turn

By the early 1980s, Japan, whose economy was export-driven, was showing a marked trade surplus with its leading trading partners, particularly the US, which was in recession. There was significant pressure from the US government to deregulate domestic markets and raise import quotas for such goods as agriculture products, electronics, motor vehicles, and car parts. Realistically, JETRO's role as a promoter of Japanese exports was no longer as relevant to

Japanese businesses as it had been in the 1960s and 1970s. Also, JETRO's role as a surveyor of foreign markets and a collector of economic and political data had, in part, become extraneous because research was being conducted by large Japanese multinationals, research institutes and MITI officials posted in embassies and Japan Chamber of Commerce offices.

However, MITI intended to continue operating a corporation that had effectively resulted in creating more territory for its officials. As a gesture of compliance with US demands, MITI began the process of re-orchestrating JETRO's function so that the organization would serve as a promoter of foreign imports and foreign investment. In 1983, JETRO set up a task force to look at import promotion.

In 1981 MITI established the Japan Economic Foundation (JEF) as a JETRO subsidiary. The JEF published the bi-monthly journal *The Journal of Trade and Industry* which is now known as *Spotlight*. The JEF website states its mission:

> to deepen mutual understanding between Japan and other countries through activities aimed at promoting economic and technological exchange. With this goal in mind, JEF engages in a broad range of activities; it provides information about Japan and arranges opportunities to exchange ideas among leaders from many countries in such fields as industry, government administration, academia and politics in order to break down the barriers to mutual understanding.

The members on the JEF board of trustees also served as the chairmen and presidents of MITI's industrial associations; the Japan Automobile Manufacturers Association, Japan Electronic and Information Technologies Industrial Association, the Japan Iron and Steel Federation, and the Japan Society of Industrial Machinery Manufacturers.

In 1984, import promotion activities such as trade fairs were held in Nagoya, Yokohama and Kitakyushu. In the same year, a second task force was set up to promote international economic cooperation for industry. In 1989, MITI completed the conversion of JETRO export promoter to JETRO import promoter with the establishment of yet another organization, the Institute of Trade and Investment. The number of JETRO's foreign offices increased to 80 in 57 countries while the domestic offices increased to 38.

Kyoto Prefecture (but not for long)

The new representative for Kyoto Prefecture was in his late thirties. Since we spoke in Japanese I could not assess his English fluency. One of our first conversations regarded his weight. He confided that he was from Osaka but his wife was from Kyoto, which has the questionable reputation for being socially impenetrable to anyone born outside of Kyoto. This is particularly true of Kyoto City, the capital. When he entered the Kyoto Prefectural Government as a civil servant he gained 20 pounds from the stress of not fully being accepted on the workplace.

The representative had lived in an area in Osaka where 50 percent of the population was Korean. His schoolmates in primary school were second and third generation Koreans who had taken Japanese surnames to avoid discrimination. After primary school some of his Korean friends were sent to Korean schools which were funded by South and North Korean organizations. Many of these schools have since been shut down due to years of political hostility between the North Korean and Japanese governments.

His father had a distribution business with Pepsi Cola and took his son to baseball games when he made deliveries. The representative's uncle had lived in New York for 30 years and a cousin lived in Los Angeles which was fortunate because the representative experienced problems adapting to his new post.

He was very nervous being alone in a big office on the 44th floor of a skyscraper. The walls creaked as the building swayed in the wind and riding the elevators which plummeted at 50 miles per hour before slowing down a few floors above the lobby was unpleasant but unavoidable for all staff. The huge windows behind his desk gave him an unobstructed view of Forty-Ninth Street but whenever rain pelted the windows he hurriedly exited the building and stayed outside until the rain had stopped.

When I interviewed him in 1994 he confessed that he had suffered from depression and had sought counselling which helped him to adapt to the stress of being in an entirely new environment for which he had been ill-prepared either by JETRO or by local government or by his predecessor who did not reveal his activities during his three-year term at JETRO New York:

> When I first came here I didn't know about many things regarding American lifestyle and how to get along here. First of all, there was a different way of thinking. Even though I understood things intellectually, I really didn't understand and experienced many difficulties. It's been two years now and there were times when I misunderstood or was misunderstood and suffered because of these mistakes. It's a relief that I can acknowledge this now. In America, in this kind of office, you must have an objective and know precisely what you are doing. In Japan, it is not clearly defined and, therefore, when I came here I didn't know what I was supposed to do.

> In Japan I didn't have to think and decide for myself. There were even situations when I didn't know what I wanted to do. Here the pressure doubled because I was alone. There is a lot of pressure because I must do something specific. In Japan, an employee doesn't act on their own volition but here one must come to a decision and report to home office that this action is what you would like to do. Then one must wait to receive confirmation. In Japan, there are proposals which are passed up to your superiors for consideration. There can be problems because decisions are not made immediately. In Kyoto, I worked together with many people so even if I didn't understand I could ask others. In a sense, it is easier. However, suddenly I am sent here and am alone. I have become used to it and I think that it has been a good experience.

The representative was certainly not alone. A number of the officials had never lived abroad and their comprehension of English was superficial. The complex Japanese language is rarely spoken outside of Japan and some of the officers were at a distinct disadvantage and on the defensive because they were unable to easily communicate with Americans. Furthermore, as did the Kyoto officer, they had worked as members of divisions and not independently, which for some officers was very stressful. The officers were dependent on JETRO management for their relocation to New York.

For several months the representative was out of the office much of the time or sitting at his desk contemplating how he should proceed. He asked me to peruse several Oklahoma newspapers for articles on Japan because Oklahoma and Kyoto were Sister-States. A Senior Trade Advisor was posted in the Oklahoma State Economic Development office. It was questionable why such a relationship had been established because the similarities between Oklahoma and Kyoto were few. The representative said that a former Japanese professor who had taught at an Oklahoma university had decided to initiate the ties. I also looked for articles in the *New York Times* and *Washington Post* but they were non-existent.

A Riddle

The work was minimal and I spent most days reading Japanese newspapers and magazines. I visited the Japanese assistants' cubicles to chat and to find out what their bosses enjoyed doing on a daily basis. Their replies were similar; in general, the representatives' schedules were relaxed and they enjoyed shopping, going to Broadway shows and being with their families if they had joined them in the US. Often they left the office by 5pm or 6pm.

I wanted to know more about MITI which western commentators and political economists were habitually lauding as the ministry responsible for policies that propelled Japan's rapid economic development. Because the US economy was flagging the international business community considered that the Japanese Inc. model of capitalism was superior. However, my experiences gave me a contrary view.

At Kinokuniya I searched for books on the bureaucracy with the hope that there would be a current assessment of MITI. The only book available was *An In-depth Research of the Bureaucracy* (*Kanryou Dai Kenkyuu*) by Tetsuo Ebato, published in 1990. Ebato graduated with a degree in economics from Tokyo University before entering Mitsui Bank. He left the company to become a freelance writer. His book regarded the Defence Agency, the Supreme Court, the former Ministry of Health and Welfare, the Ministry of Agriculture and Fisheries and MITI.

His chapter concerning MITI revealed the views of many Japanese civil servants at the time. For example, MITI officials felt that they had to continuously generate new policies and had the reputation of being skilful debaters, arguing to promote their policies. On the other hand, although MITI officials were said to be skilful analysts, their policies were often hastily planned and incomplete. National ministry officials cynically alluded to MITI as "aggressive MITI" because MITI no longer had a cogent industrial policy since the end of the Cold War in 1989 and in order to justify its budget and protect its existing administrative territory, MITI officials pursued the territory of other ministries.

The Changing of the Guard

Management announced that the president would soon be returning to Japan and that a new official would be replacing him in June. Since I had never met the outgoing president I assumed that I would not meet the new one, an elite MITI official who would serve as the figurehead of JETRO New York for a period of two years. However, without prior warning, I was introduced to him one afternoon in June by the Executive Director of Research and Planning and the director who had taken me for drinks. I was wearing a red cotton suit and a white pique blouse, appropriate attire for meeting a MITI official.

The Executive Director of Research and Planning had conceived of a monthly paper that would serve as a platform for articles regarding US–Japan relations, economics, trade and social issues. It would promote Japan's industrial and trade policies and JETRO as a trade promotion organization and would be sent unsolicited to both Japanese and American government officials, well-recognized academics and business leaders.

In order to formally receive MITI's permission, he asked the president to engage and to contribute a short editorial on the first page. He also needed other JETRO staff to contribute articles each month thus introducing me to the president as the first prospective writer.

I sat directly opposite the new president who was enthusiastic about the project. He was a graduate of Kyoto University Law Faculty before entering MITI as a career officer. A Director of Policy Planning in the Minister's Secretariat, he also served as Secretary in the Japanese embassy in Indonesia. MITI sent him to the Royal Institute of International Affairs in London for a year of study and also to the School of Management at the University of Syracuse for eight months. His interests included classical music, movies, and Japanese and English literature.

The president was without his family because his wife had to remain in Tokyo to care for their two sons and daughter who were in school and could not interrupt their studies. The two directors probably assumed that due to my musical background and bilingual skills, the president would find me interesting and easy to communicate with. We discussed the paper's format, design and the name.

A subsequent meeting was arranged in a room near the president's office. I showed the president a possible title *Japan Online* which had been printed in green on cream colored paper. He liked it but preferred his name *Inside/Outside Japan* which was more appropriate and very creative. Another meeting was scheduled for the following week.

At the meeting besides the president, and the two directors, one of whom would be the editor, were myself, the American researcher from Research and Planning and the American researcher from Industrial Research. I was the only writer not connected to MITI and the only female. I offered to write short columns on marketing and was allowed a two-paragraph blog entitled "To Market to Market" which would appear on the second page. The president wanted to engage other members of staff to contribute articles as well. The president requested that we each choose a topic and to write a piece with the word-count no longer than 2,500 words. He committed to writing a short commentary for the title page of each issue.

At a meeting the following week we offered our topics and promised to submit our articles within two weeks to ensure that the first issue would be released by end of July. Relying on my exposure to the market in Japan, I chose beer for the topic and the competition between the main Japanese producers. Titled "One Hundred Bottles of Beer on the Wall" the article received a thumbs-up from the president. Instead of the heading "Editorial" the president chose "Perspective," thus giving readers the impression that his opinions were personal and not from government.

After a scurry of activity the newsletter went out as scheduled. I used the *Nikkei Shimbun* as the source for the "To Market to Market" blog titled "The Name of the PET Food Game is Fiber!" The piece concerned Japan's growing pet food products which, in league with products for health conscious consumers tackled insufficient fiber in pets' diets. Such brand names as "Renewal" and "Healthy Dog" revived my memories of underground commuting in Tokyo and "Fresh Man."

The president's Perspective was an effort to convince readers that the government was no longer driven to catching up with the West but was intent on alleviating the discrepancy between the country's wealth and that of the populace:

> A national plan calling for vastly upgrading sewage systems and parks, bringing down the price of a home to the level five times the average annual income, and reducing, by 1996, the yearly working hours from 2,100 to 1,800. It's about time.

The editor contributed "Japanese Firms Respond to L.A. Riots" which regarded the "worst riots in U.S. history in decades" and the donation of several million dollars from Japanese affiliates based in Los Angeles for rebuilding South Los Angeles after a six-day rampage of arson, looting, killing triggered by the release of four white police officers who were indicted for brutally beating an African American. While touting the response of Japanese firms, the editor was also playing to the Japanese readers' paranoia.

Bill Whittaker was the chief correspondent in Japan for CBS Television from 1989 to 1993. When I interviewed him in 1994 for an article in *Inside/Outside Japan* he said that he was often disturbed by how Americans were portrayed on Japanese television, the reports focusing on racism, crime and the deterioration of American society. He himself was affected by what he saw on the tube in Japan and was initially afraid of returning to the US after his term was over. Although he emphasized that gun crimes were "outrageous," he also realized that he would not be a victim when he drove downtown to his office.

The American researcher from Research and Planning contributed an article about the Japan Overseas Cooperation Volunteers and Japanese youth volunteer activities in developing countries. The researcher from Industrial Research wrote about the demands of Okinawans for a big reduction of American troops from the Marine base, which to this day is still a bone of contention between the US and Japan.

The president's English remained a mystery to me until the meeting with all of the contributors where he said that he was an avid reader of English literature. When I asked him the name of his favorite Japanese author he replied Yukio Mishima which indicated his conservatism. I admired Mishima but not for his narcissistic and nationalistic views but for his brilliant use of Chinese characters and his vocabulary.

The first issue was released by Research and Planning on time at the end of July. I joined the office to help stuff the manila envelopes and to stick on the address labels for the mailing. The executive secretary and the Ehime Prefectural representative also assisted.

Getting to Know You

The first issue was considered a success and I decided to write about topics which I knew well through past work. For the August issue I contributed "The Art of Marketing-Mind-Over-Matter" which was based on the Levi Strauss Inc. and the canned coffee beverage adverts as some of the best examples of creating an image of the product being advertised.

The To Market to Market blog announced a new product developed to record a baby's first cries. "Out of the Mouths of Babes' described the "For My Baby, Memorial CD" as "perfect for parents who want to relive the joyous events of the birth of their child."

The president promised in his September Perspective that Japan's economy would recover within seven years which was the prognosis of many government officials at the time. It was also the consensus view in the international business community:

> Real estate prices continue to drop, vacancy rates of new office buildings remain high, banks are competing among themselves trying to dispose of bad loans, manufacturers are struggling to reduce excess capacity and personnel…This is not a description of the United States a few years ago, but Japan today

> Seven-Five-Three is a traditional Japanese festival for congratulating children on turning seven, five, or three years of age. But the term is now used to forecast

Japan's economic recovery: real estate will take seven years, banks five, the securities market three before regaining their footholds…The bursting of the economic "bubble" seriously injured the United States: now it is injuring Japan no less.

However, he acknowledged that his government had been too optimistic in its original forecast of economic recovery and was now going to release a stimulus package to ignite the economy:

The recovery plan, announced on August 28 provides for $86 billion to achieve four main goals: (1) expand spending on public housing; (2) increase loans to small businesses); (3) promote investment in plant and equipment; (4) to give financial institutions incentives for depreciating bad debts. The package includes $250 million earmarked for promoting imports.

My article "Oil & Art, West and East" concerned the lives of two oil magnates who were passionate collectors of art which they exhibited in their museums. J. Paul Getty (1892–1976) built a museum in Malibu, Los Angeles in 1974 for his eclectic collection of Greek and Roman antiquities, European paintings, sculptures and photographs.

Across the Pacific Sazo Idemitsu (1888–1981) the founder of Idemitsu Oil, one of Japan's biggest oil corporations, began collecting Gibon Sengai in the 1920s and housed his burgeoning collection in his museum in Tokyo built in 1966 where I had visited numerous times to see the work by one of my favorite artists.

While in San Francisco I attended my first and only auction of Japanese and Korean art objects. It was summer and there were few people perusing the exhibit, which was fortunate because hanging on the wall was what I recognized to be a painting by the 18th-century Zen Buddhist priest Sengai (1750–1837). His pictures were always combined with poems in his unmistakable script. During his lifetime he was well-known for his humorous drawings of the Zen Buddhist monastic world. He was a prolific artist and his irreverent paintings of Zen monks were held in high regard. The auction was scheduled the following week and I put in a silent bid of $500, never thinking that I would win considering that the average price for a Sengai was $10,000. A week later I received word from the auction house that I was the owner of a Sengai!

When I visited the Idemitsu North American corporate headquarters to interview the manager about Sazo Idemitsu he generously gave me a copy of the Idemitsu Oil anniversary edition of its corporate history, a book given to Japanese companies which had close relations with Idemitsu. It is a remarkable account of Idemitsu Oil's engagement in Manchuria before the Second World War. The photographs represent the infrastructure which Japanese industries installed during the Japanese occupation, a reminder of Kishi's involvement.

The To Market to Market blogs "The Two Step" announced Matsushita Electrics' dual function radio-odometer and "I Can See Clearly Now" was about Eye Health, a new product which enabled purchasers to tell when their light bulbs should be replaced.

The American researcher from Industrial Research wrote about Japan's quasi-military entrance into international peacekeeping operations (PKO) with the passage of a PKO bill in June allowing Japan to send troops overseas to engage in UN operations. The vote in the Lower House was an overwhelming 329–17 and in the Upper House at 137–102:

A basic fear that remains is that this law might open the door to militarism in Japan. It is important to remember, however, that the new law allows the Japanese government to dispatch only lightly armed contingents abroad on narrowly defined missions. Japan's participation will be limited to non-military activities such as election monitoring…Clearly Japanese leadership is committed to supplying personnel for the protection of international order.

The PKO bill was the first step of Japan's expansion of the Self-Defence Forces' (SDF) activities in the Pacific.

At the end of the last page JETRO provided details of the stimulus package. $69 billion was slated for public works and $17 billion for small business and capital investment: "The government expects the package to push up economic growth by 2.4 percent in the coming year."

"Creative MITI"

Ebato reported that the officials in the other ministries cynically referred to MITI as the "creative" ministry. *Inside/Outside Japan* created a façade contrived to support MITI's numerous objectives; to pursue other ministries' turf such as MOF and the Ministry of Foreign Affairs (MOFA), to promote and defend MITI's industrial policy and most importantly, to present JETRO as the Japanese government's trade promotion organization. The paper was a vehicle which MITI used to present itself in different ways, depending on what the audience wanted to hear while furthering its own interests.

The paper was also an effort to encourage the perception among foreign readers that JETRO was a multifaceted government-funded organization which promoted trade and investment in Japan and was managed by officials who understood Americans, their political economy and America's relationship with Japan. Simultaneously, the paper's tone promoted to readers the importance of "mutual understanding" and acceptance of the Japanese way of governing and doing business. Although the paper was, in effect, an attempt to revise JETRO's image and, therefore, maintain and increase its budget, it equally gave MITI officials the opportunity to answer US officials and the US media's contention that Japan's markets were closed to foreign business and investment.

Although some of the articles were biased in defending Japan's position at the US–Japan trade negotiations and flexing Japan's muscle in the international political arena, the articles were cleverly conceived and relatively informative. The paper provided an excellent representation of Japan's economic conditions and government policies regarding US–Japan trade relations. Incredibly, the articles forecast Japan's future economic dilemmas.

The president was very creative in his use of the paper in the promotion of his government's trade and foreign policies. He succeeded in creating a positive image of both MITI and JETRO, using methods that differed from past presidents, who primarily relied on networking personally with national and state government officials, businessmen and academics. The president preferred to supplement his networking activities with *Inside/Outside Japan* and to use the paper to disseminate information about Japanese business and promotion of government policy.

Calm before the Storm

Although the president called me "the Jane Austen of JETRO" my articles merely served to support what was essentially a propaganda sheet. The titles of my articles were famous American songs with the lyrics from the songs woven into the articles. The situation concerning my involvement in *Inside/Outside Japan* was heating up. The paper took me often to Research and Planning, the hub of JETRO New York.

Since I was working for Kyoto Prefecture, I took the lingerie manufacturer Wacoal Corporation, a company based in Kyoto, as the subject for the October 1992 article. The title "Midnight Lace and a Pretty Face Make the World Go Round" was taken from one of my husband's favorite songs "Chantilly Lace." Since the editor was a bit of a voyeur I hoped that the piece would pass muster.

This tiny article proved to be significant because the reaction to it and ensuing issues regarding my participation in *Inside/Outside Japan* spurred my decision to stay at JETRO New York:

> Can a small lingerie company from Kyoto compete in an international lingerie market? Can a manufacturer of foundation garments, exclusively designed for the Japanese female understand the needs and desires (for lingerie, of course) of the American woman?

> It took forty-seven years for Koichi Tsukamoto, founder and chairman of Wacoal Corp., to answer these questions in the affirmative. But before considering greener pastures overseas, it was essential for him to establish a strong corporate image in Japan. And in order to maintain a substantial share of the fickle she loves me-she loves me not market, he knew that entertaining the slightest hope that the consumer was telling him, "Hey Baby, you know what I like," was strictly taboo.

> Until as late as the 1960s, the bra was sometimes worn to cover and suppress the bust. But, today, the young Japanese woman has become as body-conscious as her American counterpart and enjoys emphasizing her femininity. Her revised conception of herself has radically changed the lingerie market in Japan. Although the padded bra is still the mainstay of foundation wear, the non-padded bra is gaining popularity. Nearly a million of the current hot seller, "Good Up Bra," have gone out the window. It is a ¾ cup little number, fastens in front and sharply defines the bust-line.

> The bra-burning period of the Women's Lib Movement in the late 1960s almost forced the company to close down operations. Refusing defeat, Tsukamoto shaved his head as a symbolic gesture to his disheartened employees that the brassiere would indeed prevail. "Bras will come back in fashion. After all, breasts are the most distinguishing part of a woman's body. As long as women have breasts we can sell brassieres." Wacoal came up with a seamless bra which could be worn undetected and sales were resuscitated.

> Japanese men are becoming imbued with the American spirit. They have begun to discover what American men have known for quite some time. Buying lingerie for a loved one (or a liked-one for that matter) is not such a bad idea. White Day (March 14) is the occasion when men reciprocate with a gift to women who gave them Valentine gifts. The usual is white chocolate, but forays to the lingerie department are becoming commonplace.

> Wacoal America became a reality six years ago. Its slogan, "European elegance, American fit, Japanese technology," illustrates the company's production methods for a non-Japanese market. The average bra size of the Japanese woman is 32A. The average size for an American is 34C. Bigger is not necessarily better,

but this obvious discrepancy requires that design be entrusted to the Americans…
Bra & panty sets, the bread and butter items for Wacoal America, are nearly twice
as expensive as those from other domestic manufacturers

Customers do not seem to object to this higher price for higher quality, basic-
is-best attitude. Inside/Outside Japan recently visited four major Manhattan
department stores to hear a few "just between us girls" comments from customers
and sales personnel.

"It's like a Honda. It sells itself."

"It's cult-like. Once people wear it, they never wear anything else"

"The product fits, which is strange, because they (the Japanese) are so small
over there."

The JH officer contributed an article about highways in Japan. "Highway to Heaven"
announcing the release by government of a $3.5 trillion package for infrastructure, including
highway construction to be used over a period of ten years. I learned ten years later how this $3.5
trillion package was distributed.

Occasionally the representative for JASME visited my cubicle to request help searching for
statistics on the US economy and business activities. The female non-career officer in EID/MITI
also began dropping by to ask me to help her translate the Japanese version of the new Trade
Insurance regulations. The requests from the officers were welcomed because they connected me
to high calibre civil servants and engaged me in their work. Inside/Outside Japan also helped
to establish a relationship with officers in Research and Planning and provided the opportunity
to observe the interaction between civil servants ensconced in the office, an opportunity which I
would never have had in Japan because the officers were sent from different agencies.

Despite the relaxed atmosphere at JETRO New York and despite the fact that the officers
were from separate organizations, the hierarchical structure of Japan's governing system, with
the national ministries on top and prefecture governments towards the bottom, was well defined,
as was also the case in the majority of Japanese government offices overseas.

A Slap on the Wrist

Some of the officers at JETRO New York took exception to the "risqué" nature of the Wacoal
article and I was cautioned. It was disappointing because the Japanese business community in
the US seemed to enjoy the article and I received compliments for what I considered to be an
innocuous promotion of the paper. My marketing blogs were discontinued and my article in the
November issue was limited to one page.

The president's Perspective in November 1992 preferring to ignore his bureaucracy's
complacency regarding Japan's own troubled economy, took a swipe at the US economy:

But Bill Clinton, elected next president of the United States, knew we were in
the midst of change. That's why he used "change" as a keyword in his campaign

We expect him to change the overall American stance from traditional (and highly
commendable) optimism to something less optimistic, a little more serious, a
sense of urgency in grappling with reality

American people have awakened to the need to face reality and change. We wish President Clinton success in all his endeavors.

The contribution by the researcher from Industrial Research is again entirely relevant today. The piece lauded Japan's leadership in Asia and its attempts to promote peace and improve relationships among Asian countries through the regional trade organization ASEAN. The article reported that Japan was trying to repair relations with China and Korea to demonstrate its commitment to this end. While admitting that Japan must promote China's ties with the West, the article also revealed Japan's paranoia regarding China's rapid economic development in Asia and its economic and political influence in the international community.

The article expressed concerns that issues such as China's human rights violations and arms dealings would serve to frustrate Japan's efforts to help China internationalize. Significantly, the article pointed to Japan's dependency on the US to protect its interests:

> Japan's Asian policy will have to take into consideration the concerns of its most important ally, the United States…Despite facile talk of a world splitting into trading blocs, Japan is firmly opposed to pursuing an Asian policy that isolates the United States or other Western nations. To the extent that a U.S.-Japan partnership serves to promote democratization and economic cooperation in the Asia-Pacific region, we can expect continued prosperity.

I used Mercian's Beaujolais Nouveau debacle for my one page article.

Getting to Know the Boss

The president and his editor extended invitations to me to various functions. Sometimes Japanese corporate executives from the North American corporate headquarters would attend and their submissiveness to an elite MITI official was evident. Although the president remained aloof from JETRO staff, within five months after his arrival it became apparent that he was controlling the office environment. He was well-liked and, compared to the majority of Japanese males whose stature were short and stocky, he was tall and slender. Female staff called him elegant and handsome. His executive secretary was smitten.

The editor claimed that the president was "not a typical bureaucrat" referring to his diverse interests such as writing film reviews for *Toyo Keizai* ('East-West Economics'). The editor and the president's relationship was mutually beneficial. While the president was able to rely upon the editor for polishing his prose and arranging entertaining evenings during his family's absence, the editor was given stimulating work and a position in JETRO other than serving as the in-house translator.

The president took the opportunity to introduce me to his family when they visited New York in August. I met them at the editor's flat in lower Manhattan for drinks before we went to a Vietnamese restaurant for a meal. The wife, in her early forties, was very pretty. The two sons in their teens were handsome and the six-year-old daughter was quite adorable. It must have been difficult for the family to be separated.

I introduced the president to the noodle restaurant in Soho to which he gave a five-star rating and where he continued to entertain his guests. He introduced me to his second cousin who, having left his job as an architect in one of Japan's major construction companies, was staying with him while trying to decide what he wanted to do next. He was considering getting a doctorate in environmental issues at a university in the US or Canada.

The president, who doted on Andrew Lloyd Webber whom he called the Puccini of the West, gave us tickets to Phantom of the Opera which had opened recently on Broadway with the original cast. The president also invited me to a Japanese karaoke bar in lower Manhattan because, as did the director of the Mercian wine division, he enjoyed performing before a captive audience.

Sayonara Kyoto

The Kyoto Prefectural Government representative seemed unconcerned that I was writing for the newsletter even though I was visiting the Research and Planning division, attending weekly editorial meetings and stuffing envelopes. Since he was busy acclimating to his job, he rarely asked me to engage. But I was becoming increasingly uncomfortable because the president, although very kind, was also creating a difficult situation in JETRO New York. Not only was I writing for his paper but also socializing as well with both him and the editor. In reality, I was under the president's aegis.

I began going to the office on weekends to write unobserved and to alleviate tensions. The 44th floor was empty of staff and the atmosphere eerie. The McGraw Hill building fire warden would announce over the load speaker that a fire had been reported on one of the floors below and that the elevators were not operating. Although always a false alarm it was an unpleasant experience. Sometimes the director of the JH worked in his office and on those occasions it was evident that he was suspicious of my presence.

Perhaps because the JETRO Trade Promotion Division Executive Director had conceived of the Business Support Centers (BSC) which were to open the following year he was awarded a secondment to JETRO New York. He enjoyed golf but not necessarily Americans whom he called "Whites" (*hakujin*), a mildly racist term. He urged officials to bear babies in America so that they were American citizens and thus eligible for US benefits. He was extremely displeased that his division, the promotional arm of JETRO New York, did not publish the paper. He protested vigorously to the Managing Director that *Inside/Outside Japan* usurped his division's territory.

He persuaded the representative officers from the other prefecture representative offices and agencies to lobby both the Managing Director and the Kyoto officer to terminate my involvement in the paper. He also tried to pressure the officials to prohibit their assistants from contributing. He further inflamed the situation by perpetuating gossip about my relationship with the president.

Officials began visiting the Kyoto Prefecture office to lobby the officer, plying him with lunches and other incentives. It was disconcerting being the brunt of their derogatory remarks uttered as they stood in front of my cubicle. However, their behavior sparked my curiosity about what these officers actually did for their agencies while in New York and what JETRO was all about.

By November the posting of *Inside/Outside Japan* became a monthly two-party exercise. The American researcher in Research and Planning and I stuffed 600 envelopes. One copy was sent monthly to the US Department of Justice because the paper was being published by a foreign agency. The president's and managing director's secretary abstained as did the Ehime Prefecture representative whose father happened to be the governor Sadayuki Iga. Dressed immaculately in expensive tweeds his remit was to entertain Ehime businessmen who rarely came to town. He was wise to avoid involvement because his participation was considered an affront to the Trade Promotion Executive Director and to JETRO, which was managed by MITI. I was to discover a few months later that Ehime was very dependent upon the national ministries for subsidies and that Governor Iga was a master at bringing in the cash. The unfortunate Managing Director, struggled to keep the peace and was caught in the middle of a very petty situation. Nonetheless, I was determined to continue contributing monthly to the paper because through this vehicle I could establish an abiding relationship with Research and Planning and dig deeper into the reasons for not only JETRO's existence but, also, for the other ministries corporations being represented in the office.

The Kyoto officer, who was overwhelmed by his new environment, finally acquiesced to their pressure. But contributors to the paper were sparse and the president decided to arrange my transfer to the Reference Library. He persuaded the Kyoto representative, formally yet sensitively, to allow my departure by taking the two of us to dinner at a Japanese restaurant and, afterwards, to his luxurious Eastside apartment for tea. The officers' conversation was easier because the president had graduated from Kyoto University and was raised in Shiga Prefecture, which is adjacent to Osaka Prefecture.

Although there was no allusion to my future transfer to the Reference Library, the Kyoto officer understood that he did not have a choice and that soon he would be given a new assistant. He revealed his underlying humiliation when he blurted out that I should get drunk and dance on top of the restaurant table but I had become inured to such remarks.

Crazy about Clinton: the honeymoon

Some officers seconded by the prefecture governments and by MITI's other corporations regarded MITI as a ministry weakened during the previous decade because it no longer had an effective industrial policy. However, the December 1992 issue of *Inside/Outside Japan* was a tour de force with the president promoting MITI's industrial policy by praising President Bill Clinton for his determination to fix the US economy through the restructuring of its industrial policy and for his seemingly liberal attitude towards Japan's trade surplus with the US:

> As the new administration contemplates ways of strengthening U.S. competitiveness, "industrial policy" seems to be on the lips of many policy makers. In devising and pursuing industrial policy, however, it is important to recognize that a government's role in fostering industrial competitiveness is limited…In speaking about Japan's industrial policy, the impression is often given that its function is to "pick the winner." And in noting this, it is stressed that since the government can't work better than the market, industrial policy can produce mainly errors…As has been the experience of some countries, the government arbitrarily choosing potential "winners" can lead to market distortions, as well as collusion and corruption.

No reference was made to the recent scandals of collusion between the MOC and construction companies or to some of the elements specific to Japan's industrial policy, which, in contrast to America's industrial policy, covered all of Japan's industrial sectors. Japan's industrial policy protected domestic companies from foreign competition through recession cartels, production rationalization and tax incentives to Japanese corporations who procured from domestic suppliers. The policy is implemented by administrative guidance (discussed in Chapter 15) enforced through built-in control mechanisms such as *amakudari* and MITI's industrial associations.

The president cleverly tried to persuade readers that MITI had a softer side, as the promoter of R&D for environmental protection and as a ministry which took only a peripheral role in guiding industry: "One vital point that tends to be missed, though, is that industrial policy is not the matter of choosing winners. Instead, it is a joint effort between government and industry to respond to it appropriately."

He suggested that a government "may introduce tax breaks and low interest loans for the producers of such equipment. In such government–business working schemes, competitive vitality of each industrial sector is indispensable and taken for granted. The main actor is always the industry."

The Executive Director of Research and Planning contributed a piece to the same issue which lauded Clinton's recognition that the US's trade deficit with Japan was not entirely Japan's fault nor due to Japan's "misconduct" (i.e. protected markets and non-tariff barriers) while stressing that the US must get its act together and revive its economy.

The American researcher for Industrial Research wrote a forthright piece on the state of the Japanese economy, which admitted that banks were extremely exposed to the real estate bubble and were burdened with $100 billion of non-performing loans at the end of September, a 50 percent rise from the end of March. He also confirmed that the extent of NPL was still an unknown. Ironically, the article could have been written today:

> The latest economic shock presents Japan with a task more complex than any in the past, as well as a unique opportunity…What is crucial in the process is acting quickly. At a time when the world community is expecting more leadership from Japan, quick and decisive action is likely to inspire strong confidence at home and abroad.

The president requested that I contribute a piece about MITI's promotion of protecting the environment from global warming. I was permitted the usual 2,500 words for "Beyond the Blue Horizon" which publicized MITI's programs to incentivize companies through tax breaks for the recycling of industrial waste:

> Recycling also translates into big bucks; a mayonnaise company, for example, turns egg shells from its mayonnaise and liquid egg production into palatable cookie-calcium supplements. Under the auspices of the Ministry of Agriculture, Forestry, and Fisheries, fifteen food, cosmetics, and stock-feed producing companies are doing extensive research into the extraction and refinement of DNA, the unsaturated fatty acid found in the heads of tuna and bonito, which cannot be synthesized (don't through away those fish heads).

The president was satisfied with the article. By mid-February I was sitting at a desk in the Reference Library and in the thick of it.

15

Smack Dab in the Middle

The library was the most spacious room in the office with an extensive display of JETRO's white papers on Japan's foreign business operations and trade statistics, including inward and outward investment, video tapes promoting various Japanese industries and Japanese corporate culture and management, which were loaned to schools. There were volumes of books serving as data bases of Japanese corporations who were promoted as potential business partners for foreign companies.

JETRO's services were directed to small and medium sized businesses whose owners wanted to do business in Japan but were unfamiliar with regulations, the markets and consumer culture. JETRO's import promotion programs and literature were packaged to give the corporation a glossy professional image of a Japanese government-supported agency that was earnest in its efforts to help small businesses enter Japanese markets. From the late 1980s, JETRO began publishing a series of market reports for products that found consumer acceptance such as foods, alcoholic beverages, clothing, sports equipment, cosmetics, electronic equipment, jewelry and organic products.

In 1989 JETRO released *A Survey on Successful Cases of Foreign-Affiliated Companies in Japan*. Claiming that foreign direct investment had been liberalized because the Foreign Trade Control Law had been amended in 1980, JETRO presented 13 case studies of successful ventures in Japan. The 13 manufacturers who were questioned about how they had prepared for operating in Japan replied positively about their experiences. However, they were not identified by company names but by product, the location of headquarters, location of operation in Japan, and the amount of capital investment.

In 1990 a colorful magazine was issued describing companies that had entered Japan successfully. *The Challenge of the Japanese Market* pointed to companies, such as Baccarat, Bausch & Lomb, Cartier, Jaeger, Peugeot, Rolex and Reebok, that had been accepted in Japan. However, JETRO did not advise small business owners that the main reason these companies had successful ventures in Japan was that they already had brand-name recognition among Japanese consumers before entering, and that Japanese people had traditionally been eager buyers of luxury goods when they travel overseas. The majority of the companies mentioned had originally joined with a large Japanese trading company which routinely scouted for companies with products that were ready for the market, as was the case for Mercian Inc.

JETRO offered a number of support services. In 1991, the Senior Trade Advisor Program was inaugurated in the United States, whereby former executives from Japanese multinational companies or JETRO staff were posted to the International Economic Divisions of state governments. They visited small businesses operating in their states to find products that would ostensibly suit the Japanese market. By 1994, there were 21 advisors who could also serve MITI as information-gatherers. When small business owners visited a JETRO office in the US to inquire if their products were suitable for the Japanese market, they were referred to a trade advisor assigned to the office. Owners were often advised to revise their products to meet either the Japan Industrial Standards (JIS) or consumer preferences to such an extent that the capital investment necessary for revision was often far more than the business owners could afford, given the risks of entering unknown territory.

In 1992, in response to the United States' demand that Japan open its markets to more imports MITI wrote the Law on Extraordinary Measures for the Promotion of Imports and Facilitations of Foreign Direct Investment in Japan, setting the stage for the construction of Foreign Access Zones (FAZ) throughout Japan.

In January 1993 before the inauguration of FAZ MITI International Vice Minister Yuji Tanahashi met with foreign business executives in Tokyo to discuss the implementation of FAZ and MITI's plans to modify customs laws, create a fund for industrial structural adjustment, subsidize foreign investment, defray investment costs, guarantee loans, provide additional investment information and support employee recruitment. When asked if the difficulties experienced by foreign companies to access Japan's markets were due to lack of effort, Tanahashi replied that the Japanese language could be problematic but he did point to the successful entry by large international firms such as Motorola and Texas Instruments.

Ehime and MITI: a marriage of convenience

In April when I learned that the first FAZ was in Matsuyama, the capital of Ehime Prefecture the interlocking relationship between Ehime and MITI became clear. A company comprised of government organizations and private corporations was established to manage FAZ. The Ehime Foreign Access Zone Co. Ltd. constructed a distribution center for the handling of imported goods and three exhibition halls, one of which was the largest exhibition hall in the Shikoku-Chugoku region. The hall was suitable for numerous events with conference rooms fitted with projection and simultaneous translation equipment. The entire exhibition area covered 7,300sqm. JETRO set up a JETRO FAZ Support Center in the facility to provide FAZ-specific information.

Ehime is the largest of four prefectures on Japan's fourth largest island of Shikoku. The prefecture has 5,672.5 km of coastline, the fifth-longest in Japan, facing Asia which probably was one of the reasons given for establishing a FAZ. The population at the time was approximately 1.4 million with approximately 500,000 living in Matsuyama. The primary industries are agriculture (citrus), forestry and fisheries. The secondary industries are chemicals, machinery, paper pulp and shipbuilding in Imabari where Imabari Shipbuilding, Japan's largest shipbuilder, operated in the deep waters of the Kurushima Straits. In terms of per capita income, Ehime was ranked around 35th among the 47 prefectures, 34th for personal income, 25th in industrial output, 25th for agricultural produce and 30th for the size of the budget.

Ehime is one of the most scenic areas in Japan and tourists flock to Matsuyama Castle and to Dogo Onsen, Japan's oldest hot spring which is the site of Natsume Soseki's famous novel *Botchan*. Besides being the birthplace of Kenzaburo Oe, the 1994 Nobel Prize winner for literature, Ehime is reputed to be the home of Haiku poetry.

Governor Iga had been an officer of the Ehime local government and a staunch member of the LDP. As Vice Governor under the previous administration, he was in line to succeed as governor. At the beginning of Iga's administration, one of Ehime's representatives in the Lower House in the National Diet was an LDP politician who entered Prime Minister Takeshita's cabinet in 1987 for one year as Minister of Construction. Ehime was blessed because Ihei Ochi was fortuitously in the right place and, as a consequence, the applications for public works in Ehime were accepted in the first Takeshita budget.

The governor took full advantage of Representative Ochi's connection with the MOC and the construction industry and he cultivated an interpersonal network with top officials in the ministries to promote Ehime's needs. Iga established Ehime's presence in the United States through Iyo Bank, Ehime's regional bank, opening a one-man office in Manhattan to provide offshore services to Ehime businesses in the United States. Regardless, Ehime business transactions were intermittent at best.

Iga's ties to the ministries enabled him to access large subsidies for public works which included a network of highways and tunnels throughout Ehime's mountainous terrain, and the Kurushima-Kaikyo Bridge in tandem with the Shimanami Kaido, a 60 km expressway that would link up Ehime with Hiroshima across the Seto Inland Sea and which was under the management of the Honshu-Shikoku Bridge Authority, a JH subsidiary. The bridge was due to open to the public in 1999. Iga's efforts also brought an international airport, a convention center, a modern art museum and, his biggest triumph, a FAZ.

The Managing Director was very friendly with Governor Iga's son. He took him and a JETRO New York staff on a road trip across the US. When the executive secretary confided to me that not only had the president been the recipient of the governor's hospitality in Ehime but, also, she had been entertained by the governor it became clearer why Governor Iga's son was sitting at a desk in JETRO New York. Upon his return to Ehime he became the first director of FAZ. After returning to MITI, the Managing Director was posted as the Director of the Import and Export Division, which could explain his relationship with the governor's son.

Importantly, Shikoku's only nuclear power plant commissioned in 1977 is located in the fishing village of Ikata, Ehime and supplies the island with most of its electricity. Due to the Oil Shock in 1973 and the need to reduce industries' reliance on fossil fuel the government announced that nuclear energy was a national priority. In 1974, the Three Power Source Development Law was enacted to subsidize local authorities that were willing to host nuclear power plants. MITI together with the regional utility companies and the heavy industries involved in nuclear power such as Mitsubishi, Toshiba and Hitachi, aggressively chose sites for the construction of nuclear power plants in rural, depopulated municipalities with inadequate tax bases, where the civil societies were considered weak and where subsidies to support local small businesses and maintain employment would promote the acceptance by local authorities of nuclear power plants in their areas. Ikata was a perfect representation of a needy local authority.

More Offerings from MITI

In 1993 the aforementioned Business Support Centers (BSC) opened in Tokyo, Yokohama, Kobe, Nagoya and Fukuoka to assist foreign small business owners during their visits to Japan to find buyers for their products. The BSC offered exhibition space, temporary office facilities and consulting services free of charge.

Also in 1993, the Foreign Investment in Japan Corporation (FIND) was established as a private corporation, promoting itself as "Your Foothold in the Japanese Market." Its services included the contribution of funds to foreign businesses that wanted to operate in Japan. The corporation claimed: "¥500 million in capital provided by the Japanese government (Structural Fund) and a further ¥445 million was invested by powerful businesses in the private sector and industry associations."

Among the 31 stockholders were MITI industrial associations such as the Electronics Industries of Japan (EIAJ). A MITI subsidiary, the Industrial Structure Improvement Fund, was also a stockholder. The majority of private companies who owned equity were industries that MITI regulated, including Toyota Motors, Mitsubishi Chemical Corp. Nissho Iwai Corp, Kobe Steel Ltd and Nissan Motors Corp.

It's the Image that Counts

The librarians' remit was to help visitors with their enquiries about Japan and doing business in Japan. They answered telephone calls from people requesting information about Japanese markets, the literature available about their products' applicability to Japanese markets and the JIS regulations.

I sat at the middle desk which had been occupied by a retired male JETRO local staff. The Australian woman had left before my arrival and since there was little activity in the library, she was not replaced. Although the Philippine woman did not know much about Japan nor its markets, she also served as the in-house notary public witnessing and signing-off legal documents brought to her by the directors which included applications for visas for family members, bank accounts, insurance policies, IDs etc. She tended to read novels during most of the day and chat with the receptionist and Japanese assistants.

I noticed that when visitors entered the library they were not served unless they approached the woman's desk for information and she simply pointed to the books on the shelves. When I tried to go into more detail about market access with visitors and callers she instructed me to direct specific enquiries to JETRO Trade Promotion to be handled by the Senior Trade Advisor. The visitors' ethnic diversity, which included Koreans and Russian émigrés, illustrated that America was indeed a melting pot but the Korean businessmen complained to me that their reception by the librarians had been discriminatory and that they had received poor service.

The library was empty of visitors most of the time and the daily telephone inquiries numbered less than ten. I tended to greet visitors when they entered the library and since I could answer their questions without referring them to a Senior Trade Advisor I was considered to be stepping out of line.

The library was considered JETRO proper and my new post gave me a direct pipeline to the Trade Promotion Division and to Research and Planning. As long as I continued contributing articles to *Inside/Outside Japan* I would remain semi-attached to Research and Planning. MITI officers from other divisions came to my desk to request help with analyzing data regarding US business and politics and with translating English documents into Japanese and vice versa. The work automatically made me a partner to their activities.

The officer from JASME continued to request information. The relationship evolved into a friendship with him and his new wife who had accompanied him to New York. The newlyweds were living in a small apartment near JETRO. Sometimes they invited me for a Japanese meal and occasionally we met at a restaurant. During his two-year tour the officer worked regular hours compared to the majority of officers, leaving his wife to fend for herself. She could not speak enough English to communicate comfortably with Americans and stayed in the apartment alone. She began to paint in order to pass the time and discovered that she had a hidden talent.

The female non-career officer from EID/MITI (EXIM Bank) continued to visit me for assistance with the new Trade Insurance regulations. She was the first female officer to be sent overseas by MITI and undoubtedly felt the pressure. In her forties and single, she had entered MITI as a non-career officer directly after graduating from college. Even though non-career officers are generally ineligible for promotion as directors of divisions and top positions in the ministry, she preferred focusing on her career. Her apartment was conveniently located near JETRO, allowing her to work throughout the night to communicate with EID/MITI in Tokyo. While the other officers went on holidays and were with their families, with the exception of entertaining visiting officials, she had no social life and little opportunity to see much of New York. I began escorting her to points of interest.

She enjoyed her visit to Franklin Delano Roosevelt's house and museum located in Hyde Park where there was also a museum dedicated to his wife Eleanor Roosevelt. The officer was fascinated with the exhibits in the museums which explained the New Deal and the Social Security System and, especially, the photographs of the bombing of Hiroshima and Nagasaki.

Through the work I became acquainted with her superior, a career officer who directed the JETRO EID/MITI office. In his early forties, after graduating from Tokyo University from the Law Faculty he entered MITI on the fast track. His father who was in the Coastguard relocated several times during his son's childhood which exposed the officer to diverse regions in Japan. He opted for a career in MITI because his father did not have contacts in business circles. MITI sent him to John Hopkins University for a year of study in 1982 which, according to him, was invaluable. Although he used US consultants based in Washington DC, his analytical skills helped him to produce a high standard of work during his term. When I interviewed him in January 1994 he told me about his first exposure to a person of color. His reaction was similar to the majority of Japanese:

> There were no foreign students in my school, only Japanese. When I was in junior high school, I was traveling from Tokyo Station when a foreigner asked me something. I couldn't understand anything! It was shocking to meet someone who didn't speak Japanese. He was black. I guess that even if he was white I would still be shocked. Three years of English study didn't work at all so I couldn't answer.

The officer joked that when he was staying in a Washington DC hotel, he felt that because he was Asian he was given a room at the end of a hall next to the elevator. He also was seated in a restaurant at a table next to the kitchen. When he confided to the JETRO New York Managing Director, who was a colleague at MITI headquarters, that he felt discrimination the director replied that the poor service was probably due to his disheveled student attire. I told him that single American women often experienced the same treatment.

Japan's Import Promotion Measures: MITI's promotion of MITI and JETRO?

The February 1993 issue of the paper announced a series of measures which would support the flow of exports to Japan's markets:

Japan's worry about its trade surplus is not a recent phenomenon. When the surplus continued to swell after rounds of tariff reductions and other measures to reduce procedural hurdles, Japan introduced steps unprecedented in world history and began actively promoting imports. The government's current efforts expand similar measures, with the stress on encouraging foreign businesses to come to the Japanese markets or to increase their imports to Japan. Among such import promotion programs are:

1. Special lending rates provided by the Japan Development Bank (JDB) for import-enhancing facilities and the Export-Import Bank of Japan for importation of manufactured goods
2. Set-aside-for-imports programs in government procurement.
3. Business Support Centers (BSC), to be added to JETRO. Intended to provide free "business centers" to foreign people who actually visit Japan to find leads or establish contacts.
4. Foreign Access Zones (FAZ). By March 1993 a total of seven air- and sea-ports will have expanded facilities for encouraging imports.
5. Expansion of the activities of the office of Trade and Investment Ombudsman (OTO) established to resolve problems faced by foreign markets in Japan.

The president's Perspective in the same issue was clearly in MOFA territory as he lauded former President Clinton's support for George W. Bush's military entry into Iraq:

> Future historians are likely to rate President Bush high for shaping a clear direction for the "new world order." His decision to take military action against Iraq just a few days before handing his post over to Mr. Clinton gained worldwide support, and significantly reduced the sense of instability and uncertainty in the post-Cold War international order that people began to have not long ago after the East–West schism ended in a victory for Western philosophy.

While welcoming Clinton's continuation of America's foreign policy, the president took the opportunity to emphasize that there was also the need for Japan to change from "a passive participant to an active player in the global system" and that the country was obliged to "dedicate itself to the betterment of the world with a far greater vigor than it has in the past."

My article "Sipping Sound" regarded Suntory's marketing strategy through TV adverts and the promotion of the arts.

Promotion of Industrial Policy with a Scottish Twist

In February the president asked me to access a copy of Andrew Carnegie's *Gospel of Wealth.* I found the book at the Andrew Carnegie Foundation office but I did not discover why he had requested it until I read the March issue of *Inside/Outside Japan.* Although it is an amusing interpretation of Andrew Carnegie's *Gospel* it also represents the president's "creative" promotion of MITI's Vision for the 1990s.

The essay was used as the foundation of his address "Creating Human Values in the Global Age" he delivered on March 10, 1993 to the members of the Carnegie Council on Ethics and International Affairs. In his address "MITI and Human Values" he managed to connect MITI's Vision and the release of another fiscal stimulus package with Andrew Carnegie's *Gospel of Wealth* while simultaneously presenting his ministry as a compassionate and caring agency determined on helping the Japanese realize a better quality of life.

Although it would take some stretch of the imagination, comparisons can be made between MITI, a Japanese bureaucracy, and Andrew Carnegie, a Scottish immigrant from Dunfermline who became the father of the American steel industry. He founded Carnegie Steel, the forerunner of US Steel, in 1869, a year after the beginning of the Meiji Restoration. He made his fortune in iron, coke and chemicals. The Ministry of Agriculture and Commerce (MAC) began nurturing Japan's steel industry in the late nineteenth century. However, here any similarity between Carnegie and MITI ends because Carnegie's wealth came out of his own pocket and not from tax revenue. The parks, libraries, schools, hospitals, meeting halls, universities and concert halls were personally financed. Japanese government fiscal stimulus packages are funded by public finance.

The president introduced himself to his audience by mentioning his recent visits to the Carnegie Mellon Institute in Pittsburgh and Carnegie Hall in New York, both highly visible examples of Andrew Carnegie's philanthropic activities. Then he got down to the subject of his speech, "creating human values as a form of industrial policy." Describing his ministry as a firm but gentle guide of Japan's industry, he said that MITI was sometimes called "notorious" but that he was unaware of the term's origins: "Perhaps it has to do with the way Japan's economy developed rapidly in the past five decades and MITI's supposed role in that development, which is often expressed by the very term 'industrial policy'."

The president spoke of Japan's competitive spirit as the driving force behind Japan's industrialization after the Meiji Restoration quoting the first sentence of the first essay in Carnegie's *Gospel*: "The problem of our age is the proper administration of wealth." He reflected:

> Though Mr. Carnegie was a great philanthropist, in his gospel he did not preach a "kinder, gentler attitude," he was hard-nose arguing, at one point that "no substitute [for the law of competition] has been found: and while the law may sometimes be hard for the individual it is best for the race because it insures the survival of the fittest."

The president's reference to Carnegie's generous but hard-nosed character was clever because it connected with MITI's use of administrative guidance. He insisted that Japan's post-war industrial policy included cooperation but there was a catch: "Competition is important, but a body of people – be it family, a company, or a society – cannot hope to function and grow without cooperation among its members."

The president was inferring that companies cooperated with MITI's guidance to form cartels, to rationalize production, to fix prices and to procure from domestic suppliers in order to ward off competition from foreign firms.

Although the origins of the policy to rationalize production can be traced back to 1925 and the Ministry of Commerce (forerunner of MITI) MITI used the tool known as "administrative guidance" (*Gyoseishido*) since 1952 in order to form cartels of industries designated as important to national interests, protecting them from foreign competition and to maintain a level playing field among domestic companies. The tool can be used *ad hoc* at the discretion of the ministries. There are no laws that limit the number of times "guidance" is used, giving the ministries uncommon powers to regulate. Companies will usually receive notification that they are expected to follow ministerial regulations. The directives are either transmitted in writing or by telephone, although a law in 1997 officially curtailed the use of the telephone. Carnegie's tract on distribution of wealth had a Socialist tone to it:

> under its sway we have an ideal State, in which the surplus wealth of a few becomes, in the best sense, the property of many, because administered for the common good, and this wealth, passing through the hands of a few, can be made a more potent force for the elevation of our race than if distributed in small sums to the people themselves.

Likewise, MITI's Vision and MITI's role could be characterized as Socialist. The president reminded his audience that post-war industrial policy had focused on catching up with the Western powers and on increasing Japan's competitiveness in the global marketplace. Each of these visions, in that sense, was a "how-to" guide on a grand scale.

He assured the audience that "creating human values" was very much a part of industrial policy: "after all, industrial policy…at least as practiced by MITI…is aimed to increase prosperity or a sense of well-being in the nation."

He claimed that MITI was aware that the Japanese were not enjoying the fruits of their labor and that the Vision for the 1990s was to shift the focus from "how-to" to "what-for." He listed some of the objectives of the Vision:

> Greater consumer-orientation and protection, further promotion of recycling, creating greater employment opportunities, increasing security for the elderly,

and pushing for advancement of women's social and professional status. The vision calls for vast improvement of social infrastructure, including housing (no more rabbit hutches, please), and a massive attempt to reduce excessive concentration on Tokyo and encourage regional development...the vision sets forth goals that must be achieved to secure long-term economic development that is essential to the enhancement of human values.

The speech was included as a Supplement in the March edition of the paper.

My article for the February issue "The Big Squeeze" was based on my experiences while living in Japan with the high tariffs on foreign citrus, specifically California oranges. However, I was again given a caution for what was considered a risqué approach:

Orange amateurs blatantly describe the mikan as a Tangerine without seeds. Citrus connoisseurs understand the mikan mentality and its sophisticated subtleties. Barbarians from the West will tear open its skin, ravaging its flesh, barely aware of the sublime, sweet soul within. The more refined will gently part the thin, soft, orange robe, exposing the plump succulent crescents. They will tentatively unravel the silky white, membranous threads surrounding the translucent skin and, via lips and tongue, carefully let the delicate juice, intent upon capturing its fleeting honey essence.

Nevertheless, I received a number of calls from Japanese business executives posted in New York who praised the article. My readership among Japanese was increasing.

In the April issue as a government spokesman, the president stated a recurring theme in his editorial; although Japan's economy might be regarded as stagnant, Japan was still experiencing growth of 1.5 percent GDP and that the first stimulus package of $87 billion was proving an effective measure to spark the economy but that the government would announce yet another stimulus package in mid-April. He put a spin on Japan's role in the global economy:

The Japanese economy, which has remained in the doldrums since the "bubble" burst two years ago, is finally beginning to brighten. Improvements in machinery orders which began last October are continuing.

In mid-April the Japanese government will introduce a new stimulus package. Following the $87 billion measure that went into effect early this year, the new package will aim to boost "new social capital" by inducing investments in things such as telecommunications and university laboratories...The effect of the previous stimulus package on the construction industry was evident in January, when top 50 construction companies reported a 60% increase in new orders from a year earlier.

Internationally, the continued recovery of the U.S. economy remains the key to worldwide growth. But Japan's role is no less great, especially when European countries are reeling with serious recession. Japan is implementing large stimulus measures to increase domestic demand and help the world economy grow with stability.

The year 1993 is going to be a historic one when the foundations for a new international order will be laid. Both the United States and Japan are prepared to undergo fundamental change – the United States with the keyword "sacrifice," to rebuild the domestic economy, and Japan with "global responsibility," to strengthen its international role. It is our hope that during the U.S.–Japan Summit in mid-April President Clinton and Prime Minister Miyazawa will solidify the partnership of the two nations.

Since I had received a caution, my article in the April issue "The Big Squeeze (Part 2), Can the Quitting of Quotas Cause Chaos?" was confined to one page. It regarded the lowering of tariffs on California and Florida imports of orange juice and a small reduction of tariffs on fresh oranges:

> The food and beverage industry, confident that consumers were hooked on 100% pure, quivered with eager expectation of future fresh orange juice markets when the quotas would come tumbling down, a virtual Valencia Valhalla. Processing and packaging plants in California, Florida, and Brazil were purchased. By the time the curtain lifted on April 1, 1992, at least ten major manufacturers and supermarket chains had gotten into the act....Alas, it is the "Sorcerer's Apprentice" revisited! It's Mickey's worst nightmare! Only this time around, buckets of orange juice continue to multiply and, so far, marketing magic has not been able to rectify this miscalculation of the mass market.

The Interviews

A number of the officials at JETRO New York graciously allowed me to conduct in-depth interviews with them about their education and their impressions of the United States. They were relaxed because they were away from the pressures of their home offices and thus freer to communicate candidly about their attitudes towards the United States. Also, at that time the efforts by ex-LDP politicians to reform the political system evoked a more liberal and, therefore, an easier environment.

Since I had anticipated their replies and likely to sympathize with many of their views I did not consider that my queries would intrude on their privacy. These interviews are as relevant today as in 1994. In other words, there have been no fundamental changes since then.

The interviews included a MITI official who answered the question of whether he thought that Japan could internationalize. His reply to my question why Japan cannot internationalize revealed the real picture:

> I don't think that the Japanese can internationalize. "Internationalization" is spoken about but Japanese go abroad, have experiences but return to Japan and their same way of life. Unfortunately, things from the outside will never enter Japan smoothly. I really don't understand what "internationalization" is, but I think that for Japanese to achieve a level that enables them to negotiate and interact with various nationalities is difficult.

The officer from Kyoto Prefecture was also interviewed during the same period:

> Japan is a small nation and insular. People are not open to outsiders. They build stone fences and close themselves off. Japan has internationalized in some areas like trade but for the general population, Japan has not internationalized at all.

I interviewed the president of the North American corporate headquarters of a major Japanese trading firm later that year. His insights are invaluable, particularly because Americans posted in Japan generally tend to socialize only among westerners due to the language barrier and the difference in cultures:

The Japanese who were sent here before me did not receive any education here. However, all of the Japanese who are posted here inevitably send their children to special Japanese preparatory schools (after regular school hours) as they do in Japan. They want their children to enter the Japanese education system. So even though Japan posts employees overseas for three to five years, Japan will not be able to internationalize. I don't think that the Japanese mind is too rigid but the Japanese should try to understand world affairs. Being a tourist is no good. Japanese do argue that Americans who work in Japan for American companies leave without understanding anything about the society or culture. But Americans have a pretty good sense of themselves and the world because they go out into the world. You can't compare the two countries! Japanese go to other countries on a theme: on business, on an adventure, to the desert to feel the heat, walking around the world or living in the mountains. They sport a disheveled look to fulfil a dream. But they must really enter those societies.

Getting Hotter

Although in his December 1992 Perspective the president entertained high hopes for the Clinton administration trade policies regarding Japan's trade surplus, he expressed in the May 1993 issue of *Inside/Outside Japan* some concerns when he devoted his editorial to the Clinton–Miyazawa Summit which was held in April.

He protected MITI's administrative territory by stating that Clinton was unrealistic about "result-oriented trade" or "managed trade" and that Japan was the submissive underdog at the negotiation table. Nevertheless, the president was not entirely forthright when he insisted that Japan's economy was based on market mechanisms. Even though Japan was the second largest economy in the world and the world's largest net creditor, Japan's mercantilism was creating problems in the economy that would prove to be insurmountable unless deregulation and basic structural reforms were implemented quickly. He insisted:

> The United States' position as the senior partner and founder of Japan's post-war democracy, and Japan, because of its inherent politeness and reluctance to offend.

> There is undue emphasis on select aspects of bilateral trade and ignores, for example, the fact that the imbalance in trade between Japan and the United States fundamentally results not from allegedly closed markets but from macroeconomic factors and differences in export capabilities. Forcing numerical import targets on a trading partner would be the ultimate form of market intervention – as Japanese corporations and Mr. Miyazawa forcefully argued.

The president ended with a subtle warning:

> In the new era following the Cold War, we certainly hope our amicable relationship will continue, with the United States changing itself to affect basic economic restructuring, Japan to further facilitate access to its markets and take on greater global responsibilities. This is all the more reason we must oppose demands that deliberately interfere with market mechanisms.

My article, "The Shell Game," which regarded the route taken by Blue Diamond Almonds from the 1960s to enter the Japanese market was based on my visit while living in the Napa Valley to Blue Diamond's center in Modesto where the almond growers' cooperative is located and where the bulk of California almonds are cultivated. Although the company opened a small office in Tokyo in the 1960s, in order to integrate almonds into the Japanese diet it connected with cooking schools to instruct young women how to use almonds in recipes. Blue Diamond also produced almond snacks for the Japanese palate. I concluded:

> The California almond is in Japan to stay because,

> What did that crazy goose once say? (or was it actually Frito Lay?)

> "I bet you can't eat just one!"

On the second half of the page was the announcement that the government would release a $116 billion stimulus package to "primarily improve social capital." It was 35% bigger than the previous package, the total amount equaling 2.8 percent of Japan's GDP for fiscal year 1992. It was expected to induce a "2.6% multiplier effect on GDP." The package was targeted for improving housing and sewage, as the president had promised in a previous Perspective. But he did not include that the infrastructure work would keep Japan's unemployment numbers low. The last paragraph indicated that Japan was determined to open its markets to imports: "The package also features financial schemes intended to create new facilities to promote imports [FAZ]. Among the measures to increase imports is "import sale facilitation financing," which will be made by the National Finance Corporation and the Small Business Finance Corporation."

The Sins of the US

The June 1993 issue included a special MITI report presenting the US as the culprit:

> The Japanese Ministry of International Trade and Industry (MITI) has issued the second annual report on unfair trade policies of Japan's major trading partners. The report examines U.S., Canada, Australia, and Asian nations, as well as Japan, and finds that the United States most violates GATT rules and resorts to unilateral actions.

Even though the US-Japan April trade talks were not as productive as was hoped and even though the paper served to promote Japan's interests, in his Perspective the president overstepped his remit when he used the US National Cooperative Production Act of 1993 and the National Competitiveness Act of 1993 to take a swipe at President Clinton:

> Needless to say, to truly promote industrial competitiveness, the U.S. government must do certain things that are far more visible and far more essential: to name only two, reducing the budget deficit and improving opportunities for education and vocational training. It is in these areas that we had high hopes for President Clinton; his call for change struck us as timely and convincing…We are somewhat worried therefore, that the stalemating forces in Congress are gaining influence again.

My article "California, Here I Come" was about one of my favorite Japanese confectionery producers Ezaki Glico and the Glico caramel. When I called the Glico Sales office in California to enquire about Glico's corporate history the director sent me a large corporate book released to Japanese corporate clients to commemorate Glico's 75th anniversary. It was an exquisite chronology of the company's development through photographs of pre-war factories and employees, designs and brands. It was also a history of pre- and post-war Japan. I reluctantly returned the book several weeks later.

The founder Riichi Ezaki started his company in 1921 with one product - caramels packed in a box with a toy token to entice children. His factory was destroyed during the war and in order to resuscitate the business he decided to add the California almond to the caramels and then extended the brand with more almond creations, importing 95% of the almonds from California:

> Glico's products were not always almond oriented. A best seller, Pocky, whose name nuances innocence, were two dozen chocolate-covered sinful sticks cuddled in a red and white Pandora's Box. But one way or another, the almond gets Glico and now Almond Pocky joins the pack.

At the end of the article I included the woman officer from EID/MITI:

> Is Glico's image now ALMOND? Inside/Outside Japan dropped into the office of a director who came to JETRO New York from Tokyo last year. Her elegance and sophistication are greatly admired by her colleagues. When popped the question, her lovely countenance turned pink with pleasure and "I wish I may, I wish I might" star light sparkled in her eyes. "Glico? Why, the tokens, of course!"

I sent several copies of the paper to the California office. A week later I received a call from the director who told me that the Glico CEO who was the founder's son had read my article and was very pleased with the effort. Mr. Ezaki wanted to know what he could send me to express his appreciation. Without hesitating, I requested a copy of the book. At the end of June I received a package from Glico's corporate headquarters in Osaka. A letter of thanks from Glico's corporate planning office accompanied a complimentary copy of the book, which is among my most prized possessions. Glico's support served to forge an abiding relationship with *Inside/Outside Japan* and closer ties to Research and Planning.

The LDP Bites the Dust

In August 1993, Prime Minister Miyazawa lost the no-confidence vote in the Diet (purportedly due to his proposed tax hike), and resigned from office, which marked the end of the 38 year reign of the LDP over post-war politics. Hosokawa became the Prime Minister and formed an eight-party coalition government. His domestic policy focused on the reform of the electoral system and confronting political and corporate corruption. His international policies were the antithesis of Abe's and other right-wing politicians when he formally recognized that Japan had waged a war of aggression in the Pacific. He also made a formal apology to Korea for Japan's colonization. The charismatic prime minister cut residential and income tax to alleviate the impact of the bursting of the economic bubble on the economy but was pressured by MOF to raise the consumption tax from 3 percent to 7 percent by 1997 to compensate. However, Hosokawa could not bring consensus in the coalition. The president used his Perspective to announce Hosokawa's victory:

> Japan's Liberal Democratic Party (LDP) yielded its ruling position for the first time in 33 years, creating an unprecedented opportunity for change in Japanese politics and governance. The new Prime Minister Morihiro Hosokawa, 55, is, like President Bill Clinton, a former governor.

The coalition that produced Mr. Hosokawa is made up of Socialist and seven other parties. Some people worry about the coalition's inherent instability, noting that a patchwork group of diverse views that came together mainly to remove the LDP from power

Needless to say, not everything is rosy. Just as President Clinton has run up against oppositions in his call for sacrifice, which is essential for change, so will Prime Minister Hosokawa's government have to overcome difficulties in its pursuit of change.

There were only a few writers for the August issue and I was asked to contribute two articles. "The Candy Man Can" was about the history of another favorite Japanese confectioner, the milk company Morinaga, which also produced chocolate and caramels and which I also consumed with gusto. The Morinaga caramel was based on a recipe from a confectioner in Oakland, California where the founder worked in 1868. The Morinaga caramel was introduced slightly before Glico's and was a major competitor:

The milk caramel made its debut in 1914 at a food exhibition in Tokyo, receiving rave reviews. Like the Hershey bar, it is a survivor. The packaging throughout the years has been innovative, reflecting the trends of the times. But the original yellow box still stands as an affectionate reminder of the past and a comforting affirmation of the present.

The president requested that the second article concern a school which American Honda Education Corporation, established in 1991 as a non-profit organization for potentially unsuccessful high school students in Estes Park, Colorado. "Rocky Mountain High" touted the new school a success, comparing American Honda's corporate philanthropy with American corporate philanthropy.

Liberal MITI

MITI officials were divided between two camps; the "nationalists" and the "internationalists," who were the officials sent abroad for education and to serve as secretaries in Japanese embassies overseas. Although the "nationalists" had the reputation of being more insular and more protective of MITI's administrative territory I often could not differentiate between the two camps. It depended on the officers' career objectives and if their loyalty to their superiors, who were in the position to promote them, influenced their principles.

The president was considered an "internationalist" and very liberal for a MITI official, at least in terms of his objectives for reform of Japan's political economy, clearly set out in his Perspectives. In his September Perspective he promoted Hosokawa's two initiatives for promoting economic growth. But it was questionable whether the president was agreeable to deregulation of markets to the extent of raising Japan's foreign inward investment from 2 percent, the second lowest of the 30 OECD countries to a much higher level:

The new administration believes that to further improve the Japanese quality of life and enhance creativity, expanded business opportunities are indispensable, including greater foreign participation in Japanese markets.

My article was, as usual, based on previous work experiences and explained the purchase of Ridge Winery by Otsuka Pharmaceuticals.

The November issue on *Inside/Outside Japan* was a major attempt to convince readers that Japan was set to reduce its trade surplus and to open markets to imports. "Urgency to Import Expansion" was an announcement regarding the trade conference held in October to discuss import promotion programs to reduce Japan's huge trade surplus:

> Surpluses of such magnitude invite frequent criticism from major industrial nations, which have either a huge deficit or only a modest surplus. They have pushed up the value of the yen to a breaking point, while not bringing much sense of well-being to Japanese consumers...JETRO has set up special facilities to exhibit imported houses.

The Perspective in the same issue was informative to American readers because it revealed the struggle of Japanese corporations to restructure in order to accommodate the bursting of the bubble such as a cyclical economic downturn and the rapid appreciation of the yen. It provided some facts which probably most readers were not aware of:

> there is good reason for Japanese corporations' extreme reluctance, even under unprecedented pressure to downsize, to destroy their long-standing employment system overnight. There is strong sentiment that employer-employee relations must remain equitable and stable. The average pay discrepancy between top management and a new employee is 12 to 1 in Japan in contrast to the United States where it is frequently as great as 40 to 1 or greater.

The president's Perspective in the February 1994 issue "Hosokawa Fights for Political Reform" was an optimistic announcement of the prime minister's "major victory at the end of January. He secured it only after making bruising last minute compromises. Nonetheless, for Japan's electoral system it was a major stride forward."

My article "Sally Goes Round the Sun" regarded Kyocera Corporation's ceramic engine and the company's focus on environmentally friendly products.

Beginning to See the Light

From December 1993, the editorial staff of the *Nikkei Shimbun* ran a series of articles on the front page that delved into the bowels of Japan's bureaucracy. They were triggered by the drive for political reform and the recent scandals regarding elite bureaucrats parachuting to posts in industry after retiring from their ministries (known as *amakudari* as explained in Chapter 16). I read them faithfully.

The articles were later collated for a book that was published in June 1994. *A Creaking Giant Power* (*Kishimu Kyodai Kenryoku*) examined the relationship between the bureaucracy and the National Diet as well as the power of the bureaucracy itself. It explained why bureaucrats were more influential than politicians in Japan's governing system, and why the Japanese did not believe that politicians could plan effective legislation and that there was no real leadership in the Diet. The reasons given for their lack of confidence were: i) politicians were subservient to the whims of special interest groups; ii) there was ongoing friction between political factions; and iii) politicians did not have the expertise or experience to plan effective policies because bureaucrats had been given the power to draft laws since the Meiji period.

These articles were revolutionary in terms of bringing to the public domain the environment of the post-war ministries and the vehicles which ensured that the post-war system remained intact.

16

Revelation

The articles in the *Nikkei* and in the subsequent book supported my views concerning the government administration and how the ministries' Special Status Corporations, their subsidiaries and *amakudari* served to maintain the Japan Inc. system.

Special Status Corporations: too hot to handle

Until the book was published there was little detail about these opaque entities. *Tokushu Houjin* or Special Status Corporations were off-limits and considered politically contentious and protected by the ministries. During his interview Bill Whittaker commented on the difficulties involved in accessing information from government agencies:

> I do think that the bureaucracy controls the information, not that they manipulate the story but what they choose to reveal and when they choose to reveal it. They play it close to the vest. If they do not want it to get out, it pretty well won't get out. I think that if the bureaucracy decides that the information stays within the bureaucracy, my god, that's where it stays!

There was little information regarding the operations of Special Status Corporations which were initially established after the Second World War to aid in the reconstruction of infrastructure destroyed during the war to resuscitate Japan's industrial complex. The ministries began to establish their corporations in 1947 during the Occupation at the encouragement of SCAP, which permitted the formation of the first public corporation to support the development of the match industry. The industry's representatives, fearing tight controls over their sector, issued a petition on August 10, 1947 to SCAP in protest. The protest claimed that the corporation was being formed not to support the industry but to provide jobs for bureaucrats. SCAP rejected the petition.

Four more corporations were designated for foreign trade, eight supported domestic distribution, one served to control price adjustment and two were for economic rehabilitation. Later reflecting on its decision, SCAP became concerned that the support of the ministries' corporations could serve to resuscitate Japan's wartime system of autocratic controls.

The government had difficulty defining the exact characteristics of Special Status Corporations other than that they assisted the government in promoting national interests. Nevertheless, they can be viewed as corporations that were based on a national law, which had been approved by the National Diet. The corporations were established according to certain establishing procedures through a special law, the Law of Establishment Act, Article 4-11 subject to the Ministry of General Affairs (renamed in 2001 the Ministry of Public Management, Home Affairs, Post and Telecommunications). The law was neither civil nor corporate.

The corporations were linked to the industrial sectors under the administrative jurisdiction of each ministry. Throughout the post-war era numerous subsidiaries ("children corporations") and subsidiaries of these subsidiaries ("grandchildren corporations") were established by ministry officials. It was a simple procedure because all that was needed to establish a new one was the writing of an "establish law" in the name of the corporation and a request to an obliging Diet to sanction it.

The MOC initially established ten corporations. By 1955 there were 26. During Japan's period of rapid economic growth, ten further corporations were established annually by the MOC. By 1960, the number had increased to 52 and by 1970 there were 144.

The largest corporation was the Japan Highway Corporation (JH) which was established by the former Ministry of Construction (MOC) in 1956 to award contracts through bidding procedures to construction companies to rebuild highway networks throughout Japan. Japan has been cynically referred to as the "construction country" because of the massive construction of infrastructure and public works since the early 1960s. The MOC established the Hanshin Expressway Corporation in 1959 to construct highways to connect Osaka and Kobe and the Metropolitan Expressway Corporation in 1962.

The MOC established the Government Housing and Loan Guarantee Corporation (GHLC) as a Special Status Corporation in 1950 to provide finance for the rebuilding of homes devastated by the Second World War. Until the last decade it was the biggest home lender, financing 30 percent of all houses built since the end of the war. Retail banks were unable to compete with the GHLC because of asset liability risks. The MOC established the Urban Development Corporation (UDC) in 1955 to engage in the supply and maintenance of housing.

Another 40 corporations were added to the list by 1975. By 1980 the total was 240 and by 1990 the number had grown to 326. Special Status Corporations, their "children" and "grandchildren" corporations and branch offices served to place officials from the national ministries throughout Japan. As an example, among 322 of the corporations MOC had established, 34 percent employed fewer than five people, 54 percent employed fewer than ten people, and only 9 percent had more than a hundred staff.

Nevertheless, there was one corporation employing over 700 employees. The Japan Highway Corporation (JH) had over 60 subsidiaries with such names as New Japan Highway Patrol, Sapporo Engineer, Hokkaido Highway Service, Sendai Highway Service, Number One

Highway Service, Western Japan Highway Service, Highway Service Research, Japan High Car, and Highway Toll System.

MITI established the Electric Power Development Company (EPDC) in 1952 to provide electricity nationally. The Metal Mining Agency of Japan (MMAJ) was established in 1963 to manage the mining of non-ferrous metals. MITI established corporations to support the construction of nuclear power plants and the reprocessing of spent nuclear fuel.

Japan imports about 90 percent of its fossil fuel. MITI established the Japan National Oil Corporation (JNOC) in 1967 to oversee the energy-producing industries and managed imports and refining through federations of importers. JNOC assisted Japanese oil companies with exploration and drilling for oil. The federations connected MITI to the oil refiners, who distributed to the retailers. The domestic companies cooperated with foreign firms, such as Indonesia Oil, Mobile, Shell and Abu Dhabi Oil, usually holding the larger share of the investment.

Special Status Corporations received funds from the Fiscal Investment and Loan Program (FILP), otherwise known as "Japan's secondary budget," through FILP Agency Bonds for contracts to corporations for the construction of public works, for infrastructure, for housing, loans to small and medium size companies, mortgages and life insurance. FILP was established in 1953 as a huge financial organ operated by the public sector to channel funds to key industries through newly established institutions known as FILP institutions. FILP received its capital from the Trust Fund Bureau (TFB) funded by the deposits from the Postal Savings System (PSS) and by the premiums from the public pension scheme. FILP designated institutions were state banks such as EXIM and the Development Bank of Japan and Special Status Corporations. However, I was unable to find out how the corporations distributed the FILP funds.

Creaking Giant Power's foreword began with the contention of a former MOF administrative Vice Minister that elite bureaucrats were motivated by their belief in democracy. His conviction reflected the mentality of bureaucrats who served with him during Japan's post-war period of rapid economic growth. The book also related the views of young officials in the MOF and MITI who felt that their ministries must become more egalitarian and that the relationship between the bureaucracy and politicians should be made more transparent.

The *Nikkei Shimbun* conducted another survey at the end of October 1993 of 200 bureaucrats on their views of the governing system; 147 officers answered questions ranging from devolution, and the deregulation of markets to *amakudari*. The questions about devolution brought negative replies concerning the ability of local government civil servants to plan policies. The respondents insisted that the national ministries must always bear the responsibility of governing the regions.

As for the loosening of regulations and opening of Japan's markets, 63 percent of the respondents in their twenties wanted deregulation. Fifty percent of the respondents in their fifties were also in favor of more deregulation.

The results of a public survey conducted by the newspaper in 1993 regarding how the electorate felt about their bureaucracy were included in the book. A significant percentage of people questioned revealed their discontent with elite civil servants, reflecting their reaction to the disclosures of scandals involving the ministries. The perception of bureaucrats was: i) they had a strong elitist mentality; ii) they were irresponsible; and iii) they were clever and shrewd. Twenty-two percent answered that bureaucrats were cold and uncaring. Only 3 percent believed that bureaucrats should be entrusted to plan policy independently, and an overwhelming 70 percent agreed that bureaucrats should join forces with politicians to plan policy.

Amakudari and all that Jazz

Until I worked at JETRO I was ignorant about how the *amakudari* system actually worked in terms of providing post-retirement employment for civil servants through the ministries' corporations.

Amakudari is the reemployment of retired or incumbent civil servants in private and public sector corporations or in government-affiliated entities. The literal translation of the term is "descent from heaven," which refers to the ministries' elite career officials who parachute into upper management positions in the private sector. *Amakudari* and interpersonal networks between the civil service and the private sector can be traced back to the Meiji period (1868–1912) when the bureaucracy collaborated closely with large family-owned conglomerates to develop a feudal Japan into an industrialized country in the same league as the western powers by 1928. The collaboration intensified during the Second World War when the government started to strictly regulate the economy for the war effort. Business owners would employ bureaucrats in order to determine future government directives and to also lobby interests.

Amakudari became a formalized institutional arrangement as a part of the post-war civil service system. The system benefited officials who retired earlier than staff in the private sector, usually between the ages of 55 and 60, stepping aside for the younger officials who are intent on promotion. Although the retirement age has recently been extended to 60–65, the system remains in place.

The ministries want to provide retiring officials with a source of income that supplements their pensions, which can be lower than for employees in the private sector. Ostensibly the arrangement serves as an incentive for university graduates who would otherwise seek employment in the private sector rather than the civil service. Originally, the elite bureaucrats were the main beneficiaries of *amakudari* but, gradually, officers in middle management as well as non-career officers have come to be included in the arrangement.

The system serves the interests of the ministries and their former colleagues throughout the public and private sectors and enhances the bureaucracy's power to control the implementation of economic and industrial policies. *Amakudari* expedites ministerial guidance over the businesses that are within a ministry's administrative jurisdiction. The relationship between bureaucrats and former colleagues who have migrated to businesses in a sector under their ministry's administrative jurisdiction automatically tightens the ministry's grip on that sector.

The system has served as a mutual back-scratching mechanism because the companies which hire bureaucrats have a direct pipeline to the ministries and accept officials with the anticipation that they will be treated favorably and receive useful information and subsidies, public works contracts as well as swift approval of such applications as licenses and patents. Even though companies may be reluctant to employ officials they will acquiesce to pressure from the ministries because of concerns that they will not be able to compete with businesses who have hired officials.

The editorial staff of the *Mainichi Shimbun* entered the fray as well in 1994 with a book focusing on *amakudari* in both private and public corporations. *Kasumigaseki Syndrome* (*Kasumigaseki Shindoromu*) was a surprisingly frank account of the deterioration of values among bureaucrats in terms of their objectives in establishing corporations and research institutes for the sole purpose of providing post-retirement positions for the elite retirees.

The book's most significant contribution was the reporting of how *amakudari* and the temporary posting of elite officials in branch offices of Special Status Corporations in the prefectures (*shukko*) helped the ministries to monitor local government policies. Since the bureaucratic hierarchy places officers from the national ministries above local government officers, the positioning of ministry officials at the local government level automatically induced acquiescence by local government to ministerial guidance. The book was also critical of temporary postings because there was every likelihood that the positions would become permanent.

The *Mainichi* staff detailed how the ministries maintained control over their sectors by placing conservative retirees into management in both private and public corporations. In addition, they revealed how the ministries used their Special Status Corporations to distribute contracts to companies for public works and how *amakudari* not only tied ministries to businesses but also facilitated connections between businesses and former bureaucrats, who moved first to public corporations before moving onto the private sector.

The book included a December 1993 public survey. Although 77 percent of the subjects questioned credited bureaucrats with Japan's rapid economic growth, 41 percent of the respondents regarded them in the 1990s as being greedy for power. Thirty-one percent asserted that bureaucrats worked for the benefit of their ministries, but only 18 percent felt that they worked for the good of their industrial sectors. A mere 3 percent felt that bureaucrats were hard-working, and only 3 percent considered bureaucrats to be honest and sincere.

Of the people surveyed, 60 percent wanted *amakudari* abolished while only 12 percent wanted the system maintained; 38 percent wanted the system abolished for political office and 43 percent of the people polled wanted the companies that hired bureaucrats to be subjected to strict regulations.

Variations of *Amakudari*

The National Public Service Law stipulates that bureaucrats cannot, for a period of two years, legally move directly to positions in private companies attached to the sectors their ministries regulate. However, they can move immediately to their ministries' corporations, industrial associations or research institutes supported by their ministries or by the other ministries where they linger for two years with pay before going on to the private sector. Most officials will wait out the two-year period of grace in public corporations and then slip into higher management positions in private companies although some officials may elect to remain if there are no offers from the private sector.

The variations of amakudari have evolved over a 50-year period and were regarded as the norm and not as corrupt practice by ministry officials. The system has continued for many years and, although the Japanese do not condone the system, in general they are inured to it. The ministries can cleverly manipulate the system to provide jobs for their staff in their public entities:

1. Bureaucrats can be sent by their ministries to work in their ministries' entities while they are still engaged by their ministries (and drawing salary). This practice is known as "on loan to another company" (*shukko*). Although the officials are still connected to their ministries they are identified as officers of the organizations where they have been transferred. And while the posts are considered to be temporary, they can develop into permanent positions. Essentially, *shukko* can be the catalyst for amakudari in the public corporations.
2. The ministries are not required to apply to the National Personnel Authority (NPA) in order to "loan" an official to an organization. Officials who are "on loan" to an organization can then migrate to the private sector without waiting out the two-year period of grace.
3. Bureaucrats can remain attached in some way to their ministries' public entities through their subsidiaries (as advisors or members of boards) while working for private businesses, receiving salaries simultaneously from both public and private sectors without waiting out the two-year period of grace.
4. The ministries operate research institutes where officials are "loaned" for a two-year period of grace before migrating to the private sector.
5. Positions may be given to elite bureaucrats who have not reached retirement age, but are considered to be nearing the end of their careers. The "gift" is actually a signal to officials that they will not be promoted much higher in their ministries, but that their loyalty is appreciated.

The American part-time assistant in the JETRO management section confirmed this when she told me that the presidents were considered figureheads and that MITI offered the posts at JETRO as "gifts."

The *Nikkei Shimbun* also conducted a survey in 1994 of 1,780 employees in seven Special Status Corporations that had been established by the MOC. The employees were questioned about the *amakudari* of staff members, who comprised 80 percent of the staff. The seven percent of the employees who answered that *amakudari* was necessary were in the minority; 38 percent felt that the system was a bad influence and should be abolished; 29 percent felt that nothing much could be done about the situation because of the recession; 33 percent claimed that the former bureaucrats were useless; and 50 percent answered that the retired officials were helpful to some extent. Again, a minority of 3 percent maintained that the former officers performed their duties well.

Nice Work if You Can Get It

MITI officials who are posted abroad at JETRO overseas offices promote Japan's economic and trade policies to governments, businesses, media and educators. The officials lobby governments on behalf of Japan's government international policies such as security and concerns regarding East Asia. They also promote engagement with Japanese businesses, search for patents considered applicable to Japanese business interests and for small businesses with technologies which are in need of capital investment for R&D. Most countries post commercial attachés from the ministries of commerce and industry in embassies and consulates. However, even though they serve as commercial attachés, MITI officials' interfacing duties give them the semblance of foreign attachés. JETRO overseas offices also dispense to the public both commercial and cultural information, some of it duplicating the information released by the MOFA.

When officers from the ministries' corporations were pressuring the Kyoto Prefecture representative to terminate my participation in the paper the MITI officer who searched for US patents, appalled by their behavior, confided that, although he himself worked hard, most of the officers at JETRO New York were "on sabbatical," implying that they were enjoying two to three years of R&R with their families.

The wife who accompanied her husband, a MITI official, to New York during his secondment told me that New York was considered the "Golden Apple" for a secondment. They could attend opera, Broadway shows and classical music performances at Carnegie Hall and Lincoln Center, which were located near JETRO's office. The tickets were far less expensive than in Japan and season tickets were purchased in advanced. I shared a box seat at Carnegie Hall with a MITI officer. The ticket per performance was $25.

The posting of representatives overseas in the ministries' public corporations like JETRO may not be based entirely on merit. Civil servants from both prefecture governments and the national ministries, who have displayed loyalty through their work and to their superiors, are sent abroad. Civil servants may be sent because a family member is an elite official in government or whose father-in-law is an elite ministry official. But officers may also be chosen for duty abroad because their behavior is considered outside the norm and disruptive on the workplace. The officers could be suffering from a mental disorder, or, in some cases, alcoholism, and posting them overseas serves to conveniently remove them from their colleagues.

In general, the officers' workload was far less strenuous compared to their responsibilities in Japan and they enjoyed a two- to three-year hiatus from the pressures of the home office where there is no remuneration for overtime. For the majority of the officials, a posting in the United States was an opportunity afforded to a minority of Japanese civil servants and supported by tax revenue. Similar to foreign corporate executives who are sent abroad by their firms and officials from foreign government agencies, the bureaucrats who were married were relocated with their families and they enjoyed a standard of living they would never experience in Japan. Homes can be spacious, often with gardens, a phenomenon in Japan where land is at a premium, especially in the metropolitan areas. The officers also received allowances for their children's educational needs.

Ironically, despite their concerns about safety in the United States, and, in some cases, ambiguous attitudes regarding US-Japan relations and American mores, they recognized that America offered a physically easier and mentally calmer lifestyle than the Japanese civil service. Some of the other officers, including JETRO staff, and representatives from prefecture governments coveted Green Cards and used their stay at JETRO USA offices to apply for work permits.

The MITI director of EID/MITI wanted to return to MITI and forge his career internally, which was a tough route to the top. He told me:

> There are many people in this office who say that they do not want to return to Japan. I am very glad to go. I think that I will enjoy Japan again. I know the good points of Japan. Of course, I could live here for a long time. Staying at JETRO for business is a unique experience for many reasons, including income. People can enjoy a high standard of lifestyle so maybe this is the reason they don't want to go back to Japan.

However, the majority of elite MITI officers seemed satisfied with their status, knowing that upon their return to their ministries they would receive a promotion and after their retirement they would migrate to a MITI corporation and then to the private sector. The officer stated the general view of bureaucrats regarding the post-retirement system:

> The Japanese bureaucratic system is unique. Our management system is different from the typical corporate management system. We retire earlier. Official X entered MITI in 1965 so he has retired. He worked 25 years in MITI. Of course, he got a new job in another organization [a public entity]. I have already worked for 15 years and I am sure that I'll work for ten years at least, but no more than 15 years.

The interviews in the *Nikkei Shimbun* book with politicians and bureaucrats illustrated the ministries' struggle to maintain power. Susumu Takahashi, a former administrative Vice Minister in the Ministry of Construction (MOC), was interviewed about his views on *amakudari*. Takahashi admitted that there was an alliance between politicians and the MOC and that there was indeed a relationship between the ministries and industry. However, he emphasized that denying bureaucrats post-retirement positions in industry was unrealistic because bureaucrats had to retire earlier than corporate executives and they needed supplementary income. He professed that elite officials, who were commonly referred in the press as "Old Boys" or "OBs," received benefits while they were working in post-retirement positions. Takahashi, who became the president of the Government Housing Loan Corporation (GHLC), a MOC Special Status Corporation, in 1990 after he retired from the MOC, claimed that the number of positions in Special Status Corporations was limited. However, he omitted to mention the number of positions available in the subsidiaries of Special Status Corporations or in other institutions operated by the ministries.

For the Record

If I was an official in Japan's national ministries where I would be required to work until midnight without overtime pay and where secretarial staff is usually available to only the officials holding high-level posts, I would embrace a transfer to a Special Status Corporation overseas that would allow me to escape to a more relaxed environment with my family. I would also welcome an upper management job in one of my ministry's corporations and subsequently a job in the private sector for additional income. The Kyoto Prefecture officer remarked: "The bureaucracy controls and operates Japan. I haven't thought much about the politicians but the bureaucracy controls everything and makes sure that things go smoothly."

Politicians Bash the Bureaucrats: the Naitoh Masahisa Affair

After the revelations of collusion between ministry officials and the construction industry, the bureaucracy became fair game for Japanese journalists and for politicians who were trying to wrest power from the bureaucracy.

Towards the end of March the secretary for the two MITI directors in Industrial Research presented me with a hand-written manuscript in Japanese which she had been asked to translate into English. She asked me to translate it quickly because she was too busy with other work. It was a speech to be given in early April at Georgetown University. I was also busy but took the script promising to return it to her soon.

The speech reflected on the motivations of ministry officials who worked during Japan's rapid economic growth period and who seemed inspired by their roles as the administrators of Japan's economic rebirth. The author lamented the changes in attitudes of current bureaucrats, who, he felt, had become inward and "turf-conscious," working to protect their ministry's territory rather than making policy to deregulate markets.

The address explained to the audience that the Japanese people, who had relied for centuries on either an emperor or a military to govern them, did not want to take the initiative to plan their own destiny but preferred to entrust responsibility to a bureaucracy. This submission to bureaucratic rule gave the ministries much power which was further enhanced by the close contact between bureaucrats and businessmen, who feared retribution if they did not comply with guidance. It was a significant speech and I made a copy for future reference.

While I was tussling with the script, a well-dressed Japanese gentleman in his fifties strolled through the library and peered at me. The following day he passed through again. The man seemed to know MITI officials but there was no indication of who he was. If it had not been for a chance encounter with a resident in my apartment building I would never have guessed that the gentleman was Naitoh Masahisa, a senior MITI official who, under pressure, had resigned rather than be dismissed from MITI.

One morning when I got on the elevator in my apartment building the other passenger was a Japanese gentleman in his mid-fifties. I happened to be carrying a Japanese newspaper and he struck up a conversation, identifying himself as the president of the North American headquarters of a Japanese trading company. When I told him where I worked he offered to give me back issues of the monthly magazine *Sentaku* ("Choice") which is a political economic magazine with articles reporting the latest domestic and international news and which most Japanese corporations subscribed to. A few days later he left the December, January and the February issues of the magazine with the concierge.

When I perused the February issue I recognized the man in a photograph as the man strolling around JETRO New York. He was Naitoh Masahisa. The dismissal had occurred in December and rocked the halls of MITI. It was only the second time in the history of the ministry that a high-ranking official was dismissed (the first was in 1952). Naitoh's loyal subordinates were vehemently opposed to Naitoh's resignation.

The magazine printed a four-page spread with photographs of Naitoh and Hiroshi Kumagai who was a career officer in MITI and who was serving as director-general of the Small and Medium Sized Enterprise Agency when he left in 1976 to run for political office on the LDP ticket. He won a seat in the Upper House of the Diet in 1977 and then took a seat in the Lower House in 1983. In 1991 he served for one year as the Parliamentary Vice Minister of the Economic Planning Agency before assuming several high-ranking positions in the LDP. He was one of the founders of the New Japan Party with Hosokawa in 1992 and after serving as MITI Minister in Prime Minister Hosokawa's cabinet he served as Minister of State in 1994.

Kumagai's and Ozawa's political objectives were similar, especially in regards to wresting regulatory powers from ministry officials and bringing more power to the executive office. Naitoh's dismissal was a classic example of efforts by politicians to poke holes in the bureaucracy by further inflaming public opinion against elite ministerial guidance. Although Kumagai was the front-man in instigating the incident, Ozawa was rumored to be involved as well.

When Kumagai was serving as MITI Minister in Hosokawa's cabinet he demanded the resignation of Naitoh who was said to be in line for the post of MITI International Administrative Vice Minister. Ostensibly, Kumagai's reason for demanding the resignation was that Naitoh had arranged a promotion in MITI for the son of his close friend and patron, Yuji Tanahashi, MITI International Vice Minister. The son, Yasufumi, had entered MITI in 1987. The promotion was intended to enhance his image, thus improving his chances of winning a seat in the Diet when he entered the election as an LDP candidate of Gifu Prefecture, a seat that his grandfather, a former governor of Gifu, had occupied for many years. Despite his newly polished image, Yasufumi lost the election.

Kumagai, who reportedly wanted to stop favoritism in the ministries, accused Naitoh, a civil servant, of failing to abide by the principle of non-partisan politics but realistically the affair was related to the power struggle between factions within MITI and between special interest groups in the LDP and the New Japan Party. There was also the possibility that Kumagai's ulterior motives were personal because during his time in MITI his relationship with Naitoh was said to be fractious.

Hideaki Kumano, the Administrative Vice Minister and the head of MITI, was responsible for implementing the dismissal. Although he was against Naitoh's resignation, in order to maintain calm among MITI officials, he pleaded with Naitoh to resign quietly. Initially Naitoh refused, calling the stand-off a test of the independence of the bureaucracy. However, on 23 December he resigned without apology at a news conference, telling reporters that he had simply followed the long-established custom of giving titles to ministry officials who ran for office. Although Naitoh's admission was not welcomed among the general public, who were questioning the integrity of ministry officials, it also illustrated that many ministry officials opted for political careers (as did Kumagai in 1976) and that the ties between bureaucrats and politicians could be very close.

Naitoh was well connected in the United States because he had been posted as a director of the Industrial Research Division at JETRO New York in the mid-1980s while he was negotiating with the USTR on behalf of the Japanese semiconductor industry.

When Naitoh formally resigned on April 1, 1994 he moved to Georgetown University as the Marks & Murase professor in the Asia Law and Policy Institute (ALPS) program. On April 7, 1994, Naitoh gave the speech at the Georgetown University Law Center. Marks & Murase was a law firm whose clients included Japanese businesses and government agencies.

A Creaking Giant Power carried an interview with Naitoh before his dismissal. When he asserted that bureaucrats operated independently of politicians he was asked if he thought that bureaucrats could work together with politicians to forge policies. Naitoh felt that it might prove feasible if politicians could plan strategies and the bureaucrats did the legwork, implying that administrators knew more about managing industry and economy than did politicians. He expressed disappointment that, although bureaucrats were the servants of their country, they had become isolated from society and had forgotten their mission.

Naitoh claimed that the multitude of rules and regulations did not act to effectively support MITI's control of industrial policy but, rather, the trust between bureaucrats and private businesses facilitated the implementation of policy.

Despite his sincere rhetoric, Naitoh did not mention the fact that the ministries had extended power over the political economy through their Special Status Corporations and the *amakudari* system which served MITI and the other ministries to persuade businesses to accommodate their policies. Indeed, Naitoh participated in this very system. Naitoh's post-MITI career, although more prolific, represents the post-retirement careers of ministry officials, who have found upper management and directorships in corporations linked to their ministries' administrative jurisdiction. The following June, Naitoh was reinstated by MITI as a consultant before migrating to positions on the boards of various Japanese corporations.

Kumano, who had been caught in the middle of the dispute, submitted his resignation from MITI in June to take responsibility for the upheaval in the ministry. The director of the EID/MITI division remarked that Kumano's resignation was unnecessary and unfortunate. Upon his retirement Kumano moved to MITI's Industrial Policy Research Institution (IPRI) where, in 1993, Yuji Tanahasi had also migrated upon his retirement.

The book also carried an interview with Kumano. He vigorously objected to the interviewer's suggestion that MITI was the "Number Two Ministry of Finance" (*Dai-niji Okurasho*) which implied that MITI was taking over MOF's territory by executing duties that usually fell within MOF's remit.

The US-Japan trade negotiations were becoming the hot topic in both the American and Japanese press. 1994 was going to be a bumpy year for US-Japan relations and for Japanese politics.

Although Japan was in political turmoil and although the economy was in difficulty, I knew that the *amakudari* system would be difficult to crack and that there was no political process in place to implement change. I disagreed with the majority of the international business community who naively assumed that the government together with the private sector would sort out Japan's economic woes.

17

Fanning the Friction

Japan bashing/America bashing

The term "Japan bashing" was credited to Robert Angel in the 1980s while he was the president of the Japan Economic Institute in America, a think-tank in Washington, DC and funded by the MOFA. The term was coined to counteract anti-Japanese sentiment in the US regarding Japan's trade surplus with the US and the USTR's demands to Japan to commit to numerical quotas on its exports to the US.

The three Japanese automobile manufacturers (Honda, Toyota and Nissan) agreed in 1981 to limit the number of cars exported to the US but by 1985, they had opened production facilities in the southern United States to produce larger models where workers were not members of labor unions. As the American auto industry was losing market share to Japanese car imports, American auto workers, fearful of losing jobs, protested by physically bashing Japanese cars with sledge hammers and burning Japanese flags, despite the fact that the cars parked in the staff parking lots of US car manufacturers were packed with Toyotas and Hondas.

When he was interviewed the NHK correspondent maintained that, although there had been good coverage by America media on Japan, there had also been articles by American commentators who appeared to have no fundamental knowledge of Japanese culture. Exaggerating one tiny aspect, they insisted that it represented Japan and connected these issues to trade friction.

Bill Whittaker agreed with me: "I don't think that we know beans about how Japan works or what's going on with Japanese politics. Americans are grossly ignorant about that incredibly important country."

The United States Trade Representative: who is the fairest of them all?

Japanese ministry officials grumbled that due to the end of the Cold War, the US no longer considered Japan vital in terms of a military alliance in the Pacific and that the USTR was taking a much tougher stance at trade negotiations by demanding numerical quotas. Officials also complained that one of the ways that the US was reducing the trade deficit was by selling older models of military aircraft to Japan for its self-defence forces, but not the state-of-the art models to limit technology transfer.

In 1993 the USTR was pressuring Japan again to open up markets to more processed foods, home electronics, automobiles and car parts, and to the finance, insurance and pharmaceutical industries. The automobile and car industries that were well represented by powerful lobby groups and labor unions were relentlessly pursuing the members in Congress whose constituents were businesses engaged in these industries. Trade deals seemed to relate to political need rather than to reducing America's trade deficit.

I received a call one afternoon in the Reference Library from a reporter at *Business Week* who was covering the trade talks. He began the conversation with the remark that the Japanese had a penchant for American pop culture, spending millions of dollars on movies, MacDonald hamburgers and Coco Cola. I agreed, emphasizing that there were many other American products which Japanese consumers also purchased. Suddenly, the reporter's voice darkened, "But why don't YOU people import OUR automobiles?"

The fact that the reporter identified me as a Japanese momentarily struck me as odd. I replied "That's because YOUR cars are TOO BIG for our narrow streets and the steering wheels are on the WRONG SIDE!"

Although Japan's inward investment was the second lowest among the OECD countries, importing American cars that did not suit the Japan market was not a logical solution to lowering the trade deficit.

The NHK correspondent admitted that mass media reported news in a way that it thought the public wanted to hear, putting the emphasis on trade friction rather than on the efforts by both sides to reach a compromise. He repeated the same claims made by Japanese government officials that Japan was not as important to the United States as the United States was to Japan. He was amazed at the paucity of information Americans received about Japan, including staff in President Clinton's administration, and was critical of the fact that there were no representatives in the USTR who spoke Japanese or understood Japanese culture and psychology. The correspondent expressed concerns that since Clinton regarded China as America's future market pro-Japan representatives would be absent at the negotiation table.

Bill Whitaker had a similar view. He admitted that media hype sold papers and raised ratings but because television news reported the news as it was happening the reports could be inaccurate and, at times, false. But he also thought that there was a real danger of overemphasizing the role the press played in fanning the friction between the two societies and that the people themselves should assume responsibility for the state of affairs.

The president of the North American corporate headquarters of a Japanese trading company put it in a realistic context:

> I hate mass media! The Japanese press does not transmit correct information
> about the US to Japanese. For example, Prime Minister Hosokawa came here

a few months ago and stayed at the Waldorf Astoria. President Clinton also stayed there. There was very tight security. The heavy police protection was for Clinton, not for Hosokawa. This is not done to such an extent in Japan. The Japanese press reported that the police blocking off the street didn't give Hosokawa adequate security like it did to Clinton. The newspapers from other countries in attendance didn't complain. I wasn't there, but wherever President Clinton goes, security is always tight and very disruptive. This unimportant news became fodder for criticism.

However, things that happen in Japan are very important. Everyone knew that Mr. Kanazawa [Kanazawa was a top official in the MOC] accepted large bribes from the construction industry but no one wrote about it! Everyone writes about the Waldorf Astoria and Clinton! However, the Washington Post did write about the scandal.

I don't feel that Japan and the US are equal. The interest and concerns that the Japanese have for Japan are completely different. Japan is not important to the United States. It's all right that ABC doesn't report news about Japan. But for Japan, America's very big. Trade with America is tremendous because the population in the US is tremendous and America takes huge amounts of imports. America's need for news about Japan is much less than Japan's need for news about the US.

In both countries inaccuracies in reporting are made on various economic facts. There is the excuse that reporters want to report on things as fast as possible and, therefore, cannot get the complete facts. Because of this, I don't like to read the reports. I have not seen much news on Japanese culture here. Even though Japan is the US's leading trading partner, Japanese companies produce cars and electronics here. If America's markets disappear, Japan could not exist. It would be a pitiful state. It would be ludicrous to be angry about the degree of interest Japan has for the United States and the degree of interest that the US has for Japan!

Don't Bash Us Bureaucrats!

The Japanese resented being America's whipping boy because they felt that America's economic problems were of its own making and were unrelated to Japan's economic rise and clout in international markets. An interview in January 1994 with a MITI ministry official illustrates how, not only the Japanese but, also, people in many countries consider Americans and the United States. It also reveals Japan's defensive stance regarding the US-Japan relationship.

Wherever one goes in the world, English is understood and, therefore, Americans do not have the desire to learn about other foreign countries. That's because America's bounty, America's words and America's system supports the world. It's just the way things are, I guess. America is vast, the great supporter, America, the great provider, America. We are always aware of its presence. I think that the recognition of whatever relationship Japan has with the United States is within this context.

Without referring to Japan's protectionist policies, the same official related his government's stance at the time of the negotiations:

> The latest pronouncement of the US Trade Representative is that the reason for the continuing huge trade surplus is because of Japan's position as a nation. This problem, really in terms of numbers [quotas], clearly must be solved. But if you turn things around and look at it from Japan's perspective, the United States had a huge trade surplus up until 30 years ago. Americans worked very hard and made excellent products. The trade surplus was natural. If the Japanese wanted a trade surplus, they had to develop excellent products. When comparing how open the door is to Japanese products and American markets, America's markets are far more open than Japan's. Compared to the present time, there are far more American products in Japan than before because American products are excellent. When Americans during negotiations negotiate with the contention that Japan is devious, from our point of view, it is Puritanism. Big decisions based on one standard!

A ministry official also interviewed in January was concerned that because of the trade friction the United States would abandon Japan in favor of China due to China's economic expansion, potential vast markets and its growing influence in global markets:

> Concerning America's request to Japan about the trade imbalance, America has so much it only has to think of itself. The US is now looking at China instead of Japan because it's easier to enter the market. The Chinese language has more similarities to English than Japanese. Chinese resembles English in grammar and communication is easier between Chinese and Americans. Chinese resemble English because there are many phrases and sayings that are common in both languages. In Japanese, special terms must be invented in order to communicate. Also, Chinese and American preferences are more similar than Japanese and American preferences.

Does Every Little Bit Help?

My article for the April 1994 issue of paper "Jamaica Jives in Japan" concerned a press conference held at JETRO on 26 January sponsored by the New York State Department of Economic Development (NYSDED), the National Minority Business Council and JETRO to announce the formal presentation of New York State's Global Export Market Service (GEMS) grants to ten members of the council. The grants for the members were aimed to help the small businesses engaged in the production of apparel, accessories and tableware production export to Japan. The event was orchestrated by JETRO to promote JETRO as Japan's primary promoter of foreign small business exports to Japanese markets.

The GEMS companies had already exhibited their products at the JETRO Business Support Center in Tokyo the previous October. Hiranobu Sekiguchi, the owner of a boutique in a popular, youth-oriented section of Tokyo, visited the center one day, liked what he saw and promised to place an order in January when he would be in New York. He also attended the news conference at JETRO New York, courtesy of JETRO who covered his travel expenses.

The president who hosted the event spoke briefly about the JETRO Senior Trade advisors who were posted at 19 state governments "in order to help small firms export to Japan by, for example, introducing their products in JETRO's *Import Frontier*."

The president also talked about the Business Support Center in Tokyo and its role in encouraging companies to explore Japanese markets. He told his audience: "The huge trade imbalance between the United States is real, but, it is these small but practical steps that helps reduce the U.S. trade deficit."

Among the small businesses receiving grants the craft ware company Monoco Design was chosen for a gallery exhibition in Kobe:

> Inside/Outside Japan was enraptured with the street-scene ceramics of the craft ware company Monoco Design, and especially with the owner, Noel Copeland, a Jamaican with dreadlocks, who had been spotted earlier that afternoon. Reggae is the current rage in Japan and one look told us that Tokyo would definitely take to his Rastafarian motif plates, mugs and tea pots. Mr. Sekiguchi had already reserved eight pieces for his shop. Over a breakfast of French toast the following day, Noel graciously gave us a little low-down on a life which originally included no plans of going to Japan. "I have been told that the quality of what I have to offer is most important and my race is secondary. The Japanese love the music and they love the looks so I'm expecting them to be curious about me as a person, a Rasta man with dreadlocks."

According to the artist upon his return to New York, the exhibition was well attended and he managed to sell some of his work. However, USTR representatives may have questioned whether a few pieces of pottery exported to Japan could be considered a step to reduce the US trade deficit.

Getting Hotter

The president took a more aggressive stance in his Special Supplement for the March 1994 issue of *Inside/Outside Japan. For a Better U.S.–Japanese Relationship* protested the Clinton administration negotiation tactics at the meeting between Clinton and Hosokawa in February when Hosokawa refused to agree to set numerical targets on certain Japanese imports. While defending Japan's position in the US–Japan trade talks, he was also defending his fellow bureaucrats and protecting MITI's territory. From the president's point of view, the meeting a month earlier between President Clinton and Prime Minister Hosokawa who mutually agreed to postpone decisions about numerical quotas amounted to a "breakdown" in negotiations.

His diatribe is currently relevant to: i) the fundamental reasons for Japan's current political economic conditions; ii) Japan's continuing reluctance to open markets to foreign competition and inward investment; and iii) the ministries' use of their corporations to promote their interests.

The president attacked two well-known journalists who pointed to Japan's bureaucrats for inhibiting social and economic change in Japan:

> Rather than succumb to yet another agreement to paper over the obvious differences, Mr. Hosokawa told Mr. Clinton that he could not and would not agree to something Japan was bound to find impossible to carry out, both philosophically and practically. In this, Messrs. Karel van Wolferen and R. Taggart Murphy completely missed the point when they asserted, in their joint OP-ED article in the New York Times (20 February) that it was the bureaucrats who stopped Mr. Hosokawa from going along with specified trade targets

The president also condemned the USTR's attitude toward Japan:

Evidently, American negotiators have come to believe in two things. One is that "Japan is the odd man out." In this view, the stubborn persistence of the trade imbalance between Japan and the United States derives directly from the nature of the Japanese market that is radically different from other industrialized countries. The other is that Japan's market liberalization cannot be achieved because of Japan's "entrenched bureaucracies" and wayward corporate practices.

The president bemoaned the United States' tendency to impose sanctions on countries "whenever it fails to achieve its own goals." He requested more understanding about Japan's position in trade relations and the role of Japan's bureaucracy which he felt was maligned in the American press and by the USTR. The president avoided addressing the reasons for Japan's protected markets and trade surplus, but offered:

In the decades since Japan's post-war rapid economic growth period Japan has had a trade surplus. This is mainly the result of the stupendous efforts of its manufacturing sector to improve itself and excel – although there have been macroeconomic factors such as the high savings rates that enabled Japanese industry to maintain high investment levels

The president stated the obvious:

Today, U.S. industry has regained competitiveness through restructuring and bold innovations, whereas Japanese industry has stumbled badly – in part as a result of what American industrialists call "overinvestment."

No one knows as yet whether this reversal of fortune is extensive enough to reverse the trade-balance positions of the United States and Japan. But with the compounding factor of the high yen continuing and Japanese corporations continuing to invest overseas, the trend is evidently toward a reduced imbalance. It certainly will be helped by U.S. industry's seriousness in exporting to Japan – as evident, for example, in the production of compact cars with the right-side steering wheel.

But if there was a honeymoon period between business people and bureaucrats, it was becoming a thing of the past by the early 80s…I think that it is a mistake to say, as some Americans do, that the bureaucrats are the roadblock to any social and economic change in Japan…I must emphasize that Japan has dismantled a range of barriers against imports.

The president promised:

But it is necessary to keep making these efforts, for Japan must reduce its persistent and large trade surplus. Keenly aware of this, the Japanese government is pursuing important programs: further deregulation, an aggressive implementation of antitrust statutes, large-scale public investment to enrich people's lives and promotion of imports and investment from abroad.

He concluded the article by going for the jugular:

In all these efforts, change must come from within. Short-sighted and self-serving pressure from the United States can be counterproductive. This is because it only breeds mistrust and discontent on the side that gives pressure and alienation and resentment on the side that is [being] pressured.

To ensure that JETRO's role as the government-funded promoter of inward investment and imports was duly publicized the president declared:

> JETRO has various arrangements for promoting the importation of U.S. products into Japan. To mention only two, the trade agency at present maintains a total of nineteen senior trade advisors throughout the United States who identify products with potential in Japanese markets and guide their producers every step of the way. Not long ago, it opened a Business Support Center in Tokyo which provides free space and business equipment to business people who wish to explore Japanese markets. It plans to open another such center soon.

The Executive Director of Research and Planning also took offense in a letter to the editor of the *New York Times* a week after the van Wolferen article was published:

> The "failure" of the latest round of United States–Japanese trade talks shows the simplistic and self-centered approach the United States often takes toward its "most important" international trading partner; unrealistic demands such as numerical targets, failure to obtain agreement or fulfilment, followed by threats to retaliate or a retaliatory action.

The director accused the United States of not understanding:

> the complexity of economic mechanisms and the workings of Japanese society… Take one administration official's pronouncement to the effect that Japanese bureaucracy is now the "enemy of the United States." It is naïve to assume, as the Clinton Administration apparently does, that by reshaping Japan's bureaucracy to its own liking, the United States can eliminate its deficit with Japan.

I asked him to autograph the article!

My contribution to the paper was based on my experiences in Mishima. "Row, Row, Row Your Boat" concerned Konosuke Matsushita's early years and his devotion to Zen Buddhist practice which he promoted to his employees.

Hosokawa Out!

In the April *Inside/Outside Japan* the president's Perspective "Mr. Hosokawa's Sudden Resignation" dealt with Prime Minister Hosokawa's resignation after only eight months in office which the president explained "was to take responsibility for the irregularities allegedly found in financial transactions that he had long entrusted to his personal aide." The president praised Hosokawa for his efforts to reform the political system and to deregulate Japanese markets.

Hosokawa had been implicated in the Sagawa Kyubin scandal, which had ended Prime Minister Takeshita's chief fundraiser's political career. Shin Kanemaru, the LDP major-domo, was enveloped in a series of corruption scandals. In October 1992, he publicly admitted that he had received $4.1 million in illegal contributions from Sagawa Kyubin, a trucking company that had relations with construction companies and the underworld. However, he avoided public questioning through behind-the-scenes politicking and escaped prosecution with a small fine.

Kanemaru, who was 78, was arrested with his secretary and indicted for tax evasion in March 1993. When public prosecutors raided Kanemaru's residence they discovered in his safe-deposit box gold bars and $50 million in cash and securities. Public outcry and the continuing media attention on the collusion scandals involving politicians, bureaucrats and big business forced Kanemaru to relinquish his seat and tender his resignation as LDP Vice President. A prison sentence was suspended because of his age. The governor of Niigata Prefecture also resigned from office amid allegations that he received $2.4 million in unreported campaign contributions from Sagawa Kyubin.

Hosokawa, who had received a loan from Sagawa Kyubin for ¥100 million yen, claimed that he had repaid the loan but LDP members did not believe him. Furthermore, there were problems within Hosokawa's administration, which had been weakened by political infighting among factions

Ichiro Ozawa, like Hosokawa, aggressively pushed for more autonomy for local authorities for the reform of the electoral system that would encourage fairer representation in the Lower House and result in a true two-party system which was achieved when the reform bill was passed during Hosokawa's administration. In order to preserve the Hosokawa coalition government, Tsutomu Hata, who had served as deputy prime minister, stepped in as Prime Minister.

Ozawa represented Japan's mainstream ultra-conservative political environment during Japan's post-war period that evolved through interpersonal connections between politicians and businesses to become a tangled web of vested interests, collusion and corrupt practices. In October 1992 Ozawa was also implicated in the Sagawa Kyubin scandal.

Although ministry officials were not concerned that Ozawa would be a serious threat to the ultra-conservative LDP, he was very involved in shaking up the political status quo and busting the bureaucracy. On the other hand, he was not a team player. Known as the "shadow shogun" he was regarded as a key political strategist, back-room deal-maker and a fundraiser in the same mode as Prime Minister Kakuei Tanaka (1972–74), his mentor. Tanaka taught Ozawa the importance of establishing strong relationships with smaller firms that were trying to compete with big established companies for a share of tight markets. He also taught Ozawa that a close relationship with the construction industry was essential to a politician's purse.

A right-wing reformer, Ozawa transferred to the Takeshita–Kanemaru faction after Tanaka left office in 1974. As was also the case for the Tanaka faction, construction companies who wanted to expand their operations (e.g. contracts for public works projects) contributed the major share of political contributions to the Kanemaru–Takeshita faction. Ozawa learned how to garner the support from local electorates and grassroots politics.

Ozawa, who had been implicated in the Recruit scandal in 1988 for his involvement in insider trading sanctions, was interrogated in October 1992 when Kanemaru was arrested over the Sagawa Kyubin affair. He was questioned about escorting Kanemaru to meetings with Sagawa management. His retort to prosecutors was that he was merely going along to act as barman. In December 1992 when he was still an LDP member Ozawa was implicated in a money scandal which involved Kajima Construction, one of the big six general contracting companies that had been charged with bribing numerous politicians in order to win contracts. Ozawa called a press conference to deny reports by the *Asahi Shimbun* that the contributions were illegal.

A Farewell Message

The president's Perspective in the May issue of *Inside/Outside Japan* mourned the loss of Japanese values from the Meiji Period, "encountering the West and deciding on rapid modernization and, again, in the mid-20th century."

Although the president considered that there was no longer a need to catch up with the West and that the Japanese would regain their "age-old sensibility." I recognized that the younger generation could not relate to Japan's past "sensibility."

My article "I Know Where I'm Going" was about Kazuo Inamori the founder of Kyocera Corporation, one of Japan's most sophisticated companies. Inamori was the last of the great industrialists and, like Matsushita, was a devout Zen Buddhist. He also travelled internationally to present his corporate creed, which was similar to Matsushita's. The vice president of Kyocera America Corporation in San Diego visited me at JETRO on his way to New York to prepare for Inamori's arrival. He confided that Inamori enjoyed gambling and would stop over in Las Vegas on his way to the East Coast and drop into Donald Trumps' casino in Atlantic City.

In June, the president passed the gauntlet to his successor, a MITI official who had come from San Francisco where he had served as the president of JETRO San Francisco. During that time he secured Green Cards for himself, his wife, and his daughter, allowing them to stay in the US and thus, his transfer to JETRO New York.

The title of the president's farewell Perspective "America, America" was taken from the movie by the American film director Elia Kazan. The President exited JETRO on the upbeat, lauding the US system of government, the interaction between academia "which includes think tanks and community volunteerism," and:

> Above all, I have been moved by what must be a cliché about the United States: its ability to create a milieu where people from different backgrounds can mingle with equality – regardless of race, color, religion, or national origin. This fundamental characteristic translates into the American people's spontaneous goodwill, tolerance for diversity, and the profound sense of responsibility to the world.

By sheer coincidence, my article "Struggles and Success" regarded a documentary about African Americans' experiences in Japan. *Struggles and Success* was an 85 minute documentary concerning the positive experiences of African Americans who had lived in Japan from three to 25 years and who had achieved successful careers equal to the Japanese. The documentary was partly finance by the Japan Foundation, a MOFA corporation. The film won awards and was shown twice on NHK.

I interviewed the African American director who gave a glowing account of his time in Japan making the documentary. He previously had gone to Japan for six months in 1991 as an Artist Fellow funded by the Japan-United States Friendship Commission and the Japanese Agency for Cultural Affairs to observe the work of the director of a popular television program. Although blacks are less popular than Koreans or Chinese in Japan, the article was written to support the objectives of *Inside/Outside Japan*.

> In 1986, the then Prime Minister Yasujiro Nakasone made the unfortunate pronouncement that black and Hispanics were valuing education downward. In 1988, Michio Watanabe, a ranking official of the Liberal Democratic Party, stated that blacks spend more money on credit cards and then declare bankruptcy because they don't care … Any African-American who had not been to Japan would have naturally assumed that the Japanese were racist and that blacks who visited the Land of the Rising Sun will be greeted with disappointment and perhaps danger.

I happened to be writing the piece on a Friday in early April. I was still at the office at 7pm when the weather suddenly turned wintry and snow started falling. I decided to return home before the snow piled up. Carrying a heavy briefcase and an umbrella and shoulder bag which contained my wallet, I trudged the half-block to the 49th Street and Sixth Avenue subway to catch a train. A 300-pound African American was in front of me as I descended the stairs into the station. The man descended at a snail's pace and I was unable to pass him because of his breadth. I felt a tug at my shoulder bag and, turning around, I saw that a young African American man was taking my wallet out of my bag. He began to run up the steps to the exit holding my wallet.

I dropped my briefcase and umbrella and ran after him to the top of the stairs disregarding the warning, "Lady, he has a knife!" When I exited I was greeted by two African American men in their thirties and well-dressed. I could tell that they were involved and pleaded with them politely to return my wallet which contained, besides $20, a credit card, my McGraw Hill security card and my driver's license. When they asked me if I could recognize the culprit, bowing my head respectfully in the Japanese manner, I replied that I had not.

I retrieved my briefcase and umbrella. Since I had no cash for a ticket I walked home in the snow, going first to my neighborhood police station to report the theft. The officer on duty directed me to the police station in the precinct where the theft had been committed. He added that I probably would not see my wallet again because the perpetrators were black.

I had to wait until the following Monday to report the mugging to the 49th Street precinct. After taking the details the woman officer on duty who was a Hispanic asked me if the men were black. When I replied that they were, she said that the wallet would never be returned.

When I reported the mugging to one of the JETRO management staff he automatically asked me, "Were they black? You won't see your wallet again."

I went to the DMV for another license and the following morning to the McGraw Hill security office for a new security card. That afternoon, the JETRO manager came to my desk to hand me the driver's license and security card which had been in my wallet. He told me that a man had passed them to a security guard in the lobby. Although the credit card was missing, I was relieved that the incident had not been an entirely negative experience.

Request from the CIA

On 21 June the blond receptionist transferred a call to me. The female caller identified herself as a staff in the Central Intelligence Agency Library. She requested that I send two copies of *Inside/Outside Japan* to the CIA. I worried that if the telephone call had been directed to other members of the paper, the president, the editor or to the executive director, there was a good chance that the paper would be discontinued. Recovering my composure, I replied that I would be pleased to do so. The woman told me that she would FAX the addresses to me within a few hours. However, the only FAX machine for the general office was located in the JETRO management division. Every 15 minutes I casually visited the machine to see if the CIA FAX had come through. After an hour of anxious waiting I finally recovered the FAX from the CIA before anyone had seen it.

The FAX had the CIA letter head with the date and the sender's name. It was addressed to me at JETRO New York with the message: "Thank you for your cheerfulness and help. Please send one copy each of: *Inside/Outside Japan* to the following addresses."

I posted two copies to two divisions at separate addresses that afternoon without informing anyone. The FAX indicated that the copies were to be sent only once but to be on the safe side I continued to send copies each time the paper was published in order to ensure that the CIA would not contact JETRO again.

Hello Good-bye

The president returned to Tokyo at the end of June to assume the post of deputy director for global environmental issues. The new president was the antithesis of his predecessor in terms of his career path at MITI and his cultural preferences. His predecessor was a cultural bon vivant who had been seconded by MITI three time overseas. The new president had not been sent overseas until his three-year tour at JETRO San Francisco.

After graduating from the Law Faculty at Tokyo University the officer entered MITI. He was "loaned" to JETRO Tokyo headquarters in 1986–89 where he was in charge of planning policy. After returning to MITI for a two-year stint he was seconded to JETRO San Francisco.

I interviewed him for my August article "Hello-Goodbye," bidding a welcome to the new president and a fond farewell to the outgoing president. The new president who perceived me to be under the aegis of the outgoing president was guarded. He revealed very little of himself, preferring to concentrate on his tour at JETRO San Francisco. He spoke fondly of his "new American friends" and his exposure to wine tasting, a hobby he indulged in while in California. He was skilled at creating the image of a president who was very open to new experiences:

> And in New York, the president plans to practice what his predecessor preached: "I want to enjoy the real life in New York, in the United States, and try to find the meaning of life in this country. Of course, I will continue the efforts my predecessor to be understood, to get the American people to understand what the Japanese like or what they hate, how they act and how they react. Maybe that will be my personal agenda as president of JETRO New York."

I gave a good send-off to the outgoing president:

> But the inner circle at JETRO New York knows that MITI is not what the fates have in mind for his next life and can imagine him as a music critic for the New York Times, realizing his dream to be forever at the MET. After all, he likes to refer to movies to prove a point, thinks that Andrew Lloyd Weber and Puccini are kindred spirits and is considered by some to be a little bit off the beaten track.

The new president requested a copy to check before it went to print. He returned it to me with a "thank you." I was relieved that I would continue to contribute to the paper. I was determined to stick-it-out until I understood the real situation concerning the ministries' corporations. As far as I could tell, the corporations were a waste of human resources and a disgraceful waste of public funds

Japanese-style Politics

Hata held office for only three months because of Ozawa's habit of alienating colleagues by pressuring them to accept policies he vigorously promoted like raising the consumption tax to 10 percent and more devolution for local authorities. After failing to convince the Socialists, whose party was a member of the coalition, to agree to certain policies, they left Hata's coalition and the LDP regained seats in the Lower House general elections forcing Hata to resign the following June.

In July 1994 Tomiichi Murayama, a Socialist, assumed the post, forming another coalition cabinet composed of members of the Socialist Party of Japan, the New Japan Party and the LDP. He began to push for the reform of the administration system in order to eradicate the relationship between politicians, bureaucrats and businessmen. This movement prompted a power struggle between politicians and bureaucrats, who were intent on maintaining control over the regulation of the economy.

What an Assay!

The new president requested that the title of the editorial page be changed from Perspective to "Assay." His inaugural Assay for the August issue "The Matter of Article Nine" put on the record the ultra-conservative nature of Japanese politicians and bureaucrats and the effort which persists to this day to amend the Pacifist Constitution.

> At the end of July, the executive committee of Japan's Socialist Party agreed to drop its unconditional opposition to the Self-defence Forces as unconstitutional. If adopted by the emergency party congress in early September, the decision would mark one of the most important steps for the post-war Japanese psyche.
>
> For over four decades now, the "war-renunciation" clauses of Article 9 of the Japanese Constitution and the actual existence of military forces have cast a duplicitous shadow on the minds of the Japanese people. Like many of my generation, I have had some painful experience in this regard.
>
> As a law student a quarter of a century ago, I knew I faced a dilemma when the time for taking the test on the Constitution came. The professor who administered it was a constitutional authority well-known for his unadorned view that the Self-Defence Forces were unconstitutional. What if a student had, as I did, a different view? Given in the first term, the test was regarded as the first hurdle to be cleared. After pondering the thought, I decided to hold on to my view.

The president reported that his test result was a disappointing "B." He blamed the Socialist Party, which occupied one-third of the house seats since the 1950s, for its opposition to any constitutional change:

> Once this irrational opposition is lifted, we might be able to secure more dispassionate, realistic debate on a wider range of security issues. More important, the removal of blind opposition of a party representing a sizable segment of Japanese people should usher in a new age in which similar debate is extended to all issues. If this comes to pass, Japan can claim to have changed in one crucial way.

The president was more reserved and more in the mode of a JETRO New York president than his predecessor. The executive secretary told me that she did not like him, perhaps because she did not regard him as elite as his predecessor nor did he have an outward charm. When she confided that he had removed the Apple PC from his office and replaced it with an IBM so that he could practice on it, based on my experiences at Mercian, I envisioned that his post-retirement career could be on an IBM board either in Japan or in the US. He was very savvy and used his long-term relationship with JETRO and the ministries' reemployment system to his advantage.

The president had a sharp analytical mind and made some revealing comments at meetings for the paper. When one of the contributors remarked that the news about Japan in American newspapers was subsiding, the president retorted that he thought that this was a good thing. In other words, no news about Japan's dispute with the USTR was good news.

The president's Assay in September "Japan's Industry in Peril" concerned large Japanese industries' moving production overseas due to the appreciation of the yen (¥100=$1), which was resulting in "industrial hollowing-out."

My article was another attempt to put a positive spin on the African American experience in Japan. "A Conversation with J.B. Cole" was based on an interview I conducted with Johnnetta Cole the first African American female president of Spelman College, the first college for black women in the US located in Atlanta, Georgia. Cole spoke about the Spelman College Japan Studies program, which was funded by 12 Japanese companies and the Japan Foundation. Her son had lived in Japan for six years where he taught English.

She considered that the Japanese were very comfortable with Southerners and that Japanese corporations would do well to establish operations in the South.

Assays Stick to MITI Territory

The president remained close to home with his editorials for the paper's last three issues for 1994. His message in the October issue "Trade Talks as Game-Playing" defended Japan's rejection to accept numerical targets of American imports. He emphasized that European and Asian nations had also stated that numerical targets were unacceptable:

> Similarly, Japan held on to its proposition that the areas for negotiations and agreements be limited to those "within the reach of government." Indeed as a whole, US strategy this time was a failure. Relying on a dubious "lesson" that was professed to have learned from the 1986 semiconductor agreement, the United States pursued a "results oriented" approach in earnest, itself outside the common understanding of international trade.

The president accused the USTR of "game-playing" at the negotiation table, claiming victory every time Japan accepted US requests. Even though his defensive stance was unsurprising, I was convinced that Japan would continue to postpone deregulation partly because ministry officials would lose post-retirement positions in the industries under their ministries' territorial jurisdiction.

Kobe Earthquake

On January 17, 1995 Japan suffered the worst earthquake disaster in its post-war period. The president who was brought up near Kobe, the center of the earthquake, used his January Assay to criticize his government's response:

> The government was slow in dispatching the Self-defence forces on the rescue mission; so was it in responding to the generous offers of assistance from abroad. The delays and hesitation along with the bureaucratic wrangling that was exposed through them, were heart breaking, seriously compromising Japan's vaunted ability to manage things. The fault lines in Japan's half century old institutions were exposed.

Since the president was near retirement age, his position in MITI was secure despite his hard line. For my article "Before/After: Jamaica Artist conquers Japan" I interviewed the Jamaican artist again to find out how he had fared in Kobe where his exhibition was held. Although the piece painted a very positive picture about his experiences, I purposely withheld his following remarks about his treatment by the customs officials:

> I felt stereotyped when I went through customs. I was in a long line and many people just went through without their luggage being checked and mine was thoroughly checked. The guy mentioned drugs to me. I asked why and they said that they were looking for drugs. I found that a bit strange. I found that my first experience going to Japan was rather racial. I don't know why I was singled out. Maybe it was my hair. They were expecting that because of my color I had drugs. I was almost late for the bus. I was practically the last one out because of the search.

I did not mention to him that when I went through Japanese customs at Haneda Airport in the mid-seventies carrying a Japanese pillow, a customs official grilled me shouting, "Hash? Hash?"

I also purposely did not include in the article the artist's assessment of the JETRO's Business Support Centers (BSC) which had been conceived by the Executive Director of the Trade Promotion Division. The BSC offered exhibition space, temporary office facilities and consulting free of charge. The artist who visited the Tokyo BSC, told me:

> The JETRO Business Support Center is a good idea but it needs some PR work. The location is not ideal. It's in a big office building and there is not a lot of traffic outside the building. The entire third and fourth floors have different boutiques. I was there around lunchtime and there weren't a lot of people about, only two or three people walking through. The owners who were exhibiting their works were just standing around. I spoke to two of them and they felt that they were losing money because there was not enough traffic. They were frustrated. One, I think, was from Morocco. One was American. I think that JETRO has to either publicize the place more or find a different location for the center to be successful.

At Last!

I could hardly believe it when in January the Japanese dailies reported Prime Minister Murayama's efforts to pressure the ministries to consolidate some of the smaller Special Status Corporations. The former Ministry of Agriculture, Forestry and Fisheries balked at dissolving its Raw Silk and Sugar Price Stabilization Corporation and Livestock Industry Promotion Corporation. The ministry contended that the corporations would continue to protect consumers by planning strategies that would stabilize prices. However, it was willing to merge the two corporations and in 1996 the entities were united and named the Agriculture and Livestock Industries Corporation (ALIC).

The opinion page of the *Asahi Shimbun* ran an article on January 9, 1995 reporting that when Murayama's administration conducted hearings on the restructuring of Special Status Corporations, MITI was reluctant to participate and wanted to know if the restructuring concerned the number of corporations or if the discussion was related to the financing of the corporations. The article also claimed that the ministries were changing the objectives of the corporations by contriving new roles. The paper called this "skill at disguising" (*henshin no gijutsu*), pointing to JETRO as an example of a Special Status Corporation that had been established in 1956 for the purpose of promoting Japanese exports: "Now when you phone JETRO headquarters the receptionist answers, "JETRO, import promoter.""

18

Back to the Boonies
but What a Ride

Bye-Bye JETRO?

I was sent back to the Kyoto Prefecture Representative office in March to assist the new representative who would replace his predecessor in April. The transfer came as a surprise but, also, as a relief. The Philippine librarian was antagonistic because I infringed on her relaxed environment by actively supporting visitors and callers by providing information about the Japanese markets. The JETRO Trade Promotion Division, wanting the majority of inquiries to be forwarded to the JETRO Senior Trade Advisor, was also displeased.

I regularly received complaints from callers and visitors to the library that the Japanese companies listed in the JETRO data base as potential partners with American businesses never responded when contacted. There were also complaints that the Senior Trade Advisor would recommend that they revise and relabel (in Japanese) their products for the Japanese market in order to adhere to the JIS or to accommodate consumer preferences. The majority of small business owners could not afford the costs of revising and relabeling and they threw in the towel before proceeding further.

At that stage I wanted to quit JETRO but a series of incidences encouraged me to remain for a while longer.

Fire Sale

Property values were plummeting 50 percent as a result of the bursting of the bubble. Japanese corporations who invested billions of dollars in foreign properties lost billions of dollars in the fire sales of their properties during the 1990s because of the recession and continued economic stagnation. In 1994, a debt-ridden Aoki sold its stake in the Algonquin to Starwood Capital and Goldman Sachs & Company for a mere $561 million.

Mitsubishi Estate also suffered a one billion yen loss in FY1995 when the operator of Rockefeller Center declared bankruptcy. It was Mitsubishi's first lost since its establishment in 1953. After selling its shares in 12 of the 14 buildings within Rockefeller Center, it managed to hold on to the McGraw Hill Building and the Time Life Building where JETRO was located before moving to the McGraw Hill.

There were two major reasons why the banks postponed calling in the loans. Firstly, the banks owned equity in their corporate borrowers and had members on their boards, and secondly, some of the outstanding loans were huge and if companies defaulted, the banks did not have sufficient capital to write off the debts. In other words, the companies were too big to fail. It was highly improbable that there would be any change in the relationship between the banks and their borrowers because the rigidity of the Japan Inc. system was well-established.

Kyoto Prefecture Revisited

With the exception of instructing his successor, who was visiting JETRO New York for a week, my former boss was out of the office. A recently arrived officer was posted in the JH office next door. His predecessor's wife, adhering to the Director of the Trade Promotion Division's advice to bear children in the US, had managed to have two children during her husband's term.

There was a new MITI official in the political research office. An engineer, he relied on his male American researcher and consulting firms to educate him on US politics. There were two new MITI officers in Industrial Research. One officer had graduated from the John F. Kennedy School of Management at Harvard and spoke fluent English.

The new Kyoto Prefecture Representative was a very different type from his predecessor. Around 35-years-old, he was a native of Kyoto and the son of a farming family. His initial impression of the US was hearing from his grandmother that American B-29 bombers flew over their home during the war.

He was proud of his Kyoto heritage and that he had been the first in his family to graduate from a university with a degree in accounting. Although he spoke some English, he preferred to converse in Japanese using the Kyoto dialect which was difficult to understand initially (memories of Mercian). Since he would slip into standard Japanese I presumed that the Kyoto dialect was an affectation. He confided that his superior in the Kyoto Prefecture treasury had supported his secondment to show appreciation for his loyalty. He preferred to socialize primarily with the Osaka Prefecture representative.

Unlike many of the officers who were sent to JETRO New York, the Kyoto representative had a definite remit. He was to organize a large three-day exhibition in September 1996 of venerable

Kyoto businesses engaged in the traditional Kyoto industries such as pickles, confections, arts, and crafts. Some of the firms had been operating since the seventeenth century. The exhibition was to celebrate the 1,200th anniversary of Kyoto City as Japan's first capital. Kyoto Prefecture Governor Teiichi Aramaki, the Japanese Ambassador to the US, the Japanese New York Consul General, the Governor of New York and the New York Mayor were scheduled to attend the opening ceremony. The exhibit's objective was to introduce New Yorkers to Kyoto Prefecture's finer things with the expectation that there was a market for these products in the United States. The officer who was under a lot of pressure was ambitious.

The officer was relieved that I was bilingual because I could facilitate much of his workload. His wife was about to give birth to a future American citizen after she joined him in May. He had rented a spacious home with a swimming pool in Princeton, New Jersey where he planned to enrol his first child, a daughter in a private school. Kyoto Prefecture would fund the tuition fee. Since the commute to the office was about an hour, the representative arrived in the morning at about 10:30am.

The representative was not opposed to my involvement with the paper as long as he was unaware of it. I was determined to maintain my connection with the officers in Research and Planning and wrote the articles in my cubicle when the officer was out of the office or on the weekends.

The president's Assay in March "For a 1% Discount Rate" concerned the consequences of the rapid appreciation of the yen against the dollar. He admitted that Japan's current account surplus would not decrease soon but that imports were on the rise: "I am proud to say that JETRO's import promotion is helping this development."

I interviewed Peter Simenaur, the New York Philharmonic's associate principal clarinet for my article "Who Could Ask for Anything More?" about his experience when he toured with the orchestra in Japan in 196. Leonard Bernstein was the conductor at the time. "That trip left a tremendous impression upon me. The Japanese adored Bernstein in those days and a red carpet was actually laid out! There was full press coverage."

Simenaur, who had visited Japan with the orchestra nine times repeated what I often tell my friends about cuisine in Japan: "I have found that in Japan you can get the best cup of coffee, the best pizza, the best spaghetti, the best of everything! They [the Japanese] take great effort to outshine everyone else and most of the time they're very successful."

For the first time since the initiation of the paper, I did not contribute to the April issue of *Inside/Outside Japan*. The president's Assay in the paper could be interpreted as a positive assessment about former US Secretary of Defence Robert McNamara's book *In Retrospect: The Tragedy of Lessons of Vietnam* about the Vietnam War:

> Finally, on this 20th anniversary of the end of the war, he [McNamara] has made public his examination of how he and other policy makers were gradually pulled into a dubious war. It is in this process that he repeatedly admits his mistakes. This is a courageous act. I cannot recall a single instance from among Japanese policy makers who, following Japan's defeat, did anything remotely similar.

Oklahoma Bombing

The representative encountered his first crisis several weeks after his arrival. On April 19, 1995 the FBI building in Oklahoma City was bombed. Timothy McVeigh a Gulf War army veteran drove a rented truck carrying a bomb into the side of the building. The explosion killed 168 people and injured more than 680. It was the worst incident of domestic terrorism in US history. Oklahoma Governor Frank Keaton who had served in a number of US law enforcement agencies expedited the rescue efforts. McVeigh and his cohort Terry Nichols, who made the bomb, were swiftly caught and convicted of the crime.

Since Kyoto had a Sister-State relationship with Oklahoma, the Kyoto representative was instructed by the Kyoto Prefecture government to fly immediately to Oklahoma City to offer to Governor Keating condolences from Kyoto Prefecture and to give a donation of $500. The representative requested that I accompany him and made arrangements through Japan Travel, a travel agency used by the majority of officers. The travel expenses were probably twice that of the donation.

We landed safely at Will Rogers Airport, named after the Oklahoma comedian who had died when his light aircraft crashed in Alaska. The JETRO Senior Trade Advisor posted at the State development office met us and drove us to our hotel before taking us to dinner at a restaurant for a taste of Oklahoma-style cuisine - spareribs and barbecued chicken, a first for the representative.

The following morning the officer and I visited the Oklahoma State capital and the governor's office for the meeting with Governor Keating. The Art Deco building with its gold leaf roof and the stunning interior (including the elevators) befitted the oil-rich state. We were informed that we would be meeting the Deputy Governor Mary Fallon (now the current Governor) because Governor Keating was holding a press conference. An African American woman who was Ms Fallon's assistant escorted us to the Deputy Governor's office. When we entered we saw that the JETRO Senior Trade Advisor was there as well. Assuming that I was the Kyoto Prefecture representative Ms. Fallon greeted me first to the real representative's dismay. I quickly introduced the officer who presented the governor with the check. After a photographer took a formal photograph of all of us Ms. Fallon's assistant ushered us to Congress which was in session where congressmen were voting on a bill concerning insurance regulations.

The ride on the elevator to the next floor was from a scene in the movie classic "Giant" staring Rock Hudson, Elizabeth Taylor and James Dean. The lobbyists representing the insurance industry were present in force. The congressmen wore Armani jackets, snake skin cowboy boots and Stetsons.

Following the session, the Senior Trade Advisor escorted us to a small room to show us an exhibit of Oklahoma products which he had chosen for the Japanese market. The wares were arts and crafts made by Indian tradesmen for the tourist industry. I silently assessed the collection as entirely inappropriate for Japanese consumers.

In the afternoon the representative and I visited the FBI building which had been reduced to a rubble of ash and wires. The blast was so powerful that over 300 buildings within a 16 block radius had been destroyed. Shards of glass blanketed the ground. Bouquets of flowers were attached to the barbed wire fence which kept observers a good distance away from the building. A YWCA building with a nursery school in the basement located directly across from the FBI building was almost unrecognizable. Bouquets of limp flowers were attached to the barbed wire fence in front of the school in remembrance of the children who had died. It was a sobering and somewhat morbid scene that reminded me of the local Jizo shrines in Japan where statues of Jizo, the god who protects children's souls, stand in rows with offerings of flowers and food placed at their feet.

The JETRO Senior Trade Advisor who had retired from a large trading company played host that evening at a Vietnamese restaurant which was more to the representative's taste. According to the advisor, many Vietnamese had migrated to Oklahoma at the end of the Vietnam War. He strongly recommended that we visit the Cowboy Hall of Fame before returning to New York.

The representative was reluctant to go. Although I had never been, I promised that he would enjoy the experience. We were not disappointed. The museum was a fascinating showcase of Oklahoma state history with exhibits ranging from cowboy and rodeo artefacts to exhibits replicating Oklahoma Sooner life. There was a room devoted entirely to Roy Rogers. His theme song, "Back in the Saddle Again." was piped through loud speakers and his stuffed horse Trigger was mounted on its hind legs.

The representative's wife gave birth to a girl in May. My article for the May issue *New York in Nagoya* put a positive spin on an American small business's easy entry into the Japanese housing market. The piece was based on my interview of a Japanese artist and his American business partners who took their small business converting industrial spaces into residence to Nagoya, Japan. The article also promoted the company for investment.

WOW!

In June, the Managing Director's successor arrived at JETRO New York to take over operations. He was in his early forties and divorced. We were told that his father who had been a high-ranking official in the ministry may have pushed for the secondment. The new director was a Kyoto native and extraordinarily arrogant and controlling. The Japanese assistants gossiped that his Japanese girlfriend would be joining him and that he enjoyed Flamenco and was investing in a Flamenco troop. A frequent visitor to his office was a director from Ishikawa-Harima Heavy Industries. He also enjoyed going on skiing holidays with the JH representative.

On 13 June the American researcher in Research and Planning came to my cubicle and handed me the front page of the *Sankei Shimbun*. There was photograph of JETRO Tokyo headquarters and the headline "Is JETRO Out of Control?" (*Jetero Boso?*). The newspaper's Washington, DC correspondent Yoshihisa Komori had written a stinging article pointing to the president's Assay about McNamara in the April issue of *Inside/Outside Japan*.

According to Komori, William Triplet II, an aide to Republican Senator Robert Bennett, who was a member of the Senate Committee of Foreign Relations and a recipient of the paper, took exception to the article, protesting that the president of an organization that was established to promote foreign trade and economic cooperation should not be involved in commenting on political issues.

Komori claimed that there was opposition in the National Diet to the continuation of JETRO because i) it no longer served its original function as a trade organization; ii) JETRO was an underground MITI (*kakure tsuushansho*); and iii) JETRO had in effect become the "Number Two Ministry of Foreign Affairs" (*dai-ni Gaimusho*).

The accusations that JETRO was no longer functioning as a trade promotion organization but was being maneuvered into other areas supported the *Asahi Shimbun*'s contentions that MITI was "disguising" JETRO in order to continue operations. Also, by alleging that JETRO had become a secondary Ministry of Foreign Affairs, *Sankei Shimbun* implied that MITI was using JETRO to wrest territory from the MOFA.

Komori's article confirmed my convictions that MITI was using public funds to portray JETRO as an import promoter in order to justify its budget and to justify MITI's use of its corporation to expand its territory in Japan and overseas. MITI also managed the Manufactured Imports & Promotion Organization (MIPRO) which was established in Washington DC in 1978 where MITI officials and Japanese trade delegations visited regularly.

I had thought that eventually recipients of *Inside/Outside Japan* would complain about the contents, specifically the political commentaries. And true to my prediction a few weeks later I happened to be leafing through the July issue of *Sentaku* to discover that the magazine carried a photograph of *Inside/Outside Japan* and an article claiming that the reason Triplet was annoyed with the president's article was because JETRO's activities in the United States were a source of irritation to the CIA and the FBI. *Sentaku* asserted that the CIA and FBI were watching closely the activities of the directors of industrial research in JETRO New York when they visited other JETRO offices in the United States. The agencies regarded the MITI officers as CIA-type agents from Japan and since the representatives could not be classified as either foreign diplomats or as scholars, their status was ambiguous. Also, there was a suspicion among members of Congress that the officers engaged in industrial espionage.

Another article reporting JETRO's involvement in industrial espionage in the United States followed in the October 10, 1995 edition of *Nikkei Report*. Steven L. Harmon reported that the *New York Times* had alleged that the CIA and the National Security Agency had tapped the conversations of Japanese trade representatives and automobile manufacturers during the 1995 trade negotiations in Geneva, providing evidence that Japan was engaging in industrial espionage in the United States. Harmon discovered that the FBI was focusing its investigation on JETRO's offices in Los Angeles and San Francisco, questioning former staff about their bosses' activities. Harmon claimed that a female staff member had told the FBI that espionage was "a routine part of the jobs of such Japanese posted in the United States." To counteract the bad press the Japanese press informed readers that France and Australia were the most actively engaged in industrial espionage in the US.

Officers in JETRO New York remarked cynically that Americans would sell anything for money. While I was in the Reference Library I had received enquiries from Americans who wanted to sell inventions pertinent to weapons production to Japanese companies. I replied that JETRO was not involved in procuring inventions related to military use.

Americans sometimes visited the office of the Director of Industrial Research. I advised the director to place photographs of his children on his desk to create a more relaxed atmosphere. He reported to me that the photographs were proving effective.

I was not concerned about allegations of espionage but about the appalling waste of public funds for promoting JETRO as a trade promotion organization while using its budget for activities unrelated to promoting inward investment and for planting offices overseas to serve as lobbying posts and holiday locations.

When the president was interviewed by *Japan Economic Survey* he stated that 75 percent of JETRO's budget came from public funds. Nevertheless, the expenses incurred by the relocation of representatives seconded from other government agencies was not included. But even though opponents of Special Status Corporations regarded JETRO's duties as extraneous and the offices as "empty boxes" it was unlikely that MITI would consider options to cut costs. JETRO had become a necessity.

It's the Image that Counts

JETRO, true to form, released the 1996 edition of *Success is Yours* which reassured small business exporters of processed food that entry into Japan was not difficult if certain procedures were followed. The American confectioner and maker of the famous Jelly Belly jellybeans, Herman Goetlitz Inc. was held up as an example of how a processed food producer was able to enter the Japanese market successfully. Since Jelly Belly was already popular among Japanese consumers who purchased the product in the United States, Goetlitz could count on instant name recognition and success. Sony Corporation, the distributor, would not have taken a risk with a manufacturer that did not have a solid track record. Here again, JETRO did not explain that if foreign businesses do not have a strong brand loyalty among Japanese consumers before entering the market they would have difficulty surviving unless a Japanese company was willing to take on an unknown. Although JETRO did not participate in facilitating Goetlitz's entry, readers may have assumed that JETRO was involved, since it did not state otherwise.

Success 1996 Case Studies continued to tout the success of large foreign companies in Japan that had prior recognition among Japanese consumers before entering the Japanese market. Case study 5 was entitled: "L.L. Bean Japan Entering the Japanese Market without Capital Investment." The company's outerwear was already popular among Japanese who were on extended visits to the United States.

According to the case study, in 1992, L.L. Bean joined the giant retailer Seiyu and Matsushita Electric Industrial to form L.L. Bean Japan. Seiyu put up 70 percent of the investment and Matsushita the other 30 percent, the total capital investment being ¥490 million. The study explained that L.L. Bean, a company with a large mail-order business in the US, researched the Japanese market through a consulting firm and found that Japanese consumers preferred retail outlets to mail-order. Therefore, it had to rely on large companies to market and distribute its goods in Japan. Matsushita imported L.L. Bean goods and Seiyu retailed them. Although Bean did not provide any capital nor did it take any risks, it sold its rights to sell its products to Seiyu and Matsushita, who ultimately controlled the business in Japan.

A Break from the Drama: a brief encounter with Donald Keene

I had a method for expediting a rapport with the officials I worked with. If I knew their backgrounds, where they had been born and raised, their fathers' professions, their universities and degrees and their favorite authors I could estimate quite accurately their personalities and values. If Yukio Mishima received the highest accolades among authors I guessed that the officers were conservative and prone to nationalistic sentiments. Although I considered Mishima's novels narcissistic, I regarded him a genius in his use of vocabulary and Chinese characters.

I had the great pleasure of meeting Donald Keene, who translated the works of Mishima and the 1994 Nobel Prize recipient Kenzaburo Oe at a reception given in his honor by his publisher. Keene, who is now a Japanese citizen, told me that Mishima's manuscripts were completely void of corrections or erase marks. On the other hand, the pages of Oe's manuscripts were full of corrections.

But the highpoint of the reception was a glimpse of Yoshihisa Komori, the Washington Dc correspondent for the *Sankei*. I did not introduce myself.

The FBI Comes Calling

In September I was summoned by the FBI to participate in the "Friendly Witness" program to testify about the activities at JETRO New York. I did not want to take any chances of being found out by officers at JETRO New York and requested the services of a law firm to represent me at the interview which was conducted by a young female officer at the firm's office located in the Battery. The two solicitors who attended the 30-minute session did not allow me to reply to the officer's queries about my activities nor my superiors' activities. Most likely other researchers were also questioned.

Several weeks later I received a telephone call from a man identifying himself as the director of a company in Texas. He asked if Kyoto Prefecture would like information regarding a hi-tech invention. I replied that my office was not sourcing hi-tech products. Curious to know the name of the company I redialed the number. The company was not listed.

Before he left JETRO in the summer of 1994 the first American researcher in Research and Planning who collaborated with the American in Industrial Research confided that he suspected the researcher was a CIA mole. Although the researcher had access to his bosses' schedules he did not speak Japanese, which limited the kind of information he was privy to. Furthermore, I assumed that his bosses considered him to be innocuous.

The new Managing Director was paranoid due to the attention from the CIA and FBI intrusions and he decided that, not only should the office be renovated, including the installation of a security system but, also, that all officers should clock into JETRO with new security cards. The director would then be able to assess attendance records, which pressured officers who were used to a relaxed schedule, to arrive promptly in the morning. The editor of *Inside/Outside Japan* was particularly affected by the new system because he habitually arrived late, which had always been allowed. A Japanese construction company was commissioned for the renovation of the office, which included a new meeting room. Word had it that the cost of the renovation was around $250,000. The director also replaced the computers that had been purchased two years earlier with new computers. The old ones were stored in a room never to be used again. JETRO's budget was bottomless.

Another Prime Minister Bites the Dust: reforms put on hold

On August 15, 1995, marking the fiftieth anniversary of the Second World War, Prime Minister Murayama apologized to Japan's "Asian neighbors" for the suffering and damage caused by the Japan's military. Despite this courageous gesture, Murayama's administration suffered from a sequence of events that served to end Murayama's term in office in 1996. There were the Kobe Earthquake which brought harsh criticism of the government's handling of the aftermath; the continuing recession, political infighting and the opposition of Socialist Party members to Murayama's support of the Japan–US Security Pact, which the prime minister contended was in accordance with Japan's Constitution. The rape of a teenage girl by US Marines stationed on

Okinawa did not help matters. The Sarin gas-attack by the religious cult Aum Shinrikyo in the Tokyo Underground on 20 March that killed 12 people and injured 6,000, increased Japanese anxieties about the country's socio-economic stability, impacting adversely on Murayama's administration. Voters returned to the LDP fold and the Socialist Party lost many seats in the Lower House in the 1996 election.

Murayama resigned as prime minister making way for the conservative LDP president Ryutaro Hashimoto to enter the executive office, albeit heading a three-party coalition government which included the Socialists. Frustrated members of recently established parties either returned to the LDP or joined other parties. Hashimoto, who served as the Minister of Industry in Murayama's cabinet was well-liked by MITI officials. The female non-career officer in EID/MITI told me that Hashimoto favored green leather trousers and that women over 50 were enthusiastic supporters. I was disappointed that Murayama, a reformer, had resigned. Japan Inc. was sliding into a political black hole.

Ozawa had ploughed ahead to form the New Pioneer Party in 1995, merging it with the Renewal Party. He defeated Hata in the election for secretary-general in the party but it was a meaningless exercise because Hata and the majority of members left the party to form other small parties.

Ozawa went on to form the Liberal Party, which was one of the three parties that participated in Prime Minister Hashimoto's coalition government (1996–98). He had cultivated a devout following of young supporters throughout the 1990s. Many of his lieutenants were first employed to perform menial chores in his home such as cleaning and walking his dogs. If they proved to be hard-working and loyal, they were promoted to secretarial positions in his Tokyo office.

Meanwhile, the IMF continued pressing for structural reforms and western commentators and Noble Prize winning economists were positive about Japan's recovery. By then I was confident that structural reforms would not happen.

The changing of the guard at JETRO New York took place in June when the president's two-year tour came to an end. The previous autumn he had driven his wife and me to Long Island for wine tasting at several Long Island wineries. When he departed JETRO New York he gave me a beautiful print of a portrait of a Samurai warrior and a silk brocade center table cover which is a traditional craft from Kyoto Prefecture. I framed the print in a traditional wooden frame my husband had purchased during our time in Kamakura. The print hangs on a wall in my flat. The brocade table cloth remains in its wooden box for safe-keeping.

Kyoto Comes to New York

The representative and I began to search for venues for the exhibition, using the services of a Japanese real estate agent. To his disappointment, the rooms in Rockefeller Center were too small and too expensive. To my disappointment he decided on the lobby of Number Two World Trade Center which was spacious and easily accessible to commuters. I was careful not to show my distress but I desperately wanted to avoid the World Trade Center because of the 1993 terrorist bombing of the Marriot Hotel garage in the World Trade Center. It was the first terrorist attack by Arabs with connections to Al-Qaida. I felt particularly vulnerable when I had to attend meetings with the officer in Windows on the World, a restaurant on the 106th and 107th floor of the North Building. I was not looking forward to the commute on the IRT.

I named the event "Kyoto Comes to New York." Two placards were designed by a Japanese artist. One sported a photograph of a smiling Governor Aramaki with his greeting in Japanese, which I translated in order that New Yorkers would understand his message.

Tragically, the representative's ambitions for his career were thwarted when three weeks before the exhibition his youngest daughter fell into the swimming pool. The pool was not protected by a safeguard and the child had been left unattended. The baby was rescued by a neighbor and emergency services resuscitated her. She was flown by air-ambulance to a hospital for further treatment. The baby remained in a coma for over a week before regaining consciousness. The accident left her physically impaired.

Fortunately, since the child had been born in the United States, she was eligible for Medicare and received excellent and compassionate treatment during weeks in the hospital. When she returned home Medicare continued to support her through physiotherapy. Kyoto Prefecture government insurance also supported the girl's care.

Only a day after the accident the officer, leaving his wife to attend their child, came to the office to continue focusing on the arrangements. He confided bitterly to me that he wished that the baby had died. At first, it was a shocking admission but upon reflection I could understand his reasons; he and his wife would be judged harshly in Japan for not having taken necessary precautions to prevent the accident. There was also the stigma of having a severely disabled child which could impact adversely on his career.

When the MITI officials at JETRO paid their condolences the representative was outwardly respectful but in private he told me that that the ministries regarded local governments as "beggars" always pleading for more subsidies for public works and that local government officials had to bear gifts to Tokyo to court officials. After the accident, to ameliorate the Managing Director, he offered to introduce him to his sister-in-law, an attractive Kyoto woman. It was positively feudalistic but logical in the context of the Japan Inc. system.

Prior to the opening of the exhibition a delegation from the town of Maizuru visited the officer. Maizuru is located in northern Kyoto on an inlet on the Sea of Japan. The port was established as a naval base in 1901 during the Japanese-Russo War and developed to become a city in 1943. The city's economy is supported primarily by the Coast Guard. The delegation asked what I would like to receive from Maizuru and I requested a book about Maizuru's history and a map. A few weeks later I received a beautiful hardcover volume. Strangely, many Japanese do not know that Kyoto Prefecture has a port.

The representative was determined to ensure that the exhibition went smoothly but he had to commute to the hospital regularly to support his wife as well. My workload increased substantially. I assumed much of the burden, communicating with Kyoto Prefecture government daily and assisting the tradesmen to set up their booths and hang their artwork on temporary wall set up in the lobby. Although the event was partially subsidized by government the tradesmen assumed the sizable portion of the costs of shipping their crafts to New York. Some of them had never been to the US nor could they speak English and by the time the exhibition commenced they were exhausted from the stress.

The exhibition opened to the public after the opening ceremony which was officiated by Governor Aramaki and Kyoto Prefecture government officials. The New York JETRO president put in a surprise appearance. Many Americans enjoyed their first exposure to the elegant products on display, which included Japanese confections and rice crackers. At the end of the final day, the representative gave an hour session to the tradesmen to assess the event. He was reluctant for me to attend but allowed me to sit at the back of the room.

The officer spoke at length to the business owners about the viability of their products in the American marketplace. Perhaps influenced by the JETRO news bulletins of crimes perpetrated in the US or perhaps he was unfamiliar with American consumer preferences or perhaps he watched too many TV shows, the officer characterized American consumers as couch potatoes who sat all day watching television while eating spaghetti out of cans and drinking vast quantities of beer. His analysis did not include other market information that may have given the tradesmen a more positive perspective.

The business owners left the room downcast. I was appalled by the officer's cynical view of Americans, but he had achieved what was expected of him during his posting at JETRO New York. He was also anxious about his future career. At the farewell dinner that evening I quietly offered three of the business owners to take them the following morning to upmarket boutiques and food shops where foreign products were popular and where consumers were familiar with Japanese foods and crafts and who could afford to purchase their elegant products.

The officer was somewhat distressed when he discovered that I had taken the initiative without his permission but he was mainly focusing his attention on his family situation. He began spending most of his time either with his family or visiting the branches of Kyoto businesses on the West Coast.

Reconnecting with Research and Planning

Since the officers from JASME and Ehime Prefecture were posted at desks in Research and Planning I decided to continue at JETRO New York for a while longer in order to connect with the officers and their agencies thus giving me the opportunity to confirm what I already suspected if there was an opportunity to visit them in Japan.

With the exception of an article for the September issue of *Inside/Outside Japan* my contributions were intermittent. The articles in 1995 about JETRO New York confirmed my understanding that JETRO was an extension of MITI and that a number of Special Status Corporations served similar roles. I was committed to finding out more about Special Status Corporations, especially in terms of the funding. The accounting methods in these entities appeared to be completely opaque. Indeed, when JETRO New York received notification from the government in 1996 that it would be audited in a few weeks there was a flurry of activity at the computers in the management division and huge bags of shredded paper were thrown out. After the audit JETRO New York was given a clean bill of health.

The continuous positive outlook of Japan's economy by the international business community was disconcerting as was the urging by the IMF for Japan to implement structural reforms. Only a minority of us predicted that Japan's economy would continue to be fragile and that the deregulation of markets and structural reforms would be continuously postpone not only because of political turmoil within parties but, also, because the bureaucracy was the most powerful arm of government.

Bull's Eye!

In February 1997 Japan's biggest business weekly magazine *Nikkei Business* did a cover story on Special Status Corporations, interviewing Hiroshi Kato, who was the president of Chiba Commercial College and the chairman of the government's Tax Commission in the 1980s. He emphasized that public funding of Special Status Corporations was a serious problem because the ministries had the power to use the money at their discretion without seeking consent from the Diet. The politicians supported this behavior because they solicited contracts from the corporations involved in public works for their constituencies.

Kato complained that there was no public disclosure by the corporations for accounts indicating profit-loss balances and that the accounting system used was difficult to fathom because it differed from the system used by private corporations. He recommended privatization. Some of the corporations had already been dismantled prior to 1996, when the number stood at 92.

Nikkei Business claimed that while Special Status Corporations had been founded on the precept that the work executed would serve the national interest the opposite was true for the following reasons:

1. Special Status Corporations received funding from sources that were difficult to trace.
2. The corporations could set up subsidiaries ("children" and "grandchildren" corporations) that showed profits even though the parent corporations were in debt.
3. The ministries established Special Status Corporations and their subsidiaries to provide temporary employment for staff and post-retirement positions for retired senior officials before they moved to the private sector.
4. The corporations used funds to do work that was in the best interests of the corporations.

Bull's Eye (but so what?)

The American media continued its negative coverage of JETRO New York. The American researcher with whom I spoke Japanese passed me the article in the June 16, 1997 issue of *U.S. News and World Report* with the message "Bull's Eye!"

The piece "With Friends like These" continued to probe JETRO's authenticity as an import promoter. Senior Writer William J. Holstein questioned JETRO's function in the United States. In his article, Holstein described JETRO as "a uniquely flexible organization that defies American definition." He contended that JETRO America did not serve to promote imports into Japan, but rather was a sophisticated commercial intelligence-gathering agency. He suggested that the promotional materials served to disguise the true reason for JETRO's presence. Edward J. Lincoln, who had served as a trade attaché for the former ambassador to Japan Walter Mondale and who was at the Brookings Institution, told Holstein: "At best the Japanese are being disingenuous when they say that JETRO's primary job is promoting American exports." Lincoln suggested that JETRO's "core mission" was to collect American technology and political intelligence.

In his article Holstein stated that there was a risk that products invented by small businesses would be appropriated by Japanese companies to whom they had been introduced by JETRO. He provided as an example the experiences of a Clearwater, Florida entrepreneur, Donald Lewis, whose electronic device JETRO contended in its publication *Success in the Making* it had marketed in Japan. Holstein contended that JETRO's support led to Lewis losing control over his invention to an automobile manufacturer. Lewis claimed that Toyota had agreed to use his device, and when Toyota had used it for a few days, the Japanese distributor told Lewis that it would be best to sell his stake to Toyota. Lewis felt under pressure to sell because Toyota was a giant manufacturer and very influential.

JETRO chairman Toru Toyoshima had painted a different picture when he addressed an audience of the New York Japan Society in 1993. He reported that a Senior Trade Advisor had come upon Lewis' electronic anti-rust system and thought that it would do well in Japan. According to Toyoshima, the Export-Import Bank of Japan loaned Lewis US$1.5 million to expand his operations. Toyoshima told the audience: "As some of you know, in April 1990 the EXIM Bank of Japan introduced a lending program designed to increase imports into Japan and provide financing to American companies with products that are likely to sell well in Japan. The Florida company became the first to have such financing."

When Holstein asked the JETRO New York president about JETRO's activities in the United States, the president insisted "We are promoting U.S. exports to Japan to reduce the trade gap between us." The JETRO website at the time was advertising requests from Japanese companies for such items as "used medical bed"' and "primary coat stripper for optical cable."

19

The Ties that Bind

JASME was established by MITI in the 1950s to provide loans and services to independent businesses. In the 1990s the JASME had about ¥410.9 billion in capital resources and was the primary lender to small businesses, offering long-term loans at interest rates that were lower than private financial institutions. JASME helped small businesses upgrade operations by providing finance, but the business owners had to apply through their local government authority for the loans, which, in turn, requested loans from JASME. FILP funded its budget.

The Ehime Prefecture representative and the JASME officer were not independent from JETRO and while doing work for their agencies, they were expected to engage much of the time in research for JETRO. Although the JASME officer was supposed to research small business activities in the US and the Ehime officer was researching the American retail sector, they spent most of their time glued to their desks perusing American newspapers and clipping articles to either synopsize or to send to JETRO Tokyo. Since the same articles were accessible to JETRO Tokyo staff, the two officers' work was extraneous and boring. They exemplified the waste of public funds and human resources.

The previous officer who had befriended me had returned to Tokyo. His successor was in his late thirties and was seconded to JETRO New York from the Hiroshima branch office. He had brought his wife and three children with him, renting a flat in New Jersey.

The Ehime office was in his early thirties and single. He was extremely intelligent and his English was sufficient. He was a bit of a rascal with a sardonic wit and a cynical view of life which could have been due to his job in the prefecture government that did not suit his talents. His father had also been an officer in the prefecture government but suffered from diabetes and kidney failure, forcing him to retire early. When he was 14, the representative participated in a high-school exchange program with China. The three months spent in a Chinese school inspired an infatuation with the country. He graduated with a degree in Chinese from Osaka City University and he claimed that he had travelled to China 30 times. Even though the officer was best suited to represent Ehime in China or Hong Kong his fluency in Chinese enabled him to support a JETRO director in Research and Planning to monitor America's policies regarding China and the meetings between Chinese and US government officials in Washington DC.

When I dropped into Research and Planning to invite the officers to lunch they were clipping articles from US newspapers. Since they already knew me through the paper they enthusiastically accepted.

Over a spicy meal at a Korean restaurant they spoke of their discontentment with their duties at JETRO New York. The JASME officer complained that, with the exception of finding his family a flat which was very basic and not on a par with their home in Hiroshima, JETRO management did little else to support his family to settle in the US. His wife could not speak English and was burdened with enrolling the children in schools and daily household chores.

The officers welcomed my offer to arrange visits to small businesses, banks and retailers and to coordinate the work with tours of historically important sites which would encourage a better understanding of America's political economic development. These were services that JETRO should have provided to officers who were sent to the countries where branch offices were located instead of using the budget for marketing materials and Senior Trade Advisors. The excursions would have promoted a realistic assessment of Japan's role in the international political and economic arena.

Respite from Tedium: the great escapes

The officers, apprehensive about being discovered escaping from the office, requested that we leave JETRO separately and meet outside of the McGraw Hill Building. To initiate the "escapes" I took them to Franklin Delano Roosevelt's Home and museum in Hyde Park. The officers knew nothing about Roosevelt's administration, including the New Deal or the Social Security System because Japanese textbooks relate little about America's pre-war history. They were fascinated with the aerial photos of the bombing of Hiroshima and Nagasaki and of Alamo, New Mexico.

The second escape was to the New York State capital of Albany where I had arranged a meeting with the director of the New York State Economic development Agency whom I had met in January 1994 when I covered the National Minority Business Council event for the paper. The director graciously agreed to invite a regional director from the Small Business Agency (SBA) and the director of a regional bank for a two-hour session regarding New York State's promotion of SME exports. Although the meeting was primarily for the JASME officer, the Ehime officer came along.

The scenic train ride along the Hudson River was a fine introduction to the beauties of New York State. The officer's English was passible and I translated the comments he did not understand. I also asked questions related to loans to SMEs and support from the SBA. The officer found the meeting invaluable because he could report the proceedings to his office thus gaining him brownie points. I taped the meeting and transcribed it for him, setting a precedence for future meetings.

After the meeting the three of us were escorted on a tour of Congress which was in session and introduced to the deputy majority leader. We stood for a formal photograph which was sent to us a few days later.

I took the officers to the Albany State Museum to see exhibits of the state's agricultural economy and the history of it economic development through the Erie Canal system and the railroad. The trip was a complete success and whet the officers' appetite for more "escapes."

I organized further meetings for the JASME officer with small business owners in Manhattan as well as with upper management in metropolitan banks.

Prime Minister Ryutaro Hashimoto Speaks and the NYSE Plummets

On June 23, 1997 Prime Minister Ryutaro Hashimoto gave an address at Columbia University at a luncheon sponsored by the Foreign Policy Association and Columbia's Department of International Relations. As a member of the FPA I was invited to attend and I took the two officers with me. The prime minister arrived with his wife and daughter and gave a 30-minute address.

The address "Japan-U.S. Relations: A Partnership for the Twenty First Century" regarded Japan's economy and planned reforms of the financial sector. The speech was delivered in Japanese and simultaneously translated into English. At the Q&A session a trader from Wall Street asked Hashimoto about what would happen if Japan's economy began to deteriorate rapidly. Hashimoto light heartedly replied that Japan would be pressed to sell some of its US securities. Those who understood Japanese laughed but evidently the English translation implied that Hashimoto had been serious. That afternoon, the DOW plummeted 40 points and Hashimoto was reprimanded in the Japanese press.

Viva Mexico! R&R with a Bit of Research

At lunch one day I asked the officers if they had a wish where they would like to go during their secondment in the US. They shouted, "Mexico!" I suggested against my better judgement that I would try to contrive work for them in Mexico so that their dreams were fulfilled. But getting there was a different matter. Although I could fund my airfare, they would have to source funds from JETRO for their travel expenses.

I suggested that I design a project which would enable a trip to Mexico. By coincidence, JETRO headquarters had requested data regarding the impact on American businesses in Mexico from the sudden devaluation of the peso triggered by the December 1994 financial crisis. The Mexican government began deregulating the financial sector to allow foreign banks to purchase up to 8 percent equity in Mexican banks.

I told the JASME officer to submit a proposal which would give him the opportunity to go to Mexico for four days to investigate two American banks with large operations in Mexico and their corporate strategies. I suggested to the Ehime officer that he submit a proposal for investigating J.C Penny's operations and Wal-Mart's entry into the Mexican market through connecting with the Mexican supermarket chain CIFRA, which had a close relationship with the Mexican government and suppliers.

I asked them not to mention the project or submit anything until I had arranged interviews in Mexico, the facilitation of which was doubtful. But to my surprise I managed to arrange six interviews in four days. When I called the Bank of America headquarters in San Francisco to arrange an interview with the president of the BOA's Mexican subsidiary I was transferred directly to the president of the international division. Introducing myself as a JETRO employee, I asked if a JETRO officer who had recently arrived from Japan could accompany me to observe the proceedings. He agreed to arrange the interview.

I contacted Chase Manhattan in New York to receive the contact details of the general manager of Chase Manhattan in Mexico City who also agreed to an interview. I had similar luck when I called the JC Penny Mexican Headquarters in Monterrey. Wal-Mart proved to be difficult to penetrate and I had to settle on an interview with its advertising agency in Mexico City. I then prepared the list of questions for each interview.

The directors in Research and Planning were quizzical about how the two officers had managed to enter the inner sanctums of American corporations, let alone arrange interviews. The officers, who could barely contain themselves, replied that it had been easy. When they asked me how I managed to get the interviews I replied that one had to be "as American as apple pie." Their trip was funded and the JASME officer booked plane tickets and registered a room for me in his wife's name in order to route a portion of my expenses through JETRO's budget.

Four Days of Torture

We met at La Guardia Airport and flew to Mexico City situated in a valley surrounded by mountains which, at 8,000 feet above sea level, was enveloped in a blanket of acrid smog from automobile emissions. The following day, while the Ehime officer went off sightseeing, I took the JASME officer to interview the president of BOA. In the afternoon we visited the offices of Chase Manhattan. I taped both sessions and transcribed them after returning to the hotel while the officers went off to drink tequila. The combination of Mexico's high altitude and polluted air brought on a monotonous headache and sore throat. But I was determined that the officers see as much of Mexico City as possible.

On the second day while the JASME officer went sightseeing, the Ehime officer and I flew to Monterrey to interview the president of JC Penny Mexico. His reply to my question regarding the most difficult and expensive aspect of distribution was memorable; the poor maintenance of the network of highways between the Texas distribution center and Monterrey, the frequency of vehicle breakdowns and the bandits who accosted the trucks by simply standing in the middle of the roads.

On the third day the Ehime officer accompanied me to Wal-Mart's advertising agency. Afterwards I remained at the hotel to transcribe the interview while the officers visited churches and ate masses of Mexican cuisine downed with the commensurate Corona beer. The last stop was to JETRO Mexico to pay our respects to the managing director in an effort to present the image that we had devoted our entire time in Mexico for research. And we almost succeeded. We celebrated at a Mexican restaurant that evening. When I commented that MITI was becoming weaker as a ministry, one of the officers grumbled that MITI was always creating new work.

Our celebratory mood was interrupted shortly after we returned to the hotel probably because the director of JETRO Mexico had raised the alarm. That evening, the telephone in my room rang. I picked up the receiver to hear the voice of a man asking me in broken English if I was the JASME officer's wife. I recognized the voice to be a director in Research and Planning. Although my initial reaction was to hang up, I calmly acknowledged in Japanese that I was the wife. Immediately afterwards, her husband called to warn me that we had been discovered and that JETRO New York was very angry. Both officers were frightened and distressed and I promised to sort out the mess. At least I hoped I could.

When we returned to JETRO, I was exhausted. The two officers were interrogated by their superiors and the Managing Director. They insisted that I had accompanied them to support their research. The Kyoto Prefecture representative who suspected that I had facilitated the research called me on the carpet to ask me why I had provided services for other divisions. Trying to remain calm I replied that Americans enjoyed participating in numerous activities simultaneously. My boss was left speechless and nothing more was said about the incident.

The two officers submitted their reports taken from the data I had prepared and transcribed. To their relief, the reports were assessed by JETRO Tokyo as the best that had been received for many years. Although we were exonerated, I felt that I had paid a high a price for protecting the officers. On the other hand, they felt an obligation to me and invited me to visit them in Japan at their offices. I accepted.

Ehime Knows Best: Ben & Jerry's, Katz Deli, Krispy Kreme

The Ehime representative had a sweet tooth and knew where to go for his favorite brand of ice cream. I had never heard of Ben & Jerry's until he introduced me and the JASME officer to a Ben & Jerry outlet in Lower Manhattan. Evidently, the officer knew the brand because Ben & Jerry was known in Japan as a producer who used environmentally friendly methods to manufacture its ice cream. He suggested that we try Cherry Garcia, I was not fond of cherry-flavored ice cream but it was surprisingly good.

After Ben & Jerry's the officer guided us to Katz Deli on Lower Houston not only for the giant sandwiches but, as importantly, to see where the famous orgasm scene was shot for the movie "When Harry Met Sally."

The officer liked donuts too and had spotted an article in the New York Times about a new donut shop located across the street from the Apollo Theatre in Harlem. He asked me to take him to Krispy Kreme Donuts for a taste test. I was not sure how he would react when he was surrounded by African Americans and by the obvious discrepancy between the wealth of mid-town and lower Manhattan and Harlem. The officer was duly impressed with the donuts as he gobbled the blueberry, lemon and custard cream. To mark the occasion I took photos of him in front of the Apollo Theatre. The officer obviously knew a good thing because Krispy Kreme became so popular that it soon expanded outlets to include Penn Station.

Rats Running Amok

The representative was from a rural area in Ehime where the population was Japanese and was uncomfortable in the "Golden Apple" with its ethnic diversity. He escaped to China Town in lower Manhattan to eat Chinese food, go to a Chinese barber and frequent Chinese sex shows at Chinese clubs. He told me that he planned to marry a Japanese girl in China.

Despite his dislike of the "Golden Apple" I took him to see some sites in New York City; Grammercy Park, Theodore Roosevelt's birthplace where the original Teddy Bear was on exhibit, Riverside Church which was the Rockefeller family's church, St John the Divine Cathedral, Lincoln Center and the Cloisters as an example of the Rockefeller family's philanthropic efforts. Since the officer was "researching" the retail industry, I took him to Bloomingdales, Macy's and to Wall-Mart to name just a few.

By far, the most memorable excursion in the city was to China Town where the officer introduced me to a restaurant serving Shanghai cuisine to satisfy my craving for Shanghai cooking. He often ate at the restaurant and knew the owner to whom he spoke in perfect Mandarin. We decided to walk back to our flats through the Italian district. It was about 10:30pm when we passed a Catholic church. The heavy front doors were shut. Suddenly, we saw a herd of rats escaping under the doors of the church and running down the steps onto the street. It was a scene out of a horror movie. The officer thought that the church cat was chasing the rodents. He liked cats, particularly the one he insisted he saw with a tattoo on its leg being led by its owner on a leash.

Mr M's and My America: Pittsburgh

The initial of the officer's first name was M and it is appropriate that I identify him in this way because of his need to escape from Manhattan and JETRO and my need to forge a formal yet friendly relationship with the officer and with Ehime Prefecture, representing one of the poorer prefectures beholden to the national ministries.

When he was invited by the Pittsburgh Chamber of Commerce in the spring of 1997 to contribute an article on Ehime to its magazine and to be interviewed in Pittsburgh he asked me to accompany him. I reserved rooms in the Hilton Hotel and round trip tickets to Pittsburgh on Amtrak. It was worth the eight hour trip each way just to experience the two-minute ride around the world-famous horseshoe curve at the summit of the Allegany Mountains between Harrisburg and Pittsburgh. The track was constructed in 1854.

Unfortunately, the officer had no respect for American women, especially African American women and his vulgar comments indicated his xenophobic attitudes due to lack of exposure to ethnic groups other than Asian. When we were alone, he took great pleasure asking me why African American women's posteriors were fat, and why their male partners called them "baby." His comments about Caucasian women were no less lewd. He was fascinated with nipple piercing and "breast pillows." It was so bizarre that I preferred turning a blind eye.

Most of the rooms in the Hilton had been reserved by African Americans attending a regional Baptist convention. Mr M gazed at the African American women wearing pastel and crinoline frocks and elegant hats. Their small children were beautiful with their hair tied with pastel ribbons. There was not one fat posterior in sight. The convention was held in the hotel's conference room. A gospel choir sang during the services and when I approached the assistants sitting at a table outside of the hall to inquire if Mr M and I could listen to the music we were greeted warmly and given seats in the front row with glasses of water to moisten our throats in case we wanted to join in. The choir was superb. I was careful not to speak to him about his views but I hoped that Mr M recognized all of the positive attributes of an ethnic group he had regarded as inferior to Japanese.

I took Mr M to the University of Pittsburgh for a bit of history and to lunch in the student cafeteria to observe the student body culture, which he enjoyed immensely. On to the Carnegie Mellon Institute and the Fort Pitt Blockhouse followed by a ride on a cable car up and down the Inclines. During a walk over one of the bridges crossing the Ohio River I explained Andrew Carnegie's role in the city's development and the impact on the city from Carnegie's philanthropy.

Pittsburgh? Why Pittsburgh?

I received requests from one of the directors of the Foreign Agricultural Service (FAS) in Washington DC for information about Japanese consumer culture and recommendations of the kinds of processed foods and produce which would find consumer acceptance. He included the information in the FAS monthly publication. He also referred food companies in search of market information to me for free advice. One conversation was with a marketer in Pillsbury who wanted to know if a frozen pizza would sell in Japan. I asked him if he had been to Japan to look at the frozen food section in supermarkets. When he replied that he had not I informed him that if he and his colleagues had done some on-site research they would have discovered that brands from the large domestic food producers would be tough competitors. Furthermore, the Japanese craved different toppings on their pizzas such as squid and octopus and that they tended to eat pizza as snacks and even for breakfast. I recommended that Pillsbury consider frozen bagels.

I organized a dialogue between the FAS director and the officer seconded from the Ministry of Agriculture, Forest and Fisheries at JETRO New York. Both directors found the session instructive. When I mentioned that an officer from Ehime Prefecture government was also at JETRO New York, a few months later the director invited Mr M and me to give a presentation about Ehime consumer culture to the FAS at the Food and Drug Agency (FDA) in Washington DC. Since the trip was an opportunity to escape from JETRO and since his trip would be funded by Ehime Prefecture Mr M gladly accepted. I booked train tickets and the hotel.

The day before our departure for the FAS, I went to Research and Planning to assist Mr M arrange the presentation. In my haste I inadvertently tripped over Mr M's waste paper basket and tore ligaments in my ankle. By the time I returned home, the pain was acute but I assumed if I taped the ankle, the pain would subside by morning. But on the contrary, my ankle and foot had swollen to such an extent that I could barely fit into my trainers which I wore with a proper blue suit for the trip to Washington DC.

We arrived at the FAS office by 10am and the director escorted us to a large meeting room where about 30 officers had gathered around a long table. The deputy director of the FDA greeted us, introducing me first as a writer for *Inside/Outside Japan*, adding, "And we are all looking at *Inside/Outside Japan*." Her remark struck me as peculiar and I dismissed it until the end of Mr. M's presentation when one of the officers present asked Mr. M his views on Japan – China relations. Before Mr. M could reply I interrupted stressing that our visit was to explain Ehime's agricultural industry and consumer culture. Since some of the officers who attended had high security clearance, including the wife of the captain of Airforce One, I wondered if it was known that Mr M engaged in monitoring US-China relations. On the other hand, sending two copies monthly of *Inside/Outside Japan* to the CIA may have perked curiosity about what was transpiring at JETRO New York.

After the session Mr M and I were taken by the head of the FSA, the FDA deputy director and several officers who had attended the session to the FDA commissary for lunch. I managed to hobble down the long corridor to the commissary in my trainers and blue suit, not a typical outfit for a visit to Washington DC and the FDA. The lunch conversation focused on Mr. M's experiences in the US. When he was asked his favorite American city, without mentioning that Pittsburgh was the only city he had visited outside of New York State, Mr M answered that he loved Pittsburgh. Everyone looked at me incredulously: "Pittsburgh? Why Pittsburgh?"

As we departed the FAS office, a young woman ran after me and, handing me a slip of yellow paper with a phone number, she told me that if I needed anything I should call the number on the paper. Since I could always contact the FAS director I was concerned about the motivation and discarded the paper. Upon reflection, my unique fashion statement and Mr M's love of Pittsburgh probably assuaged their suspicions that Mr M was a foreign agent and that JETRO New York was a base for industrial espionage.

Despite the ankle, within a few days I managed to take Mr M to masses of Americana. We visited the White House, the Capital Building, and took a ride on the underground tram to the Senate offices. We went to the Hall of Archives to see the original Constitution and the Bill of Rights. On to the Folger Shakespeare Library and the Library of Congress where I took out a membership. I dragged Mr M to the Smithsonian Institute, the Lincoln Monument and to see the Vietnam Memorial and the Korean War Memorial nearby.

Visiting the homes of former American Presidents seemed to be the most entertaining and the most effective means for exposing Mr M to American history. I rented a car for the drive to George Washington's home in Mt Vernon, James Madison's home in nearby Montpelier and, finally, to Thomas Jefferson's home in Monticello, Virginia. Mr M may have had difficulty understanding the tour guides' English explanations but the exhibits gave him a firm grasp of American history.

Mr M enjoyed a sail on the Chesapeake Bay on a crab trawler and eating soft shell crabs. His textbooks were void of Second World War history so I took him to the United States Ordinance Museum where old army aircraft and weaponry were on display. I photographed him sitting on a US tank and standing in front of the sign "Uncle Sam Wants You!" At the end of the trip, we visited Annapolis, the US naval college, which Mr M comfortably related to perhaps because the photographs of healthy young naval plebs and the exhibits focused more on America's present rather than on its past.

More Escapes: Philadelphia and Lancaster, the home of Woolworths and the Amish

The trip to Pittsburgh and Washington triggered a string of requests from Mr M. during 1997 to take him to other regions. He never told me how he financed his travel expenses but I assumed that he was relying on the additional salary he received for secondment. I managed to cut costs by often staying with friends and family and leasing cars for the travel. It was an expensive and time-consuming venture but I recognized that my efforts would culminate in an invaluable trip to Ehime to confirm the relationship between a prefecture and the central ministries and the use of the subsidies received from central government coffers.

Since we could not be away from JETRO for longer than two days we used long weekends for travel, departing on Friday and returning on Sunday. I tried to pack in as much history as possible choosing Philadelphia and Lancaster Pennsylvania where the first Woolworths was established to provide Mr M a reason for being absent from the office.

I took Mr M to see the Liberty Bell before going to the Benjamin Franklin Museum where he learned that Franklin had been one of the authors of the American Constitution, was the Ambassador to France and had founded the US postal system. We went to the Reading Market where he enjoyed ice cream and various cakes before going to the adjacent China Town. The railroad museum with exhibits of locomotives detailed Pennsylvania's economic development through the expansion of the railroad.

Even though the tour of the University of Pennsylvania's School of Architecture and Wharton School was mildly interesting, Mr M's best moments were spent in the university's student union watching the students of various ethnic groups engaging with each other while they ate their lunch.

Lancaster proved a success because of the Amish in their traditional dress and their horse-drawn carriages. Mr M, a foody, liked the visit to a pretzel factory. I managed to squeeze in a tour of the George Washington Museum and Valley Forge before returning to New York.

Las Vegas: not just for the slots but for the mint and more

Mr M begged me to take him to Las Vegas. Initially, I did not consider the town relevant to regional economic development but then I reconsidered. Though financed largely by the Los Angeles underworld, the city was a perfect example of how a small town in the middle of the Mohave Desert became the entertainment capital of the world.

I reserved plane tickets and one hotel room with twin beds to conserve funds. Since I was his mother's age, it was a perfectly proper solution. The plane landed at Las Vegas Airport in the evening and the town was ablaze with neon signs thanks to the diversion of the Colorado River which provides the water and the electricity. Mr M could not believe that profits from the gambling industry alleviated the need for Nevada's corporate and state income taxes.

Before heading to the casino we visited the antique car show in the hotel. I allowed Mr M two nights at the slots and only $15 worth of chips each night. Mr M relished watching gamblers standing at the "one-arm-bandits" for hours while gulping down the casino's fast food and giant plastic cups of soft drinks and beer. Of course, he sampled the food but gave it poor reviews. On all of our trips, Mr M's main pleasure seemed to be staring at people as if they were animals in a zoo. He was definitely escaping from his world. The next day we were off by bus for the 30-

mile ride to the Grand Canyon returning in the evening for a second night at the slots and a walk around downtown Las Vegas, people-gawking.

In the morning I rented a car and raced through the desert to Bryce Canyon National Park to show the magnificent red rock canyon of Southwest Utah. Mr M who was overcome by the expanse of land exclaimed, "Susan, America is too big and too rich!" which he repeated continuously until he returned to Japan. His attitude was probably similar to how many foreigners perceived the US.

Returning to Las Vegas, we boarded a flight to Reno because I wanted to show Mr M casinos which were primarily frequented by the retired community, a sharp contrast to Las Vegas. Mr M was fascinated by the grey-haired gamblers and the fact that Reno was where anyone could get divorced and then remarry in a single day.

But Reno was not the end of the line. I took him to the US mint and railroad museums in Carson City to explain Nevada's regional development through the silver mining industry and the transcontinental railroad constructed by Chinese immigrant laborers.

We made a pilgrimage to Tule Lake in northwest California where a monument commemorated one of the largest internment camps where American citizens of Japanese ancestry were interned after the bombing of Pearl Harbor. I explained that the prisoners' assets, including their farmland, had been confiscated. Ironically, the volcano Mt Shasta towered in the distance, a reminder of Mt Fuji with its cap of snow.

A Red White and Blue Fourth of July

For the Fourth of July holiday we took the ferry from Boston to Martha's Vineyard to stay with my aunt and uncle in a cottage adjacent to their renovated farmhouse. The colorfully painted Victorian clapboard houses on one side of the island had been built during the Civil War by former slaves who had escaped southern plantations via the Underground Railroad. The houses were now owned by their wealthy progeny who used them for holiday retreats. Mr M witnessed a traditional Fourth of July parade for the first time.

California Here We Come

Mr M wanted to visit the Sacramento State Fair in late August to view the livestock show and to meet several Japanese residents who were natives of Ehime. He would be able to charge the travel expenses to Ehime. This trip was a ten-day affair with the first stop in San Francisco.

The plane was scheduled to take-off from La Guardia at 7am and I instructed Mr M to wait outside of his apartment building where I would collect him by taxi at 5am sharp. Mr M was not outside when I arrived. I rang his bell several times before he answered in a sleepy voice. He finally appeared disheveled and, whispering dramatically, he claimed that he had been all night at JETRO "spying" on something regarding a top level meeting between American and Chinese officials. I guessed that he had either been at JETRO "spying" or at a club in China Town.

We landed at San Francisco Airport in the evening. Since my parent's flat could not accommodate guests, we stayed at a hotel. When Mr M complained that he could not see the Golden Gate Bridge that evening, to compensate, I called his room at 6:30am the following morning to insist that we walk across the bridge to see the sun rise over the Pacific and then to Bakers Beach for a view of the bridge. Mr M rode a cable car, walked through Golden Gate Park with an interlude at the Japanese Tea Garden for a cup of green tea, which he pronounced undrinkable, and Fisherman's Wharf where he wolfed down fresh crab and prawns for a pittance compared to Japan.

On 31 August I borrowed my parent's car for the drive to Sacramento and the State Fair where Mr M photographed a number of the livestock exhibits. We visited the Ehime residents' home where Mr M exchanged gifts with them. In the late afternoon we headed back to the city. I made a pit stop at a gas station at 6:30pm and when I entered the store to pay the tab the news that Princess Diana had been critically injured in a car crash in a Paris tunnel was blaring from the shop's radio. By the time we reached San Francisco, the princess had succumbed to her injuries.

The next morning, Mr M went alone to the Castro District which he called "Gay Town" to see how the community was reacting to the news of the death of one of the key supporters of Aids research. He photographed the colorful display of flowers laid in her memory. Mr M was enthralled with "Gay Town"and returned the following day to "gay watch."

My parents' car came in handy during the rest of the trip. On the way to my family's property located adjacent to the Point Reye's Peninsula National Seashore Mr M saw the giant sequoias in Muir Woods. We drove to the Napa-Sonoma Valley for a visit to Jack London's house because several of the author's books had been translated into Japanese.

We took the half-day trip from Fort Bragg through the redwood forests on the two-gauge Skunk Line in Humboldt Country to understand how the north-eastern California coast developed through lumber and fishing. The train made a 15-minute stop at the junction between Fort Bragg and Willets where I purchase at a kiosk a fan decorated with the American flag labeled "made-in-China."

Mr M asked to visit Stanford University to stroll around the campus and to eat in the student union so I extended the excursion to three days. On the way to Monterey I stopped in Gilroy the garlic capital of the word, where Mr M tasted the garlic-laced ice cream. We drove along the scenic Highway One to Carmel for a night before heading to Monterey where Mr M thoroughly enjoyed visiting the salt water aquarium which was funded by David Packard (the other half of Hewlett), an example of corporate philanthropy. Most likely Mr M had never read the works of John Steinbeck because SCAP had banned "Of Mice and Men." As recently as 1991 the book had received numerous complaints in Japan for its racial slurs and offensive language. Regardless, I wanted Mr M to see the internationally renowned writer's hometown. "Susan! America is too big and too rich!"

New York is a Wonderful Town but Ben & Jerry's in Vermont is better

Mr M cleverly connected the foray to Ben & Jerry's in Manhattan with a request to visit Ben & Jerry's corporate headquarters in Vermont because he wanted to "research" the corporate philosophy which focused on environmental issues. I connected the proposed pilgrimage with regional economic development.

For the three-day outing I rented a car and drove directly to Ben & Jerry's. It was October and pumpkin season. Mr M was treated with a spectacular array of trees on fire with red and orange leaves. We toured Ben & Jerry's, saw a short movie regarding the corporate philosophy and sampled a soon-to be released chocolate ice cream laced with fish-shaped marshmallows named Phish Food after the rock group. I introduced Mr M to pumpkins and maple syrup before heading to Massachusetts and Tangle Wood, the summer camp for young musicians in the Berkshires and where the Seiji Ozawa, the Japanese conductor of the Boston Symphony Orchestra conducted summer concerts. Mr M had read the Japanese translation of Moby Dick and so I took him to Herman Melville's house where the author wrote the book while gazing from his study at a mountain called the "Grey Whale."

On the way back to Manhattan I made a pit stop at a café in a small town so that Mr M could eat Sunday brunch while ogling residents on their way home from church wolfing down huge portions of pancakes, bacon, eggs and fried potatoes – a scene out of small town America.

"Susan! America is too big and too rich!"

20

Decisions, Decisions

Prime Minister Hashimoto was intent on fiscal consolidation. In order to control Japan's sovereign debt which had been increasing since 1992, he made the bold decision to raise the consumption tax from 3 percent to 5 percent on April 1, 1997. The tax hike coincided with the Asian Financial Crisis when Japan was experiencing an apparent economic recovery from the 1990 financial crisis. The country slumped into recession and Hashimoto's public support decreased dramatically. Hashimoto also made the unpopular decision to approve public funding of $6.85 billion to provide aid to seven of the home mortgage companies (*jusen*) burdened with masses of bad loans.

The *jusen* had been established in the 1970s by the metropolitan and top regional banks as non-deposit taking financial institutions which procured funds from the banks to provide loans for mortgages. Since the Government Housing and Loan Guarantee Corporation established in 1950 by the MOC provided mortgages, the retail banks could not compete because of asset liability risks. However, MOF wanted to extend lending opportunities for banks and supported this collaboration. The regulatory bodies at first were prefectural governments but in 1978, MOF took over and, therefore, the *jusen* were under the MOF umbrella.

Although in the 1980s the price of real estate spiraled, clients' collateral was rarely questioned by the banks and their affiliates. But when the asset-inflated real estate bubble burst, the losses from bad loans jumped, leaving the *jusen* effectively bankrupt.

However, the companies were not financial institutions thus their bad loans did not create another financial crisis. Nevertheless, in 1995 the NPL held by banks which had extended their real estate loans during the 1980s, amounted to $4 billion–$5 billion (¥100 = $1) and the banks could not sustain the losses from the liquidation of the *jusen*. In order to stem the losses of individual depository institutions, the financial system and the enormous burden on tax payers, the MOF pushed through relief financing, avoiding formal court hearings. Furthermore, the LDP was reliant on the substantial donations from farmers whose cooperative banks also funded the *jusen*.

In mid-1998 the LDP suffered a major loss in the Upper House election, forcing the prime minister's resignation. Keizo Obuchi, an LDP politician succeeded Hashimoto as Prime Minister but retained him as the head of administrative reforms. Nonetheless, Obuchi began his term by making a U-turn, cutting income taxes and increasing public spending in order to stimulate the economy out of recession.

The *jusen* scandal represented a critical systemic failure in the Japan Inc. system of government administration. What few realized was that Special Status Corporation served to rigidify this system because they connected the ministries with the private sector and politicians, encouraging vested interests and thus frustrating reforms. Although they were not complex organizations, people on the outside could not appreciate how the system worked because there was not much information in the public domain. Since the subject was politically controversial, Japanese academics preferred to avoid publishing papers regarding the organizations because they could risk losing government grants for their research.

Bill Whitaker commented:

> I think that what fools you, what is seductive is that on the surface it looks familiar. You've got tall buildings, freeways, subways and Western dress and all sorts of things that can lull you into feeling that you can relate to it and understand...But if you're there for a while, you begin to realize that it is just a thin veneer, that the real Japan is behind or beneath that thought, that Western thought.

A Risky Venture

I was witnessing first-hand the slow deterioration of the world's second largest economy which would struggle to recover from the impact of the 1990 Financial Crisis precisely because of the rigidity of the Japan Inc. system. But my views that nothing significant would change and that there would be a resurgence of nationalism contradicted the mainstream consensus. I considered that the most effective way to stimulate a realistic understanding of Japan Inc. while busting the myths about the infallibility of the Japan Inc. model would be to publish a book using information I had collected during my employment and putting Special Status Corporations at the center. But I was in a quandary of how to release the data into the public domain without compromising my colleagues or myself. I finally concluded that the most effective method would be to publish the book in an academic context for positive research even though the effort would demand entry into academia.

I investigated the programs at American universities but, not only would I have to pass a General Management Assessment Test (GMAT) which would take a year of study but, also, the PhD programs were for five years. The PhD programs at universities in England also demanded a GMAT. The only universities that at the time did not require a GMAT were Scottish universities. I had never been to Great Britain and Sandy Gordon was the only person I knew in Scotland. Although going the academic route would entail the inevitable continuation of a grueling schedule, I decided to visit Scotland to see if I could be at ease in an environment where I would again be considered a foreigner. It was a risky venture because even if I managed to survive the ordeal there was no guarantee that a book would be the end-product.

I asked Mr M if he would like to accompany me to Edinburgh not for sightseeing but to confirm whether Ehime government and small business owners would want to participate in a program I had designed to help them understand how small business owners in other regions operated. The International Study Program for the Implementation of Regional Development (INSPIRED) was also pertinent to small businesses located in other countries.

Since I would be able to arrange a stay at the Newington flat of the daughter of my parents' friends whom I had yet to meet, Mr M seized the opportunity to have a relatively inexpensive adventure. I suggested that he take some literature in English about Ehime in case there was an opportunity to engage with officials in Scottish government because the Scottish Parliament was scheduled to open in July 1999.

Ehime in Edinburgh: the LibDems and Hogmanay

We took advantage of the Christmas and New Year holiday period for the trip, arriving in London on 18 December. We stayed at a B&B in Earls Court and visited the Tower of London and the Monument. Mr M knew a Chinese lecturer at Sheffield University and wanted to stay overnight. I took him there before returning that evening to Earls Court on the last train. I had to transfer at Doncaster and when I asked the station master the number of the platform for the London-bound train he called me "love" which was the first time I had heard the northern expression.

In Edinburgh we stayed at the flat through the New Year. At first I was reluctant to contact Sandy Gordon because most likely he would not remember me but when I telephoned his home, to my surprise, he immediately recognized my voice and urged me to apply at the University of Edinburgh's School of Management (now the UoE Business School) where he knew the Head of School. The school was closed for the holidays and I postponed a second visit until February.

Our host entertained a close friend who was a committed member of the Liberal Democrats for many years and who participated in politics at the local level where the Lib Dems were influential at that time and whose policies included environmental protection issues and the development of alternative energy sources. The woman had been to Japan and was pleased to introduce Mr M at a Christmas party at the home of a member of the Ross family, the founders of the company that produces the confection the Original Edinburgh Rock. Lib Dem members enjoyed meeting Mr M who promoted his prefecture to Mike Pringle who was planning to stand for a seat for Edinburgh South in the first Parliamentary election and who later won against a Labor candidate.

I let Mr M experience Hogmanay on his own and he ventured out to the Royal Mile around 9pm before the action started. I waited anxiously until he returned at 2am pale-faced and in a mild state of shock, mumbling that he had gone to a pub on the Royal Mile where he met a man named Jim who said that he was a fireman in Glasgow. Mr M spent the evening in the pub with Jim while drunken revelers smashed bottles and glasses in the street outside. Mr M, who had a habit of exaggerating, claimed that broken glass was strewn everywhere. He managed to stay long enough to see the fireworks display above the castle.

But there was a bright side to his adventure. Jim had offered to be his guide around Glasgow on 2 January. Mr M took the train to Glasgow and returned that evening. He admitted that despite not understanding most of what Jim was explaining to him because of his Glaswegian accent, he kept nodding in the affirmative when Jim asked him if he understood (which was exactly how I behaved initially at Mercian).

I returned to Scotland in February to visit Glasgow University, Strathclyde, Stirling and the University of Edinburgh were I was interviewed and accepted. I did not inform the Head of the School of Management at the UoE of my connection with Sandy Gordon, preferring to gain acceptance to the doctoral program on my own terms. I decided to study at the UoE because the facilities best suited my INSPIRED program.

Meeting a Future Prime Minister

In April, the wife of a MITI officer seconded to JETRO New York took me to the Japan Society to hear an address by Naoto Kan the president of the recently established Democratic Party of Japan (DPJ). She had been invited by her friend Jun Azumi, a DPJ politician and one of Kan's assistants. Speaking in halting English, Kan energetically promoted his party's manifesto which encouraged devolution to ensure more policies were planned by local governments and the implementation of political reforms to allow fairer representation in the National Diet. There was no mention of fiscal reforms.

After the presentation, Azumi introduced us to Kan who gave us his business card, a copy of the DPJ's first manifesto and a poster with the DPJ logo which still decorates my kitchen wall. I was not impressed with Kan. Although he had a healthy ego, he would not make a strong leader. Former Prime Minister Yoshihiko Noda and Ozawa were also members. Hiroshi Kumagai joined the DPJ when it was initiated only to leave in 2000 after a disagreement with Kan to form an ultra-conservative party with four other disgruntled DPJ members.

On August 30, 2009 the Japanese electorate, in protest against the continuous corruption scandals in successive LDP administrations and the ineffectiveness of the policies to extricate Japan out of mild recession, gave the Democratic Party of Japan (DPJ) the majority of seats in the Lower House. Naoto Kan, the DPJ president became the Prime Minister. Mr. Azumi became the finance minister in Kan's Cabinet.

Kan had made headlines in the Japanese press while he was the Minister of Health and Welfare in Prime Minister Hashimoto's coalition government in 1996. When he investigated the ministry for its collusion in the distribution of blood tainted with HIV to haemophiliacs officials gave him the information he needed but on the condition that he would not release it to the public. However, Kan ignored their request. After he left the cabinet his information pipeline was cut and news regarding the investigation never went beyond the ministry's confines again.

On March 11, 2011 and the Fukushima nuclear disaster Kan, who was well-known for his deep mistrust of bureaucrats, considered the nuclear energy industrial sector to be embedded in a web of collusion between METI (formerly MITI) bureaucrats, the utility companies, politicians and submissive academics. His reliance on DPJ colleagues to advise him on the escalating nuclear crisis isolated him from the bureaucrats and politicians who were privy to more information about the conditions at the power plant. Kan's indecisiveness in dealing with the prolonged effect of the crisis on Japan's economy culminated in Kan's resignation the following August.

The DPJ manifesto focused on reforming the bureaucracy by eradicating Special Status Corporations and *amakudari*. By trying to bust bureaucratic rule Kan and the DPJ became the odd-men-out and, consequently, their policies were not enthusiastically supported by the ministries. Indeed, Kan's administration finally came to terms with the fact that in order to implement economic reforms and trade agreements it had to rely on ministerial support and began back-tracking on promises to weaken the bureaucracy.

Immediately after Kan became the Prime Minister in 2010 his wife Nobuko published *What on Earth will Change in Japan now that you are Prime Minister?* (*Anata ga Soori ni Natte, Ittai, Nihon no Nani ga Kawaru No?*), detailing her marriage and her husband's political background, which focused on politics at the grassroots level, challenging the traditional political system and environmental issues. Mrs. Kan wrote that her husband enjoyed person-to-person contact, pressing the flesh, drinking, and back-room politicking but not the homework.

Mr H's America

Mr M's term of duty at JETRO New York ended at the end of March to be succeeded by another Ehime government officer who will be referred to by the initial of his first name, "H." Evidently, Mr H recognized me as Mr M's American tour guide and he requested a similar service. Although I was preparing to relocate to Scotland I decided to continue my relationship with Ehime and take him to some events and locations that were within a reasonable distance from New York City.

Mr H was in his mid-thirties and married with two young boys of primary school age. His wife had remained in Matsuyama to attend the children. While Mr M's behavior could be considered outside of the "norm," Mr H was more subdued and reflective. But he was as keen as Mr M to see as much of America as possible during his time at JETRO.

The first escape was to the Gay Parade on Fifth Avenue, a block from the McGraw Hill Building. Mr H shot many photos of half-naked men in bizarre dress riding on outrageously decadent floats. He was fascinated by the "proud-to-be gay" police and fire brigades marching down the avenue.

I took him to an estate in the Hudson River Historic district to view a Scottish Highland Games, which occurred annually. One day we rode the ferry up the East River to Tarrytown and the home of Washington Irving, the author if *Rip Van Winkle* and *Sleepy Hollow* which were popular in Japan.

Mr H enjoyed the Atlantic City boardwalk in New Jersey and the Trump Casino. We walked across the Brooklyn Bridge to the Promenade for the view of Manhattan and the Twin Towers in the early evening. I introduced him to friends who invited us to lunch at their 200-year-old white clapboard house in a New Jersey town that was registered as a Historic Landmark.

Mr H Speaks to Primary School Students

When I took Mr H as my guest to a luncheon at the Foreign Policy Association we were seated at a table with a man and woman in their late sixties. Paul Bruehl had recently retired as the vice president of Merrill Lynch's international arm and his friend, Louise, a neighbor in Locust Valley, Long Island, a wealthy suburb which was commuting distance from banks and asset management houses. Louise was a patron of the Locust Valley Library and a volunteer at a primary school. When she mentioned to Mr H that the school's fifth grade class was researching Japan and had written reports and designed an exhibit of Japanese art which was on display at the school, Mr H expressed an interest in seeing the exhibit. Louise invited him to speak to the class about Ehime schools.

Mr H whose research included American primary education received a warm welcome from the students. After the talk, Louise and Paul entertained us for lunch at Louise's home. Paul mentioned that one of his protégés at Merrill Lynch was Michael Bloomberg who, by Paul's estimations, was a genius and who had a great future.

More Adventure: Tom Sawyer and Uncle Tom's Cabin

A half-day trip to Hartford, Connecticut to visit Samuel Clemens (Mark Twain) and Harriet Beecher Stowe's homes was a good choice because Mr H had read Mark Twain's books and Stowe's *Uncle Tom's Cabin* was popular in Japan. But he was unfamiliar with the Underground Railroad of which Stowe was one of the founders.

The visit was a prelude to a visit to Gettysburg and Atlanta. The Japanese knew about slavery in the South but mainly through American pop culture and the Hollywood version of *Gone with the Wind*. Mr H began to understand the tragedy of the Civil War when we visited the Gettysburg Cemetery and the Lincoln Memorial. But he particularly liked President Dwight D. Eisenhower's home and his wife Mamie's eclectic interior decoration, including the animal skin rugs, ruffled lampshades and the sofas upholstered in pink.

Black is Beautiful: Atlanta

Mr H's final adventure in the US was to Atlanta, Georgia, for three days for a glimpse of a political economic society he would never have seen otherwise. He was surprised to see that Atlanta's economic and business environment was significantly supported by an African American population who were well-educated successful business owners and politicians. If it had not been for the interview of Johnnetta B Cole for *Inside/Outside Japan*, I would not have known about Spelman College. By luck Martin Luther King's alma mater Morehouse College was located directly across the street. Mr H saw how the Civil Rights Movement had impacted on Atlanta's economic development to the extent that Atlanta had become a center for the corporate headquarters of CNN and Coca Cola and many multinational firms. We toured CNN and Coca Cola where we taste tested drinks produced specifically for consumer preferences in countries where Coca Cola was marketed. We also visited the Jimmy Carter Museum.

Mr H's Edinburgh

I relocated to Edinburgh in July but Mr H also wanted to visit Edinburgh like his predecessor. But since I would begin the doctoral program in October and was in the process of refurbishing a dilapidated flat I asked him to reserve a room in a B&B nearby. During the week he spent in Scotland I took him for a tour of the university and introduced him to several lecturers in the School of Management whom I had met only a few weeks earlier. One evening we joined them in a typical Scottish pub.

Mr H mentioned that he had purchased his home in Ehime at the tail end of the asset-inflated bubble when the property market was booming. He estimated that the flat's value had fallen by at least 30 percent. Although during my entire time at JETRO New York I was careful not to comment on Japan's economic stagnation and political turmoil, I took the liberty of gingerly suggesting that Japan's economy was experiencing serious problems. Mr H reacted by shouting, "What do you know? You're only an American!" I understood his reaction because he, as did Japanese in general, considered foreigners to be "outsiders" and that only the Japanese could understand their political economy. On the other hand, the Japanese feel that they are the "outsiders" when they travel abroad. Although not as insular, many societies are sensitive to such remarks from foreigners in their countries.

Support for Good Instincts: better late than never

I became confident that my conviction that Special Status Corporations linked the ministries with the private sector, local governments, and politicians when a series of books were published by Japanese activists. Tsutomu Kuji, a political and environmental activist who had written about scandals involving the Ministry of Construction and the Ministry of Health and Welfare and the connections with the industries in their respective administrative jurisdictions, published a book in 1998 about the *amakudari* practices of MOF officials. In *The Bureaucrats' Kingdom: Japan's Downfall (Kanryo Kokka Nippon no Botsuraku)* he claimed that, traditionally MOF officials served as vice presidents or directors in Special Status Corporations that were managed by the other ministries. They would move to such MITI corporations as the New Energy and Industrial Technology Development Corporation (NEDO), the JASME, the Japan National Oil Corporation and so forth. MOF officials went to the MOC's Government Housing and Loan Corporation and the Agriculture, Forestry and Fisheries' Finance Corporation. On the other hand, generally, MOF, which controlled the annual budget, was reticent to open the doors of its 900 corporations to other ministries.

Kuji wrote that in 1997, the prime minister's office announced in a "White Paper on Public Corporations" that 7,080 bureaucrats had moved to 28,089 public corporations and that 184 retired officials received upper management positions in 87 public corporations connected to MOF. Kuji maintained that even though the corporations had different names their responsibilities were remarkably similar and it was obvious that they were established as places for *amakudari*.

In 1999 Koki Iishi, a DPJ politician who held a seat in the Lower House of the National Diet, also published a book about *amakudari* entitled *Bureaucrat Heaven: The Bankrupting of Japan (Kanryo Tenkoku Nihon Hassan).* He followed this with a fine book on Special Status Corporations in 2001. In *The Parasites That Are Gobbling Up Japan: Dismantle All Special Status Corporations and Public Corporations!(Nihon wo Kuitsuku Kisiechu Tokyshu Houjin Koeki Houjin wo Zenhai Sieyo!)*.

Iishi, whose concerns centered on political and administrative misconduct, contended that Special Status Corporations and public corporations must be the focus of structural reforms. He claimed that the national ministries operated 6,879 public corporations, 76 Special Status Corporations had 2,000 subsidiaries and that local government operated public corporations which provided jobs for local government officers. He also contended that Special Status Corporations bred subsidiaries and that even though the parent corporations operated at a loss, their subsidiaries could be showing profits which were divided among the parent companies and their other subsidiaries.

His book posed pertinent questions concerning the rapid escalation of public corporations that were established through Special Status Corporations and government agencies and the employment opportunities they offered to elite bureaucrats. The reluctance of the ministries to reform these corporations, thereby preserving their territory, symbolized the rigidity of Japan's political economic system. He stressed that there had been little movement towards reform of any kind and that before structural reforms could commence Special Status Corporations had to be dismantled.

Sadly while he was serving as the chairman of the Special Committee on Disasters, Iishi was assassinated by a right-wing sympathizer in front of the National Diet on October 25, 2001.

In 2001 Tsutsumi Kazuma, a former secretary-general for the Liaison-Council of Labor Unions in Public Corporations, published a revealing report on the methods used by the ministries to ensure that their retired elite officials were comfortably ensconced in one or more of their corporations. *The Monster Ministries and Amakudari: White Paper on Corruption (Kyodai Shocho Amakudari Fuhai Hakusho)* provided a detailed account of the ministries' corporations and a chronological chart indicating the migration of retired ministry officials to Special Status Corporations who then moved on to upper management positions in private industry or other Special Status Corporations. The chart included MITI officials' migration to JETRO overseas offices.

Although very concerned about the route to academia, I knew that I had made the right decision.

21

The Last Piece in the Puzzle

The Japan Finance Corporation for Small and Medium Sized Enterprise

In the spring of 1999 I took the opportunity to visit the JASME officers in the Tokyo and Hiroshima offices and Mr M and Mr H in Matsuyama. I also wanted to conduct interviews of small business owners. The officer posted at the head office in Tokyo arranged meetings and interviews with small business owners to whom I would never have been able to gain access without the assistance of the JASME. Furthermore, I would never have been able to tape the interviews without the presence of a JASME officer.

During the two-day visit I conducted interviews with firms which produced electronic parts, car parts, semi-conductors and chemicals. The businesses produced for large domestic companies which also procured cheaper goods from foreign firms. The owners spoke about how they were coping with the recession and how they received subsidies from MITI. With the exception of the chemical firm, the owners expressed frustration with the time-consuming process involved in applying for subsidies for R&D. Furthermore, the recipients were required to submit the results to MITI which distributed them to other businesses to ensure a level playing field.

The most revealing meeting in terms of the Japan Inc. model and the significance of interpersonal networks between business and government was a two-hour interview with the CEO of a medium sized chemical firm whose father-in-law had founded the company in 1941 as a producer of special chemicals for the war effort. MCI administered the chemical industry during the war and since the company had produced for the war effort, it remained in good standing with MITI after the war. Between 1952 and 1977 the company received a number of subsidies from MITI for R&D. The founder's interpersonal network in government helped him to import new and inexpensive technologies in the 1950s and the 1960s. His strategy included creating a niche market by producing new chemical products and expanding operations overseas. His connection with MITI may also have expedited his applications for patents, licenses and permits.

By poaching an officer from the JASME as Senior Managing Director of Executive Affairs, the founder placed his company in a favorable position to receive long term, low interest rate loans from the JASME. After the founder's death, his son-in-law took over as the CEO and continued to tie-up with a major pharmaceutical firm and a clock manufacturer, supplying them with chemicals.

The new CEO, looking ahead at foreign markets, opened a sales office in Hong Kong in the early 1980s. Eyeing markets in Europe and the United States, the CEO engaged in a joint venture with a major Japanese trading company, a wise move because the trading company had long-established distribution channels but did not manufacture the same kinds of chemicals. The company supplied technical information and production acumen, and the trading company supplied investment and distribution.

To ensure an enduring relationship, the CEO hired an employee from the trading company who had been based in Europe for many years, who knew how to conduct business in European countries and who was an appropriate figure for liaising with his former employer. Another pay-off was that the vice chairman of the trading company had been an elite official in MITI, giving the company additional connections to the ministry.

Nevertheless, the CEO did not take his connections for granted, working tirelessly to maintain and to extend his interpersonal network in business and government. He was the friend of a former prime minister who graduated from the same university. He was the president of his district's Chamber of Commerce and Industry, a chartered corporation managed by MITI's Industrial Policy Bureau. The CEO also served simultaneously in other small and medium sized business organizations managed by MITI. Through this participation, the CEO was in constant contact with other business owners and with elite officials.

Ehime Prefecture

Before heading on to Ehime Prefecture I spent a day in Hiroshima to visit the offices of the JASME officer who introduced me to some of his colleagues, including the director of the office, an MOF official. I shot a short video of the officer explaining the services provided to small businesses but afterwards when he showed me a pile of brochures and leaflets describing the services, he said that they had yet to be implemented. His admission confirmed the article in *Nikkei Business* that the ministries established Special Status Corporations and their subsidiaries to provide temporary employment for staff and post-retirement positions for retired senior officials before they moved to the private sector and that corporations used funds to do work that was in the best interests of the corporations. I wanted to know how the corporation assessed collateral for loans but I thought it best not to ask.

The two-hour ferry ride across the Seto Sea (Inland Sea) to Matsuyama was as interesting as it was scenic. A gentleman who was seated on the bench in front of me wore a gold necklace and an array of tattoos. Even though I could not see if he was missing the tip of his little finger, an indication that he was a member of the Yakuza, I suspected that he was.

Mr M and Mr H rolled out the red carpet. They had booked a hotel room and scheduled two days showcasing everything I needed to confirm what I already had suspected but was reluctant to ask them in New York. After paying my respects to his colleagues at the prefecture government office, Mr M took me to interview the owner of a small business which produced car parts for one of Japan's major automobile manufacturers. The owner expressed concerns about the impact on his business from the hollowing-out of the automobile industry in Japan.

I visited Iyo Bank where I interviewed the president who entirely positive about Ehime's economy and proud of the bank's establishment of overseas branches in Manhattan and Hong Kong.

Before a visit to FAZ, Mr M escorted me to the major fish auction house on Shikoku where catches from the Seto Sea were sold daily to retailers. However, due to pollution and over-fishing, the catches were decreasing.

The installations in the Ehime World Trade Center (I.T.E.M EHIME) were extensive. Within I.T.E.M was an Ehime Products and Tourism Center divided into three areas where products from local industries where exhibited. There were paper products, towels, canned and bottled *mikan* juice and extruded fish paste known as *chikua* one of my staples in Japan. Mr M told me that towels, imported from China were undercutting the price of the towels produced in Ehime as were the "made-in-China" paper products. We could not help but laugh because every time I took Mr M to look at the merchandise at US retailers invariably the soft goods carried "made-in-China" labels.

The World Mart displayed examples of foreign goods which had been introduced to Ehime consumers. Given Ehime residents' conservative tastes I doubted that the colorful African textiles would be items on consumers' wish-lists. There were confections and Marmite from New Zealand and Vegemite from Australia, a Swiss cuckoo clock, honey and jam, and a South African bicycle, which was odd because the Japanese bicycle industry was a protected industry. A JETRO Support Center was located next door.

The exhibition hall and conference room were vacant. When I asked Mr M how often the facilities were used he replied, "That's a good question."

A second FAZ was under construction. According to the Ehime Foreign Access Zone Co. the construction "involved building a new port and roads connecting the facilities to the expressway system. The result will be a comprehensive upgrading of industrial infrastructure."

"Empty Boxes"

An Ehime Prefecture government officer drove me on newly constructed highways and through tunnels that were carved through Ehime's beautiful mountainous terrain. There was little traffic. I doubted whether a second FAZ was necessary but Governor Iga and his friends in the ministries pressed for public sector investment in infrastructure to expand Ehime's economy while also providing lucrative contracts to big businesses and employment to hundreds of Ehime residents.

The officer stopped at the Kurushima-Kaikyo Bridge due to be opened soon. It was a magnificent piece of engineering but I silently questioned how the JH's Shikoku-Honshu Bridge Authority could justify the expense. I had the same question when the officer took me to the new international airport where few passengers were waiting in the terminal.

I was hoping to go to the nuclear power plant in Ikata to see how the town had prospered since the plant was commissioned but I was reluctant to request a visit which might be considered off-limits to foreigners.

Mr H and his wife entertained me for lunch at their flat before taking me to Matsuyama Castle and to the modern art museum resplendent with mahogany toilets. But the small collection of art did not justify the expenditure not only for the museum but the expenditure for the highways, the airport, the bridge and FAZ. It seemed as if no consideration had been given to the ultimate costs of the projects, let alone the drain on local tax revenue for the maintenance of what were essentially empty boxes.

During the remainder of my visit I played the tourist with Mr M and Mr H. Mr M took me to Dogo Onsen, Japan's oldest hot spring which was the site of Natsume Soseki's book *Botchan*. I consumed a good number of Japanese cakes named after the hero, which was a major incentive for visiting Dogo. Mr H took me to Kagawa Prefecture for the prefecture's specialty Sanuki Udon.

Although Governor Iga was expected to maintain control over Ehime politics, the recession prompted dissatisfied voters to replace him in January 1999 with Moriyuki Kato, a high-ranking official in the Ministry of Education who retired from office to enter politics. The initial reaction from local businesses was positive because Kato's close ties to the national ministries would hopefully serve to facilitate the procurement of public works contracts and subsidies.

The Ehime government officer who escorted me to the bridge and airport said that Iga had gained the reputation among residents as a governor obsessed with self-glorification.

Just to Make Sure

In the spring of 2001 I returned to Hiroshima to reconfirm my initial observations at the JASME branch. There was no evidence of any change in strategy or that the services described in the 1999 brochures were available to business owners.

I went to Ehime for another look-see at FAZ. Between 1997 and 2001 there were a total of 11 international trade fairs but generally the halls at I.T.E.M. EHIME were vacant. There was no noticeable change in the range of foreign imports in the World Mart. Foodstuffs, wine, toys, sporting equipment on display overshadowed industrial goods.

Traffic was still relatively light on the new network of highways. Commuters to Hiroshima preferred the ferry rather than the Kurushima-Kaikyo Bridge to avoid the expensive toll.

In February a US naval submarine had collided with the Ehime Maru, a fishing vessel, when it suddenly surfaced off the coast of Oahu, Hawaii. Nine crew members on the fishing vessel drowned, including four high school students. Mr M was outraged that the captain had not tried to rescue the crew members and that Commander Scott Waddle had not offered an apology immediately following the accident. After a public court hearing and a naval board inquiry, Waddle was forced to resign from the Navy.

The Image of Administrative Reforms

The year 2001 was an auspicious one. Prime Minister Hashimoto was determined to streamline government administration by consolidating some of the ministries and integrating minor agencies into the ministries as of 2001. However, the mergers did little more than change the names of the various ministries. The Ministry of Construction merged with the Ministry of Transport, the National Land Agency and the Hokkaido Development Agency, which was burdened with debt. The new ministry was named the Ministry of Land, Infrastructure and Transport (MLIT). Prior to the merger the Ministry of Transport had 849 public corporations. The Ministry of Education, which had 1,811 corporations, merged with the Science and Technology Agency to form the Ministry of Education, Culture, Sports, Science and Technology (MEXT). The Ministry of Home Affairs merged with the Ministry of Management and Coordination, and the Ministry of Posts and Telecommunications to form the Ministry of Public Management, Home Affairs, Posts and Telecommunications. The ministries managed jointly the corporations which had originally been independently established by a single ministry.

MITI was left unfettered with only a minor adjustment to its name - the Ministry of Economy, Trade and Industry (METI), signifying that the ministry was going to administrate more regional economic development. MOF was also left to its own devices. The officers at JETRO New York were correct in their assessment that the mergers would prove to be ineffective in making government smaller.

Indeed, the mergers did little more than to create turmoil within the newly merged ministries regarding the restructuring of management, territorial issues, budgets and objectives. Furthermore, officials were very concerned about how the mergers would impact on their careers in terms of ranking and promotion. The mergers triggered a gradual brain drain from the ministries as officers opted to leave for jobs in the private sector or in local government where the salaries were equal to the national ministries.

The *New History Textbook*: Ehime residents versus Big Brother

On April 1, 2000 Prime Minister Keizo Obuchi suffered a stroke and lapsed into a coma until his death in May. Yoshio Mori, an LDP politician succeeded him as Prime Minister. On April 26, 2001 Junichiro Koizumi, an LDP politician succeeded Mori as Prime Minister.

Koizumi represented a breed of neo-nationalist politicians who had become a force in politics since the late 1980s. Although Koizumi was a proponent of institutional reforms, he will be remembered best for his six pilgrimages to Yasukuni Shrine where, not only Japan's military dead are buried but also Class A War Criminals. The Shinto Shrine was founded in 1869 and run by the military until the end of the Second World War, when the United States Occupation outlawed Shintoism. Infuriated by Koizumi's apparent glorification of Japan's military past and disregard for the suffering incurred by the Chinese and Koreans during Japan's wartime occupation, China and North and South Korea lodged vehement protests. Despite angering important trading partners and Japanese pacifists, as well as businessmen whose ventures were vandalized by Chinese and South Korean protestors and who were extremely concerned about the ramification to future Japanese-Chinese economic relations, Koizumi continued his visits to the shrine, ending his term as Prime Minister with a sixth and final visit in August 2006.

In 2001 Koizumi supported MEXT's approval of the controversial *New History Textbook* (edited by Governor Kato's former ministry) for high-school students which glosses over the wartime atrocities committed by Japanese military in Asia such as the abduction of "comfort women." The textbook refers to the war in the Pacific as "The Greater East Asia War," the term used by Japanese nationalists.

Besides Koizumi, other proponents of the textbook included former METI Vice Minister Keiji Furuya and former Tokyo governor Shintaro Ishihara. *Sankei Shimbun*, which owned the same ultra-conservative media group that also owns the textbook's publishers, ran a series of editorials supporting the textbook. The book's authors were academics who were members of the right-wing Society of Textbook Reform and who believed that Japan had entered Asia to liberate the region from the control of white colonists and that the so-called atrocities were merely "normal excesses" committed by all armies. Despite China's and South Korea's anger over the manipulation of facts, negative reactions from the foreign press, heated debate in the Diet and strong resistance in local governments, by 2004 the book had been adopted by a number of prefectures, including Tokyo.

Governor Kato publically endorsed the textbook in 2002, announcing that he felt that the textbook was "most appropriate to deepen people's appreciation of the history of our country." Although many local citizens were opposed to the textbook, Kato received more support from Koizumi and on May 15, 2004 at an Ehime town meeting for the revised education bill. The hall was packed with 100 educators with links to MEXT. A subsequent investigation of the event revealed the following November that 65 educators had been paid ¥5,000 each for attending the meeting and that one member was given the task of spouting statements in support of the textbook and asking questions prepared by the ministry. Despite a lawsuit filed in December 2005 against Kato by 1,000 people, including South Korean and Chinese, demanding the rejection of the textbook, it was distributed to schools in 2006.

Koizumi later admitted to organizing town meetings and paying educators to give rehearsed speeches in favor of the textbook. He also displayed his nationalistic colors by drawing up an education bill in June 2006 that for the first time revised the education bill that had been written in 1947. The new bill included the promotion of "patriotism" as part of the compulsory education. Although members of the LDP and opposition parties voted against the bill because it might promote nationalism, the bill was passed into law in January 2007 during Abe's administration. The Basic Education Law calls for singing the national anthem and saluting the Japanese flag at school ceremonies as a part of children's education. The law also gives the education minister more power over local education boards and requires that teachers renew their licenses every ten years.

Before taking office for the first time in 2006, Prime Minister Shinzo Abe published his bestseller *Toward a Beautiful Country*. In it he argued that the reporting of events regarding his grandfather's revision of the US–Japan Security Treaty was misleading and must be corrected. The initial 1951 treaty inhibited the Japanese from prosecuting Americans who perpetrated crimes in Japan (e.g. military personnel). Abe claimed that his grandfather negotiated a revised treaty that gave Japan more autonomy from the United States and gave the Japanese more power to prosecute. Abe also maintained that the history of Japan's wartime engagement in

China reported in textbooks was also incorrect and should be revised as well. The *New History Textbook* praises the bravery and patriotism of Japanese military personnel.

When Prime Minister Junichiro Koizumi took office the sovereign debt was 130 percent of GDP. Koizumi, who was the Minister of Health and Welfare in Hashimoto's cabinet was determined to implement fiscal reforms, state-sector reforms and tackle the NPL. He planned to eliminate a number of Special Status Corporations which were heavily in debt to FILP. He also planned to privatize the state banks, including the Postal Savings Agency and downsize FILP, the two institutions that funded the corporations. His struggle with the ministries and politicians is well-documented in *Special Corporations and the Bureaucracy: Why Japan Can't Reform* which was the first book in English regarding Special Status Corporations and which predicted that Koizumi's efforts would be superficial at best.

22

Special Status Corporations
No, No, You Can't Take That Away From Me!

The Image of Reform

When Prime Minister Junichiro Koizumi took office in April 2001 the sovereign debt was 130 percent of GDP. Koizumi, who was the Minister of Health and Welfare in Hashimoto's cabinet, proposed reforms which encompassed three areas: i) financial reforms; ii) state-sector reforms; iii) tackling NPL; iv) reform of the social security system; v) cutting government funding to Special Status Corporations by one-third or $1.3 billion. He planned to eliminate 50 percent of the number of Special Status Corporations which were heavily in debt to FILP. He also planned to privatize the state banks, including the Postal Savings Agency and downsize FILP by 17.7 percent ($218 billion), the two institutions that funded the corporations and whose accounting methods were said to be opaque.

By 1972, Japan had achieved a 10 percent of annual GDP growth to become the world's third largest economy in the world and, realistically, many of the corporations were no longer needed to support economic development and should have been dismantled. However, the ministries had come to rely on their corporations, because not only did they provide temporary post-retirement positions for officials while they waited for the obligatory two years before migrating to positions in the private sector (*amakudari*) but, also, they served to extend ministerial powers and increase administrative jurisdiction (namely "territory"). The connections established between the ministries' officials posted in Special Status Corporations, their subsidiaries and their branch offices throughout Japan effectively linked the ministries to the private sector. Additionally, through their officials posted at branch offices of these corporations the national ministries can monitor local government policies and guide the planning of policies. A number of Special Status Corporations continued operations for many years despite bearing large debts, which would never be repaid to FILP.

As of October 1999 the number of corporations had been reduced through mergers of insolvent with solvent corporations. Nevertheless, in 2001 there were 163 corporations (not including their subsidiaries). Some Special Status Corporations began opening their books to reveal more information than had been available before 1999. However, many of the corporations, including their subsidiaries, did not provide financial statements but due to the government's investigation of accounting practices, by 1999, the financial sheets of giant corporations, including the JH and the Japan National Oil Corporation (JNOC), revealed massive debt.

Koizumi requested that the ministries review how the corporations in debt were spending funds. His determination to cut funding by 50 percent was opposed not only by members of the LDP but by members of his own cabinet. Nobuteru Ishihara, the Cabinet State Minister of Administrative and Regulatory Reforms and whose father is Shintaro Ishihara, the former governor of Tokyo recommended that only one-third of the designated corporations should be considered for reform.

Koizumi's administration devised a scheme that would convert 59 Special Status Corporations into Independent Administrative Institutions (IAIs) with the expectation that eventually financing from FILP bonds and tax revenue would no longer be necessary and that there would be more transparency with regard to accounting methods. Many of the loans were not repaid and Seiji Ota, who was the director of the LDP office for the promotion of reforms, contended that one-third of the funds allotted to Special Status Corporations by FILP were wasted. Since MOF had been reticent to use the formal budget and tax revenue to finance the increasing number of loans throughout the 1990s, FILP was burdened with toxic debt.

Similar to the "law for the establishment of Special Status Corporations," the "Incorporated Administration Law" for the establishment of Independently Administrative Institutions was implemented on December 13, 2002.

The Ministry of Public Management, Home Affairs and Telecommunications released an explanation in English that outlined the concept of the new IAI system:

> The IAI system lies on the basic concept of public welfare, transparency, and autonomy of activities as Article 3 of the Law of the General Rules provides that (i) the IAIs must make efforts for just and effective operation under the consideration that the fulfilment of their undertaking is indispensable to people's lives, society and the economy; (ii) the IAIs must make efforts to open to the public the status of their organizations and the operations by such means as the announcement of the content of their activities as provided by this law; (iii) the autonomy of each law must be respected in accordance with the application of the Law and the laws establishing the IAIs.

The Japan Highway Corporation (JH): a tug-of-war

Koizumi focused his initial efforts on the dissolution of the former MOC's debt-ridden JH, which was referred to as "the world's largest general contractor." The expenditure in 1998 of Osaka Media Port in 1998 was $60 million, the highest of the JH's subsidiaries.

Originally, Koizumi wanted to merge the JH with three other corporations - the Hanshin Expressway Corporation, the Metropolitan Expressway Corporation, and the Shikoku-Honshu Bridge Authority, which carried massive debts. In total, the accumulated debt was $488 billion. He then wanted to privatize the single entity by 2005 and have it repay the outstanding loans within 45 years. He also wanted to cut government investment in future road construction by 40 percent because costs had ballooned to $2.46 billion annually.

The plans were admirable but the implementation of them was hindered by the vested interests of LDP law-makers, who relied heavily on contributions from their constituencies, who depended on public works projects for contracts and employment, and the bureaucrats who relied upon post-retirement positions in construction-related businesses. They demanded that the debts of the Shikoku-Honshu Bridge Authority, which could not repay the FILP loans, be separated from the other corporations, and that those prefectures where the bridges were located share the burden of the repayment with central government. Koizumi's administration was pressured to produce a watered-down version of the original package that Koizumi had hoped to get through the National Diet. The cost was estimated to be $214 billion. The repayment of the debt was doubtful.

The process of the privatization of the JH was turbulent. The president was Haruhiko Fujii who had assumed the post in 2000 after retiring as Vice Minister of the former MOC. During the period he was in both offices he was popular among LDP politicians because he expanded highway networks considerably and because of his close relationship with road construction firms. He was dismissed by Nobuteru Ishihara, the land minister at the time, after a much-publicized heated confrontation with Ishihara who accused him of being uncooperative during the process of privatization.

The four public corporations were privatized on October 1, 2005. But instead of Koizumi's one entity, there are three, each with a new name. Regardless, the Ministry of Land, Infrastructure and Transportation (MLIT) which includes the former MOC, continues to manage the highway networks. FILP agency bonds fund the Japan Expressway Holding and the Debt Repayment Agency.

Special Status Corporations: the consequences of *amakudari*

The corporations in league with *amakudari* can be breeding grounds for bid-rigging which the JH exemplified. Since the JH distributed contracts to the construction companies, bid-rigging involving large construction companies was commonplace. On September 29, 2005, the Japan Fair Trade Commission (JFTC) ordered Japanese steel bridge-builders to stop bid-rigging for contracts from government and from the JH. The JFTC alleged that 20 former officials in the JH, including former Vice President Michio Uchida and a former executive board member Tsuneo Kaneko, had received jobs in 45 companies due to their involvement in bid-rigging. Among the 45 firms named were Mitsubishi Heavy Industries Co., Ishikawa-Harima Heavy Industries and Kawasaki Heavy Industries Ltd. The JFTC announced that the contracts procured through illegal bid-rigging were worth approximately $2.35 billion. Former JH officials who were employed in the bridge construction companies had accessed unpublished information in the JH regarding toll road bridge construction projects. Uchida and Kaneko, along with officials from 26 corporations were indicted for bid-rigging.

The Government Housing and Loan Guarantee Corporation (GHLC)

Koizumi resolved to liquidate another MOC corporation (Chapter 16) because it was heavily in debt. In 2002, 40 percent of all mortgage debt was from the GHLC and FILP reforms would make the provision of long-term, fixed-rate loans by the GHLC difficult. The corporation was converted to an Incorporated Administrative Agency on April 1, 2007 and renamed the Japan Housing Finance Agency (JHF) to assess mortgage debt to enable private financial institutions to create a steady supply of long term, low interest rate loans. It is 100 percent government-funded and managed by MLIT. So far, there has been no sign of success due to the soft real estate market.

The Urban Development Corporation (UDC)

Also targeted by Koizumi for reform was the UDC (Chapter 16). It was reorganized into an Incorporated Administrative Agency in July 2004 and renamed the Urban Renaissance Agency (AR). Funded 100 percent by government, its work is no longer inclusive of urban projects and projects providing housing.

Japan National Oil Corporation: METI's zombie treasure chest

Japan must import over 90 percent of its fossil fuel. METI oversees the energy-producing industries, among them oil. The ministry manages imports and refining through federations of oil importers. The former MITI established JNOC in 1967 to assist Japanese oil companies with the exploration and drilling for oil. The corporation received funding from FILP and had 142 subsidiaries and branch offices overseas. The federation connected MITI to the oil refineries which distributed to retailers. The domestic companies cooperated with foreign firms, usually holding the larger share of the investment.

Koizumi wanted to privatize the JNOC because in 1998 when the corporation was targeted for restructuring the president Kuni Komatsu, who was a former MITI Administrative Vice Minister, divulged that the company carried an outstanding debt of $1.23 billion. However, Japan's oil refiners were opposed to private companies taking over JNOC and wanted the government to continue JNOC's operations because the corporations were financially too weak to take on the risks of oil exploration.

In August 2003, JNOC declared a net loss of $1.9 billion for fiscal 2002 and an accumulated debt of $6.17 billion due to the failure of its subsidiary, the Japan Oil Development Co. (JODCO). In 2004 METI began to dismantle JNOC, privatizing some of its subsidiaries such as the Japan Petroleum Exploration Co. and the Indonesian Petroleum Co. (INPEX Corp), a major upstream oil and gas company that was established in 1966 of which it owned a 53.96 percent share. INPEX had expanded operations internationally and was popular among foreign investors.

METI agreed to clear JODCO's debts in order to convince INPEX to take over the money-losing JODCO. INPEX merged with Teikoku Oil in March 2006, receiving 81 percent of its shares. By 2008, JODCO was fully integrated into IMPEX Holdings.

One of the major complaints lodged against JNOC was poor management by officials who did not have the expertise to direct oil and production, pointing to MITI officials who took temporary positions for two years and forged relationships with domestic and foreign oil companies, which led to permanent post-retirement upper management positions in these companies. Traditionally, a retired administrative Vice Minister from the ministry filled other top management positions, such as Vice President or Director of Finance. There were a number of migrations of officials from JNOC and from other MITI Special Status Corporations to such companies as Indonesian Oil, Japan Steel Pipe Co., Mobile Shell and Abu Dhabi Oil. The trade-off for the privatization of JNOC was that *amakudari* was allowed to continue in JETRO.

Incorporated Administrative Agencies: what's in a name?

IAIs are also regarded as Incorporated Administrative Agencies through the "Incorporated Administrative Agency Act" which is still another law which is neither civil nor corporate as stated on METI's website:

> An incorporated administrative agency is a judicial person that acts independently of the state and manages business operations such as research, inspection and trade insurance that were former performed by the state. A particular feature of such agencies is that they can independently consider how to perform their operations, and run these operations in a better, more efficient manner on their own responsibility. Specifically, each minister sets objectives to be attained by agencies under his or her jurisdiction, and each agency draws up a plan to achieve the objectives and carry out operations in line with the plan. The results obtained are evaluated by outside experts and the evaluation is reflected in management plans for subsequent years.

The explanation does not include that the government intends to review all of these agencies within a period of five to seven years in terms of efficiency of operations and management. If it is determined that the corporations are no longer viable, they may be terminated or downsized. The agencies are still in operation and it is difficult to envision that ministries such as METI, MOF or MLIT would willingly part with their respective agencies.

METI retained JNOC's oil and exploration units when it was merged with its Special Status Corporation, the Metal and Mining Agency, which in 2004 was christened the Japan Oil, Gas and Metals National Corporation (JOGMEC) as an Incorporated Administrative Agency.

In addition to JOGMEC, METI manages the following Incorporated Administrative Agencies which are energy specific and which employ retired METI officials in upper management positions or as directors on the boards:

1. Japan External Trade Organization (JETRO).
2. The New Energy and Industrial Technology Development Organization (NEDO) was established by the former MITI as a Special Corporation in 1980 for the promotion and funding of projects related to renewable energy and the development of industrial technologies. With a budget of \$2.8 billion (FY2009) NEDO employs 1,000 staff and engages in projects

overseas with offices located in Silicon Valley, Washington, DC, Paris, Beijing, Bangkok and New Delhi.

3. The Japan Nuclear Energy Safety Organization (JNES).
4. The National Institute of Advanced Industrial Science and Technology (AIST) was established in 2001 as an amalgamation of 15 research institutes that were managed by the former MITI. Its predecessor had been established in 1982. The new AIST is the largest government-supported research institute in Japan with 40 autonomous research institutes employing 2,400 researchers and 700 administrative staff.

METI's other Incorporated Administrative Agencies include:

1. Institute of Developing Economies, Japan External Trade Organization (IDE-JETRO).
2. Research Institute of Economy, Trade and Industry (REITI).
3. National Center for Industrial Property Information and Training (NPIT).
4. Nippon Export and Investment Insurance (NEXI).
5. National Institute of Technology and Evaluation (NITE).
6. Japan Water Agency (JWA).
7. Japan International Cooperation Agency (JICA).
8. Information-Technology Promotion Agency, Japan (IPA).
9. Japan Organization for Employment of the Elderly, Persons with Disability and Job Seekers (JEED).
10. Organization for Small & Medium Enterprise and Regional Innovation, Japan (SMRJ).

FILP: breaking up is hard to do

Koizumi's reforms of Special Status Corporations included the privatization of state banks which, while supporting Japan's rapid economic growth, were regarded as serving similar functions. The Japan Finance Corporation (JFC) was established on October 1, 2008 by MOF under the Japan Finance Corporation Act. JFC was the result of the integration of the National Life Finance Corporation (NLFC), the Agriculture, Forestry and Fisheries Finance Corporation (AFC), JASME and the International Financial Operations (IFOs) of the Japan Bank for International Cooperation (JBIC). However, JBIC separated from the JFC in April 2012.

The JFC is a FILP designated institution which entitles it to issue FILP Agency bonds which are guaranteed by government. Koichi Hosokawa, the current Governor and CEO was the deputy Vice Minister at MOF (2002–04). He describes the JFC: "JFC is a policy-based financial institution that aims to complement financial activities carried out by private financial institutions and contributes to the improvement in the living standards of Japanese people." Hosokawa describes FILP:

> FILP are long term low interest loans and investments by the government to achieve policies: financial support for small and medium enterprises, construction of hospitals and welfare facilities, scholarship loans, and securing of overseas resource rights.

> Procuring the capital through issuing FILP bonds, (a kind of Japanese Government Bond), FILP enables the execution of providing long term and low interest funds and large-scale and long-term public projects, which have strong

policy needs, profitability and expected returns but are difficult for the private sector to deal with. Considering the harsh fiscal conditions, FILP is becoming increasingly important as fiscal measures which do not rely on tax funding.

FILP, which is one mechanism of fiscal policy, has a function of adjusting resource allocation since goods and services are not sufficiently provided if the economy is completely entrusted to the market mechanism.

FILP supplies funds that are difficult to be procured in the private sector, to FILP agencies such as government-affiliated financial institutions and incorporated administrative agencies, and such FILP agencies play a role in adjusting resource allocation by supplying various goods and services using these funds. For instance, although small and medium enterprises play an important role in the Japanese economy, they have weak credit and collateral compared to large enterprises, and they have a difficulty to obtain necessary funds from private financial institutions alone. To solve this problem, loans are provided by government-affiliated financial institutions using FILP.

The 2012 FILP Plan issued by MOF called for continued loans to state banks such as the Japan Bank for International Cooperation (JBIC) which was the result of the merger of the former MITI's EXIM and the Overseas Economic Cooperation Fund (OECF) in October 1999. In October 2008, JBIC became the international arm of the JFC to provide loans to small and medium size companies and to larger companies for the construction of infrastructure overseas and for such operations as oil mining. In the same year, JBIC was separated from the JFC. JBIC can issue JBIC bonds which are not guaranteed by government or FILP Agency Bonds which are guaranteed by government.

The Japan Development Bank (JDB) was established by MOF in 1952 to finance Japan's industrial development by providing loans to heavy industries to support both domestic and overseas expansion. In October 1999 the JDB merged with the bankrupt Hokkaido-Tohoku Development Finance Corporation, a regional public corporation managed by MOF. The merger was celebrated with a new name, the Development Bank of Japan (DBJ). The bank's former name in Japanese translates as "Japan Development Bank" (*Nihon Kaihatsu Ginko*). Although the new name in English appears to be almost identical, the English translation of the Japanese is "Investment Strategy Bank of Japan" (*Nihon Seisaku Toshi Ginko*). The DBJ is also a *tokushugaisha*.

When I met a DBJ officer who had been sent to the University of Edinburgh Business School for an MBA in 2004 he insisted that the bank would be privatized within three years. I argued that, due to Japan's recessive economy, the DBJ would remain a state bank and continue to support struggling companies. The DBJ was one of the institutions that helped in January 2010 to rescue Japan Airlines which was on the verge of bankruptcy. The DBJ was set to be privatized in 2015, assuming a key role in supporting Japan's domestic economy and industrial expansion abroad. However, the plans are still under discussion.

The two other state banks in the FSC, which provided loans to small businesses were the People's Finance Corporation, established in 1959 by MOF, and the Corporation for Agriculture and Forestry and Fisheries also established in the 1950s by MAFA.

These state banks were revised as "special corporations" or *tokushugaisha*. The ostensible difference between Special Status Corporations (*tokushuhoujin*) and the "special corporations" is that Special Status Corporations are public corporations that were established by the ministries under a "special" law. The "special corporations" established in 2008 according to a separate "special" law are entirely government-funded but the law specifies that these corporations will eventually be privatized. The banks still provide loans to SMEs engaged in agriculture and manufacturing.

Initially, the government, which owns 100 percent of the banks, had planned to sell all of the shares within a five to seven year period. However, privatization was postponed for three-and-a-half years because of the financial crisis in 2009. The privatization of the *tokushugaisha* was again postponed for three years to deal with the aftermath of the Great Northeast earthquake in March 2011 because the banks were needed to support the regions affected by the earthquake. Despite the government's intention to reconsider the process of selling shares and the degree of influence it would reserve over banking operations, at end of FY2015 the banks were still fully funded by government.

On the surface it appears that there has been a massive restructuring of Special Status Corporations (*tokushuhoujin*) with stricter guidelines regarding the use of public revenue and how the corporations justify their budgets. However, although FILP has been downsized, there is no doubt that in the case of many of these corporations, the pay-as-you-go government gravy train system is intact.

Despite Koizumi's objectives to cut public spending through structural reforms, at the time he left office in 2006 the government debt was 150 percent of annual GDP.

Nothing Much Changes in this System

Merely changing the name of Special Status Corporations to Independent Administrative Institutions and merging some of the bankrupt corporations with solvent corporations did little to stop the wasteful spending of public revenue or the migration of bureaucrats to IAIs. In March 2007 a survey released by the Lower House reported the number of IAIs (including subsidiaries) maintained by the ministries and the number of "retired" bureaucrats, including officers on loan to these entities:

1. The Ministry of Land, Infrastructure and Transport: 834 entities, 6,386 bureaucrats.
2. Ministry of Health, Labor and Welfare: 709 entities, 4,007 former officials.
3. Defence Ministry: 207 entities, 3,917 former officials.
4. Ministry of Education, Culture, Sports, Science and Technology: 934 entities, 3,007 former ministry officials.

On 8 November the secretariat of the cabinet's headquarters for Administrative Reform released documents to a government panel of experts on streamlining public corporations. Originally, 57 corporations were set up to take over part of the operations of the ministries and agencies but this number had increased to 101, a similar pattern to that which evolved as the ministries were establishing their Special Status Corporations. The report showed that 40 out of 101 IAIs awarded contracts to their subsidiaries with more than 90 percent of the contracts completed without competitive bidding.

The documents also revealed that the 101 IAIs altogether had 260 affiliates. Companies where one-third or more of their posts were occupied by former directors and senior officials of the IAIs were among the affiliates. Also, 230 officials at the 101 corporations had assumed directors' posts at affiliates in fiscal 2005 through *amakudari*.

The lucrative salaries that top management in the public entities receive make the positions enticing to retiring officials and to officials who had left their ministries to work in the private sector. As an example, on October 24, 2009, *Kyodo News Service* reported that 98 public corporations hired officials who had retired from the ministries which managed their respective corporations. Eleven were operated by METI and seven of them, including JETRO, were headed by former METI bureaucrats. Of the seven, six were officials who had previously left the ministry to work as executives and advisors at major private companies. The average annual salary of 29 chiefs for FY2009 was $226,470.

In his book *Minshu no Teki* (*The Enemy of Democracy*) published in 2009 former Prime Minister Yoshihiko Noda stated that he had anticipated that Koizumi's administration would implement reforms and cut public debt but assessed the reforms as being no more than the image of reform of Special Status Corporations. He condemned Special Status Corporations (Noda refers to IAIs as Special Status Corporations) as a waste of tax revenue, as a haven for retired bureaucrats who landed comfortable jobs with high salaries and as impediments to the implementation of structural reforms. During Noda's administration, a bill was passed to merge JETRO with a corporation managed by the Ministry of Foreign Affairs in 2014, which I also had recommended in *Special Corporations and the Bureaucracy* (2003). However, now that Abe and the LDP have returned, it is doubtful that the merger will ever materialize.

In the book I state: "Special Status Corporations are illustrative of the basic nature of Japan's political economy. The ministries' determination to maintain territory and thus protect vested interests can be seen in the continued operations of Special Status Corporations despite Koizumi's plans to dissolve them."

Fast Forward

Despite the struggle by successive administrations to end the *amakudari* system through the National Public Service Law implemented in 2008 prohibiting the ministries from arranging post-retirement positions in both public and private sector, the system continues. On January 19, 2017 the Japanese dailies reported that the former administrative vice minister of MEXT, after retiring from the ministry in August 2015 took a position a few months later as a professor at Waseda University, a private university. In February, it was reported that over 40 officials from MEXT had received post-retirement positions in universities, a clear indication that the law is relatively toothless. Since the number of students is decreasing, as well as tuition fees, the universities will hire retiring officials hoping that the relationship will gain government subsidies. Regardless, this type of post-retirement parachuting to universities has been a long-standing practice and in many cases, a positive use of bureaucrats in educational institutions if the officials' lectures are based on their expertise. However, this individual engaged in liaison and coordination of programs of MEXT, effectively connecting his former ministry to Waseda. Nevertheless, the ministries maintain their corporations.

University graduates are increasingly unwilling to enter the civil service because of the ethos and the uncertainty of career paths within the ministries. In *Japan's Nuclear Crisis* (2012) I suggested that Prime Minister Noda could beef-up the bureaucracy through the institutional restructuring of the ministries and to cultivate technocrats who were willing to collaborate with politicians in the planning of strategy and cohesive policies. Graduates would welcome the civil service if certain conditions existed that supported a more egalitarian environment such as the discontinuation of the seniority system and the installation of the "promotion by merit" system.

Additionally, wages should represent corporate pay-scales, retirement benefits should be increased and substantial bonuses awarded for good work. Adequate administrative staff should also be provided. I even went so far as recommending that a special corporate tax be levied on the larger exporters to finance the restructuring. The reorganization of the ministries would serve to assuage the hierarchical structure and discourage patronage and a "yes-man" society.

Ministry officials work long hours without receiving overtime pay and, therefore, Special Status Corporations offer an incentive to enter the civil service. Most officials are trained as generalists and do not have specific skills which are pertinent to the private sector. The ministries still rely on their corporations as a means of taking care of their officials after they retire. Since officials want to continue earning income for their families, the ministries' corporations provide positions where they can conveniently rely on financial support.

Prime Minister Noda was correct in his assessment of Special Status Corporations but if he had worked as a ministry official, he may have concluded that there must be incentives in place to tempt university graduates to enter the ministries and something at the end of the line that would provide post-retirement salaries besides benefits. Despite the name - change to Independent Administrative Institutions or Incorporated Administrative Agencies or Special Corporations, the Japanese still refer to the ministries' corporations as Special Status Corporations.

23

Japan Inc.: Indestructible but Destructive

This chapter reinforces the analyses in the previous chapters in the context of Japan's current political and economic environment.

Whatever Happened to Mercian Inc.?

In *Japan Inc. on the Brink* the section "The Birth of the Big Zombie Companies" gave as examples the Daiei Group and Kanebo Inc. regarding how Japanese companies, despite experiencing a huge debt burden after the bursting of the asset-inflated economy, continued to borrow from their trusted and trusting creditors to diversify into businesses that deviated from their core competencies. Their main lenders who also held shares in the companies and whose executives were on the boards of directors allowed the two companies to continue operating without calling in the debt.

Although Daiei, Japan's largest retailer and Kanebo, the oldest company on the TSE, began divesting themselves of major assets by 2000, the banks were no longer able to continue providing loans, not only to Daiei and Kanebo, but also to companies that had become essentially zombie companies with loans based on questionable collateral. The section explains the process of the companies' takeover, first by a government institution which purchased equity while asking the major lenders to forgive much of the debt and finding companies to assume ownership. Daiei has never recovered despite new management and Kanebo Inc was delisted by the TSE for accounting fraud in 2005. Its auditor, Price Waterhouse Coopers, was sanctioned in Japan for six months for allowing Kanebo to essentially cook the books.

In the US companies typically appoint the majority of directors on the board from outside of the corporation as opposed to Japanese firms which are not required to appoint non-execs externally. As of 2014, of the 8113 firms registered on the TSE, 39 percent had no external directors on their boards, 39 percent had one external director, and 22 percent had two or more. Abe requested that the TSE construct a "corporate governance code" by mid-2015 to bring listed companies' policies up to international standards. However, Abe's plan called for the appointment of only one external director to serve on boards and there is no mention of directors who are in posts in companies connected through cross shareholding. Even though companies are slowly eliminating cross shareholding, the plan as it stands will not engender confidence in Japanese firms in terms of long-term commitment and investment by foreign firms.

As an affiliate of a multinational corporation Mercian was not in the same league as Daiei or Kanebo. Nevertheless, Mercian is an excellent example of how the BOJ's post-Plaza Accord monetary policy, the MOF's sloppy regulation of financial institutions, along with the institutions' willingness to provide questionable loans resulted in frenzied over-expansion and over-diversification from core businesses.

Mercian also is illustrative of many Japanese companies which failed due to shoddy management, inadequate corporate governance and is representative of companies in Japan which continued to receive loans from banks that owned equity even though the collateral was questionable.

By 1999, within a decade after Sanraku had been rebranded Mercian Inc., the company was experiencing significant problems with choppy sales and questionable management. Suzuki's message in the English version of the 1999 annual report included:

In fiscal 1999, the year ending December 31, 1999, Japan's economy, unable to make full-fledged comeback, continued to be hampered by high unemployment rates and a prolonged lull in consumer spending. To acclimatize to the age of change, a series of large-scale mergers started taking place in the financial industry. Over the next few years, the nation's economy on the whole will likely experience a huge transformation.

> During the period under review, Japan's alcoholic beverage market, affected by the trend for lower selling prices, continued to encounter intense sales competition. The Japanese wine market retreated, following an exceptional performance in the previous term. Fiscal 1999 saw a sharply growing demand for low-priced *Chuhai* drinks, while wine sales declined, affected by inventory adjustments. [*Chuhai* is a *shochu* highball beverage. Suntory was also competing successfully in the *Chuhai* market.]

Suzuki's message in the 2000 annual report revealed a continuing contraction in profits and Mercian's management problems which had been evident ten years earlier:

> Conditions in the alcoholic beverage market were harsh owing to the trend toward lower selling prices, reflecting the stagnant economy...despite rationalization measures, consolidated sales in fiscal 2000 fell 10.1%. Operating income fell 39.6%

To enhance corporate governance, we have improved the board of directors and appointed external directors, and introduced economic value added (EVA) as a key management indicator, adopted a new personnel system and a performance-based system … Price reductions are expected to continue hampering alcoholic beverages market, intensifying survival among companies. The Mercian Group is undertaking to enhance its management base … the board of directors will concentrate on policy making and operation monitoring. To this end, we have appointed external directors.

Mercian's Annual Reports in English do not include the list of primary stockholders which is included in the Japanese version. The lack of continuity in the primary shareholders listed in the Japanese version was ominous.

In 2000 Shunsuke Inamori, the chairman of Ajinomoto and Yoshihiko Miyauchi were appointed as directors on the Mercian board. At the age of 78, Miyauchi retired in May 2014 as Chairman and CEO of Orix Corporation, Japan's largest leasing firm and major provider of general financial services in Japan. Miyauchi maintained intimate networks with government and big business since the 1960s. In the same year Glenfiddich, dissatisfied with sales, transferred operations to a new Japanese distributor. The 2001 Annual Report portended Mercian's rocky conditions and that the company was under financial duress:

> the stagnant economy hurt sales of wine to restaurants, market recovery remained slow, and there was insufficient inventory consolidation in the market. Consequently, sales fell, and it was primarily low-priced products for individual users that saw increased sales this fiscal year.

> The sales of *shochu* increased from 2000, continuing to be a Mercian best seller. The Château Mercian series – Mercian's wine – again received high praise in international competition, an example of Mercian's technical merit in achieving a high standard of quality.

In March 2002 the firm of Deloitte Touche Tohmatsu was hired as independent auditors for FY2001, FY2002, FY2003 and FY2004. The auditors reported that they considered Mercian's consolidated statements to be accurate. Nevertheless, the final pages in these reports carry a "Cautionary Remark Regarding Forward-Looking Statements":

> Statements made in this document with respects to Mercian's plans, strategies, expectations about the future, and other statements except for historical statements are forward-looking statements. These forward-looking statements are subject to uncertainties that could cause actual results to differ materially from such statements. These uncertainties include, but are not limited to, general economic conditions, demand for and price of Mercian products, Mercian's ability to continue to develop and market advanced products and currency exchange rates.

A more positive statement would have been helpful.

The 2002 Annual Report Suzuki continued to put a positive spin on Mercian's conditions by touting Mercian's management overhaul and the change to Japan's new corporate accounting standards:

> We achieved the above [reduction of interest-bearing debt]…despite a harsh operating environment, including persistent deflationary conditions in the domestic economy and the global economic slowdown, which depressed exports.

These successes were made possible by the dedication and teamwork of our management and employees striving toward common goals.

Suzuki's message to stockholders in the FY 2003 and 2004 Annual Reports focused on the success of Mercian's restructuring and its core domestic liquor business. He pledged to improve operations in the feedstuffs business.

The 2004 report displayed color photographs of skin-care products Mercian was producing from grape extract labeled "Visage." But the exit of Miyauchi as a director suggested an escape from a burning building. Takei Shiina, who had been the vice president and chairman of IBM Japan Ltd., hopped on board as a director after his retirement.

Fire sale

The primary stockholders in 1999 were the financial institutions that provided loans to Mercian. The 1999 Annual Shareholders Report in Japanese shows that there were 17,012 stockholders and that there were ten main stockholders: Ajinomoto with 11.1 percent equity, Dai-ichi Life Insurance Company owned 5.5 percent, Dai-ichi Kangyo Bank (Mercian's corporate bank) and Mitsubishi Trust with 4.7 percent each, Yasuda Life Insurance and Tokyo Mitsubishi Bank with 3.8 percent, Fuji Bank owned 3.4 percent, and Sumitomo Maritime and Fire Insurance Co. Ltd. and Greater Tokyo Marine and Fire Insurance Co. Ltd. owned 2.3 and 2 percent respectively.

The major stockholders remained the same in 2000 but due to the merger of Dai-ichi Kangyo, Fuji Bank and the IBJ, the shares were transferred to Mizuho. Ajinomoto had owned 11.1 percent of its affiliate's shares until 2002 when the percentage of shares increased to 11.6 percent as indicated in the 2003 Annual Report. Also, Nihon Master Trust, a bank that was established in 2000, became a new shareholder with 12.5 percent. In 2002, Ai Oi Nissei, an Asset Administration Services took equity. Additionally, the list of key shareholders had changed from the previous year with other financial institutions holding smaller percentages of equity. Mercian's annual report for 2005 is not available.

In 2006, Kirin Holdings, Japan's top beverage producer, announced that it had purchased a 50.1 percent stake in Mercian to diversify assets outside of beer brewing.

Printed on the first page of Mercian's Annual Report for FY 2009 is a "Note Regarding Revision of Financial Statements":

In 2010, an internal investigation conducted by Mercian revealed major deficiencies in internal controls pertaining to Companywide management processes, financial accounts settlement and reporting processes, and business processes in the Fish Feedstuffs Division. As a consequence of this investigation, Mercian was obliged to revise its consolidated financial statements for fiscal 2009 and the preceding four fiscal years and to have the revised statements audited by its independent auditor, Deloitte Touche Tohmatsu.

Hiroshi Ueki, the president and CEO, who was also the president and CEO of Kirin Holdings, stated that in July 2007 Mercian had become a member of the Kirin Group of companies and that one of his primary responsibilities was to:

reinforce Mercian's corporate structure in terms of management, stimulating horizontal and vertical communication and promoting management that mirrors the perspectives of our customers. To these ends, we have implemented a broad range of measures designed to fortify our operating foundation …

Despite the positive impact of a value-based sales approach and efforts to optimize inventory and reduce sales, general and administrative costs in the wine business, and increased sales in the Pharmaceuticals and Chemical segment, the operating loss swelled to ¥1,579 million, from ¥1,303 million (¥93.50 = $1). This reflected a persistent downward trend in sales in other businesses, notably alcoholic drinks and feedstuffs segment and the worsening impact of rising prices for raw materials used in fish feed. Mercian's net loss also worsened to ¥2,117 million, from ¥1,871 million ... This was due to the application of a new accounting standard of inventories, as a result of which the differences between inventories at the beginning and the end of the fiscal year (¥795 million) was accounted for as a loss on write-down of inventories and included in extraordinary losses.

The TSE, which had been watching the company for a possible delisting, took action and delisted Mercian Inc on November 26, 2010 for the false reporting of net worth. On the same day that Mercian was delisted, Kirin Holdings announced that it would purchase Mercian Inc.'s remaining shares for $132 million in order to gain tighter control over the company, which had confirmed in May that it had inflated profits over losses for several years, booking a loss of ¥6.5 billion (¥87.10 = $1). Kirin was forced to revise down its forecast for annual net profits by 27 percent, partly to accommodate the loss. Kirin's shares dropped 1.1 percent and the Nikkei 225 average also fell 1.1 percent. Ajinomoto took over Calpis in the 2010 deal with Kirin. At a press conference Ueki told reporters that Mercian would decide whether to shut down the fish feed division. He included that he would take a 50 percent salary cut for three months to take responsibility for the false transactions and that five executives and an auditor would have their pay reduced. In 1999, Mercian employed 2,000 staff. In 2014, Mercian was employing 500 staff.

And Toshiba Too

Toshiba Corp is one of Japan's internationally acclaimed tech giants, employing 190,000 people globally. Established 142 years ago, its businesses range from semiconductors, televisions and PCs to nuclear energy. It has been engaged in the design and construction of nuclear power plants in Japan since the 1950s, including the beleaguered Fukushima power plant.

Toshiba purchased the Westinghouse Electric Corp, its US-based nuclear unit, in 2006 for a whopping $5.4 billion in expectation that the nuclear industry would continue to be a cash cow and expand its presence internationally. But the 2011 Fukushima nuclear disaster effectively halted the construction of new power plants in Japan and frustrated gaining contracts overseas. Toshiba consequently experienced a sharp fall in profits since 2013 but its major lenders continued to loan to one of their prized clients.

In 2015, Toshiba admitted that it had overstated profits to hide net losses of $1.3 billion. The accounting fraud scandal led to the resignation of the President and seven executives and to a full investigation of the company for inflating profits to conceal the dire financial state of its nuclear arm. The TSE and the Nagoya Stock Exchange began monitoring Toshiba, which has been on "stock alert" for questions of compliance. Due to the subsequent fall of share prices, four major trust banks and units of three major banks brought a law suit on behalf of its investors against the company for gross mismanagement and for failing to install an effective corporate governance system.

In December 2016 Toshiba disclosed that it had overestimated the value of shares in Westinghouse. In January 2017 Toshiba announced that the loss of $6.1 billion was greater than had been anticipated and applied to the DBJ for financing (FILP). Shares plummeted 45 percent leaving the company with a capitalization of only $7.8 billion. Toshiba also postponed submitting its third quarter earnings in December, promising to release the report by March 14, 2017. Although Toshiba's three major lenders had agreed to extend credit until March, the delay in reporting its third quarter earnings in February and then again in March forebode more bad news for shareholders, who angrily pointed to Toshiba's secretive and arrogant corporate culture. As Toshiba's shares continued to fall rapidly, citing auditing problems with Westinghouse's cost overruns on nuclear power plants under construction in the US, the date was extended to 11 April.

Its liabilities greater than its assets and pressed for cash, Toshiba had to raise at least $8.8 billion and began searching for buyers of some of its companies, including the second largest memory chip business in the world, said to be worth $13–$17 billion. The Taiwanese company Foxconn (Hon Hai Precision Industry), the largest contract electronics manufacturer in the world, initially bid $18 billion. Foxconn had bought the zombie company Sharp Corporation in 2016 for $3.5 billion, despite a rival bid from the government-funded Innovation Network Corporation. The Japanese and US governments were opposed to companies with close ties to China taking over Japanese hi-tech companies for reasons of technology transfer and the Innovation Network Corporation together with the DBJ and smaller Japanese businesses planned to enter the second round of bidding to form a consortium. Foxconn decided to up its bid to $27 billion in April and Apple was considering teaming up with Foxconn to take a 20 percent stake in order to ensure partial control of the subsidiary in the US and Japan. Among the other bidders are Western Digital Corp., and Broadcom, a California-based company. Western Digital, which has a joint venture with Toshiba in Japan, stated that a sale to competitors would violate its contract with Toshiba. However, the Innovation Network Corporation and the state bank may also team up with Broadcom to keep the chip business firmly in the control of the US and Japan.

Begging for time, on 4 April Toshiba asked lenders to delay calling in loans, offering as collateral shares in the chip business and in smaller companies such as Toshiba Tec Corp. However, regional banks were beginning to call in loans. Crumbling before its investors' eyes, the conglomerate also put its television subsidiary on the block.

In order to stem further losses Toshiba requested that Westinghouse file for bankruptcy under Chapter 11 and this occurred on 29 March. The package at the outset will cost at least $9 billion related to Westinghouse's outstanding liabilities, a sum greater than what had been forecast in December ($6.3 billion). The package is designed to keep the company afloat whilst it completes nuclear reactor projects in the US. Two days prior to declaring bankruptcy Toshiba dismissed Danny Roderick, the chairman of Westinghouse Electric, replacing him with Mamoru Hatazawa, the chief of Toshiba's nuclear division.

PriceWaterhouseCoopers Arata did not complete the auditing of third quarter earnings due to its investigation of Westinghouse upper management putting pressure on staff to make losses appear to be less than what they actually were. Nevertheless, on 11 April, Toshiba, fearful of being delisted from the TSE, submitted its unaudited third quarter earnings declaring that its projected loss for FY 2016 was $9.2 billion, one of the largest in Japanese corporate history. It is rare for companies to submit earnings reports which are not endorsed by its auditors.

On the same day Toshiba issued a statement: "There are material events and conditions that raise substantial doubt about the company's ability to continue as a going concern." If Toshiba's liabilities exceed its assets at the end of March 2018, it will be delisted from the TSE and selling its memory chip business is key to its survival. There is still the risk that Toshiba will be delisted because TSE regulators are investigating whether Toshiba's internal controls comply with TSE listing standards.

Given that the collapse is huge, Toshiba will be involved in tricky negotiations with Westinghouse and its creditors. There are also US state loan guarantees for the construction of future reactors to consider as well as American jobs. The Japanese government, namely the Trade Minister, will also be negotiating with the US Energy Secretary and the Commerce Secretary. The government is concerned that the Trump administration will use Toshiba's predicament to point to issues regarding Japanese corporate operations in the US.

Until the Fukushima nuclear disaster, Sellafield, a town located in Cumbria in the UK, was reprocessing the spent fuel not only from Fukushima but also, from other reactors in Japan. The crisis served to halt operations until recently. Moorside near Sellafield was slated to be the recipient of a £10 billion nuclear power plant constructed by Westinghouse, which purportedly would create 21,000 jobs in a region of high unemployment. The investment for the plant, which was named "Horizon," was initially under consideration by the JBIC and the DBJ (two corporations in the FSC and funded by FILP). On the day Toshiba's Chairman resigned, the President announced that the company would no longer engage in the construction of nuclear power plants but concentrate on designing, manufacturing and supplying power plants. Toshiba owns 60 percent of NuGen, which was to build the three reactors, but it was forced to buy the remaining 40 percent of shares held by the French utility company Engei, which, due to Westinghouse's bankruptcy, exercised its rights to request that Toshiba buy its interest at a cost of $138.5 million. Moorside's future was tentative until the state-owned Korea Electric Power Corp (KEPCO) announced in March that it would like to acquire Toshiba's share of NuGen and enter the UK nuclear energy market.

"Creative METI": everything old is new again

At a press conference on November 22, 2002, Nobuteru Ishihara declared that to his and the Cabinet Minister of Economy, Trade and Industry's astonishment JETRO was publishing a pamphlet advertising import promotion. Ishihara was implying that the importation of foreign goods was no longer a primary concern because of the recession and the contraction of the domestic market.

In 2007, the United Nations Conference on Trade and Development (UNCTAD) inward FDI performance index ranked Japan 137th among 141 countries, which constituted 2.5 percent of the GDP. Peter Mandelson, the former European Union Trade Commissioner, complained in a speech given at the EU–Japan Center for Industrial Cooperation on April 21, 2008 that Japan was "the most closed investment market in the developed world." Ironically, the event was sponsored by METI and JETRO its Incorporated Administrative Agency. Mandelson suggested that Japan, whilst taking advantage of the openness of foreign markets was creating barriers to foreign investment. He cited figures showing that 3 percent of Europe's total $300 million outward investment was invested in Japan, comparing it with Japan's outward investment. "For every dollar Japan invested in the UK and the Netherlands alone, European companies were able to invest a net total of only 3 percent in Japan." Since then FDI in Japan remains unchanged.

JETRO is replicating most of the services it provided in the 1990s. Market information published in the 1990s can be accessed on JETRO's current website. There are the same small business support services, the same database of prospective importers and Japanese business partners, expert business consulting services, and "a global network of company executives, advisors and more ... Because JETRO is an independent agency of the Japanese government we are able to provide many of our services for free."

The Foreign Investment in Japan Corporation (FIND) was terminated on March 31, 2002. Edward J. Lincoln wrote in his book *Troubled Times* (1999) that it had been expected that FIND would assist in a concrete way with foreign investment, but the corporation was criticized because it did little more than propose joint ventures with Japanese firms that were members of FIND. It also charged a fee for introductions. Lincoln argued that since FIND was a government corporation, it was not free to give advice on mergers and acquisitions. He concluded: "Foreign firms were less in need of advice or introduction to potential businesses than the dismantling of the real obstacles to acquisitions."

METI replaced FIND with INVEST JAPAN when JETRO was converted to an Incorporated Administrative Agency in April 2003.

The Manufactured Imports & Promotion Organization (MIPRO) was established in 1978 by MITI. As of April 1, 2013 MIPRO was renamed the Manufactured Imports & Investment Promotion Organization (MIPRO). It operates an office in Washington, DC where METI officials and Japanese trade delegations visit regularly. The MIPRO 2013 website includes a message from the president Tsutomu Higuchi:

Direct investment in Japan accounts for less than 2% of Japan's nominal GDP, which is much smaller than similar shares in other major advanced countries, and nearly 80% of such investment is made in Kanto and Koshinetsu districts. Therefore, extending foreign investment in Japan and promoting the penetration of foreign capital into Japan are urgent tasks. In cooperation with affiliated organizations, MIPRO is supporting global business activities and secondary investment in local areas by foreign companies in Japan. The investment branch wants to promote inward investment with a program called INVEST JAPAN.

INVEST JAPAN opened the INVEST JAPAN Invest Business Support Centers (IBSC) in Tokyo, Yokohama, Nagoya, Osaka, Kobe and Fukuoka which provide exactly the same services as the old Business Support Centers. The Financial Times was purchased by Nikkei Inc, for $1.3 billion in December 2015. Nikkei Inc. sponsored the INVEST JAPAN 2016 Forum run by METI and JETRO. INVEST JAPAN ran a two-page advert in the FT on December 6, 2016 promoting its services.

MIPRO's services are designed specifically to support small-lot business imports and foreign small business start-ups in Japan. MIPRO's investment division promotes inward investment in twenty designated cities in Japan's six regions. Although MIPRO's services are relevant to manufactured goods, some of them correspond to JETRO's services. For example, MIPRO publishes information regarding industrial standards, regulations, market information and market trends, direct investment into Japan, activities of foreign firms in Japan, Japanese lifestyles and consumption trends and so forth. MIPRO also offers consulting services, seminars about how to do business in Japan and introductions to Japanese firms for potential investment.

Mr. Higuchi had been the director of Policy Planning Division, Energy, Conservation and Renewable Energy in METI's Agency of Natural Resources and Energy (ANRE).

What Ever Happened to Ehime's FAZ?

The 2012 "Promising Imports Exhibition" from three Asian countries held for three months at the Ehime International Logistics Terminal (I-Lot) by Ehime Prefecture and Ehime FAZ Co. Ltd is pertinent to the waste of tax revenue on infrastructure projects and the relationship of the national ministries with prefecture governments.

The exhibition was open to 240 companies in Ehime. The Thai Trade Center in Osaka supported the exhibitors by sending samples of Thai products. Korea, Malaysia and Indonesia were also represented. The target visitors to the trade fair were Ehime retailers and wholesalers.

At the end of the three-month period the results of the exhibition were released to reveal that 85 people and 48 companies had attended. The business leads were one Thai company and two Indonesian companies. One company was interested in the Mango wood products, one was interested in the Indigo hat, and one company showed interest in the solar plants flower. A Thai company, the Oriental Beauty Charm expressed interest in exporting spa products and Ehime FAZ followed up the lead. As usual, the producer replied that it did not have the experience or the license to export cosmetics to Japan or to employ an import agent in Japan. In other words, FAZ is an "empty box."

Behold the Old World Order

On 23 July an independent lawmaker in the Upper House joined the ranks of the LDP giving the party the majority in the Upper House for the first time since 1989. Since the LDP and the Komeito control two-thirds of the Lower House there is a good possibility that the revision of the Pacifist Constitution will come to fruition.

In October the LDP voted to extend the cap on the term of the President from six to nine years. If Abe wins reelection as President in March 2018 he will be able to retain the post of prime minister to serve until 2021.

Like his grandfather, Abe's political philosophy is immersed in nationalism and his 2006–07 administration focused on promoting bills that would serve the national interest, such as the reinstatement of the Ministry of Defence and an intended revision of Article 9 in the Constitution, renouncing war, to allow the expansion of the role of the SDF. Abe has been adamant that the US–Japan Security Treaty is at the center of Japan's defence policy, which was also central to Kishi's defence policies. However, Abe's political motives focus on the perceived threat from China's rise as an economic and military power in Asia.

Kishi attempted to centralize police power and restore to the police some of their former authority such as the right to search suspected criminals. In 1960 the Japanese were still enveloped in a shroud of wartime suffering and public protests erupted against what was regarded as the resuscitation of wartime "thought control." There were strikes and demonstrations supported by labor unions. Socialist lawmakers rioted in the Diet and tried to kidnap the Speaker to prevent a vote. Three members of Kishi's cabinet resigned, forcing him to shelve the bill.

Shinzo Abe's "State Secrets Law" enacted in December 2014 harkens back to Kishi. When it was pushed through the National Diet with little public debate the Japanese media, expecting to receive gag orders from the government and to be subjected to barriers to accessing information, protested vigorously. Also known as the National Security Act, the law defined "special secrets" as sensitive information on diplomacy and counterespionage. Over 60 percent of the electorate, comparing it to the pre-war and wartime Peace Preservation Act which was implemented by government to quell political opposition, objected to the law because of its lack of detail of what constituted "state secrets" and because it indicated that the government would have more control over the population.

People who are arrested on suspicion of leaking "state secrets" can be detained in prison without trial. Those who are found guilty can be imprisoned for up to ten years and journalists who are convicted of trying to obtain classified information can be imprisoned for up to five years. Although politicians denied that the law would be used to restrict the press or the public's "right to know," Justice Minister Sadakazu Tanigaki, the former LDP president who was defeated by former Prime Minister Yoshihiko Noda in the 2011 election, did not rule out the possibility of police raids on newspapers suspected of breaking the law.

In 2016 Japan had dropped in ranking from 11th in 2010 to 59th in 2014 and now ranks 72nd for freedom of the press. The World Press Freedom Index 2016 released in April placed Japan in the category of having "noticeable problems."

Immediately after receiving approval from his cabinet for the reinterpretation of Article 9 to allow collective self-defence, Abe created a new ministerial post for security to revise existing laws and to introduce new laws in order to produce a legal framework regarding the right to exercise collective self-defence. The National Security Law implemented in September 2015 has given Abe's government the opportunity to expand the role of the Self Defence Force (SDF) to include supplying fuel and ammunition to the US military if Japan's national security is threatened. Japan's military operations now include SDF engagement overseas in South Sudan as a part of the U.N. peacekeeping activities. Initially, SDF forces were allowed to use weapons only for self-protection but now they can use weapons to protect foreign worker.

On 22 December 2016 the National Security Council approved the extension of the SDF's duties to include the protection of US military during peace times but does not exclude engaging in US military activities in defence of Japan. Defence Minister Tomomi Inada stated at a news conference that the SDF's protective duties would act to strengthen the Japan-US alliance and ensure the "safety and security of Japan." Besides the US and Australia, Japan will also supply ammunition, food and fuel to the British military, bolstering Japan's alliances in the face of China's maritime expansion in the Pacific.

Nonetheless, according to a survey conducted by the Cabinet Office between 27 October and 6 November of 3,000 Japanese nationals aged eighteen or older, only 20 percent of the respondents were in favor of the SDF engaging in UN peacekeeping activities such as in South Sudan

Abe's Army

Compared to his deputy and Minister of Finance, former Prime Minister Taro Aso, Abe can be considered a "dove." Aso's right-wing ultra-conservative ideology and glorification of Japan's colonization days in East Asia replicates Abe's. Aso's opinions have been well publicized in the press during his political career. Despite his frequent public outbursts espousing his neo-nationalist sentiments, he remains as Abe's second-in-command. In 2005, he touted Japan as a mono-culture with one race, one language and one civilization, excluding other ethnic groups such as Chinese and Koreans.

When he ran for president of the LDP in his bid for the office of Prime Minister in 2005, Aso's platform regarding foreign relations was "Arc of freedom and prosperity: Japan's Expanding Diplomatic Horizons" which may also be interpreted as a reiteration of the Meiji slogan, "Prosperous Country, Strong Country, Strong Military." In 2006, Aso warned the Japanese that China, with a population of one billion people, possessed nuclear bombs and had expanded its military budget by double figures for seventeen consecutive years.

During Aso's term as Prime Minister in 2008, the Western media reported that Aso Mining had forced 300 Allied prisoners to work without pay in the Aso Mining Company in 1945 and that two Australian prisoners had died. Furthermore, 10,000 Koreans were recruited to work under cruel conditions, many of whom had died. Although former laborers requested an apology, Aso refused to reply.

Aso continued his nationalist rhetoric at an ultra-conservative conference in Tokyo on July 29, 2013. He criticized the lack of support for revising Article 9, stating that the Japanese should follow the example of the Nazis who, in order to avoid protests, secretly revised the Weimar Constitution to the Nazi Constitution. Aso recommended that the Japanese should learn from these tactics. He also encouraged secret visits to Yasukuni Shrine in order to avoid diplomatic outbursts. Aso refused to apologize or resign from office but retracted his statement, blaming misinterpretation by *Kyodo News* the newspaper which reported the event.

Abe's appointment of Tomomi Inada as Minister of Defence in August was not welcomed by South Korea because of her blatant ultra-nationalist views. A right-wing revisionist, she denied the military atrocities committed in Nanjing in 1937 and claimed in a 2007 advertisement in the Washington Post that there was no evidence that Korean women were forced to serve as "comfort women." In 2014 she was photographed with the leader of the Japanese pro-Nazi party. She claimed that she had met the leader only once. Inada, who visits Yasukuni Shrine annually, also supports prime ministerial visits.

In February, a major scandal engulfed Abe, his wife Akie and Inada. Moritomo Gakuen an ultra-nationalist operator of a kindergarten in Osaka Prefecture had purchased land in Osaka for the construction of a second kindergarten for £950,000 or 14 percent of the appraised value. It also received millions of yen in government subsidies. The objectives of the school's curriculum is to instil patriotism with the daily singing of the national anthem, bowing to a portrait of the Emperor, and memorizing the 1890 imperial edict on education, which calls for loyalty and sacrifice for country and had been banned by SCAP. The children are taken to military bases and Shinto shrines. The parents of former students have lodged complaints regarding the harsh treatment of their children and the abusive language used in newsletters regarding the Chinese people and Korean residents.

In a video shot in 2015 Mrs. Abe told her husband that the school's curriculum was excellent. She was appointed "Honorary Principal" the following year. In 2016 Inada, who had formerly denied any connection with Moritomo a year earlier, admitted to serving as legal counsel for Moritomo when it filed a civil lawsuit in 2004. The scandal pressured Akie to resign her position. In March, as his public approval rating plummeted from 67 percent to 36 percent, Abe denied unequivocally the accusations that he had donated funds to Moritomo and pledged to resign from office if he was found culpable. Abe will likely survive because he has strong support from within the LDP, from the New Komeito and, according to a public survey conducted in March by the Nikkei Shimbun, 60 percent of respondents claimed that they were satisfied with their society.

The Propaganda Machine

The Nippon Hoso Kyokai (NHK) is a public broadcasting system and, similar to the BBC, is supported by license fees collected from everyone who owns a television. Although the NHK is ostensibly an independent broadcaster, the twelve-member board of directors is appointed by Parliament, which also approves the NHK annual budget.

In the autumn of 2013, Abe appointed four ultra-conservative officials as members of the NHK board. The four officials then assisted Abe to appoint Katsuto Momii as governor who succeeded Masayuki Matsumoto after Matsumoto suddenly announced that he would not seek another three-year term as had been anticipated. The media reported that he had been admonished by Abe's administration for allowing National Broadcasting System (NHK) coverage to be too critical of nuclear energy and American bases on Okinawa. Abe also established a new NHK Management Board in 2013 and appointed Michiko Hasegawa, a right-wing nationalist, to the board.

Right-wing nationalist sentiments are now being expressed openly by the directors on the board of the NHK. After only two days on the job as the governor of NHK, Momii stated at a news conference that the 200,000 women who had been forced to serve as sex slaves during the war was common practice in any country engaged in war. Momii cited France and Germany as examples. He later retracted his statement when he was grilled in Parliament. But Momii refused to retract his other statements, which included his support of Japan's territorial right to the Senkaku Islands and rejected the view that NHK should cease criticizing the secrecy law. Despite the controversy sparked by Momii's remarks, two days later Naoki Hyukuta, a novelist and who also was chosen by Abe as one of the twelve governors of NHK, stated that in 1938 Chiang Kai-shek had blamed the Japanese army for the Nanjing Massacre and that the event did not occur. Hyutaka also reiterated Momii's statement regarding "comfort women."

After the Kumamoto earthquake in April, Momii instructed staff to focus only on the government's explanation of the safety of nuclear reactors in the neighboring prefectures and to dismiss the analyses of "outside" experts. There is significant pressure on the government from citizen groups for his dismissal. Momii will be replaced at the end of his term by board member Ryoichi Ueda who was the CFO of Mitsubishi Corp.

The Japanese media is expressing deep concerns that Abe and his right-wing colleagues are interfering with freedom of the press and freedom of speech through the political appointment of people who will silence criticism of government policies, including restarting the nuclear reactors and denial of Japan's wartime atrocities. The Japanese are increasingly worried that Abe is using the NHK as an organ to control the flow of information and as a mechanism which supports his political agenda.

Spreading the "N-Word"

Abe is also determined to spread his nationalist ideology in the ministries. In 2014 Abe established the Cabinet Bureau of Personnel Affairs which choose the appointments of 600 elite ministry officials for positions in their respective agencies. The previous system allowed the prime minister and his chief cabinet secretary to select 200 elite ministry officials for top posts in the ministries but the new bureau gives Abe and Chief Cabinet Secretary Yoshide Suga the power to screen and appoint 600 elite ministry officials for top positions in the ministries.

Suga, who is Abe's closest ally and who is known for his penchant for interfering in personnel affairs, explained that the objective of the bureau was to "cope with various issues quickly and in a united manner." The new system allows Abe and his right-wing colleagues to spread an ultra-conservative, right-wing ethos in the bureaucracy through the appointment of senior elite officials who have similar political views and objectives. As an example, traditionally, a senior official in the Cabinet Legislation Bureau was appointed to the position of director-general but Abe preferred to appoint an official who would promote the reinterpretation of the Constitution to allow collective self-defence.

Newer History Textbooks

In my 2012 and 2014 books I detailed Japan's relationship with China and South Korea and the territorial disputes with China which claims sovereignty over the Senkaku Islands and with South Korea which claims sovereignty over Takeshima. The government's assertion that the islands belong to Japan was emphasized in the revised *New History Textbook* as well as in twenty four additionally authorized books published in 2014 by five publishers. The texts include claims regarding territorial conflicts which also include the Russian-occupied Northern Territories off of Hokkaido. The education ministry requested that the publishers avoid specific issues such as the Nanking Massacre and to include the government's posture on compensation for forced wartime labor from China, for example "comfort women." The 1890 Education Imperial Edict and *Mein Kampf* are also included as educational material. In other words, the publication of the first *New History Textbook* set the foundation for this nationalist propaganda.

China lodged a formal protest to the Japanese government for what it referred to as "historical errors," claiming that the Nanking Massacre was an atrocity committed by the Japanese military and, also, that China had inherent rights to the Senkaku. South Korea also lodged a protest.

The media continues to cover Ehime. On 16 March 2016 the Ehime Prefecture board of education reached a unanimous decision that high school students who intend to participate in off-campus political activities must give prior notice to their schools. The new rule coincides with the government reducing the age of voters from twenty to eighteen and the Upper House elections in the summer. The risk is that if students violate the regulation, they could face disciplinary action. The scare tactic will ultimately inhibit political awareness among young voters.

The Power of the State

Abe's "Basic Energy Package" declares that nuclear power is an "important base load electricity source" but it does not state specifics about the development of alternative energy sources, suggesting a long-term commitment to nuclear energy.

Japan's Nuclear Crisis: The Routes to Responsibility (2012) exposed the former MITI-affiliated agencies and research institutes which have been at the core of the nuclear and electric power industries since the 1950s. The book examined how these and other ministries' affiliated institutions served to promote interpersonal networks between ministry officials, politicians, the utilities and the nuclear energy industrial sector to answer why the nuclear crisis was an impending disaster, why the regulatory supervision failed and why there were fifty-four nuclear power plants on earthquake-prone zones.

Until the nuclear crisis the Nuclear Industry Safety Agency (NISA), established in 2001 was a division in METI. NISA's website promoted itself as "an institution dedicated to ensuring nuclear power safety." NISA declared that it was dedicated to "making a sustained effort towards on-site safety" and assured the public that it was committed to keeping the public informed. NISA claimed that first and foremost its mission was to recognize the impending risks that are intrinsic in nuclear installations and through regulatory measures to ensure the safety of the public. NISA also maintained that its objective was to respond quickly to accidents in order to control damage and the acceleration of events.

However, the vested interests in the nuclear energy industry shielded the utility company operators who falsified data regularly regarding the structural safety of their nuclear power plants such as radioactive leaks and cracks in the infrastructure. Following the crisis NISA was terminated and replaced with a new agency, the Nuclear Regulatory Authority (NRA) which charged the utility operators to install new safety measures to ensure that the plants would withstand tsunami and earthquakes.

Abe replaced two outgoing commissioners with advocates of nuclear power in order to ensure that the NRA would approve the restarts of a number of reactors. The independence of the NRA from government and the impartiality of the commission is questionable because the commissioners either received large endowments from the nuclear industry for research or had close relations with the nuclear industrial complex. Since the research and development of nuclear energy is protected by the state as one of its industrial policies and since it is also connected to issues of national security it is unrealistic to presume that the NRA can be separated from government and that guaranteeing a transparent and unbiased inspection of power plants is unrealistic as well.

The Tokyo Electric Power Company (TEPCO) admitted to falsifying reports sent to NISA which would have otherwise exposed the structural problems in the reactors. Ministry officials also refused to accept the claims of an engineer involved in the construction of Fukushima that the No 1 reactor was structurally flawed. After the crisis TEPCO continued to withhold data revealing the volume of nuclear waste seeping from the reactor. *Japan's Nuclear Crisis* predicted that the government would continue to fund the consequences of the Fukushima disaster and that the burden would be assumed by the public who, in September, were advised that they would be invoiced in their electricity bills for the cleaning up of Fukushima and the decommissioning of reactors. The bill is estimated to be $118 billion, double that anticipated.

The book forecast that despite assurances from the government that evacuees would be able to return to their cities after a clean-up, the majority of evacuees from the cities affected by the nuclear event would either be unable to return to their homes, compelled to live in temporary housing or move to other regions. Sadly, the forecast was correct. The operator TEPCO continues to struggle to contain the leakage of radioactive waste and the towns near the plants are still contaminated with radiation levels similar to Chernobyl.

I predicted that the nuclear power plants would be reactivated as soon as new safety regulations had been established but due to vociferous public protests and the reticence of political parties to take a stance (even though both the LDP and DPJ were pro-nuclear prior to the Fukushima crisis), with the exception of four, the majority of reactors remained idle until this year. Despite the recent earthquake in Kumamoto Prefecture, the NRA, supported by the Supreme Court, has given the thumbs-up to restarting a number of reactors, including several commissioned 40 years ago and scheduled for decommissioning.

SHOW US the MONEY

A chapter in the 2012 book discusses pork barrel patronage in the prefectures and the consequences on the proliferation of nuclear power plants in less well-endowed regions. The towns where the nuclear plants are located which relied on subsidies and tax breaks for hosting the plants are now requesting the reactivation of the plants to ensure employment of workers and continued subsidies and tax breaks.

Abe's administration targeted Ehime Prefecture's Ikata as the first plant to go online as soon as the NRA gave the all-clear. In October 2006 when METI requested that Ehime host a pluthermal plant to become fully operational by 2010, in spite of vehement protests from civic groups, Governor Kato welcomed the project since Ehime's economy would undoubtedly benefit from substantial government subsidies of ¥6 billion ($51.7 million). This was a hefty sum, especially for a prefecture which generated only about 36 percent of its expenditure through tax revenue. On October 13, 2006, after obtaining the consent from Ikata mayor Kazuhiko Yamashita, the governor presented a written agreement to the President of Shikoku Electric Power Company (YODEN) which owns and operates the power plant.

Three years later, refusing to capitulate, on January 19, 2009 the Association of Ehime Prefectural People for Cooperation together with other citizen groups demanded that METI's former Nuclear Industrial Safety Agency (NISA) force YODEN to cancel its plans for the pluthermal reactor. Their appeal was ignored and YODEN began commercial operations in March 2010. Kato expressed confidence about YODEN's safety measures and his belief that the central government's pluthermal policies were practical.

On August 3, 2011 *Mainichi Shimbun* reported that a retired METI official who headed the public relations in NISA admitted that NISA had asked YODEN senior officials to request that staff attend a seminar in Ikata in June 2006 to promote using MOX in Ikata's No. 3 reactor in order to influence a positive response from attendees.

Kato's successor was Torihiko Nakagawa, a local lawyer, who won the 2010 election on the LDP ticket. Applauding the initiation of a pluthermal plant, he agreed with Kato that the government's screening methods and government nuclear policy were reliable. Although concerned about the safety issues, the majority of Ikata residents, many of whom worked in nuclear-related jobs and who were adversely affected financially due to the loss of subsidies and jobs, were clamoring for the restart of the reactors. In an interview in March 2014 Mayor Yamashita said that he would accept the restart of the plant if the NRA confirmed that the plant was safe. YODEN submitted an application to government to restart number three reactor which is 100 percent fueled with MOX.

In the summer of 2015 the NRA approved Yoden's safety measures for No. 3 reactor and on October 26, 2015 Governor Nakamura, despite the opposition from 54 percent of Ehime residents' and appeals to the Supreme Court for an injunction, gave the all-clear for the resumption of the reactor. Ikata's mayor followed suit. Commercial operations formally commenced on 25 August with 16 units of mixed oxide (MOX) in the 157 fuel assemblies. In the eventuality of an earthquake, evacuation of the 120,000 people living within the 30 km radius of Ikata is problematic because of the likely collapse of the transportation infrastructure which would serve to cut-off the escape routes. Citizen groups from Hiroshima and Matsuyama, continuing the fight, filed yet another request to the district court in Hiroshima for a temporary injunction to halt operations at the No. 3 reactor but it was rejected on March 30, 2017.

YODEN decided to decommission No. 1 reactor because of the price tag of rebooting the 40-year-old reactor. The decommissioning is expected to take 40 years at a cost of ¥1 billion and government subsidies to Ikata will decrease by ¥400 million.

Despite the anti-nuclear protests and grave concerns about the reactivation of the Hamaoka Nuclear Power Plant (Chapter 2), otherwise known as "the most dangerous power plant in the Japan.," which had been taken off-line, CHUDEN, after constructing a sea wall standing 22 meters high and1.6 km long at a cost of $3.56 billion, will reboot the reactors in the near future. According to records kept by the head of a residents group, the town received $28.3 million for over two decades from CHUDEN as "cooperation money." The amount in government subsidies and tax breaks was not included.

Other prefectures are also caving in to the need for continued subsidies. Even though the neighboring Kumamoto Prefecture suffered a powerful earthquake in April, Kagoshima Governor Satoshi Mizazono accepted the restart of operations at the Sendai Nuclear plant paving the way for KUDEN to reboot the plant in December. Fukui Prefecture has also given the green light to the restart of the forty year old Mihama Plant even though the Fast Breeder Reactor has had a history of nuclear incidents.

In February 2017 the NRA confirmed that Kansai Electric Company's (KEPCO) Oi plant In Fukui Prefecture had met the new safety standards and will give final approval in April for the plant to go online after public approval. Nevertheless, a seismologist and formerly one of the five commissioners on the NRA warned in June that the standards did not fully recognize that potential of a big earthquake in the vicinity of the plant. After the Osaka High Court overturned a lower court's 2016 injunction to suspend operations of KEPCO's Takahama reactors No. 3 and 4, the reactors will go online.

In March, the mayor of Genkai in Saga Prefecture, supported by the town assembly, agreed to the restart of Genkai 3 and 4 reactors. If the governor approves, the plants will go online.

The Kashiwazaki-Kariwa nuclear power plant located in the town of Kashiwazaki-Kariwa in Niigata Prefecture is a classic example. The late Prime Minister Kakue Tanaka, a consummate user of FILP funds, represented the prefecturein the National Diet for many years and used his political muscle to bring numerous infrastructure projects to his constituents while realizing large personal profits through land-flipping transactions. Despite serious accidents, the plant continued to operate until the Fukushima nuclear crisis when it was taken off-line. TEPCO, the operator is pressuring government to restart the plant.

On 17 October, Ryuichi Yoneyama who ran on an anti-nuclear platform was elected governor. However, on 20 November Masahiro Sakurai who is pro-nuclear, won the mayoral election for Kashiwazaki-Kariwa. He will approve a restart "if the safety is confirmed," which, after his initial meeting with TEPCO management, could take several years, according to a government spokesman.

Japan's Nuclear Crisis predicted that as a consequence of the decline in the construction of nuclear power plants domestically, the nuclear divisions of the heavy industries would struggle to earn revenue and the government would aggressively promote the export of nuclear technologies and equipment to emerging markets. There was little success until November 11, 2016 when Japan signed a civil nuclear energy agreement with India. Toshiba, through its Westinghouse subsidiary, was set to build six nuclear power plants in India.

Since India possesses nuclear weapons, anti-nuclear activists and pacifists were protesting vigorously at the outset of the negotiations in 2010. But the government and the heavy industries were determined to seal the deal.

There are concerns that the government has been storing plutonium for military purposes. On June 7, 2014 *Kyodo News Service* confirmed that Japan had omitted declaring 640 kg of unused plutonium to the International Atomic Agency (IAEA) in 2012 and 2013. Japan possesses as large an amount of plutonium as countries with nuclear weapons and is closely monitored by the IAEA. On 17 September the cabinet office reported that Japan's stockpile of plutonium was 47.1 tons, up 2.9 tons from the end of 2013 and enough to produce 6,000 nuclear weapons.

The Public Pension Investment Fund: the big squeeze

The prefectures where the nuclear plants are located were experiencing depopulation for years and the majority of residents in many towns were senior citizens. *Why Japan Can't Reform* (2008) argued that an aging population together with a decreasing population and the rise of welfare costs would increase public spending and serve to raise the government debt. The low fertility rate at the time was causing major worries since 25 percent of the population was over 65 and the longevity rate was the highest in the world. In 2005 the National Institute for Population and Social Research predicted that the portion of the population aged 65 and older would rise to 27.8 percent in 2020 while those aged 15–64 would fall to 60 percent. There were also concerns that with little immigration and a birth rate that was below replacement (at 1.32), the population of 127 million was already shrinking. Pension and healthcare pay-outs were swelling as the number of elderly was increasing. The productive population was shrinking and premium payments were also decreasing.

According to a survey released by the Ministry of Internal Affairs and Communication (MIC) on April 15, 2014 the total population of Japan fell 0.2 percent from the preceding year and the main working population fell below 80 million as of October 1, 2013, for the first time in 32 years.

As of September 2016, 27.3 percent of the population was 65 years or older. The decline in the working population aged 15–64 was significant and, therefore, wage-earners will be burdened with the responsibility of paying for the social welfare costs of retirees. MIC reported in July 2016 that Japan's population had fallen to 125,891,742 as of 1 January a decline for the seventh straight year. To make matters worse, the number of babies born during 2016 fell below one million for the first time on record. Statistics published in April 2017 by the National Institute for Population and Social Research projected that by 2065, the working population will fall by 40 percent, a trend that predicts a demographic catastrophe and an unsustainable burden on the state pension unless the retirement age is extended.

Abe's "Industrial Revival Plan" promised a long-awaited overhaul of the public pension investment fund (GPIF) to reduce exposure to JGB and invest in other assets that promised higher returns. In 2014 the $1.3 trillion fund, which is the largest in the world, invested 50 percent in both domestic and foreign equity and returns were initially positive at 12 percent. However, due to the downturn in global equities, the fund suffered a $52 billion loss in FY 2015, the biggest since the global financial crisis. The GPIF managed to recoup some losses in the third quarter of 2016 when it posted its first profit of 1.8 percent due to the rise of domestic and foreign shares on the stock markets. Nevertheless, the turbulence in global markets is an ongoing concern.

Will He or Won't He?

The OECD reported that the ratio of Japan's primary debt balance to GDP for 2015 was 4.84 percent, the worst figure among the thirty five OECD member nations. It is projected that the government will be unable to wipe out its primary balance deficit by 2020 which is calculated to be approximately $53 billion because of decreasing tax revenue. It had urged Abe to pursue structural reforms and to raise the consumption tax in 2015 from 8 percent to 10 percent.

Former Prime Minister Noda who criticized Abenomics as "voodoo economics" stated in his book in 2009 that the consumption tax must be raised to 15 percent by 2013 in order to fund burgeoning welfare costs.

At a press conference on 13 June 2014 Abe announced that the government would decide by year-end whether to raise the consumption tax to 10 percent. However, even pressure from business leaders and members of his cabinet to raise the tax did not dissuade Abe from postponing because he feared that a hike would trigger a recession close to the elections. To justify the postponement of raising the consumption tax in 2017 and to justify further QE, in March, Abe called on Paul Krugman and James Stiglitz, both proponents of stimulus. Without considering that minus interest rates were counterproductive and served little more than to monetize the sovereign debt, both economists, signaling the global economic downturn, advised Abe to freeze the consumption tax, consider other forms of taxation and indulge in more stimulus, but with the caveat that consolidation with fiscal policy was essential. Their recommendations conveniently gave Abe leave to announce in June 2016 that he would postpone the tax hike from 2017 until 2019.

Getting it Right about the Sovereign Debt: QE

In all of the books I focused discussion on Japan's escalating sovereign debt, asserting that it would continue to rise because of the BOJ's accommodating monetary policies. In 2002, the sovereign debt was 140 percent of annual GDP and by the end of Koizumi's term in office (2006) it had climbed to 180 percent. When Prime Minister Abe entered office in 2006 government debt had escalated to over 200 percent. In 2016 it stands at 250 percent. Sixteen years have passed void of little fiscal rebalancing or structural reforms of the administrative system. FDI is still the same at 2–2.5 percent.

Currently, fiscal consolidation and rebalancing is not being given serious consideration as Abe's fiscal policies continue to mirror policies implemented since the 1990s with huge stimulus packages and secondary budgets to support infrastructure projects, benefiting the larger companies and exporters and gaining support in key constituencies.

Former BOJ Governor Masaaki Shirakawa was opposed to further purchases of JGB which is referred to as QE or "quantitative easing" but he suggested the purchase of riskier assets such as exchange-traded funds, real estate investment trusts (REIT) known as "qualitative easing" (QQE). Nevertheless, he expressed concerns in May 2011 that Japan would lose market confidence if the government failed to deal with its finances. He also worried that the weakening of confidence in the private sector financial firms, which were heavily invested in JGB, would lead to higher borrowing costs. The economy would suffer, tax revenue would fall and the government would have difficulty paying off its debt. The following July, the BOJ was not prepared to guarantee more JGBs to fund growth because it would undermine the trust in the currency, increase long-term interests rates and pose difficulty selling JGB on the market.

Shirakawa emphasized the limits of an enormous increase in the monetary base particularly within the context of Japan's deflation and other economic problems and that fiscal policies must complement monetary policies. He urged the government to address Japan's slowing growth rate and low productivity as well as the rapid decrease of the working population and to implement structural reforms. Shirakawa retired from office in April 2013, two months before Abe installed a new governor who was enthusiastic about QE as a means to end deflation and to depreciate the yen. When Haruhiko Kuroda, a former MOF international vice minister became the new governor he wholeheartedly supported Abenomics and set an inflation target of 2 percent within two years.

In April 2013 the BOJ began its extreme monetary easing measures by purchasing large amounts of corporate bonds from banks and companies. By December 2013 as Japan's money supply had reached $1.83 trillion just short of the $2 trillion targeted, the BOJ purchased additional assets while the government launched a $910 billion package to compensate for the April 2014 rise in the consumption tax from 3 percent to 8 percent. Even though BOJ Governor Haruhiko Kuroda was not concerned about a 2 percent rise in long-term bond interest rates, at a news conference on April 8, 2014 Kuroda told reporters that, although the BOJ was not considering exiting from QE, spare capacity in the economy was "approaching zero." His hint that the BOJ might cut asset purchases caused bond interest rates to spike briefly. Some of the bonds purchased are so-called *Zaito* bonds, also referred to as FILP bonds or FILP agency bonds (Chapter 22) and issued by designated *Zaito* institutions similar to the FSC. However, these bonds are not guaranteed by the government.

On June 18, 2014 the BOJ announced that at the end of FY 2013 the bank was Japan's biggest debt holder with 20.1 percent of JGB or $1.97 trillion, the highest on record. According to the report, insurance companies held 19.3 percent of JGB, followed by small and medium size financial institutions with 13 percent, government public bodies with 8.9 percent and households holding only 2.1 percent. The BOJ is purchasing JGB worth $750.32 annually. QE continues, effectively transferring interest-risk from the private sector to the bank and bringing the relationship between the BOJ and government even closer.

Nevertheless, in an interview with the *Wall Street Journal* in May 2014, Kuroda was beginning to sound like his predecessor. He stated that Japan's medium-term growth was less than 1 percent: "Unless this growth potential is raised, the end result will be only the 2 percent inflation target achieved but real growth is meagre."

Kuroda also expressed his concern that despite 2 percent inflation, growth would be tepid and urged Abe not to rely on monetary policy alone but to implement structural reforms that coincided with BOJ's policies.

As of October 17, 2016 the BOJ-held bonds exceeded $3.8 trillion for the first time. In January 27, 2017 the BOJ increased purchases of five to ten year JGBs. The bank's bond-holdings are 40 percent of all outstanding JGB and it is projected that it will hold over 50 percent by 2018. In other words, the BOJ is assuming much of the government debt.

Since inflation is a mere 0.3 percent and since its policy tools of minus interest rates and purchasing JGB has failed to spur the economy, in order to shore-up the TSE, the BOJ is expected to purchase more exchange-traded funds and release more stimulus.

Getting it Right: QQE and QQE2

On January 29, 2017 the BOJ announced that it would hold interest rates for long-term bonds at zero percent and pull 3–6 month bonds into minus interest rates (QQE2). Since yield is "zero" or lower foreign asset management houses and private investors are exiting the market and domestic institutional investors and asset management houses are following suit. Since the demand for loans is low the FSA is concerned that negative interest rates will cost the three largest Japanese banks $2.96 billion. If interest rates go further into negative territory, the banks' profits will decrease even more as they struggle to pay-off savers. Regional banks are particularly vulnerable because the banks cannot sustain losses due to zero and minus interest rates. It is forecast that by 2025, 60 percent of regional banks will be in the red.

Japan Post Insurance which is listed with the Japan Post Bank on the TSE holds three-quarters of its assets in domestic bonds, of which 50 percent are JGB. But this year it is shying away from traditional investment and avoiding the purchase of negative yield government bonds and investing in stocks and foreign bonds, including junk bonds, private equity and real estate trusts (REITs). Other institutional investors are actively searching for profit-bearing investments and avoiding JGB. The BOJ will struggle to sell government bonds on the open market.

But the bank is facing yet another obstacle. It is running out of the means to continue its stimulus policies through JGB and riskier exchange-traded funds. When there were indications in 2016 that the BOJ might reduce its purchase of long-term bonds, yields spiked briefly. The spree of risky asset purchases has resulted in drying up the amount of assets available in Japan and REIT assets are proving even riskier because of the weak real estate market.

I have been cautioning colleagues for years that Japan's escalating sovereign debt should be of major concern because Japan owns considerable equity in foreign markets and is one of the world's largest net creditors. In order to avert a funding crisis, Kuroda, who is due to retire in 2018, has accepted that his extreme policies have not served to raise inflation and he has given up on a 2 percent inflation target. Kuroda announced again at a news conference in December 2016 that there is no limitation to loose monetary policies but that monetary and fiscal policies must be consolidated in order to bring the economy out of deflation. To put it mildly, monetary policies alone cannot correct the deep seated problems besetting the Japanese economy.

In January 2017 Abe's government continued fiscal stimulus for FY 2016 with a third extra budget to support disaster relief and missile defence. It can be argued that Abe is asking the BOJ to soak up the debt but as the debt continues to rise, as the economy continues in mild deflation and consumerism is weak, as the population continues to decline, and as liquidity dries up and cheap credit is exhausted, the government will become a pauper and the BOJ will ultimately be pressured to create new money to fund the budget.

Nevertheless, Abe whose cabinet had received over a 66 percent public approval rating in March, will either ask Kuroda to continue as governor after his term expires in 2018 or appoint a governor who will continue to pursue stimulus policies.

The Same Old Story

In June 2010 METI released its "Industrial Structure Vision" which stated the ministry's objectives to "launch a nationwide effort to boost its industry's global competitiveness" to stimulate Japan's economic recovery. METI's aim included a shift in industrial structure to encourage "potential strengths in businesses, the creation of jobs by aggressive globalization and by building world-class business infrastructure" and to change the government's role to "win the fierce competition to acquire added value among countries."

The vision, which described Japan as a "deadlocked economy," included data from the IMF World Economic Outlook Database that showed the general deterioration of Japan's competitiveness in global markets and the effects on the stagnated economy. IMF figures revealed that Japan's global ranking in terms of GDP per capita was third in 2000, falling to twenty-third in 2008. In 1990, Japan's share of the global GDP was 14.3 percent while in 2008 its share had decreased to 8.9 percent.

The METI vision reported that, although the economy was growing during 2000–07, wages remained stagnant or had declined. The number of companies going out of business exceeded the number of start-ups. MOF data revealed that while outward investment had increased, domestic capital expenditure had decreased. From 2006, domestic investment plummeted 37 percent. There was a significant shift by businesses to produce abroad. In 2011, Toyota was producing 50 percent of its cars outside of Japan and Honda and Nissan were each producing 70 percent of their vehicles abroad.

According to the World Economic Forum's Annual Global Competitiveness Report released on September 28, 2016, Japan slipped from sixth place to eighth in the ranking of 138 countries. The reasons given were: i) difficulties in firing staff; ii) ratio of women to men in the workforce; and iii) difficulty attracting foreign talent.

METI announced that industrial output in February 2016 this year had fallen 6.2 percent month on month, the worst since March 11, 2013. The big manufacturers were cutting capital expenditure for FY 2016 and their business sentiment was the lowest since June 2013.

The Tankan quarterly survey taken by the BOJ in September 2016 also revealed the continued deterioration of business sentiment due to the failure of Abenomics to eliminate deflation and fuel economic growth. The reasons given were the slowdown in demand for manufactured goods from China and weak domestic consumption. Almost 80 percent of the top 100 companies viewed Japan's economy "at a standstill." The yen's appreciation was also eating into profits for exporters. One of the reasons for the currency's appreciation in spite of QE was its role as a safe haven given the uncertainties in the global economy.

Exports fell in October 2016 for the thirteenth consecutive month due to the currency's appreciation. But in November the rapid depreciation of the yen against the dollar (¥105 to ¥114) would give exporters some relief. However, real growth depends upon consumer spending which accounts for 60 percent of GDP and the annual CPI fell 0.2 percent for the first time in four years, a decline for the consecutive tenth month. Although the unemployment rate is 3 percent, wages remain flat despite Abe's pleas to corporations to raise wages.

Devolution: too late?

The government's push for devolution should be considered within the context of Japan's continued severe economic conditions and not because the national ministries prefer passing the powers to local authorities to plan and implement policies.

In order to downsize subsidization and conserve national budget outlays, the government is requesting that local authorities assume more of the financing of infrastructure, public works projects, education and welfare thus reducing the dependence on central government support. The Ministry of Internal Affairs and Communication (MIC) acknowledged on its 2010 website that Japan's economy had been in a state of recession since 1992:

> Regional finance therefore plays an extremely important position, so to speak, as one of the two wheels of a vehicle together with national finance. Increasingly important will be the roles of local governments and accompanying financial measures, such as promoting regional sovereignty reforms, supporting nursing, medical parental cares designed for the society with a declining birth rate and aging population

Regional finance totals the finance of about 1,700 local governments, most of which are financially weak municipalities. The shortage of funds for regional finance increased swiftly in and after fiscal 1994 due to the decline in local tax revenues:

Moreover, the balance of loans in regional finance grew rapidly in recent years due to the decline in local tax revenues, compensations for tax cuts, and the increased issuance of local bonds for stimulating the economy. The end of fiscal 2011 saw the loans growing to 200 trillion yen, accounting for 41.4% of GDP. This marked a 2.9-fold increase since fiscal 1991, showing an increase of 130 trillion yen.

Local governments, especially in the weaker localities, shared with central government about 30–40 percent of tax revenue, the costs for public works, educational programs and social welfare. However, now the tables are turned to accommodate "such a severe financial situation." Although local authorities must still adhere to ministerial edict, local governments are expected to assume more of the finances because they are being given more "autonomy."

Since the structure of Japan's governing system remains hierarchical with the national ministry officials at the top and local government officials on the lower rungs of the governing ladder, since ministry officials regard local government officials as generally inadequately prepared to plan policies and since many local government officials have for over a century been pressured to accept policies planned by the national ministries, the pace of "a government that can adapt to changing circumstances in an economic society during such a severe financial situation" will take decades.

Back to Basics

Blaming BREXIT for having a negative impact on the economy, in September 2016 Abe announced the planned release of a stimulus package worth $265 billion to spur the stagnant economy and induce consumer spending. The package is slated for construction of infrastructure projects and supporting local and national governments.

The government also blames Donald Trump. When President Trump announced his intention to withdraw from the Trans-Pacific Partnership (TPP) Abe's hopes that the trade pact would serve as a buffer against China's economic and military expansion in Asia were shattered. Abe's visit to Hawaii to hold talks with President Obama on 27 December was choreographed with a visit to Pearl Harbor to express his "deepest remorse" and "sincere condolences" to the victims of Pearl Harbor. Suga emphasized that Abe's visit should not be interpreted as an apology because the victims of the US atomic bombing of Hiroshima and Nagasaki were civilians. Undoubtedly, Japanese conservatives were not happy with Abe's visit but Abe wanted to "use the opportunity to signal the value of Japan-US reconciliation" and "to send to the world that we will further strengthen and maintain our alliance towards the future." Abe also took the opportunity to pay respects at the memorial for the nine crew members of the Ehime Maru. A day after Defence Minister Inada returned from Pearl Habor where she accompanied Abe, she visited Yasukuni Shrine, a move which served to nullify Abe's conciliatory PR objectives. Her visit was sharply criticized by China, South Korea and, also, by the US.

Abe, on the defensive, was clearly concerned that the US would gradually begin to pull out of the security treaty, leaving Japan to fend off China's encroachment on the East China Sea. Abe also expressed concerns that Trump's administration would ask Japan to assume more of the budget for the US military presence in Japan. On his visit to Japan on 3 February, Secretary of Defence James Mattis reassured Abe that the US was committed to the US-Japan Security Treaty. Although he praised Japan for its "cost sharing" of the budget (74.5 percent) he avoided commenting about the possibility of Japan paying more for the maintenance for US bases. On 18 January the PHP Institute, founded by Konosuke Matsushita, released a report stating that rather than footing the bill of US military operations in Japan, the government's budget for defence spending should be increased to 1.2 percent of annual GDP. But Abe's government had already announced Japan's record defence budget at $43.6 billion for FY2017, an increase of 1.4 percent, putting further pressure on national finances and driving up the sovereign debt.

Déjà vu

On January 17, 2017 the *Asahi Shimbun* released a public poll revealing that 48 percent of Japanese surveyed were pessimistic about Japan-US relations, partially because of President Trump's criticism of Japan, China and Mexico for America's trade deficit. Japan was given a taste of things to come when Trump tweeted a month before he took office that Toyota would pay a "border tax" if it went ahead with a planned production plant in Mexico to build cars for the US market. Toyota argued that it had been a "good corporate citizen," investing $21.9 billion in expansion in the US, employing 136,000 workers and producing 25 million vehicles over 30 years. Several weeks later, Toyota announced plans to invest $600 million in its plant in Indiana, adding 400 jobs.

Trump had previously warned both Ford and General Motors that the manufacturing of small cars currently produced in Mexico to take advantage of low wages should be relocated to the US. Ford, while denying the Trump effect, announced that it had cancelled plans to build a $1.6 billion small car factory in Mexico.

Trump's renegotiation of the North American Free Trade Agreement (NAFTA) will have a big impact on the 1,000 Japanese companies producing in Mexico, where they produce more than in any other Latin American country. The companies use Mexico to export mainly automobiles to the US and Canada.

Suga also stated that Japanese investment provided a "vitality to the US-Japan economic relationship." The Japanese government emphasized that the trade deficit with the US had shrunk to less than half of what it was in the 1990s and its cumulative investment in the US was $47 trillion while China's was a meagre $15 billion. Japanese companies were employing 890,000 US workers while China employed only 38,000.

Trump, highly critical of Japan's automotive industry and monetary policies, claimed that the US was at a disadvantage in trade relations. The Trump administration will focus on bilateral trade policies which, once again, will return Japan to one-on-one negotiations with the USTR. On 25 January, Abe announced that Japan would be willing to engage in bilateral trade talks with the US, lowering tariffs on beef and pork on the condition that the US would deregulate certain markets.

Abe needs US support both economically and militarily. When Abe met with Trump on 8 February he bore gifts to soften Trump's stance both on bilateral trade and the deregulation of Japan's markets. Ironically, METI officials did not accompany the Prime Minister. He proposed a $150 billion investment in US infrastructure projects such as a high-speed railway system between Texas and California which he promised would create 700,000 jobs. Loans for the projects would be partially funded by Japanese mega-banks and government-affiliated financial institutions and by its Special Accounts. Abe, ever fearful of China's military build-up, proposed that Japan import more US military equipment to contribute to the American economy and cut the US-Japan trade deficit.

METI is relieved that the newly appointed US Ambassador to Japan is William Hagerty, a businessman who spent several years in Japan with Boston Consulting group. Hagerty, who is positive about Japanese investment in the US, may take a softer stance on US-Japan trade relations. Trump also appointed Wilbur Ross, the billionaire investor who is known for taking over and restructuring failing companies. In 1999, Ross's company took over the failing Osaka-based second-tier regional bank Kofuku, operating 81 of the bank's 123 branches. It is still early days to predict any results of Ross's efforts to implement bilateral trade with a country that protects its markets but he visited Japan in April to begin talks regarding the agricultural and pharmaceutical markets. The Commerce Department and the USTR initiated a 90-day review of the factors which contribute to America's massive trade deficit, such as dumping, misaligned currencies and "non-reciprocal" trade practices. In terms of trade surplus with the US, China leads with $347 billion whilst Japan comes in second with $68.94 billion.

Robert Lighthizer is the newly appointed USTR trade representative. He was the deputy trade representative under Ronald Reagan and participated in the US-Japan trade disputes on autos and steel in the early 1990s. He probably had met Naitoh Masahisa during the semiconductor negotiations in the 1980s. Most likely JETRO will invite Lighthizer's colleagues to seminars on doing business in Japan, escort them to the BSCs and even to FAZ to explain how Japan is trying to deregulate markets, increase imports and increase inward investment to three percent of GDP. *Inside/Outside Japan*, which was terminated at the end of 1990, may go online!

Foreign asset management firms are questioning the existence of the "third arrow." Well-invested in Japanese equities, the firms were pulling out of the market to the tune of $46 billion by April 2016. The Japanese are tired of peddling their economy with no relief in sight. But Japan Inc. is mired in a system that is unforgiving. Regardless, Abe will not be deterred. At a news conference on January 4, 2017 he emphasized that his chief priority was the economy: "We will keep shooting the three arrows of monetary policy, fiscal policy and growth strategy to beat inflation."

Other commentators are beginning to agree with me. Notably, Oliver Blanchard, the former chief economist of the IMF wrote recently in the Telegraph that there would be an "ugly end game" in Japan in relation to its debt spiral. The consequence of Japan's ongoing financial woes matters. It is the world's third largest economy by far, is the largest holder of US Treasury Securities reported in October 2016 to be $1.13 trillion and holds substantial foreign assets. The repatriation of funds could happen at any time, creating instability in the global financial system.

Index

E

F

G

H

About the Author

In 1988, at the height of the asset-inflated economic bubble in Japan, Dr Carpenter was employed as the first non-Japanese staff in a major Japanese pharmaceutical and liquor producer to launch foreign brands onto the Japanese market and to negotiate joint ventures with foreign producers. During the first Gulf War Dr Carpenter worked in a Japanese commercial television station and, during Japan's first "lost decade," she worked for Japanese government agencies, including the primary lender to SMEs and the state import-export bank that provided trade insurance to Japanese heavy industries.

She holds a doctorate from the University of Edinburgh Business School where she lectured on Japanese political economy and served as the Director of the MSc in International Business and Emerging Markets. Dr Carpenter operated a small business in New York State with a former Vice President of Nippon Telephone and Telegraph (NTT). Carpenter Kano Associates consulted on regional high-tech small business development for Japanese industry. From 2009 to 2016 she was the CEO of International Markets Analysts Ltd. The company conducted political and economic country risk analyses of international financial markets and engaged in the development of Scottish start-ups.

Lightning Source UK Ltd.
Milton Keynes UK
UKHW02f1346011217
313681UK00009B/48/P